INTROD
TO EDU
GERONT

SERIES IN DEATH EDUCATION, AGING, AND HEALTH CARE

HANNELORE WASS, CONSULTING EDITOR

ADVISORY BOARD

Herman Feifel, Ph.D.
Jeanne Quint Benoliel, R.N., Ph.D.
Balfour Mount, M.D.

Benoliel—*Death Education for the Health Professional*

Corless, Pittman-Lindeman—*AIDS: Principles, Practices, and Politics, Abridged Edition*

Corless, Pittman-Lindeman—*AIDS: Principles, Practices, and Politics, Reference Edition*

Curran—*Adolescent Suicidal Behavior*

Davidson—*The Hospice: Development and Administration, Second Edition*

Degner, Beaton—*Life–Death Decisions in Health Care*

Doty—*Communication and Assertion Skills for Older Persons*

Epting, Neimeyer—*Personal Meanings of Death: Applications of Personal Construct Theory to Clinical Practice*

Haber—*Health Care for an Aging Society: Cost-Conscious Community Care and Self-Care Approaches*

Lund—*Older Bereaved Spouses: Research with Practical Applications*

Prunkl, Berry—*Death Week: Exploring the Dying Process*

Riker, Myers—*Retirement Counseling: A Practical Guide for Action*

Sherron, Lumsden—*Introduction to Educational Gerontology, Third Edition*

Stillion—*Death and the Sexes: An Examination of Differential Longevity, Attitudes, Behaviors, and Coping Skills*

Stillion, McDowell, May—*Suicide across the Life Span—Premature Exits*

Turnbull—*Terminal Care*

Vachon—*Occupational Stress in the Care of the Critically Ill, the Dying, and the Bereaved*

Wass, Berardo, Neimeyer—*Dying: Facing the Facts, Second Edition*

Wass, Corr—*Childhood and Death*

Wass, Corr—*Helping Children Cope with Death: Guidelines and Resources, Second Edition*

Wass, Corr, Pacholski, Forfar—*Death Education II: An Annotated Resource Guide*

Wass, Corr, Pacholski, Sanders—*Death Education: An Annotated Resource Guide*

Weenolsen—*Transcendence of Loss over the Life Span*

IN PREPARATION

Bard—*Medical Ethics in Practice*

Bertman—*The Language of Grief and the Art of Communication*

Brammer—*Coping with Life Transitions: The Challenge of Personal Change*

Leenars, Wenckstern—*Suicide Prevention in Schools*

Leng—*Psychological Care in Old Age*

Leviton—*Horrendous Death, Health, and Well-Being*

Lindeman, Corby, Downing, Sanborn—*Dementia Day-Care Handbook*

Lonetto—*Explaining Death and Dying*

Papadatos, Papadatou—*Children and Death*

Salloway, Matthiesen—*The Chosen Daughter: Women and Their Institutionalized Mothers*

INTRODUCTION TO EDUCATIONAL GERONTOLOGY

Third Edition

Edited by

RONALD H. SHERRON
Virginia Commonwealth University

D. BARRY LUMSDEN
University of North Texas

●HEMISPHERE PUBLISHING CORPORATION
A member of the Taylor & Francis Group

New York   Washington   Philadelphia   London

INTRODUCTION TO EDUCATIONAL GERONTOLOGY: Third Edition

1 2 3 4 5 6 7 8 9 0   E B E B   8 9 8 7 6 5 4 3 2 1 0 9

This book was set in Press Roman by Hemisphere Publishing Corporation. The editors were Amy Lyles Wilson and Deanna D'Errico; the production supervisor was Peggy M. Rote; and the typesetters were Wayne Hutchins, Linda Andros, and Bonnie Sciano. Cover design by Debra Eubanks Riffe.
Edwards Brothers, Inc. was printer and binder.

Library of Congress Cataloging-in-Publication Data

Introduction to educational gerontology / edited by Ronald H. Sherron,
    D. Barry Lumsden. — 3rd ed.
        p. cm.
    Includes bibliographical references.

    1. Gerontology—Study and teaching—United States. 2. Aged-
-Education—United States. I. Sherron, Ronald H. II. Lumsden, D.
Barry.
HQ1064.U5159 1990
305.26'07—dc20   89-15563
ISBN 0-89116-057-4 (cloth)
ISBN 1-56032-039-7 (paper)
ISSN 0275-3510

To my children, Gina and Danny, whose seemingly overnight growth and development serve as a constant reminder of my own aging (DBL)

To all of us who are certainly aging (RHS)

CONTENTS

Preface   **xiii**

chapter 1

A HISTORY OF THE EDUCATION OF OLDER LEARNERS
David A. Peterson   **1**
    Education Today   **1**
    The Development of Educational Gerontology   **3**
    Education Programs for Older Learners   **8**
    Implications of Education for the Aging   **15**
    Future Education for the Aging   **16**
    References   **19**

chapter 2

EDUCATION AND THE LIFE CYCLE: A PHILOSOPHY OF
AGING   *Harry R. Moody*   **23**
    Experience   **23**
    Dialogue   **29**
    Transcendence   **34**
    References   **39**

chapter 3

REMINISCENCE AND LIFE REVIEW: THE POTENTIAL FOR
EDUCATIONAL INTERVENTION   *Sharan B. Merriam*   **41**
    Introduction   **41**
    Reminiscence Defined   **42**
    Reminiscence and Age   **44**
    The Function of Reminiscence   **47**
    Other Functions   **50**
    The Rationale for Educational Intervention   **51**
    Techniques of Educational Intervention   **53**

Conclusion   55
References   56

chapter 4

THE COMMUNITY OF GENERATIONS: A GOAL AND A
CONTEXT FOR THE EDUCATION OF PERSONS IN THE LATER
YEARS   *Howard Y. McClusky*   59
   The Concept   60
   The Procedural Dimension   62
   The Substantive Dimension   64
   Examples   73
   The Meaning of the Examples   80
   Conclusion   82
   References   83

chapter 5

INSTRUMENTAL AND EXPRESSIVE EDUCATION: FROM NEEDS
TO GOALS ASSESSMENT FOR EDUCATIONAL
PLANNING   *Carroll A. Londoner*   85
   Introduction   85
   A Sociological, Theoretical Framework   88
   A Psychosocial Interpretation of Adult Participation   90
   Three Underlying Assumptions   96
   Literature Review   97
   Analysis and Assessment of Needs and Goals   101
   The Educational Planner's Responsibility   104
   References   106

chapter 6

RELIGION AND AGING AND THE ROLE OF EDUCATION
J. Conrad Glass, Jr.   109
   Introduction   109
   Religious Involvement of the Elderly   111
   Social and Psychological Influences of Religion on the
     Elderly   113
   Barriers to Participation   114
   The Elderly in the Local Church or Synagogue   116
   Objectives of Older Adult Ministry   118
   Older Adult Ministry   119
   The Role of Education in Aging Ministry   123
   Conclusion   129
   References   131

chapter 7

INSTRUCTING EXPERIENCED ADULT LEARNERS
Christopher Bolton   **135**
    What We Know About Instructing Older Adults   **136**
    Two Factors That Affect Older Adult Education   **137**
    Authority-Focused Teaching Methods   **139**
    Learner-Focused Methods   **141**
    Redesigning Adult Education   **143**
    Conclusion   **147**
    References   **147**

chapter 8

UNITING THE GENERATIONS   *Josie Metal-Corbin
and David E. Corbin*   **151**
    Introduction   **151**
    Rationale for and Benefits of Intergenerational Programs   **154**
    Development of Formal Intergenerational Programs   **157**
    Implications for Planning, Implementing, and Maintaining
        Intergenerational Programs   **162**
    Strategies for the Future   **164**
    References   **167**

chapter 9

EVALUATION OF EDUCATIONAL PROGRAMS IN SOCIAL
GERONTOLOGY   *Thomas A. Rich*   **171**
    Growth Problems: Academic and Federal Issues   **172**
    Background Issues in Gerontology   **174**
    Recommendations   **181**
    Summary   **184**
    References   **185**

chapter 10

CAREER EDUCATION FOR THE PREPARATION OF
PRACTITIONERS IN GERONTOLOGY, WITH SPECIAL
REFERENCE TO ADULT EDUCATORS
Margaret E. Hartford   **187**
    The Changing Future   **190**
    Curriculum Design for the Future   **195**
    The Future Begins Now   **199**
    References   **200**

chapter 11

CREATIVE BEHAVIOR AND EDUCATION: AN AVENUE
FOR LIFE-SPAN DEVELOPMENT   *Joy H. Dohr
and Margaret Portillo*   **201**
   Introduction   **201**
   An Integrative Framework for Creativeness and Aging   **203**
   Definitions of Creativity: Person, Process, and Product   **206**
   Timeframes of Development   **207**
   The Public Sphere   **208**
   The Private Sphere   **210**
   Purposeful Product   **214**
   The Role of Social Exchange   **217**
   Educational Interpretations: Concerns for Planning
     Programs   **219**
   Conclusion   **222**
   References   **223**

chapter 12

THE POLITICAL ECONOMY OF HIGHER EDUCATION FOR
OLDER LEARNERS   *Scott A. Bass*   **227**
   Introduction   **227**
   Sociological Theories of Schooling   **229**
   Theoretical Perspectives About Older Learners   **230**
   Equal Opportunity and Access   **233**
   The Economic Role of Older People in the Work Force   **234**
   The Economic Role of Formal Education   **237**
   Adapting Higher Education to the Older Learner   **238**
   Conclusion   **239**
   References   **240**

chapter 13

MODELS OF COGNITIVE FUNCTIONING IN THE OLDER
ADULT: RESEARCH NEEDS IN EDUCATIONAL
GERONTOLOGY   *Gisela Labouvie-Vief*   **243**
   Idealism in Adult Developmental Theory   **244**
   Psychobiological Maturation and Cognition in the Elderly   **249**
   Sociohistorical Context and Adult Intelligence   **254**
   Criteria of Development and Maturity   **258**
   Conclusion   **263**
   References   **263**

chapter 14

LEADERSHIP TRAINING FOR RETIREMENT EDUCATION
Carl I. Brahce and Woodrow W. Hunter   **269**
   Historic Developments in Education for the Elderly   **272**
   The Role of Institutions   **277**
   Training Retirement Educators   **281**
   Learning Progression in Later Years   **288**
   Programming   **289**
   Trends   **292**
   References   **293**

chapter 15

A 21st CENTURY CHALLENGE TO HIGHER EDUCATION:
INTEGRATING THE OLDER PERSON INTO ACADEMIA
*Ben E. Dickerson, Dennis R. Myers, Wayne C. Seelbach,
and Sue Johnson-Dietz*   **297**
   Introduction   **297**
   Historical Perspectives on Older Learners   **301**
   Participation Rates of Older Learners   **304**
   Characteristics of Older Learners   **306**
   Characteristics of Higher Education   **314**
   Characteristics of Social Institutions   **318**
   Questions Facing Higher Education in an Aging Society   **322**
   Guidelines and Recommendations for Integrating the Older Person
      into the College or University Setting   **325**
   Conclusion   **326**
   References   **328**

chapter 16

EDUCATIONAL GERONTOLOGY AND THE FUTURE   *James A.
Thorson and Shirley A. Waskel*   **333**
   Preface   **333**
   Introduction   **334**
   Rising Expectations of the Elderly   **337**
   The Social Problem of Isolation   **339**
   Technology and the Future of Education for the Aged   **342**
   The Role of Educational Institutions   **345**
   Educational Gerontology as Intervention   **348**
   References   **350**

Index   **355**

PREFACE

When we put together the first edition of this introductory volume in 1978, we had little reason, if any, to think a second and third edition would follow. The longevity of books is generally far less than that of journals, and the mortality rate of books normally exceeds that of scholarly periodicals. But for whatever reasons, this book continues to live and do well. We, of course, like to think it is because educational gerontology is at least here to stay, if it is not in fact the wave of the future.

Educational gerontology continues to be a dynamic, fast-growing branch of gerontology. Around the world today public and private agencies are becoming increasingly aware of their responsibilities, both delegated and voluntary, to provide training opportunities for laborers in the field and educational experiences for older adults themselves.

The major purpose of this third edition continues to be to provide an overview of some of the major issues and problems affecting the contemporary practice of educational gerontology. This edition has been thoroughly updated in two important ways. First, most of the chapters that carry over from previous editions have been significantly revised to reflect changes in the disciplines and the profession. Second, new chapters have been added to round out and even increase the comprehensiveness of the first and second editions.

It is our hope that this new edition will excite its readers as much as its development did its editors and contributors. It is also our hope that in some significant ways the book will further establish educational gerontology as a legitimate and academically respectable branch of social gerontology. We would like to hear from you, our readers, concerning your perceptions of the strengths and weaknesses of this third edition. Should time and circumstances dictate the necessity of a fourth edition, your comments and criticisms will be considered in our efforts to produce an even better piece of work.

Ronald H. Sherron
D. Barry Lumsden

1

A HISTORY OF THE EDUCATION OF OLDER LEARNERS

DAVID A. PETERSON

University of Southern California

EDUCATION TODAY

Older people have participated in instructional activities for as long as educational programs have existed. Historically, education was directed primarily toward adults, and participants were individuals with available time and interest. Older people were part of this group and were involved as both learners and teachers in the discussions. Education, then, is not foreign to older people, but only recently in the United States have conscious attempts been made to recruit older participants and to design educational experiences that are exclusively for people in this age group.

Education is a widely used word, and its general meaning is understood by all. Unfortunately, its widespread use has diluted its clarity and the word has taken on inappropriate and indistinct meanings. Here *education* is used to mean planned learning that occurs apart from maturation and that is seriously undertaken. Education is different from learning. Although both may result in changed knowledge or behavior, education is distinct in that the change is identified beforehand by the teacher or the student or by both. Unlike learning, which can occur in an unplanned, spontaneous, serendipitous manner, education is a consciously designed program. It usually involves at least four components: a plan of what is to be learned (curriculum), a design of how the learning will take place (methodology), a leader who knows the plan and method (teacher), and a goal or end that is desired (objective). The consciousness of purpose is the characteristic that distinguishes education from incidental learning and forces the educator to carefully consider alternative approaches to the instructional endeavor.

Another characteristic of education is that it is an important, serious, and

1

difficult endeavor (Moody, 1976). Lasting and meaningful change generally does not occur without effort; education is a lengthy and continuing program of self-improvement, and it requires consistent and conscientious application of the student's emotional and intellectual faculties toward the understanding and integration of new knowledge, skills, concepts, and behaviors. For this serious learning to occur, the student must implicitly accept the fact that his or her state of functioning in a particular area is less effective or efficient than desired or possible. This awareness aids in opening the student to new understanding and enables real learning to occur.

Education can employ multiple approaches, but the desired outcomes generally improve awareness, understanding, skill, or behavior in an area where a weakness has been identified. Whether the learning is directed toward acquiring a new skill, continuing a lifelong interest, or developing one's psychological and social relationships, education offers a means for better comprehending the complexity of life and relating oneself more adequately to that complexity. Much that passes for education does not meet these criteria. There are many occasions when programs that are more correctly described as recreation, diversion, or pacification are presented under the title of education. They may play a very helpful role in the lives of some individuals, but they need to be separated from an attempt to understand and to know, and to do that takes effort, time, and direction.

In contemporary America the population is realizing more clearly the need for this type of intellectual growth as the rapidity of social change, the complexity of urban life, and the developmental changes of the individual force more and more adults to seek assistance. The availability of increasing amounts of leisure time and greater financial resources have allowed students of all ages to enroll in a variety of educational settings, leading to what has been called "a learning society." This view that learning and education must continue across the life span is becoming more widely accepted. As community colleges, voluntary agencies, membership organizations, business and industry, proprietary schools, the public school systems, and government programs encourage the acquisition of new knowledge and skills, individuals find themselves increasingly engaged in education regardless of their age.

Older adults have not been the first clientele of these developing programs, but they are becoming increasingly visible in educational settings. Programs designed especially for them are growing in number, and as the older population expands, increasing enrollments are resulting. The learning society, however, includes not only those individuals who are enrolled in formal education activities, but also people who are cultivating their personal growth and development by pursuing their interests and solving their problems through conscious learning. Older people, as one portion of this total audience, continue their involvement and may be expected to become far more numerous participants in continuing education in the years ahead.

In this chapter I outline the developmental stages of education for older people. Although I refer to specific programs, it is not my intent to mention all or even most of the numerous educational activities currently under way. Rather, I attempt to provide some understanding of the antecedents of instructional programs for older adults, to indicate some of the philosophical positions that have been taken, to show their relation to the larger field of adult education, to describe a few of the key events of the developing field, to suggest some implications and current trends, and to speculate briefly on the future developments that may occur in this dynamic and important field.

THE DEVELOPMENT OF EDUCATIONAL GERONTOLOGY

Educational gerontology refers to the study and practice of instructional endeavors for and about the aged and aging. This definition has been used previously (Peterson, 1976), indicating an attempt to integrate the institutions and processes of education with the knowledge of human aging and the needs of older people. As an area of practice, its purpose is to prevent premature decline, to facilitate meaningful roles, and to encourage psychological growth; as an area of knowledge, its focus is on the intellectual changes that occur throughout later life, the instructional adaptations required for older students, and the motivational factors that determine educational participation or nonparticipation. Educational gerontology, then, is an attempt to apply what is currently known about aging and education in order to extend the healthy and productive years and improve the quality of life for older people.

Educational gerontology can be both instrumental and expressive, both formal and informal, both for older people and about them, both a study and a practice, both remedial and preventive—but it is designed as a positive approach to helping people better understand and assist themselves. It is a "positive domain" (McClusky, 1971) in which the potential of the individual is accepted and developed in order to ensure continuing growth throughout the life span. Educational gerontology includes three major areas: instruction for older people; instruction for general and specific audiences about older people; and instruction for people who will work with older people, such as professionals or practitioners employed in the agencies and institutions that plan for and serve the older client. This chapter deals only with the first of these three categories: instruction for older people. Consequently, it excludes major portions of the field of educational gerontology but emphasizes the area that is currently so vital and expansive that educational institutions and community programs are rapidly instituting relevant activities.

Florio (n.d.) has suggested that there are three main categories of education for older people. These categories, which are based primarily on the emphasis of the instructional offerings and the manner in which they are designed, are as follows. First, programs in which special privileges for seniors are provided. These are regular course offerings of an organization or institution, but they are provided at a reduced cost or without fee to older people. Second, existing programs that include a few courses adapted or modified to fit the special interests of older adults. These offerings may be designed primarily for the older participant, or they may be the typical course with a new title or time assignment intended to attract a few more older students. And third, programs that have been designed, packaged, and offered especially and often exclusively for older people. Frequently, they exist apart from other offerings of the institution and are presented in a manner and at a time most appropriate for older people.

Values and Purposes of Education for Older Learners

Because educational programs for older people are offered through a variety of institutional settings, it is not surprising that there are multiple purposes and that the results lead to quite diverse outcomes. Education may be preparation for a new task such as a job, volunteer assignment, or changing role in the family. It may be directed toward psychological growth whereby the individual attempts to explore innate capabilities. Education may be a primary mechanism used to prevent the physical, psychological, and social decline of the individual. Likewise, it may be used to evaluate lifelong experience and provide insights regarding the importance and meaning of that experience. It may be the opportunity to discover meaning in the individual's knowledge and experience and translate that to a higher level of abstraction and understanding.

Moody (1976) has theorized that human service professionals and educators make one of four general presuppositions about education and older people. These basic attitudinal positions provide an understanding of, and a means of analyzing, contemporary programs in education for older people.

1. Rejection   People who take this position perceive older people as being limited in economic value and as representing the antithesis of what society values— productivity, power, beauty, and youth. Essentially, older people are seen as expendable in a technological society. An attempt is made to isolate them on the grounds that they have little value or meaning in modern America. This attitude invalidates all rationale for educational concern or service. Because older people are seen as worthless to society, it becomes inappropriate to expend economic resources to educate them. Obviously this view would be rejected by most people in the field of gerontology today.

2. The Provision of Social Services   Based on the belief that the problems of older people must be ameliorated by changes in public policy, this orientation leads to the implementation of transfer payments or social programs provided by professionals, generally at government expense. The projects are based on contemporary society's liberalism and the belief in a welfare state in which social justice and equality are highly valued. Too often the emphasis is placed on attacking the symptoms rather than correcting the causes of the social problems faced by the elderly. Older people often passively receive services rather than honing the skills that will enable them to initiate their own, more effective programs. In addition, social service programs may lead to segregation of people of different ages and disengagement of these older individuals from their traditional roles and relationships. Programs may become mere activities rather than providing older individuals with opportunities that will ultimately enable them to improve their own lives. On an educational level, these instructional programs are often designed to keep people busy and to improve social relationships. This may provide meaningful activity for some individuals but often discourages many others.

The social services presupposition may be carried somewhat further if the educational programs are directed toward specific problems such as illiteracy and inability to handle the stresses of contemporary daily life. Birren and Woodruff (1973) suggested that this type of remedial education is extensively needed by contemporary older people and that a major contribution can be made through helping people overcome current problems. The value of education that will assist individuals in coping with contemporary situations was also indicated by McClusky (1971), who saw this as the first and most comprehensive category of educational need that should be addressed by instructional programs.

3. Participation People of this orientation contend that older people should continue to participate in the mainstream of American society because they have skills and abilities that may help overcome some of the societal problems facing the nation. In this view, education is directed at the normalization of roles for the elderly and the preservation of individual dignity. These are largely political values and can be realized through activity that is meaningful to the individual and to society. Educational programs based on this position encourage and facilitate such activity by helping to increase societal participation, by preparing individuals for second careers, and by expanding volunteer roles for people who are outside the work force. Through meaningful participation, older people can improve the quality of life in the country generally while assisting themselves and their age-mates in adjusting to their changing circumstances.

One application of this participative strategy was emphasized by Frank (1955) in his description of education as a means of increasing the citizenship capabilities of older people. Such education can play a meaningful role in a democratic nation by preparing the large number of recent immigrants for successfully performing their political and citizenship roles. In addition to preventing the waste of human resources, involving older people in conducting the nation's affairs provides excellent role models for younger people.

4. Self-actualization This category emphasizes psychological growth and spiritual concerns as major outcomes of educational programming. Moody suggested that there are unique possibilities in old age, which can be realized only through a combined psychological and spiritual quest for meaning and insight. Old age can be considered a symbol of closure—an attempt to determine the meaning of experiences and integrate understanding acquired through life. In this sense, disengagement from activity may be a positive goal if it leads to contemplation and resynthesis of the self. This type of psychological growth in later life has been emphasized elsewhere (Donahue, 1955; Erikson, 1980) and is perhaps the highest goal of instructional programs. It is difficult to describe and conceptualize instructional methodology or program content, however, because individuals may vary greatly in their interests, needs, and levels of insight.

Moody, along with many others, has made a compelling case for the value of education across the later adult years. That education for the elderly meets personal and social needs is apparent, and the positive effects of such education should provide strong support for utilizing human and financial resources in this manner. Education offers a major potential for expansion and contribution, although the diversity of possible outcomes, purposes, and methods leaves one somewhat bewildered as to how best to describe or understand this growing phenomenon.

Education for older people is a developing area of study and activity that is occurring within and between the fields of education and gerontology. Studies in a variety of disciplines and professions through numerous settings and institutions are providing support for the belief that education offers much to older people. Although the values of education for individuals in our society have long been recognized, only recently has this belief been implemented in relation to middle-aged and older individuals. We are now entering a time when this practice is becoming widespread. As this occurs, greater knowledge is needed to ensure that the quality of instruction continues to improve and that the most effective and efficient learning processes are used.

These developments are of interest to policy makers and agency heads, as well as the public, because they offer the hope of preventing some of the decline that often occurs in later life and the opportunity to assist older people in maximizing their potential. Success in these endeavors will have major significance for the continued employment of older people, for their integration in the fabric of society, and for the type of health and social services that must be provided in the future. We are only beginning to glimpse the significance of education for the aged, but the potential effect is truly great.

The Development of Adult Education in the United States

Education for older people developed primarily from the adult education movement of the United States. As old as the nation itself, this movement has its roots in the social, cultural, and political concerns of the 18th century. Our earliest leaders believed that American democracy rested on the educability of its citizens and that public decisions could be improved through widespread education. Thus, education became a citizen's right, and discussion regarding it dealt not with whether the general public should be educated, but how this education could be most effectively provided.

Early adult education, then, had an underlying concern for the development of good citizenship; the capacity to read and write was cultivated so that the individual could participate in the decisions of the nation. This was often associated with a religious emphasis because the ability to read was closely tied to an understanding of the Bible and the desire to gain salvation. Thus, much of the religious education had a decidedly political and civic orientation, and much of the political discussion had close ties to Christianity, if not to a specific denomination. Political and religious leaders took an active interest in education, and the elementary and secondary school system reflected this concern.

Benjamin Franklin played a key role in developing one of the first adult education activities in this nation. In 1727 he formed a small study and discussion society, later called the Junto, which lasted for 30 years (Grattan, 1955). It was composed of 12 persons who met weekly to discuss community and social considerations. The group clearly had an intellectual orientation but was interested in problems or issues then current in Philadelphia. The Junto led to the formation of the local lending libraries, which made available a variety of books to all citizens and greatly expanded the accessibility of printed material. The Junto also served as the stimulus for the establishment of a national organization later called the American Philosophical Society. However, the local discussion group in which each of the members took responsibility for the preparation and presentation of materials was Franklin's major contribution to American adult education.

Approximately 100 years after the creation of the Junto, another adult education innovation began to reach popular acceptance. This was the Lyceum, a lecture series that introduced adult citizens, especially those in small and rural towns, to scholarly knowledge, generally in an applied context. These lectures attempted to raise the educational level of adults who had not had the opportunity to complete an elementary education, and the movement became a strong supporter of common schools in each community. Much of the Lyceum program was provided by traveling lecturers who dispensed both enlightenment and inspiration through well-prepared and well-delivered orations. The Lyceum movement lasted more than 100 years and was the means for bringing intellectual stimulation into many of the rural areas of the nation, especially the Midwest.

The Chautauqua movement followed the development of the Lyceum by 50 years and provided a combination of religious orientation, liberal education, and the performing arts. Founded as a summer assembly on the shore of Lake Chautauqua, New York, in 1874, it provided training for Sunday school teachers, enlightenment for church members, and the basis for a national series of tent performances over several decades. Although it had been established by the Methodist Episcopal Church, the summer assembly was basically nondenominational and drew audiences from a wide area. Music, drama, lectures, discussions, and individual study were encouraged in a pleasant and relaxed atmosphere, which proved to be appealing to many people. The "tent Chautauquas" provided similar programs across the nation but did not include the residential aspect of the original New York setting. The summer learning retreats remain popular today and provide the setting for many education programs for older people.

There is little reason to believe that the Junto, Lyceum, or Chautauqua were primarily designed or operated for older learners. The Lyceum was principally oriented toward younger people, and the Junto included people of all ages. The Chautauqua may have appealed more frequently to older people because it was a summer resort where people frequently stayed several days to several weeks. Today many of the people in attendance are of retirement age, but this may be a recent phenomenon. These programs, however, provide the basic orientation of most of the current programs for older adults—liberal education, religious education, vocation and personal education, and civic and community education.

EDUCATION PROGRAMS FOR OLDER LEARNERS

Educational programs for older people today reflect the history and heritage of the adult education movement. They include a variety of program types and purposes as wide as Moody's categories. Many have been in existence for several years and have developed distinctive formats and extensive offerings. It is not surprising, then, that these programs are so difficult to characterize and that their history has been reviewed so infrequently. The diversity of programs makes them very troublesome to describe and the lack of a formal history offers the reviewer limited clues to their collective genesis. There are several reasons why description is difficult: the lack of agreement about what education comprises; the diversity of agencies and institutions that offer these programs; the lack of a national association to coordinate and facilitate these programs; the variety of funding sources that support programs; and the lack of a continuing collection and presentation of data on program content, enrollment, and budget.

The weakness of the field in these five areas clearly indicates the present limited institutionalization of this type of program. Educational offerings for older people have diverse sponsors, program types, audiences, and content. There is no central system of support for or monitoring of these activities, so their patterns depend on the preferences of administrators and the needs of local communities. This often makes them very responsive to the wishes of the clientele, but it does not facilitate development of easily described categories of programs, nor does it provide much assistance in replicating a program with other sites and sponsors.

An additional reason for lack of clarity in this developing area is the unevenness of program reporting. Those few fortunate organizations that have received financial support from a federal agency or foundation have frequently been required or encouraged to report their results in monographs or journal articles. Many of these reports are available and constitute the best sources for assessing the state of the field. Most programs, however, have been built on local funding without being expected or required to disseminate information about their progress. Consequently, descriptions are not likely to be found in the literature, and the programs are less visible beyond their own boundaries and may be overlooked in any summary of activities in this general area.

However, a number of surveys have been conducted that were designed to provide insight into the extent and type of instructional programming (American Association of State Colleges and Universities, 1974; Chelsvig & Timmermann, 1979; DeCrow, n.d., 1978; Edelson, 1976; Glickman, Hersey, & Goldberg, 1975; Hendrickson & Barnes, 1964; Institute of Law and Aging, 1978; Korim, 1974; Rappole, 1978; Sarno, 1975; Scanlon, 1978; Sprouse, 1976). Although each of these report on some of the information collected, most emphasize that the response rate was too small for the data to be generalizable. Thus, the researchers resort to the method of describing selected programs as models of what can be done in specific settings and content areas. This provides extensive understanding of the history and operation of an individual institution's project, but it does not offer much insight into the comparative aspects of program development or the general extent of educational programming for older adults. We are left with a very partial view of the programs both historically and currently. We must be guided by both what is said and not said and balance it with general knowledge and personal experience, hoping that the true pattern of development is not too different from what is described here.

Early Programs

Educational opportunities for older people developed as an extension of other community-based adult education programs. The earliest comprehensive survey of such activities (Donahue, 1955) indicated that a wide variety of instructional programs were under way by the mid-1950s but that many of these began by simply including older people in the organization's or agency's existing offerings. As in Florio's first category of educational programs, older people were not the primary audience but were included in programs designed originally for other age groups. Later these programs were modified to make them more appealing to, and more specifically oriented toward, older people.

The breadth of institutional sponsorship 35 years ago is truly surprising, for adult education activities then as today were diverse in both content and sponsorship. Donahue's summary describes instructional programs offered by public schools, colleges, university extensions, agricultural extensions, correspondence, libraries, state agencies, federal agencies, employment agencies, institutions, business and industry, government, and unions. Each of these sponsors reported that older participants were receptive to the programs. Few of these programs included a separate administrative base for their operations. Most were sponsored by an organization or agency designed for some purpose other than education for older people. Older adult education was still an adjunct to their primary mission, and although there was major commitment to the programs that were operating, there was little commitment to develop a separate organizational structure that would ensure their long-range maintenance.

It is not surprising that the number of participants reported was very small. Often programs attracted only a few dozen people and succeeded or failed based on the continued interest and participation of the local citizenry. Program development began with the first correspondence course at the University of Chicago in 1952; the first preretirement education program about the same time; the first community needs survey in 1949 by the University of Michigan; and numerous other events that led to later expansion and refinement.

In the 1960s programs spread into a greater number of agencies and institutions. Although the types of programs changed little, it became less difficult to identify local programs that were providing educational services to older people in any part of the country. The extent and pervasiveness of programs grew rapidly as interest in the problems of older people expanded. Because the 1960s were a time of social concern for many underprivileged groups, it is not surprising that instructional efforts for older people took on a social service orientation (in Moody's terms). Educational programs emphasized the crisis aspects of adjustment to retirement and the need for outside assistance to overcome the trauma of role change. Program rationales emphasized the needs of older people and the responsibility of social institutions to meet these needs.

One example of this type of instructional program can be seen in the preparation for retirement programs developed at the University of Chicago and the University of Michigan in the early 1950s. Within both industry and higher education, counseling and instructional programs were developed in order to provide assistance to the older worker who was considering retirement. Hunter's work at the University of Michigan was the most visible of these activities, and his surveys of programs as well as his longitudinal research on program outcomes provided much of the literature available at the time (Brahce & Hunter, 1985). Retirement education was rapidly expanded with the passage of the 1978 Age Discrimination in Employment Amendments (ADEA). It has continued to develop and now emphasizes life and career planning.

The ADEA amendments, which have virtually eliminated mandatory retirement, have also encouraged the development of retraining programs for older workers in business and industry. Although such projects have existed for many years and have been described and refined by Belbin and Belbin (1972), interest in them has grown slowly since the passage of the recent legislation. Dennis has contributed to this literature through the publication of *Retirement Preparation* (1984) and *Fourteen Steps in Managing an Aging Work Force* (1988). Although some employers have begun investing in the retraining of older workers, the area has not developed as rapidly as anticipated and has yet to play a major part in the education of older people.

A shift in the social service orientation can be noted in the background paper to the 1971 White House Conference on Aging. In it McClusky accurately reflected the new orientation of the 1970s when he changed the emphasis by pointing out the positive nature of education and the potential of every person, regardless of age. His statement that education is an affirmative enterprise resulting in positive outcomes has been quoted on numerous occasions and proved to be the orientation of the field through much of the decade.

Conferences and Publications

Educational programming for older adults continued to develop during the 1970s and was encouraged through a variety of conferences and publications. Florida State University was an early entrant into this area, offering annual conferences in the late 1960s and early 1970s designed to train leaders in education for the aging. It is interesting that each of these early conferences had a heavy dosage of introductory gerontology, including an overview of the physiological, psychological, and social aspects of the aging process. Also included were the educational interests of the elderly, program planning, and experiences of other programs. These conferences often resulted in a publication of the presentations, which was widely circulated for later reference and use.

The New England Gerontology Center held similar conferences in 1974 and 1975, which brought together many educators and program planners from that part of the country and gave impetus to the developing programs in the Northeast. Other conferences (at the University of Michigan in 1968, the University of Southern California in 1972, and Virginia Beach in 1975) have added to the visibility of the area and have provided stimulation to its continuing growth.

Regional and national meetings of gerontological and adult education associations have also helped the process. The Western Gerontological Society (now the American Society on Aging) has made education for older people a major part of its annual conferences for several years. Because the organization is oriented primarily toward the practitioner, workshops and symposia have dealt with program design and operation rather than with research. The Gerontological Society of America, through the auspices of its Education Committee, held several well-attended symposia on education and training in aging at its annual meetings in the early 1970s. These tended to focus on research and conceptualization of program purposes. National policy issues regarding funding of these programs were also a major consideration and took a substantial portion of the time.

The Adult Education Association of the U.S.A. (AEA) had a section on Aging since its establishment in 1951 and has generally included some sessions on older participants in its annual conferences. The AEA was active in developing publications in the area of education for the aging, including Donahue's (1955) book; Grabowski and Mason's *Education for the Aging* (n.d.); and Jacobs, Mason, and Kauffman's summary of the field and bibliography (1970). There were few other major publications before the mid-1970s. Thus, AEA and its Aging Section may be given credit for developing publications that provide much of our knowledge of activities before 1970.

The conferences and workshops, as well as individual project reports, provide a number of guides for the development of instruction for older people. Most of these include an overview of the changing demographic nature of the U.S. population, a rationale for the development of such programs, and some recommendations for program development (Academy for Educational Development, 1974; *Adventures in Learning*, 1969; Claeys, 1976; Cross & Florio, 1978; DeCrow, n.d.; Edelson, 1976; Glickman et al., 1975; Hendrickson, 1973; Hendrickson & Aker, 1969; Hixson, 1968; Myhr, 1976; Scanlon, 1978). Most of these reports were published in paperback and generally have had limited distribution. It is interesting that until the 1980s there were so few volumes offered through commercial publishers that provided the "how to" of educational programming for older people.

Several books on the topic have been published recently. The second edition of *Introduction to Educational Gerontology* (Sherron & Lumsden, 1985) provides background material on educational philosophy and psychology as well as on program planning, instructional methods, evaluation, and intergenerational programming. A second book by Lumsden, *The Older Adult As Learner* (1985), deals primarily with instructional considerations in working with older people. A recent volume published in England, *Educational Gerontology: International Perspectives* (Glendenning, 1985), provides an overview of international thinking and developments of the field.

Peterson's *Facilitating Education for Older Learners* (1983), is one of the few books that has been written by a single author and thus provides a more integrated view of the field although without the diversity of perception that is included in other volumes. Peterson, Thornton, and Birren (1986) have recently edited *Education and Aging*, which deals with several aspects of the field. Although it is more abstract and theoretical than most other publications, it does include broad coverage of thinking in this area. Lowy and O'Connor (1986) have contributed *Why Education in the Later Years?*, which examines that issue as well as other aspects of older adult instruction.

Lumsden made another substantial contribution to the field through the establishment of a journal, *Educational Gerontology: An International Bimonthly Journal*. Although the international orientation is not often in evidence, the journal has provided an enormous service to researchers and practitioners who wish to share their results, insights, and thoughts regarding the design and operation of education for older people. Since its beginning in 1976, the journal has consistently published high-quality papers covering the subject from a variety of perspectives. It has published special issues on old age and literature (1977), training (1979), reading (1979), rural aging and education (1980), international perspectives (1984), socioclinical geriatrics (1986), cognitive development (1986), gerontological education (1986), and religion and aging (1988). These have provided comprehensive and useful treatments of these areas, and its regular feature on learning resources is a relevant and helpful summary of recent publications and materials. Although it is not the product of a scholarly organization, the journal has done more than any other single source during the decade to make the field of research and practice of education for the aging visible and respected.

Another journal, *Gerontology and Geriatrics Education*, tends to elicit articles that deal with gerontology instruction, but occasionally it includes articles dealing with instruction for older people. Other journals such as the National Council on the Aging's *Perspective on Aging* (1987) and the American Society on Aging's *Generations* (1987–1988) occasionally publish special issues on education for older people.

Recent Developments in Education for Older Adults

In 1970, community colleges became the focus of the expanding instructional network on aging when the Administration on Aging provided a grant to the American Association of Community and Junior Colleges (AACJC) to encourage that organization "to develop an awareness of the needs of older Americans and to explore ways in which these community-oriented institutions might contribute to an improvement in the quality of life in the nation's elderly population'' (Korim, 1974, p. 5). This project involved several conferences and workshops, a survey of current activities, and the publication of several documents designed to help the local college understand the needs of the older person and how it might help meet them.

It is not possible to determine the specific effects of this project, but it is fair to say that the mid-1970s saw the development of many new programs for older people by community and junior colleges. These programs were not all educational in nature, but they did indicate the increasing willingness of the community college system to include older people in existing programs and to design special ones for older people in their service area. Some of this development would have come without the AACJC project, but its activities were initiated at an ideal time and the dynamic leadership given it by Korim provided a major impetus to the development of programs in two-year colleges across the nation.

Another major development of the 1970s was the rapid growth of residential education for older persons. Through the Elderhostel Program, week-long programs of instruction, discussion, and entertainment are provided for older people by colleges and universities across the nation. These programs have grown rapidly in the past five years and have attracted thousands of people to learning activities reminiscent of the Chautauqua movement. There are few other examples of residential education for older people, but the response to this offering has proven once again that a combination of stimulating atmosphere, congenial company, and varied activities is both desired and appreciated by older people. Basically a return to the liberal arts programs of the past with a sprinkling of civic instruction, its future growth may prove to be one of the most significant trends in senior adult education. It is a start toward Moody's category of self-actualization and a clear step into full participation.

The growth of educational programming for older people was not a result of funding from any single source. Most of the activity occurred under the sponsorship of local agencies and institutions with support from their regular program budget. In other words, program developers and administrators initiated these new programs for older adults in addition to continuing whatever other responsibilities they had. It was doubtless common for an individual staff member to subsidize the program development until the organization could be convinced that the program was worthwhile.

From the national point of view, two funding sources added substantially to program growth. One source, the federal government, has supported education for the aging in several ways. Title I of the Higher Education Act of 1965 has been used by colleges and universities to direct their resources and staff to program development for older people. Although many additional types of community programs were funded under this title, programs for the aging have been developed in many parts of the country and have become a major part of the overall education pattern. The Administration on Aging has also funded many educational programs. Initially under Title III, and later as part of the Nutrition Program and Model Projects, numerous educational components of other projects and specific instructional programs were supported. There has not been any continuing or national strategy in these grants; they have stimulated much action and interest but have resulted in relatively little insight into the most effective means of designing, implementing, or conducting education for older people.

The second funding source is private foundations. Although many foundations have given local awards, only a few have devoted large amounts of money to this area and continued the support over several years. The Edna McConnell Clark Foundation chose to support a few projects, especially those involving the design of volunteer and employment opportunities for older people. Through the Academy for Educational Development and several local projects, the foundation attempted to show what can be done by consistent support. Several of their publications indicate the value of educational programs and describe the steps involved in their development, but the information does not provide much insight into the best means of developing such a project. The Charles Stewart Mott Foundation from 1981 to 1988 supported a number of second-career coordinating agencies that conducted training in job seeking and career development for older people. This project involved conscious goal setting within the field of education for older people and the continuation of funding for several years (Mott Foundation, 1988).

An understanding of the development of education for older people is not possible without at least a mention of the impact of one individual. Although many people have contributed, including several of the authors of this book, one person's involvement clearly stands out: Howard Y. McClusky, Professor Emeritus of Education at the University of Michigan. In reviewing conferences, symposia, workshops, and papers on education for the aging, McClusky emerges as one of the major speakers and thinkers in the field. His background paper for the 1971 White House Conference on Aging has already been mentioned. His many articles and papers are widely used, and his influence has also been felt in terms of his personal assistance. No other individual whom I have had the opportunity to know has so consistently and tirelessly helped others develop programs for older people. At conferences and meetings, in his office or his home, in the classroom or at workshops, he was continually supportive and enthusiastic about the great potential of education for older people as a positive force to be developed and directed in the years ahead. His personal support of individuals who planned programs and his willingness to listen, share, and compliment has led to the establishment of many programs based on his original ideas and continuing encouragement. His support of education and individuals is similar to his belief that education will ultimately change the social patterns of the nation and improve the involvement of older people in daily life. He has given to the field the notion of education as an affirmative enterprise, which builds on the possibilities and potential of older people; he has also given to hundreds of individuals the belief that they can succeed, and that through their faith in education and in themselves they can make the world a better place to live.

IMPLICATIONS OF EDUCATION
FOR THE AGING

Educational programs for older people have now developed to such a point that we can begin to gain some perspective on their growth and to identify some trends that have emerged. The history of the movement thus far produces several implications, four of which I discuss. First, there now seems to be general acceptance that we are living in a learning society, in which people of every age will be required to continue to expand their knowledge and skills in order to survive and prosper. This is the foundation for the support of instructional programs for older people. Although major needs remain in terms of financial resources for this activity, hesitation about the involvement of older people in programs of educational and community institutions and agencies is rapidly disappearing. Discussions are more likely to center around whether age-segregated or age-integrated education is preferable, rather than whether there is a value in including older people in educational programs.

This change is especially clear in the nation's community colleges, where literally thousands of older people register each semester. It is apparent to most community college administrators that their close relationship with residents of the geographic area they serve will require them to respond to the needs and interests of those residents, many of whom are old. Some colleges are now enrolling a large proportion of their total student body in classes especially for older people. Other agencies, such as public schools, universities, libraries, museums, and recreation centers, are also seeking older participants, because they are a consistent and receptive clientele.

The era has passed when gerontologists and leaders of older persons' organizations must explain the need for institutions and agencies to provide services to older people. Sponsors are now seeking opportunities on their own and developing programs without demands from outsiders. We have been successful in gaining recognition of the needs and wants of the older group and now face a period when concern for quality will replace concern for program existence.

The second implication is that the acceptance of the rationale for education for older people has modified the orientation of many instructional programs. No longer do the introductory statements of programs deal only with the difficulties that arise in old age; more frequently they stress the ability of people to grow and develop throughout their entire lives. Older people are seen as individuals with potential who can contribute and serve as well as cope and survive. This change in orientation has led to many more programs oriented toward Moody's category of self-actualization and growth. Liberal education, psychological growth, and broadening experience are becoming a greater part of the programs; lifelong planning is replacing adjustment to retirement.

Third, education for older people is no longer a modest undertaking rating little time or interest and relegated to the smallest division of an institution. Higher level administrators are realizing the potential of this education and are increasingly involved in its development. As more older people enroll, the staff and budget will increase and so will the program's influence in the organization. To date, however, although the number of participants is high, most budgets are still very limited. Those directly administering the programs are doing so with minimal staff, and only through their own extensive commitment do the programs succeed. The size of the enrollment is beginning to have an effect, and financial support, staff size, and professionalism are starting to increase.

Finally, as the enrollment of older people increases, institutions that in the past have simply encouraged older people to participate in their regular programs are beginning to develop special offerings exclusively for them. These new programs fall into Florio's second and third categories, resulting in separate administration, program, and budget. As this occurs, recognition of the other needs of older people has developed. That is, when older people are included in the regular courses or programs of an institution, they are often treated like everyone else. However, it is now apparent that they often will not accept the difficulties of admission, registration, and tuition that others have tolerated. For older students, these bureaucratic processes must be streamlined and abbreviated. Major modifications of the usual administrative procedures will follow an awareness of this problem.

Likewise, those individuals teaching courses that include older people will discover the need for special knowledge of them as students. Adjustments for changes in vision and hearing will be insufficient; instructors also must understand the role of experience in the older students' lives, their educational background, self-image, desire for relevance, and need for slower pacing. Ideally this will lead to in-service education of faculty and to development of knowledge about the older person as a student and learner.

FUTURE EDUCATION FOR THE AGING

The task of educators and program planners over the past decades has been to encourage the development of instructional programs that would attract older people, and to secure organizational support for these programs. To a large extent this has been accomplished. As Donahue reported, "our colleges are slowly but surely beginning to set up a wide variety of courses, institutes and research studies aimed at the ultimate goal of making man's later years his golden years" (1952, p. 119). That statement was made by the New York state Joint Legislative Committee on Problems on the Aging in 1949, and it is still true 40 years later. This part of the task is rapidly being completed, for awareness and programmatic adaptation are quickly expanding.

The future holds more of this development. The number of people reaching age 65 will be larger and they will have higher levels of formal education, higher socioeconomic status, better health, and greater involvement in adult education. Each of these qualities is positively associated with participation in education in later life, so older peoples' demand for instruction should continue to expand.

Likewise, there is reason to believe that our educational and service agencies will increase their willingness to serve older people as their younger clientele decline in numbers. Although there are still misconceptions about later life and negative attitudes toward the potential of older people, as extensive knowledge about aging is widely disseminated it will become harder to resist including older people in any educational enterprise. Institutions will welcome them and make provision for special services, and trained instructors will be prepared for the unique circumstances of teaching this group.

There remain, however, several major concerns and issues in the development of educational programming for older people. The first of these deals with the stigma that is still attached to old age and the elderly. Some educators refuse to offer courses dealing with the topic of aging, or to list their courses as being specifically for older people. They believe that older people should not be segregated in any way and prefer to offer their programs to all adults, although the students are almost exclusively older people. The Elderhostel Program, for instance, does not include content about aging. Although the program is restricted to people over age 60, its directors do not believe that these people want to study gerontology. Other providers attempt to ignore the age of their clientele, choosing euphemisms for their programs that omit any mention of old age. This reluctance to admit that the clients are old or that this time of life involves any uniqueness reinforces the stereotypes that old age is to be avoided, ignored, or denied. A preferable strategy would be to admit that one is serving older clients, to provide both age-segregated and age-integrated instruction, and to treat old age realistically, as a period including unique problems and opportunities.

A second major concern for the future is the method by which educational activities for older people will be financed. Federal and foundation funds are not nearly sufficient for the number of programs currently operating and being planned. Long-range funding will have to come from the states or from the sponsoring institutions themselves. This will require a recognition that education for this group is appropriate and valuable and will require revising program priorities. Public institutions will require state support for this to occur. Typically, state support has been primarily for credit students, with noncredit enrollees paying most of their own program costs. Because older people generally are not willing to pay high tuition for noncredit courses, either new support mechanisms or new definitions of credit courses will be needed.

Third, increased funding will be needed to improve the quality and efficiency of instruction. As indicated previously, reports on education for older people are largely anecdotal, providing little in the way of clear evaluations that may apply to other settings. We have limited insight as to why certain programs fail while others succeed. The many questions that need systematic study include the long-term effect on a program of top administration's involvement; the importance of a charismatic leader; the effect of outside funding being withdrawn; the value of advisory committees; the best mix of classes in personal development, liberal education, and coping skills; the effects of educational participation on the lives of older participants; the effect of a senior citizen program on voting behavior in local elections; the most effective types of instruction for various groups of learners; and the effect of older people's involvement in traditional programs.

Today we have only fragmentary data on these and dozens of other questions regarding the development and conduct of instructional programs for older people. Over the past 40 years, the many programs that have been established have met local needs and have been guided by local organization guidelines. The developmental stages have been reported infrequently, and little insight into the unique circumstances and activities has been gained. Few research projects have examined the outcomes of the procedures, and none has compared the approaches of several administrators or instructors.

Currently no government or private group regularly collects data on the extent, type, and budget of existing programs. The surveys done by the National Center for Educational Statistics (1978) in 1969, 1972, and 1975 provide some insight into the changing enrollment of older people in adult education, but this is the only panel study that has attempted to indicate trends. Various studies such as those by Johnstone and Rivera (1965) and Harris and Associates (1975) can be compared, but differing samples, instruments, and analyses make gleaning insights difficult. What is needed is a continuing collection of data on older people in educational programs.

A fourth concern for the future lies in the expanded use of the media for educating older people. There have been several television programs designed exclusively for middle-aged and older people. These include *Over Easy, Old Friends/ New Friends*, and *Winslow House* (Davis, 1980). The impact of these programs on the older segment of our population remains unknown, but they have the potential for raising the level of consciousness as well as the knowledge about many aspects of aging. The programs clearly are aimed at older people, so they are surely avoided by some people who refuse to consider themselves in this category. How these people can be reached remains to be seen. Funding is a problem for these endeavors, and their long-range success may depend on government and foundation funding rather than on commercial assumption of the costs.

A fifth area where attention is needed is the new-found interest of business and industry in the creation of training programs for middle-aged and older people. Corporations that once limited their activities to preretirement education are now retraining older workers, training people who supervise them, and upgrading personnel staff who work with them. The 1978 Amendments to the Age Discrimination of Employment Act have made compulsory retirement before the age of 70 illegal. Although most people will probably choose to retire before age 70, others may exercise their rights to continue working and thereby create major training responsibilities for business and industry. Little experience in this area currently exists, and substantial future development is likely.

A sixth concern is the need for inclusion of older participants from all socioeconomic levels in the educational programs. Today, a majority of the older participants are those with the highest levels of education, income, and employment. We have been relatively unsuccessful in attracting those who have the greatest need for education. With the expansion of the older population and the increasing interest in education, it should be relatively easy to design programs and recruit increasing numbers of older people of higher socioeconomic status. These programs must be balanced with those for people with less education, limited literacy, little knowledge of English, and fewer coping skills. Financial support from the federal government and foundations should give first priority to these individuals and programs.

Finally, continued discussion, debate, and clarification are needed to determine the highest priorities for educational programs. Education is interventionist by nature; that is, it is undertaken to bring about change, preferably for the better. We have not reached general agreement on which changes are most needed, which programs are of greatest importance, and which outcomes are most desired. The possible results of education are almost limitless. Which should we seek most diligently? Birren and Woodruff (1973) suggest three: elimination of illiteracy, skill development for problem solving, and prevention of future problems. McClusky (1971) adds the development of contributive skills and those needed to influence society. The Academy for Educational Development suggested new roles both in employment and volunteerism. Moody (1976) urged self-actualization through liberal education.

Each of these suggestions is appropriate and has a place in the future development and refinement of educational programs for older people. Growth will probably occur in all areas. However, the trend seems clear from the past: as long as funds are limited and institutional commitments come grudgingly, program designers will choose those activities that appeal to the most people with the least expenditure of resources. These are the classes that are recreational, social and enjoyable, light and entertaining. These programs are valuable and should be continued, but they should be supplemented by courses of greater substance, with outreach aimed at nonparticipants and with outcomes of social value. Older people can continue to make social contributions throughout their lives. Education has a responsibility to see that they contribute as extensively as possible.

REFERENCES

Academy for Educational Development. (1974). *Never too old to learn*. New York: Author.
Adventures in learning. (1969). Providence, RI: University of Rhode Island.
American Association of State Colleges and Universities. (1974). *Alternatives for later life and learning: Some programs designed for older persons at state colleges and universities*. Washington, DC: Author.
American Society on Aging. (1987–1988). *Generations, 12*.
Belbin, E., & Belbin, R. M. (1972). *Problems in adult retraining*. London, England: Heinemann.
Birren, J. E., & Woodruff, D. (1973). Human development over the life span through education. In P. Baltes & W. Schaie (Eds.), *Life span developmental psychology* (pp. 305–337). New York: Academic Press.
Brahce, C. I., & Hunter, W. W. (1985). Leadership training for retirement education. In

R. H. Sherron & D. B. Lumsden (Eds.), *Introduction to educational gerontology* (2nd ed., pp. 275–301). Washington, DC: Hemisphere.

Chelsvig, K. A., & Timmermann, S. (1979). Tuition policies of higher educational institutions and state governments and the older learner. *Educational Gerontology, 4,* 147–159.

Claeys, R. R. (1976). *Utilization of college resources in gerontology: A program guide.* Upper Montclair, NJ: Montclair State College.

Cross, W., & Florio, C. (1978). *You are never too old to learn.* New York: McGraw-Hill.

Davis, R. H. (1980). *Television and the aging audience.* Los Angeles: University of Southern California, Andrus Gerontology Center.

DeCrow, R. (n.d.). *New learning for older Americans.* Washington, DC: Adult Education Association of the U.S.A.

DeCrow, R. (1978). *Older Americans: New uses of mature ability.* Washington, DC: American Association of Community and Junior Colleges.

Dennis, H. (1984). *Retirement preparation.* Lexington, MA: Lexington Books.

Dennis, H. (1988). Fourteen steps to managing an aging work force. Lexington, MA: Lexington Books.

Donahue, W. T., (Ed.). (1955). *Education for later maturity.* New York: Whiteside.

Donahue, W. T. (1952, January). Education's role in maintaining the individual's status. *The Annals of the American Academy of Political and Social Science,* pp. 115–125.

Edelson, I. (1976). *The role of state university systems in opportunities for senior citizens.* Albany, NY: State University of New York at Albany.

Erikson, E. H. (1980). *Identity and the life cycle.* New York: Norton.

Florio, C. (n.d.). *Education and work programs for older persons.* Unpublished manuscript.

Frank, L. K. (1955). Education for aging. In W. T. Donahue (Ed.), *Education for later maturity,* (pp. 1–18). New York: Whiteside.

Glendenning, F. (1985). *Educational gerontology: International perspectives.* London, England: Croom Helm.

Glickman, L. L., Hersey, B. S., & Goldberg, I. I. (1975). *Community colleges respond to elders: A sourcebook for program development.* Washington, DC: National Institute of Education.

Grabowski, S. M., & Mason, W. D. (Eds.). (n.d.). *Education for the aging.* Syracuse, NY: ERIC Clearinghouse on Adult Education.

Grattan, C. H. (1955). *In quest of knowledge.* New York: Associated Press.

Harris, L., & Associates. (1975). *The myth and reality of aging in America.* Washington, DC: National Council on the Aging.

Hendrickson, A. (Ed.). (1973). *A manual on planning educational programs for older adults.* Tallahassee, FL: Florida State University.

Hendrickson, A., & Aker, G. F. (1969). *Education for senior adults* (ERIC Document Reproduction Service No. ED 032 511). Tallahassee, FL: Florida State University.

Hendrickson, A., & Barnes, R. E. (1964). *The role of colleges and universities in the education of the aged.* Columbus, OH: Ohio State University.

Hixson, L. E. (1968). *Formula for success: A step by step procedure for organizing a local institute of lifetime learning.* Long Beach, CA: Institute of Lifetime Learning.

Institute of Law and Aging. (1978). *Survey of national law school programs and materials in law and aging.* Washington, DC: George Washington University, National Law Center.

Jacobs, A. L., Mason, W. D., & Kauffman, E. (1970). *Education for aging: A review of recent literature.* Washington, DC: Adult Education Association of the U.S.A.

Johnstone, J. W. C., & Rivera, R. J. (1965). *Volunteers for learning.* Chicago, IL: Aldine.

Korim, A. S. (1974). *Older Americans and community colleges: An overview.* Washington, DC: American Association of Community and Junior Colleges.

Lowy, L., & O'Connor, D. (1986). *Why education in the later years?* Lexington, MA: Lexington Books.

Lumsden, D. B. (Ed.). (1985). *The older adult as learner.* Washington, DC: Hemisphere.

McClusky, H. Y. (1971). *Education: Background and issues.* Washington, DC: White House Conference on Aging, U.S. Department of Health and Human Services.

Moody, H. R. (1976). Philosophical presuppositions of education for old age. *Educational Gerontology, 1,* 1–16.

Mott Foundation (1988). *Coordinating older worker programs: An update and guide to Mott Foundation resources.* Flint, MI: Author.

Myhr, P. J. (1976). *The older adult's training program: A report on the 1975–76 developmental year.* Seattle, WA: University of Washington.

National Center for Educational Statistics. (1978). *Participation in adult education: Final report.* Washington, DC: U.S. Department of Health, Education and Welfare.

National Council on the Aging. (1987). *Perspectives on aging, 16.*

Peterson, D. A. (1976). Educational gerontology: The state of the art. *Educational Gerontology, 1,* 61–73.

Peterson, D. A. (1983). *Facilitating education for older learners.* San Francisco, CA: Jossey-Bass.

Peterson, D. A., Thornton, J. E., & Birren, J. E. (Eds.). (1986). *Education and aging.* Englewood Cliffs, NJ: Prentice-Hall.

Rappole, G. H. (1978). An overview of community college programs for elderly Texans. *Educational Gerontology, 3,* 35–59.

Sarno, M. R. (1975). *Activities in the field of aging as reported by representatives of colleges and universities in Ohio.* Columbus, OH: Columbus Technical Institute.

Scanlon, J. (1978). *How to plan a college program for older people.* New York: Academy for Educational Development.

Sherron, R. H., & Lumsden, D. B. (Eds.). (1985). *Introduction to educational gerontology,* (2nd ed.). Washington, DC: Hemisphere.

Sprouse, B. (Ed.). (1976). *National directory of educational programs in gerontology.* Washington, DC: U.S. Government Printing Office.

2

EDUCATION AND THE LIFE CYCLE: A PHILOSOPHY OF AGING

HARRY R. MOODY

Hunter College of the
City University of New York

We shall not cease from exploration
And the end of all our exploring
Will be to arrive where we started
And know the place for the first time.

T. S. Eliot

EXPERIENCE

In the art and iconography of cultures the world over, we find a recurrent symbol, a special form of the circular *mandala* called the *Ouroborus,* which depicts a snake eating its own tail. This is an image of the human life cycle: a circle that returns to its origins and completes itself only upon arrival at the starting point. In old age, too, there is a closure, a completion of the life cycle, with an opportunity to "arrive where we started" and "know the place for the first time." With this goal in mind, I would suggest that education of older people should be grounded in life experience: in the history and the life cycle of the learner.

Older people bring to the learning situation a lifetime of personal experience that can be not only their greatest resource but also their greatest stumbling block. The ancient Greeks understood the problem well: the tragic flaw of the dramatic hero serves to remind us that our greatest strength is also our hidden flaw and deepest weakness. So too with the life experience of the older person: experience may lead to wisdom or it may lead to dogmatism. In any event, experience is the unavoidable condition of learning for the older person, and so, as teachers, we ignore it at our peril. I believe that education for older adults will achieve its purpose only when we situate our educational objectives within a conception of the human life cycle as a whole.

Old people have been around a long time, and when they come to subjects like literature or history or psychology, they have already had a wide experience of the phenomenon under study. They are not necessarily knowledgeable about the disciplines we have to offer, but they have another strength. The older person who comes to study these subjects at age 60 or 70 is in many ways much better equipped than the typical 18-year-old college student to appreciate what literature or history or psychology really have to offer us through broadening or deepening our understanding of life. The older person may come to the subject in a deeper way than might have been possible at another point in the life cycle. Too often the learning process of the older adult is examined exclusively from the standpoint of losses: memory, perceptual functions, cognitive deficiencies, and so on. What we need to do is, first, to recognize the special strengths that older people can bring to the classroom, and, second, to use these strengths to enrich the learning experience.

I began with some lines from T. S. Eliot's (1971) poem the *Four Quartets,* a profound meditation on the meaning of time, self, and aging. Among other things, Eliot's poem is a bitter condemnation of the sentimental idea that old age necessarily brings with it wisdom. The poet asks:

> *What was to be the value of the long looked forward to,*
> *Long hoped for calm, the autumnal serenity*
> *And the wisdom of age? Had they deceived us*
> *Or decieved themselves, the quiet-voiced elders,*
> *Bequeathing us merely a receipt for deceit? (p. 26)*

It is the tragic flaw of old age to believe that life experience—the experience of the past—automatically has continued meaning in the present. We have all seen how experience distorts our perception, conditions our responses, and reduces flexibility and ability to learn: we see a thing and we've seen it all before; we know the answer before we have even heard the question. Eliot (1971) writes:

> *There is, it seems to us,*
> *At best, only a limited value*
> *In the knowledge derived from experience.*
> *The knowledge imposes a pattern, and falsifies,*
> *For the pattern is new in every moment*
> *And every moment is a new and shocking*
> *Valuation of all we have been. We are only undeceived*
> *Of that which, deceiving, could no longer harm. (p. 26)*

Every teacher of older people is familiar with the escape maneuvers, defense mechanisms, rigidities, and anxieties that Eliot summarizes in his phrase "the knowledge that imposes a pattern and falsifies." In rigidity, we sense the anguish of old people who feel all too keenly that time has passed them by, that their experience belongs to a world that no longer exists, and that they as people are obsolete and their experience without value or meaning. These people, who often feel "ignorant" because they lack formal educational credentials, are only a mirror image of other old people who glorify the past as a defense mechanism for coping with an uncertain present and a threatening future.

The defense is entirely understandable. The economy and the technological system of our society place decreased importance on life experience and tend to favor skills and knowledge that must be continually updated to avoid obsolescence. Outside the technological sphere, in the domain of customs, values, and family life, old people also find themselves at a disadvantage: their life experience is of less and less value in a world of rapid social change. If old people try to preserve lessons derived from life experience, they are in part simply trying to preserve themselves and their sense of who they are. Yet this very attempt at self-preservation can destroy the possibility for growth and adaptation in the present. As teachers of older adults, we are compelled to understand this predicament because it is our role to facilitate the conversion of life experience from an obstacle, into a source of strength, through education.

Our attitude toward our own past deeply affects the quality of life, whether we hold on to it too dearly or disown it too readily. To *disown the past* means to act as if age makes no difference at all, as if life experience were irrelevant. Don't think about the past too much; be actively engaged in projects and new activities; look to the present and to the future: Such seems to be the advice of Simone de Beauvoir. We often see this approach advocated for older people who return for education in retirement, to discover new hobbies, second careers, or leisure-time activities. Their past, their life experience, is forgotten, by teacher and student alike.

This attitude toward the past is common in America, a country dominated by the image of the future. The past represents what is used up, what is bypassed and rejected. Old people feel it too: how often we meet old people who simply deny that they are old! This, too, is a defense mechanism, a form of denial, that deprives life of its meaning and rejects the irreversibility of the human experience of time. By contrast, consider the older people we know who are emotionally healthy. They have neither the dogmatism that comes from living too much in the past, nor the illusion of an endless present that denies the past and avoids the future. Instead, we find in such people a vivid acceptance of life in the present, a present that includes past and future. Perhaps the deepest definition of successful aging is simply this: to repair the past and prepare for the future by living in the present. To be alive and aware in the present is indeed the key, but this process should not mean avoiding the future—which for all of us is death—but rather, preparing for it in the deepest way possible. It should not mean disowning the past but repairing it instead by extracting from it a kind of insight that allows us to affirm its continued meaning. T. S. Eliot (1971) writes:

> It seems, as one becomes older
> That the past has another pattern, and ceases
> to be mere sequence—
> We had the experience but missed the meaning,
> And approach to the meaning restores the experience
> In a different form ... I have said before
> That the past experience revived in the meaning
> Is not the experience of one life only
> But of many generations ... (p. 39)

What would it mean for education in old age to make use of the past, of the learner's life experience? Here is the touchstone: the past ceases to be a mere sequence of events; we elicit from it something of universal significance. "Old men ought to be explorers," says Eliot, but he adds that "the end of all our exploring / will be to arrive where we started / And know the place for the first time." To arrive where we started is to discover in the pattern of life experience a meaning quite different from what it first appeared to be. "The meaning restores the experience in a different form ..." because the form of education is the universality of knowledge that makes each single human life into a microcosm for all generations. To *repair* the past means to discover in one's own life history something that is timeless. When we study the history of our immigrant forebears, we understand something about all immigrant groups; when old people read *King Lear,* they understand something about the recurrent conflict between parents and adult children. The past is then encompassed in knowledge that is liberating because it is simultaneously both personal and universal. This type of educational experience means neither to be imprisoned by the past nor to disown it, but rather to discover in life experience an unanswered question: the question of *meaning.*

It was Robert Butler who called attention to this point about the value of reminiscence in old age when he described the process of *life review.* In psychodynamic terms, the process of life review constitutes the major developmental task of old age, and it is the fundamental question for any philosophy of aging. Old people looking back at their life experience—just as all of us must, of whatever age, if we are honest with ourselves when we think about our past, about 5 years, 10 years, 50 years ago—cannot help wondering, What did it all mean? What did it amount to? What was the result of all those efforts that seemed so important at the time? This is the universal experience of time and aging that we find expressed in the opening lines of Neihardt's (1961) life story of a Sioux Indian chief, *Black Elk Speaks:*

> *My friend, I am going to tell you the story of my life, as you wish; and if it were only the story of my life I think I would not tell it; for what is one man that he should make much of his winters, even when they bend him like a heavy snow? So many other men have lived and shall live that story, to be grass upon the hills. . . .*
>
> *This, then, is not the tale of a great hunter or of a great warrior, or of a great traveler, although I have made much meat in my time and fought for my people both as boy and man, and have gone far and seen strange lands and men. So also have many others done, and better than I. These things I shall remember by the way, and often they may seem to be the very tale itself, as when I was living them in happiness and sorrow. But now that I can see it all as from a lonely hilltop, I know it was the story of a mighty vision given to a man too weak to use it; of a holy tree that should have flourished in a people's heart with flowers and singing birds, and now is withered; and of a people's dream that died in bloody snow.*
>
> *But if the vision was true and mighty, as I know, it is true and mighty yet; for such things are of the spirit, and it is in the darkness of their eyes that men get lost. (pp. 1, 2)*

The haunting eloquence of this last line expresses our dilemma: "It is in the darkness of their eyes that men get lost." Black Elk, telling the story of his life, sees clearly that the events of his experience—the travels, the adventures, the encounters with people—all of this amounts to nothing at the end. "These things I shall remember by the way, and often they may *seem* to be the very tale itself, as when I was living them in happiness and sorrow." The pattern of the past is not the mere sequence of events, even though it may seem that way as we are living those events. Old age has conveyed to Black Elk the vision to see it all "as from a lonely hilltop." Now he can grasp the pattern of *life as a whole*, and in this process of reviewing his own life, he finds the universality of the human condition. The circle is completed.

Contrast now this autobiography of a wise Indian chief with a work of modern literature such as Samuel Beckett's play *Krapp's Last Tape*, where we find an old man rummaging through tape recordings of intimate thoughts made in previous years. Now, in his old age, he finds the unlabeled tapes scattered through his bedroom. He is unable to put them into any kind of order, and as he listens to them, he cannot even recall what the talks were all about. The tape recordings, our subjective memories of the past, have become a meaningless jumble, like names and faces we can no longer remember. This is the image of old age in the contemporary world: the frightening possibility of total despair, a despair of life that has become meaningless, where time is a mere succession of moments, the future an abyss.

It is this image of the experience of time in old age that Simone de Beauvoir (1972) describes so vividly in *The Coming of Age*:

> *The past is not a peaceful landscape lying there behind me, a country in which I can stroll whenever I please, and which will gradually show me all its secret hills and dales. As I was moving forward, so it was crumbling. Most of the wreckage that can still be seen is colourless, distorted, frozen: its meaning escapes me. Here and there I see occasional pieces whose melancholy beauty enchants me. They do not suffice to populate this emptiness that Chateaubriand calls "the desert of the past." (p. 365)*

Life experience, in and of itself, furnishes us with no intimation of wisdom, only with an appalling recognition of "the desert of the past." As Simone de Beauvoir (1972) describes it, the fate of old age is bleak indeed:

> *A limited future and a frozen past: such is the situation that the elderly have to face up to. In many instances it paralyzes them. All their plans have either been carried out or abandoned, and their life has closed in about itself; nothing requires their presence; they no longer have anything whatsoever to do. (p. 378)*

Samuel Beckett and Simone de Beauvoir portray the existential anguish of the modern world: a complete rejection of the traditional image of old age as a period of wisdom. It is a protest that must be taken seriously. *The Coming of Age* is a profoundly important book, though I believe it will be clear that I disagree with Simone de Beauvoir's conclusions.

If our past is "frozen" wreckage, as Simone de Beauvoir suggests, and if our memories are like scattered tape recordings, then ideed the past becomes a "mere sequence" of events without meaning or purpose. As we look back at our own past, each of us inevitably finds a part of our experience that falls under this description. Our experience *is* puzzling, incomplete, fragmentary; we *do* lack the wholeness, the ego integrity, that is properly associated with the idea of wisom, but this is not the whole story by any means. The past is not finished, is not "frozen," as long as its meaning still escapes me: as long as I recognize in myself the capacity to discover in that past elements of universal significance. It is this sense of discovery that gives the process of life review its true significance and its relationship to continuing education throughout the life cycle.

If we accept this process of life review as being the major developmental task of old age, it must become the starting point for any theory of education that we might evolve. We will need to pay the closest attention to how older people use their life experience in the learning process in order to build on the strengths of experience in old age. As matters stand now, education for older adults tends to follow the pattern of adult education in general: an indiscriminate proliferation of courses based on student interest, guided only by the implicit faith that curiosity and new interests are intrinsically desirable. To date, educators have not been very creative in finding ways to *use* the student's own life experience to enhance the learning process. Many older people would just as soon forget the fact that they are old, and all too often our educational options for them encourage that tendency. We have yet to discover ways of integrating the rich life experience of older people into the classroom, of tying the lessons of experience to the conceptual structure of subject matter, instead of sacrificing one to the other. This observation leads me to my second major point, which concerns the methods of educating older adults, and here I want to focus specifically on the method of *dialogue.*

DIALOGUE

I have said that the unique strength of older people lies in their life experience, which, if we could find a way to unlock it, would unfold remarkable possibilities of growth and understanding. But where to turn for a model to accomplish this? I turn back to the origins of the Western philosophical tradition, to the thought of Plato, and in particular to Plato's (1966) dialogue, the *Meno,* perhaps the earliest treatise on the philosophy of education. This problem addressed by the *Meno*—Is it possible to teach virtue?—turns out to be essential for the education of older adults.

In the dialogue, we find Socrates interrogating a young boy about the principles of geometry. The boy professes to know nothing about geometry: he's never studied the subject, but under Socrates' skillful questioning, he successfully reconstructs a theorem describing the relation between the area of a square and its diagonal sections. The ignorant boy turns out to be not so ignorant as he himself had imagined. He has answered Socrates' questions on his own and yet just a few minutes before he did not "know" the correct answers. Thus, concludes Socrates:

> So a man who does not know has in himself true opinions on a subject without having knowledge.

Meno: *It would appear so.*

Socrates: *At present these opinions, being newly aroused, have a dreamlike quality. But if the same questions are put to him on many occasions and in different ways, you can see that in the end he will have a knowledge on the subject as accurate as anybody's.*

Meno: *Probably.*

Socrates: *This knowledge will not come from teaching but from questioning. He will recover it for himself. (p. 370)*

A whole Platonic epistemology is implicit in this fragment of the dialogue. All of us have opinions arising from our experience of the world. Over and above such opinions stands the realm of systematized knowledge: of science and scholarship. When we consider this realm of systematized knowledge, these opinions derived from life experience are likely to seem but confused, partial renditions of a complex reality. Thus we are inclined to devalue life experience and defer instead to the experts, the scholars, the "people who know" those disciplines that describe the world of our everyday experience. We see this tendency to devalue life experience—and to defer to "the professor"—especially among older people who have been away from school for many years.

Yet, like the slave boy in the *Meno,* all of us possess much more than we realize, and this is especially true for older people whose life experience has given rise to opinions about the world described by formal disciplines such as history or literature or psychology. In our teaching of older people, we need not be so much concerned to convey new knowledge or information as to elicit a new understanding of what is already present in the learners. The model for accomplishing this is given in the structure of the Socratic dialogue itself. Through questions put to the student "on many occasions and in different ways," we discover that the older student "in the end . . . will have a knowledge on the subject as accurate as anybody's."

If life experience is to be the basis for learning in this way, then it demands that we see the role of the teacher differently. In a late dialogue, the *Theaetetus,* Socrates describes his own role as "the midwife of ideas": the man who does not proclaim himself wise but who instead gives birth to wisdom in others through the relentless questioning of the Socratic method. In this view, the teacher's role is neither to accept nor reject altogether the answers given by the pupil. Rather, the answers—the dogmatic conclusions furnished by life experience—are to be turned back upon themselves to discern their premises and thus to expose their limitations. Upon cross-examination, the framework of concepts dissolves into uncertainty *(aporia),* as the pupil recognizes that to have an opinion, even a true opinion, is not the same thing as to have real knowledge. What is the difference? In the *Theaetetus,* Plato proposes the notion that a true opinion becomes knowledge only when it can "give an account of itself." The Greek term here is *logos*—"language, word, concept"—and it is the guiding role of *logos* that determines the validity of the educational enterprise.

There are some important implications here for education with older people. When older adults appear "opinionated," the point is not necessarily to reject the false opinions and certify the true ones. Even if the opinions derived from life experience happen to be true, they are still not yet knowledge. The whole purpose of education is to convert these true opinions into knowledge by revealing their roots in life experience and their connections with a wider context of life. This knowledge is *justified true belief*, or an opinion that can "give an account of itself." As the dialogue unfolds, we realize that knowledge is characterized by qualities of depth, generality, and power to illuminate unforeseen features of the world. Knowledge, in other words, is a leap beyond the empirical facts of a given situation or an individual life history to disclose a wider horizon that may have been missed in the course of life experience but is implicit in it just the same. "We had the experience but missed the meaning," as Eliot puts it.

It is through the process of dialogue that life experience is converted into knowledge. The teacher, like Socrates, points the older people's attention back to their own life experience until "true opinion" is exhibited in its connection to a wider field of facts or beliefs. It is in this sense that knowledge as "justified true belief" serves, not only to justify the conclusions of life experience, but also to explain the experience itself, whenever the teacher of older people is willing to use this life experience in the educational process. For example, consider the case of an older adult who expresses in the classroom a belief that "People are better off trusting their own ethnic group than trusting government officials." The teacher of sociology or political science who treats this opinion with seriousness will urge the student to examine it, to justify it, perhaps to qualify it. If the process of dialogue achieves its goal, the older person ends up by embedding a formerly dogmatic belief in a wider context of social reality. What is more, to justify the belief is also to explain the experiences that gave rise to it: for example, the need for family or ethnic solidarity of immigrant groups facing an alien society. What had previously been a fragmentary opinion becomes generalized and systematized until the student glimpses a larger rhythm of history that served as its background.

Older people cannot enter the classroom simply to receive a ratification of their previous opinions; indeed, one should expect that these opinions will be challenged at the same time that they are taken seriously. To become educated, as Plato realized, is more than to have opinions, even true opinions, about the world. Education, Plato argues in the *Republic*, means to be led out of the shadow world of opinions (whether true or false) and to discover the fundamental ground whereby we can know *why* our opinions are true or false. To have knowledge is to have a justified true belief about the world, and this means to have adequate evidence for holding some beliefs and not others. It does not mean simply to have had certain experiences or even to extract from life experience generalities or regularities: the empiricism of common sense.

This common-sense empiricism is exactly what Socrates describes as the "dreamlike quality" of newly aroused opinions that have yet to be converted into self-conscious knowledge. The danger of a "dreamlike" opinion is that it "imposes a pattern, and falsifies, / for the pattern is new in every moment" (Eliot, 1971, p. 26). By contrast, the Platonic dialogue itself is a return to the origins, a circle that turns back on itself when the older person's life experience itself becomes the basis of learning: "This knowledge will not come from teaching but from questioning. He will recover it for himself."

If older people learn for themselves how to recover knowledge from their own life experiences, then they become both teachers and learners at the same time, and this demand is actually implicit in the fact that Plato did not write treatises, but dialogues. Now, the dialogue form is not a mere literary device but is itself a model for an educational process based on both speaking and listening: Students speak while listening and listen while speaking. In speaking out loud, students listen inwardly and criticize their own opinions instead of simply allowing life experience to voice dogmatic opinions. In listening, students are also inwardly speaking, or actively responding to new ideas presented, not as mere information, but as an evocation of what was already implicit in life experience. True listening includes speaking, includes an active dimension, just as true speaking includes this critical self-consciousness that we might call "thinking out loud," wondering about our opinions, examining ideas in the very act of expressing them.

How can students learn to do this? Not by dogmatic assimilation of new facts or true opinions, but by internalizing the process of dialogue itself, by speaking and listening at the same time. For this reason, Plato describes thinking as "the dialogue of the soul with itself." For older people, thinking means a dialogue between past and present, between the memory of life experience and the structure of the subject matter. Neither element is sacrificed for the other, but both are present, dialectically unified. The past "speaks" through old people but so does the active learning of the moment. To be in dialogue with the past means to be in touch with feelings and opinions, not to subordinate them to the subject matter or to reject them as useless or irrelevant.

This kind of educational experience is immensely difficult to achieve. Everyone, including old people, tends to be dogmatic when speaking from experience. On the other hand, we are all aware of the older person who becomes subservient to "the professor" by casting teachers in the role of people who know all the answers, all the facts. Let us admit as well that many faculty members are comfortable in this superior role. Education based on dialogue means that older people must be *both* teachers and learners, just as those of us who direct the educational process must be both teachers and learners. If we begin to become isolated behind the safety of the subject matter, the discipline, then we too quickly stop listening to the students' own experiences. We are no longer speaking and listening at the same time, but merely speaking—as the professor—while the older people listen to us. As soon as speaking and listening become polarized into the roles of teacher and learner, we become locked in our roles and no longer find a way to legitimize the value of life experience for the classroom. What we really need instead, as Gattegno put it, is "the subordination of teaching to learning."

But can this Socratic model be applied to the education of older adults in our contemporary world? I believe it can and I point to the work of Paulo Freire, the Brazilian educator, whose books, *The Pedagogy of the Oppressed* and *Education for Critical Consciousness,* have much to teach us about education for older adults. Freire's work grew out of his experience in education for literacy among Brazilian peasants. As he worked with these people, he discovered that a persistent block in their learning to read was a deep-seated negative self-image: a feeling that they could not learn, that they were not capable of acquiring the "high culture" of literacy, and that what they did know from their own experience was worthless. The peasants had internalized a negative self-image that systematically devalued their life experience.

There are significant parallels here with the learning situation of older people. In our culture, many older people have internalized a negative self-image that says, "You're too old to learn," or "Your experience is obsolete and worthless." These false messages cannot be overcome simply by putting older people in a classroom and filling them up with new information. Freire, in particular, castigates this "banking model" of the learning process, in which learning is seen as acquiring more and more information, like money saved up in a bank. The point is, rather, that adults, especially older people, already have a lifetime of experience that is rich with meaning if only we could unlock its hidden potential.

The way to do this is not to expose older people to new information, but to initiate what Freire describes as a problem-*posing* education based on themes already implicit in the life experience of the students. This approach is not the same as a problem-solving, technocratic education in which students acquire new skills or analytical methods to solve preestablished problems. Instead, argues Freire, one must *problematize* the entire social, cultural, and historical reality in which we are immersed. To do this, we must identify the *generative themes* that emerge from students' own reality and own life experiences and then, through the process of dialogue, elicit what is universal and significant in those life experiences. Students, in other words, must take responsibility for their own learning processes, not in the absence of a teacher, but in partnerships in which the teacher is a learner as well. Freire insists on the need to free educators from their artificial roles as experts who know all the answers, and at the same time to free the students to be no longer passive objects of education, but rather its essential subjects.

Freire's ideas are of the greatest importance in the education of older people. Like the Brazilian peasants, older people tend to be robbed of their self-worth by being denied a meaningful role in society. The systematic devaluation of life experience leads many to feel that their past is worthless; in Simone de Beauvoir's terms, they face "a limited future and a frozen past." It is no wonder that older people risk dogmatism or despair or else escape it only by disowning the past. Freire's approach of problem-posing education means that we have to "problematize" this situation and challenge the stereotype of old age in our society. In this way, the generative themes implicit in life experience can become the center of the educational process, and older people will no longer be passive learners, but rather, active contributors to their own learning and to society at large.

TRANSCENDENCE

This appraisal of Freire's contribution, however, leaves some important questions unanswered. Freire's methods are in certain respects simply a systematic, philosophical account of effective adult education, or indeed of good education in any setting. Although the idea of generative themes elicited by dialogue gives us a method, it does not provide us with any content for a curriculum. It describes a process or a means of reaching a goal, but it does not tell us what our goal should be. In fairness to Freire, he would probably respond that the goal is simply *praxis,* or "reflective engagement in worldly activities." In the case of oppressed groups, *praxis* takes the form of political struggle and revolutionary consciousness aimed at transforming the world, but it is activity or engagement that remains primary. Is this goal of continuous activity a viable one for older people? It certainly represents one answer to the dilemma of old age in our society, an answer given by Simone de Beauvoir at the conclusion of *The Coming of Age* (1972):

> The greatest good fortune, even greater than health, for the old person is to have his world still inhabited by projects: then, busy and useful, he escapes both from boredom and from decay. The times in which he lives remain his own, and he is not compelled to adopt the defensive and aggressive forms of behavior that are so often characteristic of the final years. His oldness passes as it were unnoticed. For this to be the case he must have committed himself to undertakings that set time at defiance.... (pp. 492-493)

For Simone de Beauvoir, the solution to the problem of aging is rooted in an existential philosophy derived from Sartre and Marx and sharing similarities with Freire's concept of *praxis.* It is only the existential project, she tells us, that gives life its meaning, and this requires that older people must avoid turning inward, must transcend their own past by engagement in the present. In contrast to theorists who speak of disengagement from social roles in old age, Simone de Beauvoir insists that it is only through involvement and participation that people remain healthy in old age. But is there not implicit here a subtle rejection of the condition of old age itself? Note the phrase "His oldness passes as it were unnoticed." It seems that for Simone de Beauvoir there are no distinctive strengths or tasks uniquely associated with the condition of age. The answer to the question of what to do in old age is simply "more of the same."

A different point of view is possible, a point of view rooted in a developmental conception of the human life cycle. The great insight of progressive education, from Rousseau to John Dewey, is an insistence that the educational process be adapted to the changing developmental needs of the learner. Progressive education argued that we begin with the psychological growth of the child, not the abstract demands of the subject matter. This means that age is not an accidental, but an intrinsic, part of the learning process. We have not yet found a way to apply this principle to adult education for the very understandable reason that, by the large, we lack a detailed developmental psychology of the adult life cycle. What Freud and Piaget have done for the stages of child development needs to be done for the adult as well. As we look at language, sexuality, moral development, and logical reasoning in the child, we see a growth process tied to norms or developmental tasks mastered over time. Is there something analogous in the developmental process of adulthood and old age? Some psychologists, in particular Carl Jung (1963) and Erik Erikson (1963), have argued that there is.

Jung, for example, observes that the psychological demands of the second half of life are distinctively different from those of the first half. The first half of life is devoted to achieving a stable ego-identity associated with work and family, but the second half of life requires that we divest ourselves of the *persona*—"the mask of adult roles and social performances." The goal of the second half of life is a process of psychological *individuation* or self-realization: returning to our origins to become the total, unified personality symbolized by the archetype of the self: a circle, as in the image of the Ouroborus, a snake swallowing its own tail. In the first half of life, we go outside of ourselves to establish an identity through activity; in the second half, we turn inward to achieve wholeness. Interestingly, Jung warns that the psychopathologies of maturity and old age result from a failure to accept these changing developmental tasks of the life cycle. The aging playboy, the old person who lives in the memory of past glories, the old person who refuses to modify the lessons of past experience: all these represent a failure to live in the present, a failure to transcend the past.

But a developmental process that leads us to transcend the past must be rooted in acceptance of that past. It cannot be an escape or an evasion of the unresolved conflicts of life experience. We cannot disown the past, and this is simply to recognize the immutable law of the return of the repressed: the need to master each developmental stage in sequence, as Erik Erikson (1963) describes it in his chapter "The Eight Ages of Man," in *Childhood and*

Society. For Erikson, the distinctive task of old age is expressed in the polarity of *ego integrity* versus *despair*. Ego integrity means "acceptance of one's one and only life-cycle as something that had to be and that, by necessity, permitted of no substitutions" (p. 268). This sense of self-acceptance means working through the meaning of past experience, as in Butler's notion of life review.

These indications from Jung and Erikson point in their different ways toward a common thread that distinguishes the position of old age from other phases of the life cycle. As Simone de Beauvoir (1972) puts it:

> *In childhood and youth, life is experienced as a continual rise; and in favorable cases—either because of professional advancement or because bringing up one's children is a source of happiness, or because one's standard of living rises, or because of a greater wealth of knowledge—the notion of upward progress may persist in middle age. Then all at once a man discovers that he is no longer going anywhere.... There comes a moment when one knows that one is no longer getting ready for anything and one understands that the idea of advancing toward a goal was a delusion. (p. 491)*

In other words, with the arrival of old age, there is a fundamental alteration in the human experience of time, in which the "mirage of the future" disappears and one realizes "one is no longer getting ready for anything." In our future-directed, achievement-oriented culture, this realization can precipitate a tremendous psychological crisis. For the person facing sudden retirement, for example, the crisis may literally be life threatening: What do we live for if time is shrinking and we can no longer believe in the future? Whether we have reached our goals and been perplexed by success, or whether we have discovered that we will never become the person we imagined in youth: in either case, life closes in about itself and demands that the goals of the past be transcended.

The key concept here is *transcendence:* transcendence of the past, transcendence of previous social roles, transcendence of a limited definition of the self. For this reason, Simone de Beauvoir's prescription of "more of the same" (more activity, more projects) simply will not do. If there is to be participation and activity, it will have to be participation with a different qualitative experience of human time, with a recognition of finitude as intrinsic to the human condition. As Gray Panther leader Maggie Kuhn once remarked, the political activity of older people ought to be very different from ordinary interest-group politics. In an age of nuclear weapons, people have been urged to vote for a President who has grandchildren, as if to underscore the fact that our interest in the future does not end with our own life-span. If old people are "the elders of the tribe," then as an interest group, they have the potential of recognizing interests that transcend any single generation. If we educate older people for new roles and activities, it must be based on acceptance of the limitations of time, and it must include the selfless striving of preparation for future generations or creation of conditions for social justice in a world the old people will never live to see. To acknowledge our own finitude and death and still to strive for social change is already recognition of the dimension of transcendence.

Transcendence is acceptance of the past as finished and unfinished at one and the same time. It is a paradoxical attitude of suspended judgment about one's life. To transcend the past means to let go of it, to acknowledge it as finished, not to be repeated, as "the one and only life-cycle," but at the same moment that I am letting go of it, it begins to speak to me; my past speaks and tells of things I did not know before. It is speaking and listening at one and the same time. As the listener, I am in dialogue with my past, neither identified with it nor separate from it. My past is finished, but it is also unfinished because its meaning is never exhausted. It is not frozen, not worthless, but still rich with reflected light that can illuminate the present.

Was this *persona* simply a mask, an accidental covering of the self? Was the past a mere sequence of events without meaning or purpose? If the archetype of the self means completeness, totality, then it means acceptance of the *whole* of myself; it means that nothing can be discarded, nothing rejected as alien or "other" than me. I return to the origins. The value of life experience lies in what I can continually draw from it, as from an inexhaustible well.

Transcendence means overcoming one's previous role and definitions of the self; it means recovering them *in order* to let them go. The enormous value of education in old age lies in the way in which each subject studied can illuminate an aspect of this unrecovered self. For example, the history of the last 40 years allows older people to recognize themselves in the events that shaped their own life histories. The study of psychology or literature allows them to see, objectified, the same forces and conflicts that run through all our lives, to see that the story of the human race is one story. A liberal education is an education that is liberating, that discloses other cultures, other historical epochs, other values, in such a way that we discover, in this "other," our very own selves. Life experience is the starting point because the process of dialogue can begin anywhere and with any person. This educational enterprise is immensely important; it is serious; and above all, it is *difficult*. Perhaps I object to the notion of leisure-time education because it is ultimately demeaning; it seems to suggest that education in old age is not quite serious. The interesting fact is that, from the standpoint of the life cycle, older people have even less "leisure time" than the rest of us: the sense of time is more constricted and choices must be made with this recognition of finitude in mind.

This altered sense of time—the intuition of human finitude—provides the key we have been looking for. It situates the goal of the educational enterprise within the last phase of the life cycle and points to the developmental task defined by Erikson (1963) in the term *ego integrity:* "It is the ego's accrued assurance of its proclivity for order and meaning... an experience which conveys some world order and spiritual sense, no matter how early paid for" (p. 268). The continuing assurance of order and meaning demands that life experience be taken as the indispensable contribution and strength of older people. Yet to confront the real meaning of that life experience is to glimpse in experience itself something unsatisfied, something unknown. It is this intuition of the unknown, combined with self-acceptance and transcendence of the past, that stands out in the concluding passage from Jung's (1963) autobiography, *Memories, Dreams, Reflections,* written at age 85, at the very end of his life:

> *I am satisfied with the course my life has taken. It has been bountiful, and has given me a great deal. How could I ever have expected so much? Nothing but unexpected things kept happening to me. Much might have been different if I myself had been different. But it was as it had to be: for all came about because I am as I am... I cannot form any final judgment because the phenomenon of life and the phenomenon of man are too vast. The older I have become, the less I have understood or had insight into or known about myself.*

> *I am astonished, disappointed, pleased with myself. I am distressed, depressed, rapturous. I am all these things at once, and cannot add up the sum.... There is nothing I am quite sure about. I have no definite convictions—not about anything, really. I know only that I was born and exist, and it seems to me that I have been carried along. I exist on the foundation of something I do not know. In spite of all uncertainties, I feel a solidity underlying all existence and a continuity in my mode of being. (pp. 358-359)*

The fact that there is something incomprehensible or unknown about our life experience need not lead to the despair of *Krapp's Last Tape.* It is precisely *because* we come up against this mystery that we must have *hope.* As Jung puts it: "In spite of all uncertainties, I feel a solidity underlying all existence and a continuity in my mode of being." This is the meaning of Erikson's ego integrity and this is the reason why, in the end, Black Elk and Jung come to a common recognition. As Erikson (1963) says: "A wise Indian, a true gentleman, and a mature peasant share and recognize in one another the final stage of integrity" (p. 269).

Every old person in our classrooms will not be a Black Elk or a Carl Jung, and yet I have always found in conversation with old people, at bottom what each person wishes is to be able to tell his or her own story: to tell the story to himself or to herself and to know the teller of the tale. We all need to tell our stories, and if we bear this burden alone, then this is despair. Each of us wishes to be known and to know ourselves, and when we speak of individuation or ego integrity, this is the immmense task of old age: to know ourselves as a whole, as we really are, in the light of finitude and at the horizon of death.

In this chapter, I have spoken of experience, dialogue, and transcendence: the origin, the way, and the goal. Experience is the indispensable resource; dialogue releases the truth of experience and points toward a transcendence of our previous understanding. Experience, dialogue, transcendence: each phase moves on to the other until the circle completes itself as "we arrive where we started and know the place for the first time." If life experience is an unanswered question, then transcendence means to *live* the question, as Rilke (1963) says:

> Be patient toward all that is unsolved in your heart and try to love the questions themselves like locked rooms and like books that are written in a very foreign tongue. Do not now seek the answers, which cannot be given you because you would not be able to live them. And the point is, to live everything. Live the questions now. Perhaps you will then gradually without noticing it, live along some distant day into the answer. (pp. 34–35)

An education that teaches us to love the questions themselves will also teach us to tell our own story and, God willing, teach us to bear the burden of our own existence as an infinite labor of perfection. This education alone is worthy of the last stage of life.

REFERENCES

de Beauvoir, S. (1972). *The coming of age*. New York: Putnam.

Eliot, T. S. (1971). *Four quartets*. New York: Harcourt.

Erikson, E. (1963). *Childhood and society* (2nd ed.). New York: Norton.

Jung, C. G. (1963). *Memories, dreams, reflections*. (A. Jaffe, Ed., and R. Winston and C. Winston, Trans.). New York: Pantheon.

Neihardt, J. G. (1961). *Black Elk speaks, being the life story of a holy man of the Oglala Sioux*. Lincoln: University of Nebraska Press.

Plato. (1966). *Meno* (W. K. C. Guthrie, Trans.). In E. Hamilton & H. Cairns (Eds.), *The collected dialogues of Plato*. New York: Pantheon.

Rilke, R. M. (1963). *Letters to a young poet* (rev. ed.). New York: Norton.

3

REMINISCENCE AND LIFE REVIEW: THE POTENTIAL FOR EDUCATIONAL INTERVENTION

SHARAN B. MERRIAM
University of Georgia

INTRODUCTION

A person's identity is, to a large extent, defined by the nature and extent of his or her life experiences. Developmental psychologists and adult educators have recognized the centrality of life experiences to one's being, as well as the role past experiences play in continued growth and learning. How well one deals with the transition and crises of adulthood, for example, is thought to be a function of how one has handled life events and problems in the past (Neugarten, 1973). Adult developmental psychologists while seeking to identify the commonalities of human experience at the same time recognize the uniqueness of each individual. It is somewhat ironic that the past experiences of older adults lead to both increased diversity and increased commonality. The older one grows, the greater the amount and variety of experiences one has accumulated. A group of 60-year-olds will be less alike than a group of 40-year-olds, and a group of 40-year-olds will be less alike than a group of teenagers. But while adults become more diverse in interests, personality, and life style as they age, those who live the longest are typically better educated, have higher incomes and better health (Troll, 1975). Thus survivor bias—those who continue to outlive their peers—becomes a basis for increasing commonality.

The importance of past experiences in enhancing one's learning has been addressed by numerous educators. John Dewey (1971, pp. 92-93) in fact defined education as the "continuous reconstruction of experience." He wrote that education was both retrospective and prospective. That is, "it may be treated as a process of accommodating the future to the past, or as an utilization of the past for a resource in a developing future." Adult educators, in particular, urge teachers to make use of their adult students' past experiences as a learning resource. According to Knowles (1980), an adult's life experiences is one way child learning is distinguished from adult learning:

> *To children, experience is something that happens to them; it is an external event that affects them, not an integral part of them. If you ask children who they are, they are likely to identify themselves in terms of who their parents are, who their older brothers and sisters are, where they live, and what school they attend. Their self-identity is largely derived from external sources.*
>
> *But adults derive their self-identity from their experience. They define who they are in terms of the accumulation of their unique sets of experience. So if you ask adults who they are, they are likely to identify themselves by describing what their occupations are, where they have worked, where they have traveled, what their training and experience have equipped them to do, and what their achievements have been. Adults are what they have done. (1980, p. 50)*

While many writers point to the value of recalling past experiences in the service of learning or psychological development, in reality, such activity is frowned upon in our culture. Recollecting the past, especially by older persons, evokes a negative image of escapism, encroaching senility or psychological decline. Butler (1963, p. 66) observes that "occasionally, the constructive and creative aspects of reminiscence are valued and affirmed in the autobiographical accounts of famous men," but for the most part, the "usual view of reminiscence is a negative one." To change our culture's negative view of reminiscing, people must first come to understand what it is, and what function it has in an older adult's development. The purpose of this chapter is to first review what is known about reminiscence, or recalling the past, and then speculate as to how this knowledge might be used to structure effective educational and counseling intervention strategies with older adults.

REMINISCENCE DEFINED

The dictionary defines reminiscence as "the recall to mind of a long-forgotten experience or fact" or "the process or practice of thinking or telling about past experiences" (Webster's Third International Dictionary). Such a definition, however, leaves unanswered the following questions: How far back in time must one go to be reminiscing—ten minutes, yesterday, last month, three years ago? Is reminiscing the same as remembering, or is it only an aspect of memory? How is reminiscing differentiated from other mental processes such as daydreaming, therapy, hypnosis, nostalgia, or recollecting?

Turning to the research and writing on reminiscence does little to clarify the concept. In one of the more thorough studies conducted by Havighurst and Glaser (1972, p. 245), reminiscence was defined as "dwelling on the past" and "retrospection, both purposive and spontaneous." It could be oral or silent but reminiscence did not include recalling facts in order to make a decision or daydreaming about the future. The authors further asserted that reminiscence was an aspect of memory but not identical with memory. Lewis (1971, p. 240) conceptualized it as involving the process of memory "with the added action property of reaching out to infuse others with these memories." Lewis designated subjects as reminiscers if over 40% of their sentence unity referred to events five or more years in the past. Others have defined it as "the remembered past" (Lieberman and Falk, 1971), and the "act or process of recalling the past" (Butler, 1963).

With few exceptions the issue of time is ignored in the literature. Coleman (1974), in addition to Lewis mentioned above, used five years as a criterion for reminiscing. McMahon and Rhudick (1967) classified responses referring to the "remote" rather than "recent" past as reminiscence, but failed to specify what constituted "remote."

Although the questions relating to reminiscence remain puzzling, a few writers have brought some understanding to the phenomenon by delineating several types of reminiscing. Coleman's schema (1974) presents the clearest framework for pulling together much of the literature on reminiscence. According to Coleman, there are three categories of reminiscence: simple, informative and life review. Simple reminiscing—"linguistic acts of referring to the remote past" (p. 285)—is what most of the research has investigated. Informative reminiscing is akin to storytelling (McMahon and Rhudick, 1967) and its main purpose appears to be entertainment or, as Coleman notes, "using the past to teach others the lessons of experience" (1974, p. 283). In addition, folklorists and oral historians have long depended upon the reminiscences of the elderly to preserve a culture's history and folklore. Coleman's third category, the life review, was first proposed by Butler (1963) and includes the dimension of analysis. That is, older persons in the face of death rework or analyze their past experiences in order to achieve an integration and acceptance of one's own life.

Butler's concept of the life review deserves more attention since it has precipitated much of the recent work on reminiscence. For Butler, the life review and reminiscence are not synonymous. Rather, the life review includes reminiscing. Prompted by the realization of approaching death, the life review is

a naturally occurring, universal mental process characterized by the progressive return to consciousness of past experience, and, particularly, the resurgence of unresolved conflicts; simultaneously, and normally,

these revived experiences and conflicts can be surveyed and reintegrated.
(Butler, 1963, p. 66)

Butler's life review operationalizes, to some extent, Erikson's concept of ego integrity in old age. According to Erikson (1950), the awareness of death precipitates a need on the part of older persons to review and evaluate their life experiences. If one can accept "one's one and only life cycle as something that had to be and that by necessity permitted of no substitution" (1950, p. 268), then one feels a sense of integrity in later life, rather than despair. As with the life review, this task involves reminiscing about the past from an analytical and evaluative perspective.

REMINISCENCE AND AGE

It is commonly thought that older persons reminisce more than younger people and that older persons dwell upon their childhood more than other stages of life. Such thinking is reinforced by the media, by writers, and by researchers themselves who, for the most part, have used only aged subjects when studying reminiscence. One can only speculate as to the reasons for this view of the aged and reminiscing. Perhaps it is thought that older persons have more time to dwell on the past, and less of a future to think about, or perhaps it is because of a better long term rather than short term memory, or perhaps it is usually the older person who records a life history, writes an autobiography or gathers memorabilia. The handful of reminiscence studies conducted with subjects of all ages suggest, however, that reminiscence is not unique in content or amount to old age.

Giambra (1977) in a large scale study investigating the tendency of 1,275 adults aged 17-92 years to daydream about the past, present and future, found no relationship between age and daydreaming about the past. Neither was there a tendency for the elderly to daydream about the more distant past than younger members of the sample. Giambra cautions people dealing with the aged to avoid attributing any special reminiscing tendency to the aged. Reporting essentially the same results as Giambra, Cameron (1972) conducted a series of studies on the time orientations of teenagers through the elderly. Cameron found that all ages think more about the present than either the past or future and that "there is clearly nary a hint that the old think more retrospectively than any other age group" (1972, p. 118).

In a comprehensive study of several dimensions of reminiscing with over 300 adults aged 18-90, Merriam and Cross (1982) found no systematic differences based on age. Questions which probed the time of life reminisced about revealed that increasing age merely offers more stages of life about which to reminisce. That is, older persons do not dwell disproportionately upon childhood. In fact, people over 60 reported reminiscing more about the last years of their work career and their middle adult years than their

TABLE 1 Mean Scale Responses by Four Groups to Questions Addressing
the Life Stages about which One Reminisces

Statement	Age group			
	(18–22)	(23–34)	(35–59)	(60–90)
1. Childhood	3.9	3.7	3.2	4.2
2. Teen years	5.5	4.4	3.8	4.4
3. Early adult life	4.9	4.9	2.3	4.7
4. College life	4.7	4.4	3.0	3.2
5. Early work career	3.4	4.5	3.7	4.5
6. Middle adult years	1.7	3.3	4.2	4.8
7. Last years of work career	2.0	3.1	3.6	4.7
8. Retirement years	2.2	2.6	4.7	2.9

Note. Directions to respondent: Circle the number 1 (never) through 7 (always)
which represents how often you reminisce about the period of life.

childhood. As can be seen in Tables 1 and 2, adults, whether they be 18 or
90, reminisce about events throughout their entire life span.

In the same study Merriam and Cross (1982) attempted to discern
the objects or events about which different-aged men and women most
frequently reminisce. Table 3 presents a list of 24 events, topics, or objects to
which respondents were directed to indicate how frequently each was a focus
of their reminiscing. Most of the items were generated by the researchers but
some were suggested by Havighurst and Glaser's study (1972).

The mean responses for each age group are given. Again, there was no
systematic pattern with regard to age in frequency of topic reminisced about.

The above studies investigated what Coleman called simple reminiscing.
Butler (1963), it might be remembered, has proposed the life review as one of
the developmental tasks of old age. While it can be observed in younger
persons anticipating death, it is more commonly characteristic of older persons
in the process of adapting to changing circumstances at the end of life.

TABLE 2 Recency of Events about which People Reminisce

Age group	Past event (years)								
	2 or less	2–5	6–10	11–15	16–20	21–25	26–30	31–35	36 or more
18–22	34	40	12	2	2	0	0	0	0
23–34	13	22	27	18	10	5	1	0	0
35–39	14	9	13	17	21	10	8	5	4
60–90	14	11	8	10	7	12	10	6	15

Note. Directions to respondents: About those events you most enjoy thinking about, how
long ago did they happen?

TABLE 3 Mean Scale Responses to Questions Addressing the Topics about which One Reminisces for Four Age Groups

	Age group			
Statement	(18–22)	(23–34)	(35–59)	(60–90)
1. Popular music or song of the past	4.6	4.4	4.3	3.9
2. Favorite stage or screen star	3.0	3.0	3.1	2.8
3. Favorite book	3.0	3.7	3.9	3.7
4. Political events	3.2	3.4	3.7	3.7
5. Some event in which you were successful	5.1	4.7	4.3	4.5
6. Some event in which you were unsuccessful	3.7	4.0	3.1	3.3
7. Some event in which you were embarrassed	4.0	3.8	3.2	3.1
8. Something you did in sports or games	4.7	3.9	3.8	3.2
9. Something you did in dramatics	3.1	3.2	2.7	2.3
10. Experiences with the opposite sex	5.8	4.9	4.1	3.1
11. Experiences with the same sex	3.4	3.3	3.1	3.3
12. A tragedy of some kind	3.8	3.7	3.0	3.5
13. Objects from childhood	3.4	3.2	2.8	2.9
14. A major decision	4.7	4.5	4.0	3.9
15. A family celebration	4.3	4.0	4.3	4.8
16. A trip	5.1	4.8	4.7	4.9
17. The neighborhood where grew up	4.4	4.3	3.6	4.6
18. War time	2.2	2.6	3.2	3.9
19. A pet or animal	4.1	3.3	4.6	3.7
20. A marriage	2.2	4.3	4.3	5.0
21. A time of year	4.3	4.4	3.7	3.9
22. Your favorite teacher	3.1	2.9	2.9	3.1
23. An exciting experience	5.5	4.9	4.4	4.1
24. A family outing or trip	4.2	3.9	4.2	4.5

Note. Directions to respondent: Circle the number 1 (never) through 7 (always) which represents how often you reminisce about the following topics.

Research by Lowenthal, Thurnher, and Chiriboga (1975), however, raises the question whether this form of reminiscing is as limited to old age as Butler suggests. These authors postulate that life reviewing, as an analytic, integrative process peaks during periods of crises and transition, regardless of age or stage of life. Just as Kübler-Ross' stages of dying (1969) are applied to many kinds of loss, not just death, perhaps Butler's life review could be viewed as an adjustment or coping device utilized throughout adulthood.

In summary, the few studies which have investigated reminiscing across age suggest that older persons are probably little different than other ages in their reminiscent behavior. Much more needs to be done in terms of defining and conceptualizing the phenomenon before firm conclusions with regard to age differences can be advanced. With this caveat in mind, the remainder of the chapter will return to focusing on older adults and their reminiscing. Most of what is known about reminiscing comes from studies with older adults and it is this base which allows us to speculate as to how it functions, and what interventions might be used with the elderly to facilitate the activity.

THE FUNCTION OF REMINISCENCE

There is quite a bit of speculation in gerontological literature as to how reminiscence functions in the lives of older people. More specifically, much of the writing addresses how such an activity can enhance the psychological and social well-being of the elderly. In addition, some suggest that those persons who come in contact with the elderly, such as social workers, family members, and nursing home staffs, will benefit in various ways through an older person's reminiscing. This section will first discuss the functions of reminiscence which have been actually studied by researchers, and then review some proposed functions which have yet to be empirically investigated.

The dozen or so studies conducted on reminiscence can be loosely placed into the following categories: life satisfaction, adaptation to stress, cognitive functioning, and ego integrity. That is, researchers have proposed that there is a relationship between life satisfaction and reminiscence, for example, or that reminiscence can bring about ego integrity or extend cognitive functioning.

With regard to life satisfaction, there appears to be a positive relationship between frequency of pleasant reminiscing and one's satisfaction with life. Havighurst and Glaser (1972) using three samples of adults investigated the frequency, content, and affective quality of older persons' reminiscing. They concluded that there exists "a syndrome" of good personal-social adjustment as measured by a Life Satisfaction Inventory, positive affect of reminiscence, and a high frequency of reminiscence (1972, p. 252). Oliveria (1977) also focused upon life satisfaction and reminiscence. In this study, 40 elderly participants were classified as either high or low reminiscers. Oliveria found that those who reminisced a lot felt better about their past life and were more satisfied with the way they had lived than low reminiscers. High reminiscers liked to reminisce, felt relaxed when they reminisced, and reminisced more about pleasant experiences than the low reminiscers. Both groups, however, were satisfied with their lives, were very active, and were making plans for pleasant activities in the future.

Merriam and Cross (1981) also found that life satisfaction correlated with positive affect of reminiscence. Respondents in their sample who placed greater emphasis upon reminiscence as an enjoyable activity tended to have a higher life satisfaction score as measured by the 17-item Philadelphia Geriatric Morale Scale. Conversely, those who reported using reminiscence as a way of coping with loneliness, boredom or stress, tended to have lower life satisfaction scores. While all three studies report positive relationships between life satisfaction and reminiscence, causality was not investigated. That is, it is not known whether pleasant reminiscing leads to life satisfaction, or whether being satisfied with one's life results in pleasurable thoughts about the past.

Reminiscence as a coping mechanism with regard to stress was explored in a study by Lewis (1971). Lewis hypothesized that when faced with a socially threatening situation, reminiscers would show a greater consistency in self-concept than non-reminiscers. This study was conducted with 24 men over age 65. From an analysis of a taped non-directive interview, subjects were designated as reminiscers if over 40% of their sentence units referred to events five or more years in the past. Measures of one's past self-concept and present self-concept were recorded prior to, and after, placing the subjects in a stressful situation. Reminiscers, when their expressed opinions were threatened, showed a significant increase in the correlation between their past and present self-concepts compared to non-reminiscers. Lewis concludes that reminiscing might contribute to successful aging by supporting the self-concept in times of stress.

Lieberman and Falk (1971) explored reminiscence and stress with three samples of aged: those who were living in a community setting; those who were waiting to enter homes for the aged; and those who were long term residents of institutions. They found that those in an unstable life context facing imminent change (i.e., the waiting list sample) were considerably more involved in reminiscence than either of the other two samples. In investigating the role of reminiscence and adaptation to the stress of moving into an institution, no relationship was found, however. The discovery that scores on reminiscence indices were unrelated to subsequent adaptation or non-adaptation to stress led the authors to conclude that "the adaptive function of reminiscence activity is questionable" (Lieberman & Falk, 1971, p. 138).

In an interesting study of the time perceptions of centenarians, Costa and Kastenbaum (1972) suggest that a sense of continuity in one's life might serve as a coping procedure for accommodating emotion and tension. The researchers analyzed interview data on 276 centenarians to items asking respondents to recall their earliest memory, the most salient historical event in their lives, and the most exciting event in their lives. They then correlated the three memories with items related to future ambitions. They found that centenarians "who were able to offer responses for all memory items more frequently stated future ambitions than did their peers who had less command over the past" (1967, p. 16).

In addition to increasing life satisfaction and reducing stress, it has been hypothesized that encouraging older persons to reminisce might contribute to greater mental acuity. This notion was supported to some extent in a study investigating the effect of a structured reminiscence program with 105 volunteer participants (Hughston & Merriam, 1982). Females, but not males in the reminiscent treatment group significantly improved scores of cognitive functioning as measured by a culture-free test of intellectual capacity (Raven Standard Progressive Matrices). McMahon and Rhudick (1967) in a study of 25 very old subjects (average age, 84) explored, in a different manner from Hughston and Merriam, the relationship between reminiscence and intellectual functioning. Working from the commonly held notion that reminiscence is somehow a symptom of intellectual deterioration, subjects were rated with regard to this factor using the deterioration quotient derived from the Weinsler-Bellevue Intelligence Test. The tendency to reminiscence was found to be unrelated to level of intellectual competency and decline of intellectual abilities.

McMahon and Rhudick (1967) also explored the relationship between reminiscence, depression, and survival. They discovered that the nondepressed subjects reminisced more than those who were depressed. Furthermore, seven out of nine subjects rated as depressed or suspected of depression died within a year of the study, while only one of the 16 nondepressed subjects had died.

Finally, of the studies conducted on reminiscence, two have explored the life review or ego-integrity dimension of reminiscence. Boylin, Gordon, and Nehrke (1976) administered a questionnaire on reminiscing to 41 elderly institutionalized veterans along with a scale to assess ego adjustment. They reported a positive relationship between the amount of reminiscence and ego-integrity—that is, those who reminisced more scored higher on the ego-integrity measure. Interestingly, it was found that remembering painful or negative past experiences also correlated with the ego-integrity measure. The authors suggest that the subjects were indeed engaging in a life review, which, according to Butler, includes both pleasant and unpleasant aspects of past experiences. They concluded that the results support Erikson's theory of ego-integrity, and point to a linkage between reminiscing and adjustment in old age (Boylin, Gordon, & Nehrke, 1976, p. 124).

Coleman (1974) in a study of elderly men and women in supervised housing for the aged in Great Britain investigated simple reminiscing, life reviewing, and informative reminiscing. These three types of reminiscing were related to measures of past and present life adjustment. Those who were dissatisfied with their past lives reviewed life to a greater extent than did those who were satisfied with their past lives. There was no relationship between life reviewing or simple reminiscence and present adjustment. Informative reminiscing was related to adjustment only in the men. Coleman concluded that reminiscing alone was not an adaptive mechanism in old age, but that life reviewing in the sense of working through past conflicts helps older persons deal with an unsatisfactory past life.

In summary, several studies, if taken together, suggest that reminiscence functions as an adaptive mechanism or facilitates personality reorganization in late adulthood. Reminiscence appears to play a role in life satisfaction, coping with stress, enhancing cognitive functioning, and facilitating the life review process. Research in these areas is still sparse, however, and little can be stated with any certainty about the nature and strength of these relationships.

OTHER FUNCTIONS

The value of reminiscing might well go beyond the four areas discussed in the previous section. Several writers have made observations from practice, others have advanced theories as to the potential usefulness of the activity. Lewis (1973), for example, (whose study on using reminiscence to maintain a self-concept in times of stress was mentioned earlier) proposes using cognitive dissonance theory to explain why older people reminisce. Dissonance theory postulates that when there are inconsistencies between one's behavior and self-concept, dissonant elements are disowned so that the self-concept and reality become congruent or consonant. One way to reduce dissonance is to convince the self and others that inconsistencies in a situation are really consonant. Recalling the past in ways which will restore consonance to the present is thus a coping mechanism, especially for older people who often must accommodate losses related to social roles, health, living arrangements, and so on.

That reminiscence functions as a coping mechanism in later life is a fairly common theme in gerontological literature. As suggested by Lewis' (1973) dissonance theory, reminiscence helps older persons transcend present worries, facilitates the resolution of grief related to loss, and helps overcome physical limitations and unpleasant living conditions. There is, of course, no reason to assume that the coping functions of reminiscing are limited to the aged. It is rather that older persons by virtue of their stage in life are more likely to encounter loss, physical problems, and less satisfactory living conditions. Hence, the increased used of reminiscence is hypothesized for this period of life.

Reminiscence might also be looked at from two perspectives: its value to the individual and its value to others. In addition to the functions already addressed, it has been suggested by one writer who leads reminiscing groups, that the activity expands one's concept of time, allows for self-actualization through creative expression of the individual's experiences, expands consciousness, and aids in the development of a philosophy of life (Ebersole, 1978). Moody (1978) also speaks to the need for self-actualizing and consciousness expanding opportunities for older persons. This need is perhaps greatest in old age because "with the arrival of old age, there is a fundamental alteration in the human experience of time, in which the 'mirage of the future' disappears and one realizes 'one is no longer getting ready for anything' " (p. 44). Transcendence of the past, of previous social roles, of a limited definition of the self is, for Moody, the key to education in later life. He writes:

> Transcendence is acceptance of the past as finished and unfinished at one and the same time. It is a paradoxical attitude of suspended judgment about one's life . . . my past speaks and tells of things I did not know before. It is speaking and listening at one and the same time. . . .
>
> Transcendence means overcoming one's previous role and definitions of the self; it means recovering them in order to let them go. The

enormous value of education in old age lies in the way in which each
subject studied can illuminate an aspect of this unrecovered self. (p. 45)

There are several ways in which an individual's reminiscing might be of
value to others. Ebersole (1978) suggests that it allows for identification of
universal themes of humanity. Reminiscing, especially the informative type,
allows for the transmission of culture and cultural values from the older
generation to the younger generation and between groups of one cultural
orientation and those of another. Lewis and Butler (1974) see reminiscing in
life-cycle group therapy as one means of bringing about intergenerational understanding. The aged as group members can make the following contributions:
(1) be a model for growing older, (2) offer solutions for loss and grief,
(3) creatively use reminiscence, (4) exhibit a sense of the entire cycle, and
(5) possess historic empathy (Lewis & Butler, 1974).

McClusky (1978) also addresses this theme of the value of older persons
interacting with young people in educational situations in particular. His
concept of the *community of generations* is based upon the assumption "that,
although separated by time and experience, each generation nevertheless has a
common stake with other generations in relating itself to the wholeness of the
life-span of which it is a part" (p. 50). McClusky then discusses what
particular contributions each generation can make to the other. Older persons,
in any given instructional setting, can contribute their expertise, "can relate
the learning of the classroom to the realities of everyday living," and "will
possess a perspective on a wide range of human concerns that only a direct
encounter with historical events can provide" (p. 58).

Finally, it has been suggested that reminiscences of the elderly might be
used in training nursing students (Safier, 1976), by social workers who wish to
establish good rapport (Pincus, 1970) and by geriatric facilities that seek to
heighten trust between residents and staff (Hala, 1975).

Thus, in addition to the functions studied by researchers reviewed earlier
in the chapter, there are several other values and potential uses attributed to
reminiscence. While its consciousness-expanding possibilities or its role in stimulating intergenerational dialogue have not been empirically tested, these and
other functions have been advanced, for the most part, by practitioners who
have seen the impact reminiscing has upon the elderly themselves, and upon
those who work with them. The potential for enhancing the lives of older
persons through reminiscing is certainly worthy of further attention by researchers and practitioners.

THE RATIONALE FOR EDUCATIONAL
INTERVENTION

The rationale for structuring opportunities for older persons to reminisce
is based upon knowledge available from empirical research studies and the

first-hand experiences of gerontologists and educators. The rationale also forms a summary of the material covered in this chapter thus far. The following four points can be made in support of structuring reminiscence activities for the aged.

1. Reminiscing might lead to a better old age. While the data are not conclusive, studies have shown that reminiscence is related to life satisfaction (Havighurst & Glaser, 1972; Oliveria, 1977; Merriam and Cross, 1981), helps one cope with stress (Lewis, 1977; Costa & Kastenbaum, 1973), is unrelated to intellectual decline (McMahon & Rhudick, 1967), and may in fact sharpen mental acuity (Hughston & Merriam, 1982), and may facilitate personality reorganization through the life review (Boylin, Gordon, & Nehrke, 1976; Coleman, 1974).

2. Reminiscing appears to be a therapeutic acitivity especially with those elderly who are most withdrawn. Liton and Olstein (1969, p. 263) write that "particularly responsive to the therapy of reminiscence are senile persons who have become withdrawn because their failure to respond to conventional approaches has caused them to be passed by." Reminiscence, the authors feel, can help "the aged person recapture that part of his self-image that is the deepest value to him" (1969, p. 268). One is reminded of Kenneth Koch's (1977) success in getting even the most withdrawn nursing home residents to write poetry. Responses were evoked through exercises in which residents recalled their place of birth, their childhood, their first date, and so on. And, in a particularly poignant example of reminiscence's therapeutic value, Roger Hiemstra (1980) writes about his encounter with a withdrawn nursing home resident:

I noticed a person slumping in an outer reception room chair. He was in a fairly disheveled state, clothing awry, and not noticing anything around him. I asked a nurse about his condition and she said he was having senility problems but enjoyed sitting in the lobby to watch the people go by.

I approached him, got his attention, and eventually started a conversation. After some difficult starts I got him talking about himself. It turned out he was seventy-six years old, his wife had been dead for five years, and his children were all living on the West Coast. He, too, had been an agricultural specialist until his retirement ten years prior. We talked about his experiences, his grandchildren, and his views on today's agriculture. During the hour long conversation he transformed before my eyes into the image of my other interviewee. He slowly straightened up in his chair, became animated, straightened up his clothing, ran his hand through his hair. He smiled, he talked wisely, he wished for the future, he became alive! (p. 34)

3. Reminiscence is a good method for professionals to know better the older persons with whom they work. Those in the helping professions can come

to understand both the diversity and commonality of the aging experience. By knowing something of an older person's past, their values, their attitudes, a helping person can make more informed decisions about the resident or client in their charge. Pincus (1970) makes the interesting observation that reminiscing operates significantly in helping the older person deal with interpersonal relationships. That is, it is used to negotiate age and status differences between oneself and one's social contacts. In a setting with a younger social worker, for example, a client can recall experiences that can either accentuate differences, and thus widen the gap, or that can stress similarities which would have the effect of establishing a closer relationship. Pincus (1970) advises social workers to be sensitive to clues in an older person's reminiscing which might reveal their needs and mental condition. Such awareness can lead to more effective assistance.

4. Using past experiences as a learning resource is good adult education. The older one becomes, the greater depth and breadth of experiences one accumulates. A person's past can be used to augment, to understand, to deal with the concerns of the present. In an educational setting older persons can add a personal dimension to the study of history, politics, literature, philosophy and so on, not obtainable through books alone. In more skill oriented settings past experiences with like challenges can be applied to the learning of new skills. But using past experiences is also a process whereby life experiences are more than a *basis* for new learning. Life experiences, through dialogue, can become converted into knowledge:

> *If older people learn for themselves how to recover knowledge from their own life experiences, then they become both teachers and learners at the same time. . . . For older people, thinking means a dialogue between past and present, between the memory of life experience and the structure of the subject matter. Neither element is sacrificed for the other, but both are present, dialectically unified. The past 'speaks' through old people but so does the active learning of the moment. To be in dialogue with the past means to be in touch with feelings and opinions, not to subordinate them to the subject matter or to reject them as useless or irrelevant. (Moody, 1978, p. 40)*

TECHNIQUES OF EDUCATIONAL INTERVENTION

Both research and practitioner experience suggest that there are several reasons for encouraging older persons to reminiscence. A large number of specific activities can be used to stimulate reminiscence. The following nine activities are regularly incorporated into the activity program at the Hebrew Home of Greater Washington in Rockville, Maryland (Weisman & Shusterman, 1977). Each offers a core idea which can be expanded into a full educational intervention program.

1. Oral history project. Volunteers interview elderly residents and ask them to sum up their feelings about life. Life histories can also be recorded and returned to the interviewees "thus providing them tangible evidence of the validity and durability of their life experiences" (Myerhoff & Lufte, 1975). Experimenters with this technique conclude that it allows the older person to integrate his or her past and heighten his or her sense of identity. Younger interviewers/recorders also benefit by gaining a sense of history and life cycle continuity (Myerhoff & Lufte, 1975).

2. Holiday celebrations. Residents are encouraged to relate how they used to celebrate a particular holiday. Holidays provide a common basis for beginning a reminiscent acitivity and can be used to point out both the commonality and diversity of human experience.

3. Art therapy. Residents at the Hebrew Home discuss their earliest memories and draw pictures of them. This appears to be a particularly good technique for furthering the personality reorganization of the life review process. In an article entitled "Life Review in Art Therapy with the Aged," Zeiger (1976) reports two case examples in which art therapy facilitated the life review.

4. Music therapy. Memories of the past are relived when residents hear and sing familiar melodies.

5. Trigger film series. Films are selected which encourage residents to remember and discuss past events.

6. Antiques of yesteryear program. Old household implements are brought to a class and used to stimulate residents' memories.

7. Night school. History classes are conducted in which each stage of American history is correlated to the personal experiences of class members.

8. Poetry class. Poetry readings in group sessions stir old memories. Poetry *writing* is also a tested technique for stimulating reminiscence. Speaking of this activity with nursing home residents, Koch (1977) writes:

> *I saw, even in their very difficult circumstances, possibilities for poetry—in the lives old people looked back on, in the time they had now to do that, and to think, and with a detachment hardly possible to them before. . . . Poetry, if they did write it, would have to come from memory and from what happened and from what we could help make happen right there in the nursing home. (p. 4–5)*

Koch's success in getting older persons to write poetry was in part due to approaching it as art, rather than therapy. "As therapy it may help someone to be a busy old person, but as art and accomplishment it can help him to be fully alive" (p. 44). Koch comments on the changes in residents' behavior as a result of the workshops:

> *What we noticed in the poems and in the class was apparently going on outside the class also—the students seemed to have more concentration*

and more confidence. They spoke more clearly and had more to say to us, to the social workers, and to each other. Eagerness to talk about what they thought and felt had replaced reticence, vagueness, and, for some, even silence. (p. 53)

9. Residents' journal. Many of the articles in the monthly home publication are stories residents have written about their earlier years. Journal writing in which people are asked to record past experiences and present thoughts about those experiences can, of course, be utilized in a variety of settings ranging from structured classroom activities to individual therapy.

All of the above suggestions for stimulating reminiscence can be carried out by older persons themselves, in dialogue—that is, an older person with an instructor, therapist, human service worker or student, or in groups. Ebersole (1976) points out that group reminiscing can facilitate an individual's sense of ego integrity and self-esteem as well as be a socializing stimulant. Using reminiscence groups as a means of increasing socialization may in turn have a positive effect on each individual. One study of a reminiscent group therapy project in a geriatric facility reported that the groups led to an increased level of participant interaction which transferred from the group to other aspects of institutional life (Hala, 1975). Ebersole (1978) lists eight specific goals for reminiscing groups. These goals include: enhancing a cohort effect, stimulating socialization, stimulating memory, increasing self-esteem, reducing generation gaps, recreation, self-expression, and self-actualization; facilitating a positive life review; and launching other types of working groups.

In Ebersole's experience (1976), reminiscence groups typically move through stages as they become cohesive. The first stage is trusting the leader. Most group members seek direction, careful planning and acceptance by the leader. The second stage is establishing the importance of self; realizing that one has something valid to contribute leads to sharing with others. The third stage consists of extending trust to group members, and the final phase involves the working through of painful as well as treasured memories.

There is much to be said in favor of group reminiscing. Such sharing encompasses two of the three types of reminiscing delineated by Coleman (1974)—simple and informative. It may even involve the third type—life reviewing—when conflicting past memories are worked through with the help of the group and group leader. Whether the activities suggested are conducted individually, in dialogue, or in groups, is less an issue, however, than encouraging older persons to recall their past, to use it for creating new knowledge, and perhaps a new sense of the self.

CONCLUSION

The purpose of this chapter has been to propose the use of reminiscence as a basis for educational and therapeutic interventions with older persons.

Recalling the past because it is a pleasurable activity or because it helps one cope with the present is at least related to, and may in fact bring about, a more satisfying life. There is certainly no evidence that recalling the past is detrimental to a person's psychological well-being. Even the life review which processes conflicts and painful as well as pleasant memories leads, its proponents feel, to reintegration and a sense of integrity in later life.

The research which has been reviewed in this chapter as well as practitioner experiences with reminiscent-type activities suggest that it might lead to a better old age, is therapeutic especially with elderly who are withdrawn, is a good method for professionals to know better the persons with whom they work, and is "good" adult education. Past experiences can be both the subject matter *of*, as well as a resource *for* enhancing and enlightening learning activities.

The final section of this chapter presented techniques for stimulating reminiscing from recording oral histories to bringing antiques to class to writing poetry in nursing homes. In closing, practitioners as well as researchers in education and gerontology might make use of these activities either in individual, dialogical or group form, by recording the effect of the activity on a person's well-being, self-esteem, intellect, or other important variable. Such information is needed to reverse the popular negative view of reminiscence and to more effectively structure educational intervention.

REFERENCES

Boylin, W., Gordon, S. K., & Nehrke, M. F. (1976). Reminiscing and ego integrity in institutionalized elderly males. *The Gerontologist, 16*, 114–118.

Butler, R. N. (1963). The life review: An interpretation of reminiscence in the aged. *Psychiatry, 26*, 65–76.

Cameron, P. (1972). The generation gap: Time orientation. *The Gerontologist, 12*, Part 1, 117–119.

Coleman, P. G. (1974). Measuring reminiscence characteristics from conversation as adaptive features of old age. *Journal of Aging and Human Development, 5*, 281–294.

Costa, P., & Kastenbaum, R. (1967). Some aspects of memories and ambitions in centenarians. *The Journal of Genetic Psychology, 110*, 3–16.

Dewey, J. (1917). *Democracy and education*. New York: Macmillan.

Ebersole, P. (1976). Reminiscing and group psychotherapy with the aged. In I. M. Burnside (Ed.), *Nursing and the aged*. New York: McGraw-Hill.

Erikson, E. (1950). *Childhood and society*. New York: Norton.

Giambra, L. M. (1977). Daydreaming about the past: The time setting of spontaneous thought intrusions. *The Gerontologist, 17*, 35–38.

Hala, M. (1975). Reminiscence group therapy project. *Journal of Geriatric Nursing, 1*, 34–41.

Havighurst, R. J., & Glasser, R. (1972). An exploratory study of reminiscence. *Journal of Gerontology, 27*, 235–253.

Hiemstra, R. (1980). *Preparing human service practitioners to teach older adults*. (Info. series No. 209). Columbus, OH: ERIC Clearinghouse of Adult, Career and Vocational Education.

Hughston, G., & Merriam, S. (1982). Reminiscence: A nonformal technique for improving cognitive functioning in the aged. *Journal of Aging and Human Development, 15*, 139–149.

Knowles, M. (1980). *The modern practice of adult education*. Chicago: Association Press.

Koch, K. (1977). *I never told anybody*. New York: Random House.

Kübler-Ross, E. (1969). *On death and dying*. New York: Macmillan.

Lewis, C. N. (1971). Reminiscing and self-concept in old age. *Journal of Gerontology, 26*, 240–243.

Lewis, C. N. (1973). The adaptive value of reminiscing in old age. *Journal of Geriatric Psychiatry, 6*, 117–121.

Lewis, M., & Butler, R. (1974). Life-review therapy: Putting memories to work in individual and group psychotherapy. *Geriatrics, 29*, 165–173.

Lieberman, M. A., & Falk, J. M. (1971). The remembered past as a source of data for research on the life cycle. *Human Development, 14*, 132–141.

Liton, J., & Olstein, S. (1969). Therapeutic aspects of reminiscence. *Social Casework, 5*, 263–268.

Lowenthal, M. F., Thurnher, M., & Chiriboga, D. (1975). *Four stages of life*. San Francisco: Jossey-Bass.

McClusky, H. (1978). The community of generations: A goal and a context for the education of persons in the later years. In R. H. Sherron & D. B. Lumsden (Eds.), *Introduction to educational gerontology*. Washington, DC: Hemisphere.

McMahon, A. W., & Rhudick, P. J. (1967). Reminiscing in the aged: An adaptational response. *Psychodynamic studies on aging: Creativity, reminiscing and dying*. New York: International Universities Press.

Merriam, S., & Cross, L. (1982). Adulthood and reminiscence: A descriptive study. *Educational Gerontology, 8*, 275–290.

Merriam, S., & Cross, L. (1981). Aging, reminiscence and life satisfaction. *Activities, Adaptation and Aging, 2*, 39–50.

Moody, H. R. (1978). Education and the life cycle: A philosophy of aging. In R. H. Sherron & D. B. Lumsden (Eds.), *Introduction to educational gerontology*. Washington, DC: Hemisphere.

Myerhoff, B., & Lufte, V. (1975). Life history as integration. *The Gerontologist, 15*, 541–543.

Neugarten, B. (1973). Personality and change in late life: A developmental perspective. In C. Eisdorfer & M. P. Lawton (Eds.), *The psychology of adult development and aging*. Washington, DC: American Psychological Association.

Oliveria, O. H. (1977). *Understanding old people: Patterns of reminiscing in elderly people and their relationship to life satisfaction*. Unpublished doctoral dissertation, University of Tennessee, Knoxville.

Pincus, A. (1970). Reminiscence in aging and its implication for social work practice. *Social Work, 15*, 47–53.

Safier, G. (1976). Oral life history with the elderly. *Journal of Gerontological Nursing, 2*, 17–22.

Troll, L. (1975). *Early and middle adulthood*. Monterey, CA: Brooks/Cole.

Weisman, S., & Shusterman, R. (1977). Remembering, reminiscing, and life: Review-
    ing in an activity program for the elderly. *Concern in the Care of the Aging, 3,*
    22–26.
Zeiger, B. (1976). Life review in art therapy with the aged. *American Journal of Art
    Therapy, 15,* 47–50.

4

THE COMMUNITY OF GENERATIONS: A GOAL AND A CONTEXT FOR THE EDUCATION OF PERSONS IN THE LATER YEARS

HOWARD Y. McCLUSKY*

University of Michigan

The present is in every age merely the shifting point at which past and present meet, and we can have no quarrel with either. There can be no world without traditions; neither can there be any life without movement . . . .

There is never a moment when the new dawn is not breaking over the earth, and never a moment when the sunset ceases to die. It is well to greet serenely even the first glimmer of the dawn when we see it, not hastening toward it with undue speed, nor leaving the sunset without gratitude for the dying light that was once dawn.

In the moral world we are ourselves the lightbearers, and the cosmic process is in us made flesh. For a brief space it is granted to us, if we will, to enlighten the darkness that surrounds our path . . . . As in the ancient torch race . . . we press forward torch in hand along the course. Soon from behind comes the runner who will outpace us. All our skill lies in giving into his hands the living torch, bright and unflickering, as we ourselves disappear into the future . . . .

Havelock Ellis

Because of the incomplete and provisional state of our knowledge, this chapter is necessarily exploratory in character and makes no pretense of constituting a definitive statement of the field. It is offered here primarily as a

*Deceased.

means of opening up a new domain of practice and inquiry for the agenda of both the educational gerontologist and the general educator.

THE CONCEPT

The concept of the *community of generations* is an intentional variation on a life-span approach to comprehending the wholeness of life. It is based on the assumption that, although separated by time and experience, each generation nevertheless has a common stake with other generations in relating itself to the wholeness of the life-span of which it is a part. In more operational terms, a community of generations is not a community of "equals" or "similars." It is not an association of persons necessarily similar in performance, ability, social class, or ethnic origin. Moreover, it is not an association of persons necessarily in agreement on substantive matters. On the contrary, it is, to coin a term, a *community of differents,* i.e., an interacting collectivity of people occupying both adjacent and widely separated stages in the progression from the beginning to the end of life. The thesis in this chapter is that this difference is of such a character as to make the achievement of a community of generations a viable possibility. It is this difference that makes an experience of the wholeness of life more comprehensible. It is also this difference that accents the common and compelling need the generations have to learn from one another. Finally it is the celebration of the creative potential of this difference that generates the dynamics for establishing the community of generations as a goal and a context for the education of Persons in the Later Years.

Reservations

Before proceeding with an exegesis of what is essentially an optimistic and developmental view of the potential of instructional processes, we should be prepared to face some of the hard-nosed realities with which any intergenerational effort must contend. In the first place, we must reckon with one of the most pervasive features of human existence—the direction of the flow of responsibility between the generations. In infancy, childhood, and, in our culture, during most of the period of youth, growing individuals are dependent on the generation immediately ahead of them for support and protection. The people of this generation are usually their parents or parent surrogates with whom they necessarily maintain a kind of dependent, or debtor, relationship. This must be so because of the irreversible progression of stages through which people must move in the life cycle. This relationship is, of course, by no means wholly devoid of educational outcomes. For one thing, parents are probably the most important teachers in children's lives. For another, the children, far more than most people admit, are at least implicitly but no less effectively, teachers of their parents. In other words, the family is still the basic educational unit in society. The point, however, is that the dominant-dependent nature of the relationship between the parental generation and the adjacent younger generation can be, and often is, a barrier to productive communication and must be properly handled if its educational potential is to be achieved.

In the second place, in making a case for the idea of the community of generations, we must deal with another feature of the human condition: the facts that, generally speaking, people interact and communicate more readily with their generational peers than they do with people of other generations and that the greater the generational distance, the less the likelihood of communication. One explanation for this point is the fact that the dominant-dependent relationship leads young people to seek the company of their peers in order to achieve a balancing sense of autonomy. This reaching out is especially strong during adolescence, and, as one way of achieving a sense of identity, it accounts in part for the dynamics of the youth culture. A collateral and perhaps more persuasive explanation for a preference for communicating with peers is that people occupying approximately the same stages of life confront, to use Havighurst's terminology, similar *developmental tasks* or *dominant concerns* and therefore have more in common about which to communicate. For example, few experiences produce a greater sense of community among parents than that of being members of a parent-teacher group concerned with the well-being of their children in the same elementary school.

A third major factor responsible for an ideological separation of generations is the outcome of a feature of our educational system—the pervasive practice of segregating the ages in both the curricular and administrative dimensions of educational programs. This practice was consolidated when the school system in the United States adopted the Prussian model of an age-graded organization in which, for example, members of the first grade are 6 years old, members of the second grade are age 7, third grade youngsters are age 8, and so forth. (The growing support for expansion of the ungraded elementary school is a reaction against the rigidities of the prevailing Prussian model.) A plausible case can be made for some grouping according to developmental stages for instructional purposes, especially when we consider the developmental distance between the 6-year-old and the prepubescent 12-year-old or between the pubescent 13-year-old and the 16-year-old. The reason, however, for calling attention in this context to the historic practice of age segregation in the educational system of the United States is that, in proposing the implementation of the concept of the community of generations, we confront a long-established tradition based on the assumption that education occurs more effectively when it is confined to interaction with members of the same generation than when it is designed to encourage communication between the generations. It does not serve the implementation of the community of generations, to romantically ignore some of the tough realities with which any effort at maximizing the potential of intergenerational relations must contend.

Boundaries

The concept of the community of generations could apply to the interrelationships of any combination of generations we might wish to examine, and from an educational standpoint, each combination would present a set of issues and opportunities unique to it as well as the issues and opportunities relevant to the entire life-span. For purposes of this discussion, however, I am concerned mainly, though not exclusively, with the interrelationships of the generation of childhood and youth with the generation of the later years.

The concept of the community of generations as applied to the educational enterprise has both a procedural and a substantive dimension. Procedurally, it suggests both motivations and strategies whereby the subject matter of instruction may be more effectively internalized. Substantively, it suggests a somewhat innovative approach to the determination of what the subject matter of instruction might be. In both cases, as already indicated, the differences between the positions of the respective generations are regarded, not as a liability, but as a decisive asset in enhancing the influence of educational processes.

THE PROCEDURAL DIMENSION

It is my premise that, if properly arranged, interaction between the generations can be productive for invigorating and broadening the thrust of the teaching-learning process. This premise is based on the fact that each generation occupies a different stage in life-span development and is a product of a somewhat different set of societal forces. I also postulate that these two factors will tend to lead each generation of people to approach an issue or area of subject matter in a way unique to its stance.

Before proceeding further with my argument, I should be careful not to overplay this point. For instance, it can be plausibly argued that a developmental stage (i.e., a stage en route to maturity) and a difference between cohorts would make little difference in approaching such cognitively pure examples of subject matter as mathematics and the physical sciences or perhaps some meticulously objective treatment of the empirical data of history or geography as well. Also, it might be argued that there is often as wide a difference in the viewpoints of members of the same generation as there is between members of different generations. Finally, many issues will, for many people, transcend generational differences. There may be people in both the later and earlier years who feel equally strongly about such problems as protection of the environment, involvement in foreign affairs, or discovery of new sources of energy.

It is sufficient for my case, however, to point out that, for many people, a variation in the stage of life-span development, combined with a difference in the surrounding environment in which successive generations are immersed, can lead to a difference in approaching those aspects of learning for which life-centered experiences possess a unique relevance. If we can accept this hypothesis, we can assemble a substantial volume of psychological theory and research to support it and to explain the dynamics of its operation.

There are several kinds of evidence from the field of psychology that can be employed to account for the dynamics of instruction that differences between the generations might generate. One kind is derived from a study of the operation of *perceptual contrast.* For example, a sound, even of moderate intensity, following a period of prolonged silence, will attract more attention than a sound following a continuous series of sounds; e.g., the bark of a dog or the song of a bird in a silent forest, the crack of a gun fired under the silence of a desert sky. Conversely, a moment of silence abruptly following a period of sustained noise will attract more attention than silence that is merely more of what already exists; e.g., at a noisy sports event the moment of quiet in honor of the memory of a distinguished citizen, the stillness of a night sky at the end of an explosive display of Fourth of July fireworks. Similar results may occur in reaction to contrasts between light and darkness, between movement and rest, and, in more generic perceptual terms (especially important to our argument), between figure and ground.

Another kind of evidence comes from our knowledge of the phenomenon of *homeostasis,* the tendency of the organism to seek to maintain a steady state of equilibrium. If this equilibrium is upset, the organism goes to work to bring about its restoration. For instance, when we are well fed, we are in equilibrium; if we are hungry or starving, our gastronomic system is thrown off balance, and we seek food to regain our preferred state of steadiness. So it is with water when we are thirsty, or rest when we are fatigued, or heat when we are cold, or cold when we are hot. Although our knowledge of homeostasis has been largely physiological in character, many psychologists believe that homeostasis is just as relevant to the understanding of the dynamics of personality as it is to the understanding of bodily conditions. For example, stress, anxiety, fear, or blows to self-esteem upset the steady state of an individual's adjustment; as a consequence a person will strive to remove the source of these threats in order to recover a sense of well-being.

Still another kind of evidence that can be used to explain the dynamics of intergenerational differences may be found in the theory of *cognitive dissonance.* Simplified, this theory holds that if ideas (i.e., cognitions) are perceived by a person as incongruous (i.e., dissonant), that person will employ various strategies to realign the ideas into some state of acceptable, cognitive harmony.

By this time, the reason for making use of the insights that may be derived from psychology should be clear: Diversities of experience and outlook that may result from occupying a different stage in the life-span lend themselves to the use of contrast, disequilibrium, dissonance, and other kinds of inherent or contrived discrepancies as a means for motivating and broadening the processes of instruction. With proper arrangement of the instructional situation, this technique can be accomplished well within the range of acceptable toleration. To paraphrase a well-known cliché, I am simply asserting that the *variety* of intergenerational differences, can be the *spice* of the teaching-learning process. Let me operationalize the argument by illustrating what this point might look like in practice.

First, consider how the reactions of a 10-year-old child, or a 16-year-old youth, or a 25-year-old young adult would compare with the reactions of a 70- or 80-year-old adult upon (1) perceiving a flower, (2) viewing a picture of some historical event, (3) reading a story, (4) solving a problem, or (5) empathizing with some instance of acquisition or loss, or of success or failure.

Second, consider the following questions as topics for a panel discussion in which representatives of the ages indicated are participants: What is best and what is worst about being age 15 or age 25 as opposed to being age 65, or 75, or 85? What is best and worst about being a woman or a man at age 25 and at age 75?

Third, consider what a resourceful teacher could do with Arthur Miller's *Death of a Salesman* in a class where a sizable number of the members has first-hand knowledge what it means to be occupationally frustrated, while others in the class have yet to be employed in a permanent job. Consider what a teacher of political science could do with a course in local government in which some class members have participated in a party caucus or have served on the city council or are veterans of the program of the League of Women Voters, whereas others have yet to vote.

Finally, consider how an intergenerational mix of students affords opportunities for a variety of additional strategies for the stimulation of instruction; e.g., the reversal of intergenerational positions in role playing; the alternation of persons of different generations in observing the processes and content of group discussion; the use of intergenerational teams in planning projects, data collection, and outreach programs of research and community service.

My hypothesis, then, is simply that the combination of differences accommodated by a community of generations would greatly enlarge the scope of procedures available for instruction and, at the same time, result in outcomes ranging from clarification of issues to the production of a creative dialectic.

THE SUBSTANTIVE DIMENSION

In attempting to deal with the substantive dimension of the community of generations, I can make no pretense of offering a definitive statement about such a highly speculative domain. Moreover, I cannot pretend that what

I have to offer is uniformly applicable to all people of all generations. I intend the following points to convey generic and ideal themes in order to indicate the kind of substantive outcomes that may emerge from an involvement of different generations in a common, instructional experience.

I am attempting to formulate an answer to the question What can one generation learn from another generation? More explicitly, What can a Young Person (YP) learn from a Person in the Later Years (PLY) and what can PLYS learn from YPs?

What Persons in the Later Years Can Learn from Young Persons

First, PLYs can, in the course of interacting educatively with YPs recover some of the idealism they probably had in the earlier years of their own childhood and youth. At the risk of being stereotypical, a case can be made for the fact that, in general, YPs have high expectations, dream dreams, and are idealistic. On the other hand, members of the adult generation are generally prone to trim the aspirations of their youth and to adjust to the frustrating realities with which any implementation of ideals is compelled to contend. Perhaps YPs expect too much, but it is also possible that adults of the middle and later years expect too little. Is it not possible, then, that some exposure to the idealism of youth would stimulate those in the pragmatic, adult years to lift their sights and renew their faith in the vision of a better life? Although it is not inevitable, the probability is great enough to justify a revival of effort.

Second, by associating with YPs in common tasks of learning, PLYs can go far toward renewing a sense of intellectual discovery. In the early stages of life, much of living must necessarily be devoted to processes of discovery. Encountered for the first time, everything is new and must be sampled, tested, and learned. Hence, things, people, events, machines, nature, are all novel to the young and are generally objects of exploration. It would be easy at this point to be naive and forget that much of what, to a YP is frontier must become habitual in order to free him or her for the performance of more mature tasks. As the years pass, however, those objects, people, skills, and procedures necessary for survival become learned so that what was once a matter of discovery becomes a process of maintenance, i.e., sheer performance rather than growth in learning. The law of least effort makes understandable why it is easy for adults to restrict their living to the repetitive performance of procedures already learned and to gradually lose the inclination to break new paths, entertain new thoughts, and explore new frontiers. Again, is it not possible; when and where there are so many new things, facts, technologies, and procedures to be learned as well as a mass of equally exciting and relevant old things not yet learned; that sharing with YPs the challenge of discovery will induce PLYs to achieve a new sense of intellectual adventure? Although it is not inevitable, it certainly seems worth a try.

Third, in working with YPs there is a strong probability that PLYs can rekindle their interest in and achieve an extended sense of a viable future. There comes a time, perhaps about midway in life, when people become aware of the fact that they have a past and aware that the sense of unlimited time that characterized their outlook in the days of youth is giving way to a realization that life is not forever, that time is beginning to run out. It is not surprising, therefore, that when people move into and through the last quarter of life, more and more of their waking hours are absorbed with the increasing volume of the apperceptive past, mixed with a growing awareness of an existential now, together with a sense of a rapidly diminishing future. I use the word *rapidly* here deliberately to reflect the well-nigh universal experience that the longer life lasts, the more rapidly time seems to pass.

In contrast, from the perspective of the life-span, the lives of young people are drastically incomplete. Because of this incompleteness, youth are rich in life expectations. The years stretch out before them in lines of development that they have yet to experience. It is understandable, therefore, that YPs should be activated by a sense of the future so compelling that it dominates their entire outlook on life. It is also understandable that they should devote so much of their effort to anticipating what may lie ahead; for instance, how they will earn a living, the family they hope to establish, or a possible return to education. Recent research (Olmsted, 1976) indicates that even as early as the middle and late teens, YPs are capable of projecting a realistic schedule of major events likely to occur in the full span of their own lives. By associating with young people and by empathetically assisting them to envisage their lives, PLYs could, under favorable circumstances, be more likely to develop an extension of a sense of their own future and achieve the ability to transcend, in part, the perceived limitations of their decreasing life expectancy.

Fourth, by interacting with YPs in educational activities, PLYs would be more likely to maintain a meaningful contact with the stream of societal change. This point goes far toward underscoring the fragility of the status of PLYs in a period in human history when change is so rapid, pervasive, and dominant and promises to become increasingly so in the years ahead.

Let us consider how some of the decisive events in the course of life tend to remove PLYs from the mainstream of change. There is the impact of retirement. When people retire, they automatically lose the day-by-day, face-to-face contact with fellow workers that constituted a major link to the changing world. If they formerly belonged to a labor union or an organization of employees, this association, with its publications and programs of events, tends to weaken. Retirement means, for practical purposes, removal from a part of society, namely the world of work, that perhaps more than any other part reflects the tide of societal change. Then there is the fact that as people gain in years, links with systems of kinship tend to decline; children, formerly a source of communication with the world outside the home, grow up, leave home, and establish their own independence and their own families. Furthermore, because of the growing trend toward geographic mobility, brothers and sisters, uncles and aunts, cousins, and other members of the clan are likely to be living in widely scattered locations throughout the country. As a result, PLYs suffer another gradual erosion of ties with the outside world of change. There is also the problem of transportation and the trend toward living in relative isolation that contribute to weakening the bonds of PLYs with the stream of contemporary change as they gain in years.

In contrast, one of the distinctive features of the world of youth is that, by virtue of their unique location in the life-span, YPs are strategically positioned to reflect and transmit the tides of change. To use an analogy from chemistry, YPs are both the litmus paper and the catalyst of societal change. After all, we live in a youth-oriented society, and whatever else they are, YPs are contemporary and live in contemporary culture, and to be contemporary is to keep abreast of change. They absorb the new language, alternatives in life-style, occupations, and recreation like a sponge absorbs water. So, one of the ways in which PLYs can keep up with a rapidly changing society is to maintain a viable contact with YPs, and this can be most meaningfully accomplished by joining them in a community of inquiry.

What Young Persons Can Learn from Persons in the Later Years

Let us now turn to the question of what YPs could, under favorable and appropriate circumstances, learn from PLYs. The answer to this question stems almost wholly from the generic and obvious fact that PLYs have lived longer than YPs. PLYs' advantage as potential instructors is largely due to the advanced position they occupy in the life cycle. In effect, they have had more experience and know more about the wholeness of life. I am not proposing that all PLYs will demonstrate the advantage of their advanced position, nor do I assert that they will all embody the ideal behavior described in the following discussion. I am writing about the ideal expectations and possibilities, some of which some PLYs will be able to approximate, if not achieve.

In the first place, some, possibly many, PLYs in any given instructional setting will have an expertise they can contribute to an educational program, depending, of course, on the level and subject of instruction. In some instances, this expertise may consist of a highly developed skill or craftmanship, the possession of which was much more common 50 years ago than today. In other instances, their expertise may consist of some areas of specialized knowledge, a knowledge that is the product of a lifetime of practice and study. In still other cases, a PLY may possess unusual competence in the management of human relations. These three examples are merely illustrations to which many more could be added. Whatever the nature of the extensive experience of the PLYs, it can be an enormous advantage in working with young people in an educational setting. In fact, it should always be kept in mind that in many situations any number of PLYs may possess a competence in some departments far in excess of that possessed by the instructor of a class. This is another way of saying that probably the only dimension in which an instructor, presumably a younger adult, can be certain of being more competent than a given PLY student, is in the subject matter around which the class is organized. A PLY may express this expertise in various ways: by insightful contributions to a group discussion; by serving as a counselor to younger fellow students; or by serving as a short-term, ad hoc instructor when some topic on the teacher's lesson plan coincides with that expertise.

In the second place, because they have lived longer and have known more of life, with its mixtures of frustration and success, disappointment and fulfillment, PLYs will be in a better position to relate the learning of the classroom to the realities of everyday living. Learning, to them, will not be a thing apart, embalmed in books and libraries and restricted to laboratories and workshops. Learning will, to the PLYs, become a vital part of the exigencies of daily existence. Thus they will demand and be able to contribute relevance to the instruction to a degree that cannot possibly be matched by YPs because of the limitations of experience with which they are compelled to contend. PLYs will be in a much more favorable position to translate theory into practice than YPs, and YPs will in turn be the beneficiaries of this competence.

In the third place, PLYs, as potential instructors of their younger colleagues, will have the advantage of having lived through a most fantastic and turbulent period of history. In consequence, they will possess a perspective on a wide range of human concerns that only a direct encounter with historical events can provide. Take, for example, the history of United States involvement in war. This generation of PLYs will have listened to the recital by their parents or grandparents of stories based on a living participation in our Civil War. Anecdotes and names associated with the battles of Bull Run, Antietam, and Gettysburg and with the surrender at Appomattox will be vivid in the memories of their childhood days. Somewhat later, they or their parents will have taken part, directly or indirectly, in the first worldwide war in the chronicles of the human race. They will have actual photographs or living memories of the battles of the Somme, the retreat to the Marne, the stalemate at Verdun, and the surrender negotiated in the railway car in the forest of Compiègne near Paris. Some will have been there; others will have heard about it from those who were there. Then there was the attack on Pearl Harbor and World War II. This time, some PLYs, but in most cases their children, were caught up in the mobilization of forces. This time the war effort took four years (1941-1945), not one (1917-1918), and the conflict occurred, with new, sophisticated weapons, on three continents and their bordering oceans, rather than just in Western Europe. Since then, there have been the Korean War and the war in Vietnam.

For another example of the historical perspective PLYs can provide, take the very practical, down-to-earth behavior of money. This generation of PLYs will recall when $1 was considered to be a fair wage for a ten-hour day's work. They will also remember the shock causing howls of consternation in the industrial world when Henry Ford advanced the wage rate to $5 a day. Because of these memories, they will have qualms and some reluctance about paying $25 for one hour of the time of a plumber to repair a faucet in the kitchen sink. They will remember what it felt like when the banks were closed during the early days of the depression, and what it was like to be unemployed without insurance or compensation, or what it was like for their own parents and grandparents to face retirement without the support of social security. Some of the current PLYs may wonder why the National Youth Administration (NYA), or the Civilian Conservation Corps (CCC), or an equivalent is not revived in order to check the rise of unemployment among youth.

Communication provides still another example. The PLYs generation will be able to tell about the time when they had to turn a crank at the side of a wooden box to get the attention of the telephone operator instead of being able to dial directly to phone stations in most quarters of the globe, as we can today. They will also be able to tell us about when the radio and television first arrived; what it was like as these twin technologies brought instant news and information into the privacy of their homes from the most distant parts of the world; and how this and the advent of jet airplanes have transformed the image of the world as a potential community, an image, more of fact than of experience and acceptance, with which we have yet to come to terms.

I could continue with an elaboration of the changes that have occurred in the last 65 years or so in transportation, sources of energy, international relations, education, population, food supply, human relations, women's liberation, sexual behavior, civil rights, religious attitudes, family life, etc.; but to do so would only be piling up evidence for the point that by this time should be well established—that this generation of PLYs has had an opportunity to observe and take part in transformations of living that have been massive in scale and dramatic in impact. They are, therefore, living historians of an incredible, recent past, and as such, they are in a position to make an authentic contribution to any learning experience that they might share with YPs and to which the historical dimension is relevant.

Those who have lived through the last amazing and transforming 65 or more years of history will, because of this fact, have much more to offer as potential educators than just a knowledge of historical happenings. They will have achieved a sense of time past and time to come, giving them an outlook that will place issues, problems, and the stream of events in an enduring and stabilizing perspective—a perspective some regard as one of the most valuable outcomes of an educative experience. For instance, they will not necessarily be dismayed when at times everything seems to be going wrong, because they will have known periods like this before and have survived. On the other hand, they will not be unduly swayed by ebullient promises, however attractive, of better things to come, because they have had to retreat from high expectations before and life has continued to be reasonably good. Thus they should be able to help YPs not to panic when the door slams shut or to become too excited when the door blows open.

This attitude could also help YPs to secure a stabilizing grip on the impact of change. Earlier in this discussion, I stressed the point that young people live in a culture of the contemporary and reflect change like a sponge absorbs water. This is obviously a fact, but it is not necessarily a virtue and certainly no cause for celebration, because in extreme forms, being contemporary can border on the pathological. Being an 18-karat contemporary can lead a person to act like a weather vane responding, without the slightest display of autonomy, to every shift in the wind. Being contemporary can mean rushing desperately from passing fad to passing fad, or jumping on every bandwagon that comes in sight without asking where it is going or discovering what it will do after it arrives. This malady is a mild form of neurotic behavior that is not necessarily confined to the younger generation inasmuch as it often strikes adults, especially in mid-life when they suddenly discover that time is running out, whereupon they attempt to secure a new grasp on the meaning of life. It is, however, a kind of malady, an escape into meaningless activity, for which some YPs, in their efforts to be "with it," are especially susceptible.

PLYs, with their perspective, can be a positive force in keeping this drive for the contemporary within constructive bounds and in reminding YPs that change qua change is not necessarily constructive; that much of what appears to be new is simply a return, under a new label, of something that has been around for a long time; and that, in some cases, virtue is more likely to be embodied in something that has stood the test of time, than in something, like a roman candle, that has suddenly caught the attention of people but will soon be lost in the darkness and forgotten. YPs may ask, Is it new? but PLYS may ask the more fundamental questions, Is it important? Will it last? for PLYs will have lived long enough to know that many more start a race than finish it and those who finish are in a better position to know how to get there than those who drop out soon after the bang of the starting gun.

These three broad areas of contributions PLYs can make to the education of young people by no means exhaust the possibilities. To the points already made I could add the role that PLYs could play in helping YPs validate an internalization of enduring values, the pursuit of which gives meaning to life, or to be more operational, I could formulate recommendations that PLYs could submit to YPs looking forward to successful

aging in their own later years, but instead I conclude this section of my
presentation with an exegesis of what is probably the most important
contribution that PLYs can make to the educational development of YPs:
helping them to achieve some understanding of the interactive wholeness of
the life-span and to see how this understanding can facilitate lifelong
development.

To make this point as secure and acceptable as possible, I am prepared
to concede that we should not expect people in a world of growing
complexity and change to be sufficiently clairvoyant to anticipate with any
degree of certainty the paths the future may dictate. Under such circumstances, the wisest strategy is to make the best of every event and task as they
appear and to trust that a successful response to their demands will equip
people to deal adequately with succeeding demands as they come along. This
policy makes good sense for practical, short-run purposes, but it fails to take
into account that, whereas society may be changing in unanticipated ways, the
critical events, requirements, and turning points of the life cycle are,
nevertheless, much more predictable. Because of this fact, individuals can
secure a much better grasp on the direction of the years ahead if they are
disposed to view the future in the context of the wholeness of lifelong
development.

Before we allow ourselves to be carried away by a euphoric acceptance
of this point, let us briefly examine some of the trends in contemporary living
that stand in the way of its implementation. In a society in which babies are
born and the elderly die in hospitals and not at home; in which little children
are placed in day-care centers or nursery schools; in which 6-to-12–year-olds
are segregated in a six-grade elementary school; in which youth in the 12-to-14
and 14-to-18 age brackets are separated in junior and senior high schools; in
which people 18 years of age and older are scattered in community and
far-flung four-year colleges; in which more mothers are working at part- and
full-time jobs; in which both mothers' and fathers' jobs are usually separated
from the home in both function and location; in which grandparents and
great-grandparents are usually living alone in single housing units or segregated
in housing complexes for "seniors" or in retirement villages often located in
distant parts of the country; in such circumstances, how can the society and
its people gain an adequate understanding and appreciation of the developmental, life-span wholeness? Obviously, an adequate and realistic answer to
this question will require fresh action on many fronts, e.g., community,
planning, housing, transportation, kinship system, etc. We are confronting,
here, a problem grounded in some of the basic features of modern living and
for which an adequate solution will require more than a reordering of the
educational enterprise; but properly conceived and properly arranged, educational institutions could go a long way to relieve the situation just described
and to recapture some of the sense of life-span wholeness that our
fragmenting society is leading us to lose.

In taking this stand, I am not naively proposing that achieving a sense of developmental wholeness will come easily or that its achievement will ever be perfect. I do claim that such an achievement can be approximated and that its approximation should become a goal *deliberately* chosen to give direction to instructional programs. In pursuit of this goal, PLYs would have a unique function to perform and would have an exclusive advantage in doing so.

The uniqueness of their function stems from a point I have stressed before, namely that PLYs have lived longer and experienced more of the totality of life than people who are now young but have yet to experience middle and old age. PLYs, though now old, were once middle aged and young. Thus, because of their apperceptive memory bank, they have the capacity to comprehend much better what life in its wholeness is all about than young people with their lack of experience possibly could.

How would this advantage be expressed? In at least two ways: (1) PLYs could help YPs take a long view of some of the inevitable happenings and turning points they will, in the course of the unfolding years, be compelled to confront, and (2) even more important, PLYs could, through processes of educational exchange and also by serving as models of successful living, assist YPs to view their own later years as a period of progressive development. Thus, they could anticipate their future, not as a plateau followed by an over-the-hill decline, but rather as an ascending spiral with the potential culmination being lifelong fulfillment. To use the formulation of Erikson (1963), YPs could look forward to the middle years as a period for generation and the avoidance of stagnation, and to the later years as a time for the achievement of a sense of ego integrity rather than despair. To borrow from Maslow (1970), YPs could be assisted in perceiving the later years as a time when a person becomes "fully human" and "fully mature," with potentialities "fully realized." Self-actualization would be regarded as a unique and exclusive achievement of PLYs. To quote Maslow (1970):

> *Self-actualization does not occur in young people. In our culture at least, youngsters have not yet achieved identity or autonomy nor have they had time enough to experience an enduring, loyal, post-romantic love relationship, nor have they generally found their calling, the altar upon which to offer themselves. Nor have they worked out their own system of values; nor have they had experience enough (responsibility for others, tragedy, failure, achievement, success) to shed perfectionistic illusions and become realistic; nor have they generally made their peace with death; nor have they learned how to be patient; nor have they learned enough about evil in themselves and others to be compassionate; nor have they had time to become post-ambivalent about parents and elders, power and authority; nor have they generally become knowledgeable and educated enough to open the possibility of becoming wise;*

nor have they generally acquired enough courage to be unpopular, to be unashamed about being openly virtuous, etc. (p. xx)

EXAMPLES

To illustrate the kind of community of generations I have been advocating, I am concerned here with examples of intergenerational projects that are primarily educative in character, although I am not committed to any formal model of instruction. In some instances, the principal learner is a PLY, and the YP is the teacher. In other cases, the direction of exchange is reversed. In still other situations, both YPs and PLYs interact as peers engaged in a common task of learning. I have selected five projects for review. To indicate the range of potential in the field, two projects are located in settings outside the formal school system and three within. In the former category, one project is an innovative venture of the Girl Scouts, and the other is a product of a "rest home." In the latter category, one project takes place at the level of the elementary school, another in a high school, and a third in a college specializing in the baccalaureate degree. I offer none as ideal models, and none embody all of the values I have earlier ascribed to the outcomes of intergenerational education. All are, however, authentic, real-life examples of how YPs and PLYs can get along together in a shared task of inquiry.

Girl Scouts

For a number of years, local Girl Scout troops, as a part of their regular program, have organized projects involving the association of young Scouts with PLYs. These separate efforts became so attractive that the national organization of Girl Scouts, with funds from the Administration on Aging, decided to make this kind of activity a matter of national emphasis and gave it the title Hand-in-hand: Cross-age Interactions (Girl Scouts of the U.S.A., 1975). Some excerpts from the report of the first year of the national project illustrate what actually happens when the young and the PLYs share their interests and contribute their respective talents to activities designed to improve the quality of living for those participating as well as those being served.

Let us begin with a look at the program of the Santiam Girl Scout Council of Salem, Oregon. In Salem, the Scouts collected oral histories from the PLYs, conducted games that both the Scouts and the PLYs could enjoy, and set up an adopted grandparent program designed to foster enduring, one-to-one relationships. The initiative, however, did not always originate with the YPs. For example, one elderly woman, although arthritic and confined to a wheelchair, taught a Scout troop how to knit; at a potluck dinner-concert given by the Scouts' families, a group of senior guests entertained the audience by playing their own brand of recycled instruments and by presenting a skit in which Tiny Tim was the featured character (according to the recorder, everybody "loved it"). Girl Scouts also participate by visiting the elderly in their homes and assisting them with shopping. In cold weather, the older Scouts help PLYs by installing storm windows in their homes. Participation in the Salem project increased 1000% in the first year of its operation.

The Girl Scouts of Lathrup Village, Michigan have organized a day-camp program for the elderly of the area in which the elderly are the campers and the Scouts are the counselors. Activities range from just enjoying the sun and being out in the country to arts and crafts. At the same time, the "campers" ((PLYs) teach the Scouts how to fish and study nature. The Lathrup Village program is not all camping, however. Back home, the Scouts have organized a friendship circle that involves, among other things, the girls telephoning PLYs to offer their services, to learn how they are getting along, or just to talk. As a result, some very close and gratifying relationships have developed.

In Marquette, Michigan the Girl Scout Council is involved with an already established group of PLYs called the Merry Mixers. The two groups are diverse, not only in age, but also in background. The PLYs have spent their entire lives in the Marquette area, whereas members of the Scout troop from Sawyer Air Force Base have lived in such faraway places as Morocco, Germany, and Turkey. This variety in background has turned out to be a great asset in program development. From the PLYs, the Scouts have learned about the past by living history. Crafts are also a source of mutual enjoyment for both the Scouts and the PLYs. Their creations, which are often the product of cooperative effort, are sometimes sold to help cover the costs of the project. From the Scouts, the PLYs receive some much-needed and appreciated services. For example, the girls help partially disabled PLYs with such chores as housecleaning and snow shoveling. They also assist with a hot lunch program that operates out of a school cafeteria. A Cadette troop regularly visits a nursing home, and another troop is helping to locate PLYs who might need health care. As a result, both the PLYs and the young Scouts have been delighted in developing new friendships.

Eureka, Illinois, Rest Home

Let us next examine another kind of program that is outside the formal school system and that is the product of a kind of agency in which we would least expect such a project to occur, namely, a "rest home." The program is the Prairie Crafts workshop, located at the Maple Lawn Homes, a Mennonite rest home in Eureka, Illinois. The project got under way when Ellen Braucht, the Home Extension advisor for Woodford County, received a request from some young homemakers for a workshop on quilt making. Braucht knew that many of the residents of the Maple Lawn Homes were experts in the disappearing skills of quilt making, knitting, crocheting, embroidering, and weaving; she had also observed a growing interest among young homemakers in the creative homemaking skills of the past, so the Prairie Crafts workshop was born. The residents of the Maple Lawn Homes are the instructors and the young homemakers are the students.

Beginning with 50 young homemakers and 12 residents, the project has grown to involve 200 homemakers and 60 residents. There is no charge for instruction. The instructors range in age from 80 to 96; the students are 19 and older. A few young mothers bring their small children to the workshop. This attracts some of the residents who are not involved as instructors, so there is no lack of sitters to take care of the children while their mothers learn how to make quilts. Interest in the project has been high, and soon more quilts were produced than the homemakers could use. As a result, Earl Greaser, the Maple Lawn Homes administrator, arranged to partition off and enclose with glass windows one end of the activity room and named it "Granny's Cupboard." Items in Granny's Cupboard are for sale. According to the latest report, the women of the home have a substantial backlog of orders for their products.

So it happened that a young, alert, Home Extension advisor brought together the skills of a group of women 80 to 96 years of age—skills that are the product of another era—with the needs of a group of young women interested in improving the culture of their own homes. As a result, friendships developed, interests expanded, over 60 elderly women got a new lease on life, and—for a substantial number of young families in the area of Eureka, Illinois—traditional American crafts were preserved to be enjoyed and passed on to future generations.

Fairhaven College—The Bridge Project

To introduce the second category of examples of intergenerational education, we now turn to Bellingham, Washington, the location of Fairhaven College, which for the past few years has been experimenting with the inclusion of a number of people over 60 years of age in the student body. Called the Bridge Project, it attempts to overcome the differences in understanding that presumably exist between the generations. The project began modestly in October, 1973. When the PLYs first arrived on the campus, they and the students were a little wary of each other, but uncertainty soon disappeared. The students found that they could continue to live the way they had been living and that the older people were not apostles of yesteryear seeking to reform them. The older people were relieved to find the students friendly and polite and respectful of their attitudes and viewpoints.

The older people were attracted to the Fairhaven campus by the prospect of classes, concerts, films, plays, lectures and recreation ranging from billiards to mountaineering. In addition some felt that from their own store of knowledge and experience they could contribute to the understanding and awareness of younger people. For others, the greatest appeal was sitting across the tables from youthful faces. And a few thought that at Fairhaven they might be able to satisfy their curiosity about hippies.

The pre-retirement occupations of the Bridgers vary considerably: businessmen, farmers, secretaries, teachers, a meat inspector, a college dean, a military officer, a postman. According to answers given to two questions on their applications, however, occupation had no bearing on their attitude toward age. When asked if they considered themselves old, they all without exception answered no. When asked which period of life they considered the most satisfying they all had difficulty singling out any one particular span of years.

Approximately half of all the participants in the Bridge Project hold Bachelor's degrees, but for the others the Bridge is their first experience with college.

The relaxed atmosphere at Fairhaven, the working and learning together and the "feeling of belonging" that it begets is an integral part of the functioning of the Bridge Project. Perhaps as a result of it the Bridgers have taken the initiative in involving themselves in campus life. One woman organized an arts and crafts fair; another together with a student set up a seminar on tutoring and wrote a tutoring manual for para-professionals. Another Bridger taught an accredited course entitled "Perspective on Aging."

Fairhaven history professor Michael Burnett looks at the Bridge Project from the point of view of his own classroom. "The older people tend to be more anecdotal than analytical in their approach to subject matter! This can slow things down, but it does amplify and does provide more humanity to a class. The Bridger in the classroom has a stabilizing effect; he takes the long view. When students become pessimistic after analyzing a situation, the older person can say 'That's not new. I remember that happening before.' They provide a continuity that students don't get any other way."

The students regard the Bridge Project as good for Fairhaven and good for them personally. Some mention that the Bridgers have given them a broader perspective of themselves, that they have been helped by knowing that these older people have gone through some of the same experiences that they are now going through. Others no longer think of people over the age of sixty as conservative and hard-of-hearing. Says one young man, "Now when I see old people on the bus, I'm more comfortable and ready to talk to them. I feel I might have something in common with them."

The Bridgers too regard their participation in the project as a valuable learning experience. For some the most important learning is academic; for others it is one of personal relationships. Connie Miller, a retired medical secretary leans toward the latter persuasion. "So many of us" she says, "were so busy living day to day during the years of raising a family we had little time for cultural activities. Those of us who worked saw the same people steadily for the last twenty years. At Fairhaven we meet a new group of people; we don't live in the past. We have a chance to grow. I think when we leave here we will be prepared to continue to broaden our acquaintances and to be more understanding of young people and young ideas." (Davis, 1975, pp. 8-9)

Mildred Henry, of the Center for Research and Development in Higher Education at the University of California at Berkeley, has conducted an evaluation of the Bridge Project (in Davis, 1975). In her report, she writes that "Young people are looking for a dependable philosophy to live by and . . . the Bridgers as a whole seem to have a special philosophy for living." She concludes, "The Bridge Project might well be considered highly significant because it is working amazingly well. Certainly it is providing a needed, lively, healthful option to the usual options available in our country to individuals of retirement age."

Brighton High School, Boston, Massachusetts

If we had been in the Allston-Brighton area of Boston on Thursday, October 19, 1972 and had looked at the local newspaper of that date, we would have seen the headline of an article, "This Year, History Takes a New Start at Brighton High School" (Kelsrud, 1972). Had we been in Boston on November 2, 1972, two weeks later, we would have seen a similar headline in the *Boston Globe:* "Young Learning about Age in Brighton Class" (Kriceland, 1972). These headlines refer to an intergenerational venture in education in which high school students join PLYs in reliving recent, twentieth-century history. The project started with the organization of a small group of PLYs who wished to examine the possibility of bringing their real-life experiences into a high school setting. According to the coordinator of the project, Edith Stein ("Elders, High Schoolers," 1974):

About fifteen older people said they were willing to try it and decided on subjects and methods during an eight week orientation period. . . . As a part of the training procedure, tape recorders were used to enable them to listen to and criticize themselves, improve their diction and presentation.

Only twelve students signed up originally for the opening class. . . . But opening day brought forty students for the class. We were overwhelmed.

The first class meeting was devoted to getting acquainted. In the next meeting, on entertainment in the twenties, a retired vaudeville performer drew on her experience to describe the world of entertainment before television. In the third meeting, devoted to the history of organized labor in the thirties, a labor organizer, now retired, but active in the early thirties, outlined the status of the labor movement at that time. The topics of the remaining meetings were: "The Boston Police Strike of 1919," "The Big Depression," "Social Changes in Our City," "What Do Older People Do Now?" and "Does It Have Any Value in Your Life?" As Stein said ("Elder, High Schoolers," 1974):

> By the third class, students had to be turned away. This was just a beginning. . . . We know new ventures are frightening, but we now know they are worth the effort, building a new role for elders which says—"You are important, your experiences give new meaning to all our lives in the community."

> The elders now see themselves as pioneers of a new venture which is effecting their lives daily in many ways. They have been called on by Harvard Divinity School to help in a seminar geared to sensitivity training for students who would be ministering to elders. They have appeared on television shows which they and the students have planned and worked on together.

> Their entrance into the mainstream of community life by going into the high school with a program of their own design has significantly altered the community. Students at the high school never will look at the elders as they did previously.

As a postscript to the preceding description of the Brighton high school project, Stein (1975) indicates that a very important clue to the success of the project is the eight-week orientation period in which those PLYs taking part were carefully trained for reentry. Stein warns that if anyone intends to replicate the Brighton project, "The most important aspect is the preparation of the elders for entry into the public schools." She continues, "If the persons who are invited to come and tell the history of the 20th century through their own life experience are limited to those who can do so easily and well—the whole idea is void! The main thing is to refresh and encourage those who are now depleted by the segregation of aging."

The Teaching-Learning Community, Ann Arbor, Michigan

For our last illustration, let us return to the Great Lakes region of the Midwest and learn how "grandpersons" are participating in an authentic

Teaching-Learning Community sponsored by the Ann Arbor, Michigan public school system. "Grandpersons" is the name given to 120 older volunteers currently involved in programs in seventeen of Ann Arbor's public schools.

In one recent three-month period, 246 separate projects were completed under grandperson guidance; they involved fine arts, graphics, crafts, woodworking, carpentry, photography, filmmaking, pottery, weaving, rug-hooking, music, movement, reading, story-telling, environmental arts such as gardening, flower arranging and plant care, and even the forgotten art of lace making.

The volunteers are average older citizens simply using the skills of a lifetime in a new environment, the schools. They come from single dwellings, public housing, retirement and nursing homes. They range in age from 60 to 87, are multiethnic, of every social background and occupation, and become a part of T-LC simply by saying "yes" when invited.

According to Dr. Harry Howard, superintendent of the school system doing the inviting, "Children learning from grandparents, and grandparents thriving on such a relationship may be 'innovative' in the formal educational sense of the word. However, the concepts embodied in T-LC are virtually timeless. Almost by definition, it had to work."

Project Director Carol Tice started it all five years ago by transporting three senior volunteers from school to school in her own car. She now has a project staff of five, a number of aides, and a substantial Title III grant to develop and evaluate T-LC concepts.

Tice says, "When Ralph Waldo Emerson wrote 'Youth is everywhere in place, but age requires fit surroundings,' he was not looking forward to the time when the aged would be expected to live in isolated ghettos with no further social function. 'Fit surroundings' for grandpersons simply means organizing time and space to accommodate their individual interests and needs.

"One of these needs is certainly the need to contribute, to be seen as givers of an important human and historical connection. T-LC creates that type of 'fit surrounding' for older citizens in the public schools."

Whether a retired furniture maker is developing balsa wood models, or a retired photographer is helping kids produce great shots of Ann Arbor's latest yellow fire truck; whether patchwork pillows are being made of authentic Early American designs, or the creation of puppets leads to the writing of scripts and the performance of grandpersons 'on stage', all of these activities have one thing in common: Grandpersons are seen as individuals with important skills to offer.

Each school "setting" is individually fine-tuned to a grandperson's skills, interests, energy level and mobility. The classroom teacher takes the initiative for inviting senior citizen participation, and then, through friendly informal conversations, discovers the range of activities that can be undertaken. The age and size of the student group, as well as the contact frequency, are adjusted to suit the senior volunteer.

As project activities commence, some senior volunteers sit quietly and let the children come to them. Others take the initiative for organizing students around an activity. Most T-LC grandpersons participate once or twice per week, for half day sessions.

T-LC has shown that grandpersons can be plugged into the public schools with important benefits to all concerned. In comprehensive tests by Project Evaluator Dr. James Doyle, an amazing statistic has resulted: 98 percent of participating schoolchildren respond enthusiastically to "their" grandpersons. They express opinions ranging from "Grand-persons are funner people" to the hope that "T-LC can go on forever" and "be on a daily basis."

Observers also have noted that grandpersons often spontaneously effect "cures" on hyperactive children, resulting in calmer, more receptive learning; and that the health of active T-LC participants improves and their medical needs decline. One older volunteer who could barely move across the room to a chair one year ago now arrives from her nursing home pushing the chair of another volunteer.

Whether grandpersons help to make rugs, rediscover lacemaking, or give form to a child's fanciful design, they are an important part of the neighborhood family that schools can build. Teaching and learning thrive where kinship and community are shared with grandperson volunteers (Mehta, 1976, pp. 60–61).[1]

THE MEANING OF THE EXAMPLES

What do the projects I have presented in the preceding section tell us about the organization and operation of programs of intergenerational education? First, in all of the above examples, and in every other instance (not reported here) with which I am acquainted, the initiative for the inter-generational venture did not originate with the PLYs but with the agency or institution involved. This is not surprising. PLYs have no affiliations, no precedence, and no power base that would enable them to walk in the front door of an organization or school without invitation and offer their services

[1] Reprinted from *NRTA Journal.* Copyright 1976 by The National Retired Teachers Association.

with the expectation that they would be accepted. Because of this fact and the reticence with which PLYs usually perceive their roles as volunteers, the organization taking the initiative must go out of its way to make them feel welcome and make certain that the conditions for involvement are as favorable as possible.

Second, in all the cases reported above (and in all others, I examined), there was an initial feeling of what might be called "autistic anxiety" among the participants at both ends of the age scale. Working closely with people widely separated in ages was, for both the YPs and the PLYs, a new experience, so new that they had little background for anticipating how to behave, what to say, or what the results would be. As a consequence, members of both generations approached their involvement with a mixture of curiosity and anxiety. This fact itself tells us a great deal about the attitudes that the generations usually hold toward each other. Typically, the generations coexist in a state of mutual toleration with little experience in meaningful and sustained interaction. This means that an educational community of generations will not just happen or arise spontaneously out of existing instructional programs; it will come into existence only by the sustained and careful preparation of arrangements in which both the young and the PLYs will feel at home.

Third, once the ice is broken, the introductions are completed, and the members of each generation have had an opportunity to feel out and sample the behavior of the other, anxiety quickly subsides and gives way to feelings of genuine delight and appreciation among each generation for the presence of the other one. This reaction was common to all the cases reported. It was due not merely to the relief that usually follows a discovery that the cause of an initial anxiety is not as malign as imagined; it was due also to the fact that members of each generation discovered an intrinsic and authentic interest in the activity that brought them together. The implication of the related facts that, when the generations learn to work together, (1) anxiety subsides and (2) interest increases, is that people expecting to set up projects of intergenerational education should have confidence in the potential of the positive motivation that cooperation between the generations will ultimately produce, because *once they try it, they will like it.*

Fourth, the programs I have reported on above were good education for the young as well as for the PLYs. That is, in order to accommodate the needs and make use of the talents of PLYs and make sure that they are engaged in a rewarding experience, it is not necessary to compromise the educational quality of the programs for YPs. In fact, all those in a position to know agreed that the programs generated by the projects were not only educationally superior, but probably better than comparable programs involving only a single (usually young) generation. In other words, the instruction of YPs was not watered down or sacrificed in order to involve and entertain the PLYs. The programs produced quality experiences for the PLYs as well. Thus both generations were rewarded with superior instruction as a result of working effectively together.

CONCLUSION

At this point, I return to the opening paragraph of this chapter. As I cautioned the reader there, information about the field of intergenerational education is incomplete and extremely limited. This limitation may be attributed to the facts that (1) relatively few systematic and sustained efforts have been made to integrate any combination of generations in a collaborative approach to learning, and (2) the few efforts that have been made have occurred so recently that there has been very little time in which to prepare a report of their activities. As a result, it is not yet possible to definitively delineate a full-blown implementation of the idea of the community of generations. Many questions of practice remain to be answered, and many issues of policy remain to be resolved. Despite the sketchiness of the information, however, I believe that enough has already been accomplished to establish the feasibility and importance of my thesis and to support the proposition that the concept of an intergenerational community of inquiry holds great promise for the instruction of people at all stages of the life cycle.

For all practical purposes, the generations usually have little educational commerce with one another. The best that can be said of their relationship is that the generations coexist in a state of mutual toleration. Typically, they walk different paths, which often diverge but rarely converge. It is my premise that this lack of meaningful interaction constitutes a grave loss for both individuals and society. I concede that there are probably some subjects that can best be studied and issues that can best be resolved in instructional situations in which the learners are similar rather than diverse in generational status, but I believe that there are many areas of inquiry in which a mixture of generations could lead to a superior level of educational performance.

In decision making and problem solving, for instance, it is quite possible that YPs would be more likely to suggest innovative solutions, whereas more mature people would be better at evaluating suggestions and anticipating the consequences of their adoption. Similarly, the young might be better at divergent thinking, whereas mature people might be better at convergent thinking. Or take the process of relating time past (history) to time to come (future). Presumably, PLYs are the historians, whereas YPs are the futurologists. Is it possible that PLYs can be taught to extrapolate from their knowledge of history in order more explicitly to anticipate the future, while YPs can be taught to search history more imaginatively for the antecedents of their predictions? Would these respective approaches lead to a higher level of educational performance if they were done interactively rather than separately? I think so. In fact, I believe that the application of an intergenerational approach to education would open an entirely new domain of research theory and practice for the agenda of both the educational gerontologist and the general educator.

According to one of the cardinal principles of gestalt psychology: The whole is more than the sum of the parts. To conclude, I summarize the thesis of this chapter by paraphrasing this well-known principle: The wholeness of intergenerational relations will give rise to more significant educational outcomes than the random collection of coexisting generational parts. We shall see!

REFERENCES

Brahce, C. I. (1975). Art bridges the age gap. *Innovator, 7*(2), pp. 1, 3–5.

Davis, C. C. (1975). Fairhaven's senior freshman. *American Education, 11*(4), 6–10.

Elders, high schoolers, join in Bay State teaching program. (1974, March–April). *Aging*, p. 17.

Erikson, E. H. (1963). *Childhood and society.* (2nd ed.). New York: Norton.

Girl Scouts of the U.S.A. (1975). *Hand-in-hand: Cross-age interactions.* (p. 40). New York: Author.

Havighurst, R. J. (1974). *Developmental tasks and education.* New York: McKay.

Kelsrud, P. (1972, October 19). This year history takes a new start at Brighton High School. *Allston-Brighton Citizen* (Item B).

Kriceland, P. F. (1972, November 2). Young learning about age in Brighton class. *Boston Globe.*

Maslow, A. H. (1970). *Motivation and personality* (2nd ed.). New York: Harper and Row.

Mead, M. (1970) *Culture and commitment: A study of the generation gap.* Garden City, NY: Doubleday.

Mehta, M. (1976, July–August). How to be a grandperson. *NRTA Journal*, pp. 59–69.

Olmsted, M. (1976). *The influence of a unit of instruction in gerontology on the attitudes, knowledge and perceptions of high school students of the aging process, the aged and their own aging.* Unpublished doctoral dissertation, University of Michigan.

Sokoloff, J. (1972, November 9). Generations exchange gifts at Brighton High. *Allston-Brighton Chronicle-Citizen.*

Stein, E. (1975, September). Personal communication.

5

INSTRUMENTAL AND EXPRESSIVE EDUCATION: FROM NEEDS TO GOALS ASSESSMENT FOR EDUCATIONAL PLANNING

CARROLL A. LONDONER
Virginia Commonwealth University

INTRODUCTION

Preparing a chapter for the third edition of this book has given me the opportunity to review the latest developments in instrumental and expressive orientations as a means for assessing people's educational needs throughout the life span. Although there have been a few dissertations related to the subject over the last 15 years, few have extended the initial conceptions I presented in the first edition of this book (Londoner, 1978). Indeed, Peterson (1983) viewed those conceptions as the only major attempt so far to develop a theoretical framework for examining the educational wants of older people. I view this situation with both pride and sadness—pride in what I was able to contribute conceptually to the area, and sadness that others have neither extended nor refuted the theoretical base. Although program planning has grown increasingly more sophisticated (Caffarella, 1988; Knowles, 1980), the same cannot be said for the area of needs assessment for adults and specifically for persons of later years (PLYs). Much of the literature has confined itself simply to describing needs assessment techniques and strategies that program planners can use in creating educational activities for PLYs.

I am sincerely grateful to Professor Hiemstra, who compiled and wrote the original literature review and developed the "Data Collection Matrix for Educational Program Planning" (Figure 4) for the first edition of this book. His initial encouragement to develop this chapter, based on our earlier collegial endeavors, led to a sharpening of my own theoretical position, and this revised chapter builds on his earlier efforts.

The purpose of this chapter is to clarify some of the ideas and extend some of the conceptualizations that were presented in earlier editions of this book and to examine some of the more relevant literature. I believe that the ideas are still conceptually relevant even though the theoretical base may not be clear to the general reader. Most likely this is because the ideas emerge from the discipline of sociology rather than from the disciplines of education and psychology with which most readers are familiar. Those looking for an immediate answer to a pressing educational problem will not find it in these descriptions. Rather, the purpose is to provide a sound theoretical rationale and structure for assessing the needs of PLYs. Additionally, I hope that these ideas from sociology extend the foundation upon which needs assessment in general is practiced. I have always believed that the very best practitioners allowed their philosophical and theoretical underpinnings to guide their practice. Too often one finds that people in the field who have been trained in adult education simply ignore what they know is right in the interest of expediency and time. My position concurs with that of Lewin (cited in Marrow, 1969), namely, that nothing is so practical as a sound theory that guides one's professional practice.

The search for a theoretical framework for needs assessment is in its seminal phase. Because many older adults are still active in a variety of social settings, any needs assessment theory and approach should consider the social setting and the older person's needs jointly. Too often the strategy focuses solely on the individual's needs with little thought given to the organization's or agency's requirements to meet those needs. The discipline of sociology reminds us that individuals operate within social systems that have collective expectations of its constituents.

A number of theoretical constructs exist from the fields of psychology and social psychology that are useful in analyzing the older person's needs. Generally, these constructs assume internalized energizing mechanisms that push or impel a person to participate in activities. Inherent in these constructs is the notion that people meet their needs by interacting with the environment in some meaningful way. These constructs are based on a needs reduction paradigm that perceives the individual to be responding to some internal drive mechanism that triggers overt behaviors in society. These ideas have been helpful in developing educational programs but appear to me to contain only part of the behaviors that should be examined. Another set of constructs focuses on the notions of positive striving whereby the individual proactively seeks to obtain some specific goals from various social settings. Thus the person is pulled toward some specific target or objective rather than being pushed by some psychological need. Melding these two positions might better serve us in creating a theoretical base.

Both as a practitioner and as an academician I have been interested in the education of adults of all ages. Why, when one has undertaken a recognized needs assessment strategy, do people not respond to the educational program? It was this kind of question that led me to examine extant literature in the field and eventually to develop the ideas for this chapter. The search for a theoretical framework for needs assessment led me to the early works of Havighurst (1964, 1969), who had used the terms *instrumental* and *expressive educational activity* in a sociological framework. Researching the source of these terms led back to the work of Parsons (1951/1964), a leading sociologist of the structural–functional school of analysis. Parsons's major contribution was the development of a systems analysis approach to the study of social structures and the motivational behavioral orientations of people who interact within social structures. He developed an exhaustive set of analytical categories for all levels of social systems that focused on the notion of an *action frame of reference* and the ways individuals and collectivities of individuals interact with each other in various social situations.

Of great interest was Parsons's discussion of the gratification people receive when they participate in activities as they strive to meet their goals and objectives within society. Some activities yield immediate gratification simply by participating in them. These he termed *expressive orientations*. Other activities provide delayed gratification upon completion of some desired future goal. These activities he termed *instrumental orientations*. These sociological terms were used in an earlier article by the author (Londoner, 1971). I proposed adopting these sociological terms as a theoretical construct for identifying and assessing the needs of older adults (Londoner, 1971). Furthermore, I have argued that instrumental educational activities should be given priority over expressive activities because they provide needed coping and growth competencies for meeting the challenges of the later years.

From that original theoretical framework Hiemstra (1972, 1973) developed and contributed to several empirical studies that examined the educational preferences of older retired people according to the expressive and instrumental dichotomy. These and other studies provided educational gerontologists with information concerning whether PLYs would prefer instrumental or expressive forms of educational activities. Hiemstra (1975) found that generally the older people sampled preferred instrumental over expressive educational activities. These early findings seemed to strengthen my thesis that instrumental adult education activities for PLYs provided the essential competencies for survival and growth in interaction with the social environment.

Later studies, however, conflicted with these data and left the issue somewhat up in the air (Peterson, 1983). That is, some older people wanted expressive educational activities, whereas others wanted instrumental ones. I review these data later in the chapter. Peterson (1983) made a helpful distinction between the educational needs of older people and their wants. Often these are not the same. Needs are identified by the professional educator through an analysis of the older person's circumstances, whereas wants tend to be the strong desires or preferences expressed by PLYs. Wants may appear to be too recreational or social to educational planners and not sufficiently educational in nature. Also, these wants may appear to be too whimsical and tentative and change so quickly that they seem to provide little indication of the real wants of PLYs. I return to this distinction later in the chapter.

These early empirical findings were criticized for their reliance on the two terms as the theoretical framework for needs assessment. The criticism may be justified on the basis of the simplicity of the either/or dichotomy when compared to other theoretical frameworks. However, it has been suggested that some of the critics, lacking a sociological orientation, misunderstood the meanings of the terms as they were used by Parsons from his action frame of reference to social systems analysis. In the remainder of this chapter I will clarify these terms further, thereby providing a more detailed theory for educational needs assessment, especially as it relates to PLYs. I present a motivation–participation model based on a construct that includes social–psychological needs, the social system, and goal gratification. I then review the most salient literature on the research of instrumental–expressive orientations and present a goals/needs assessment model to aid educational gerontologists in developing educational programs for PLYs.

A SOCIOLOGICAL, THEORETICAL FRAMEWORK

At the outset, readers must discipline themselves to think in the sociologist's thought patterns; sociologists employ ideas and clusters of ideas quite differently from psychologists and educators. Educators and psychologists view people in very individualistic ways; sociologists do not. Sociologists analyze people's patterns of actions and interactions within many levels of social situations. Individual behaviors are of interest solely because they reveal *orientational* and *relational* patterns people use to structure their activities to achieve personal and collective *motivational goals*. Sociologically, the focus of interest is always that of an action frame of reference that stresses the interaction of people as they manifest their values, roles, and goals in specific social situations. Social action theory does consider the importance of subjective meanings as people interact within society. However, these subjective meanings are analyzed in light of the individual's internalized values and their expectations of the reactions of others in various social relationships.

Parsons (1964) defined his use of a social action frame of reference for analyzing social systems as follows.

> *A system of action . . . is a system of the relations of organisms in interdependence with each other and with non-social objects in the environment or situation. It is in order to keep this system distinct from the organism as a physiochemical system that we prefer, instead of referring to the "action of the actor" and instead of using the term environment, to speak of the situation of the action. (p. 545)*

The social system, then, is a major focus of interest for sociological analysis. Parsons (1964) best articulated this frame of reference by saying that

> *a social system consists in a plurality of individual actors interacting with each other in a situation which has at least a physical or environmental aspect, actors who are motivated in terms of a tendency to the "optimization of gratification" and whose relation to their situations including each other, is defined and mediated in terms of culturally structured and shared symbols. (pp. 5–6)*

Of major importance is the notion of the optimization of gratification evaluated by each person. Parsons called this the gratification–deprivation balance and believed that it plays an important part in motivating people. People select among alternatives available according to their potential for maximizing gratification and minimizing deprivation. A social system situation that tends to maximize gratification for the individual will naturally prove more popular with that actor. Individuals can maximize their gratifications through a system of self-expectations related to their needs and goals and by the possibility of attaining these gratifications by interacting with others in various social-system situations.

Every *action situation* presents a variety of alternative actions to the individual. These alternatives cause personal dilemmas, because individuals must weigh the costs of postponing the immediate gratification in lieu of some future goal that may produce an even greater degree of gratification once the desired goal is achieved. That is, in the light of two mutually desirable goals, the actor must choose between having immediate gratification by participating in an activity or postponing the gratification for a later time when the other goal may be obtained.

From the social-system action perspective, the *goal-directedness* of one's action is vital. It indicates a future state of affairs one is motivationally committed to achieve proactively. Accordingly, motivation is understood to mean *goal-seeking behavior*. Intrinsic motivation is based on an expectation of direct and immediate gratification of one's desires, because gratification stems directly from the goal activity undertaken and is inherent in the activity itself. For example, one may take a class on cooking because one thoroughly enjoys the process of creating wonderful culinary delights. Extrinsic motivation, on the other hand, is based on an expectation of indirect fulfillment of a person's desires, because the activity undertaken to achieve the goal has no inherent or immediate gratification. Rather, the activity is perceived as instrumental in obtaining a desirable goal. Others may take that same cooking class because they want a job as a chef in a first-class resort hotel. The gratification will come when one gets the job of choice. Therefore, it is imperative to know the temporality of the goals in order to analyze the motive actions of the individual.

This implies rather clearly that the goal, end, or desired objective toward which an actor is striving is the place to begin analysis of the motivational interactions of people in social-system situations. Moreover, from this theoretical framework, it is imperative to examine these desirable goal gratifications in relation to the activities of which they are functions and not to confuse nor infuse them with subjective psychological interpretations.

It is at the point of goals analysis that Parsons (1964) raised the issue of instrumental and expressive action orientations and when the goals and their gratifications are to be achieved and obtained. Parsons summarized his position as follows.

Action may be oriented to the achievement of a goal which is an anticipated future state of affairs, the attainment of which is felt to promise gratification:

*a state of affairs which will not come about without the intervention of the
actor in the course of the event. Such instrumental or goal-orientation intro-
duces an element of discipline, the renunciation of certain immediately potential gratifications. . . . Such immediate gratifications are renounced in the
interest of the prospectively larger gains to be derived from the attainment of
the goals, an attainment which is felt to be contingent on fulfillment of certain
conditions at intermediate stages of the process. (p. 48)*

For Parsons, therefore, instrumental action orientations assume the givenness
of a goal that requires a self-evaluation or prioritization of gratifying desires. It also
requires knowledge of the conditions essential to attain the goals despite the person's
desire to take advantage of the immediacy of the opportunity for gratification, even
though such action could interfere with the achievement of a future goal. Thus,
people find themselves in the dilemma of having to choose between two mutually
desirable goals, the actions required to achieve them, and when to actualize the
desired gratification through immediate or delayed goal achievement.

Parsons understood *expressive action orientations* to be related to the immediate time dimension wherein one participates in an activity in which goals gratification is immediately available. Hence, it can be said that doing the activity itself is its
own emotional reward. Again, the notion that people evaluate and prioritize their
desires surfaces because they do not postpone gratification for some future goal.
Instead, they choose the positive emotional response inherent in the activity at hand.

To summarize, Parsons devised a system for classifying the motivational gratifications people receive when participating in activities as they strive to attain their
goals and objectives. Some activities yield immediate gratification simply by participating in them. These are the expressive orientations. Other activities provide gratification at a later date when a desired goal is achieved. These are the instrumental
orientations.

Apparently Havighurst (1969) developed his ideas concerning the action orientations of people engaged in educational activities from these ideas. He stressed
the idea that instrumental educational activities are those in which the goal of learning lies beyond the immediate activity. Expressive educational activities are largely
participated in for their own sake and gratification is immediate.

A PSYCHOSOCIAL INTERPRETATION
OF ADULT PARTICIPATION

The following discussion is an attempt to explain, in part, what motivates
adults to participate in educational programs that use the ideas of instrumental and
expressive action orientations to achieve goal gratification. Readers are cautioned to
remember that there are any number of ways of explaining and interpreting human
behavior. This is merely one way of interpreting the behavioral patterns we observe
daily.

Life may be portrayed as a temporal line that extends from our past through
our present daily activities and into our future (see Figure 1). What we see and

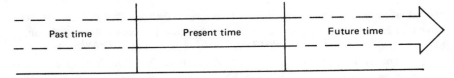

FIGURE 1   Life conceived as a temporal line.

experience in daily, present-time living are the behaviors of individuals acting and interacting with each other. Mentally, we cluster these daily behaviors together into meaningful explanations and suggest that one has needs that cause these behaviors. Further analysis of these needs that trigger behaviors suggests that people strive to achieve personal and collective goals that gratify their needs. Meeting our needs by achieving our goals normally creates a change in our daily behaviors. Thus, it can be said that daily behaviors are changed in light of the goals we strive to achieve because the goals tend to meet our needs.

An example familiar to the majority of graduate students illustrates what has been stated. If social scientists were to study the participation and motivation patterns of graduate students, they might make the following anecdotal comments: Graduate students exhibit a variety of behaviors in their daily (present-time) activities that can be clustered together logically. One can see the students making appointments with their advisers to plan their graduate programs. These students go through the matriculation process, attend classes (often at night to accommodate their work patterns), and complete weekly reading assignments, examinations, class reports, and term papers in order to receive an acceptable grade for the class.

Social scientists see these complex clusters of graduate student behaviors and surmise that these students apparently have some needs they are trying to fulfill. When the students are interviewed it is learned that they are meeting the educational requirements for a given graduate program to obtain an advanced academic degree. That is, these students have educational needs (the successful completion of all required courses) that triggered the many graduate student behaviors observed by the social scientists in the present time. Further questioning reveals that the students want or need the advanced degree for professional growth or to enter another profession. Thus, they participated in graduate school activities to achieve some future goal that will satisfy their personal and professional needs.

In the psychosocial literature this description of the motivational patterns of educational participation is referred to as a *needs → social system → goal gratification* hypothetical (or theoretical) construct. There are some important implications of hypothetical/theoretical constructs, especially as they are related to the idea that life may be portrayed as a temporal line stretching from the past, through the present, and into the future.

Hypothetical constructs are understood to be imagined underlying factors that social scientists postulate to explain human behaviors exhibited in daily activities. In reality these factors do not exist; they are merely the products of someone's imagination to aid in thinking about the behavior being studied. Constructs should be

viewed as abstract elements of theories of human behavior. That is, they are perceived as inferred causal phenomena accounting for behavior observed in daily
living.

All of us are familiar with theoretical constructs and use them in everyday
conversations. Words such as *intelligence, motivation, attitudes,* and *love* are examples of such constructs that are used to explain daily behaviors. Regrettably, too many
people treat these constructs as if they were real events or objects. One need only
point out the indiscriminate use of Maslow's schema for a "hierarchy of needs" as a
way of explaining human behavior. Too many people treat these needs as concrete
realities; however, Maslow (1954) merely postulated inferred, underlying, causal factors that might explain behavior. But these needs simply do not exist as concrete
objects for study as do, for example, the internal organs of the body.

Because the human mind apparently desires to superimpose logical order and
create explanations of behavior, endless psychosocial systems of thought abound to
explain why we do what we do. These postulated systems of thought are the imaginary
hypothetical constructs we rely on to explain observable human behavior. The proposed *needs* → *social system* → *goal gratification* model for educational participation
suggested here is another system of thought to explain behavior. Therefore it too relies
on hypothetical constructs. Essentially, the model suggests that people have needs that
trigger clusters of present-time behaviors. These behaviors are designed to achieve
goal gratification either immediately or at some later time. When the goals are
achieved and people are gratified, we conclude that people have met their needs.

As simple as this model seems, when it is combined with Parsons's instrumental and expressive action orientations, it becomes a fairly complex paradigm for
explaining why we do what we do. In Figure 2, several new elements are added to
the temporal lifeline depicted in Figure 1. Social systems is placed in present or
real-time portion of the figure and is subtitled "human behaviors exhibited within
social systems". Needs is lodged in the past portion of the temporal lifeline and is
subtitled "inferred causal states or conditions". Finally, goals is located in the
future portion of the figure and is subtitled "inferred gratifications".

Figure 2 should be read in the following manner: The only realities people
can observe occur in the present or real-time. These observable realities are the
human behaviors one sees as people act and interact within society's various social
systems. Because of the inclination to confer meaning on observed behaviors, we

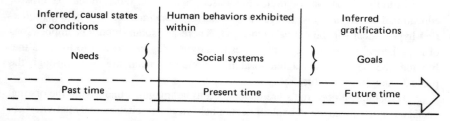

FIGURE 2 The temporal lifeline integrated with the needs → social system → goal gratification
model of participation.

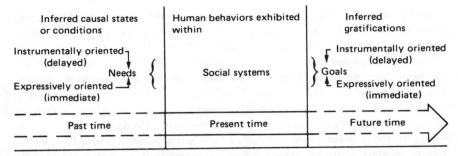

FIGURE 3   Needs → social system → goal gratification model of participation further delineated by instrumental and expressive action orientation.

mentally cluster them into meaningful patterns and infer their causes. Reflection suggests that these causes are unobservable needs that initiate participatory behaviors within various social systems. These needs are placed in the past portion of Figure 2 to indicate that they occur before present-time behaviors and, therefore, may be inferred causal linkages to the observed behaviors. As theoretical/hypothetical constructs, these needs may be thought of as the stimuli in the stimulus–response chains of events. They presumably act as the initiators of participatory behaviors within social systems. I say "presumably" because it must be remembered that needs are fabricated from our own logical thought process and postulated as the presumed initiatory stimuli of the participatory behavior.

Goals are placed in the future portion of Figure 2, showing that they are as-yet-unachieved expectations. Their subtitle, "inferred gratifications", indicates that their fulfillment (by acting and interacting in social systems) will gratify someone by meeting his or her needs, which are also inferred constructs. Thus, goals, like needs, are products of the mind. From all the range of existing possibilities one postulates an unachieved, yet anticipated event, and reasons that present behaviors are future oriented. The tendency to invest observed behavior with meaning permits logical clustering of the behaviors to form goal-seeking patterns of future-oriented desirable states of affairs. Accordingly, we are likely to say a person is motivated (a theoretical construct) to achieve some goal by participating and interacting with others in social systems. When the goal is achieved, goal gratification is obtained, thus satisfying the needs that triggered the observed participatory behaviors that occurred within social systems.

Figure 3 represents the fully developed model. Note that new elements have been added to the needs and goals sections of the model. Needs and goals are now divided into instrumentally and expressively oriented needs and goals. It is now possible to relate the fully developed model to Parsons's idea of instrumental and expressive action orientations of actors who are motivated to optimize and actualize their goal gratifications.

The graduate student example used earlier helps to illustrate the fully developed model as displayed in Figure 3. Recall that a social scientist was observing graduate student participation behavior in a university. The students had matriculated in order to obtain an advanced degree. Possessing the degree permits either entrance to a higher level professional position or to a new career. The social scientist deduces that the students were motivated by instrumentally oriented goals. That is, the scientist perceives graduate students' interactions within an educational system to be oriented toward achieving an anticipated future state of affairs. Clearly, the students had to discipline themselves to delay, and possibly renounce, more immediate gratifications in the interest of the larger gains derived from possessing the degree.

The social scientist then postulates a hypothetical construct termed instrumentally oriented needs to account for the observed behaviors of graduate students in the university. These instrumentally oriented needs are meaningful, however, only when they are linked with their instrumentally oriented goals and subsequent gratifications achieved when the goal is obtained. In other words, the researcher had to have some idea of what the students were anticipating in the future in order to suggest what their needs might possibly be.

Suppose, however, that the investigator also interviewed some students enrolled in the same graduate courses and found that these students were not degree oriented. They participate just because they enjoy the intellectual stimulation of the graduate course itself. Their goal gratification is immediately available to them by virtue of their class participation. Their goals, the immediate gratification from the learning itself, should be classified as expressively oriented goals. That is, the learning activities yield immediate gratification simply through participation.

Again, the researcher may postulate another underlying theoretical/hypothetical construct termed expressively oriented needs to account for the observed behaviors of the students. These needs do not exist, of course, in real-time because they cannot be directly observed or measured. They are, however, envisioned as the imaginary inferred causal states or conditions that initiate participatory behavior (taking the courses) because of the immediate gratification derived from the participation. These expressively oriented needs are meaningful, however, only when they are first linked closely with the person's expressively oriented goals. Thus, goals and needs must be linked together logically for the participatory behaviors of people in educational systems to be understood from an action frame of reference.

By now it should be clear that establishing a functional theory of and for needs assessment is a difficult matter. Perhaps that is why so little has been done in this area. The natural desire of the busy educational planner for a cookbook, show-me-how-to-do-it approach is a desire for an easy way out. Why spend valuable time with so heavy a theoretical orientation? Furthermore, professors inevitably hear from their students that what is practiced in the "real world of work" hardly ever follows what is taught in the university. Why work so hard to understand theory when it is not practiced on the job? The clear answer is that a good deal of current needs assessment and subsequent programming is erratic and often fails to attract the target audience. Worse still, the clients often attend a few sessions and then drop out because the "program does not meet their needs." This very unevenness in assessing needs, the dichotomy between what is taught and practiced, and the subsequent drop-out phenomena requires us to look for a functional theoretical approach to goals and needs assessment.

It should be clear to the reader by now that I am rejecting the standard needs assessment approach, because the psychological paradigm of looking for variables or factors that drive or push people into participating in educational programs does not explain these behaviors sufficiently. To postulate underlying needs states that drive, force, or impel people toward activities seems rather diabolical. It suggests that people are out of control and simply cannot help themselves because of these powerful psychological urges. Furthermore, I reject the standard approach because I believe that most people do not know what they need. In many instances there are a variety of factors that may be working that may explain one's reasons for participating in an educational activity. To ask someone to identify one or two underlying needs impelling them to participate in something seems fruitless. That is why standard needs assessment approaches fail. The educator dutifully collects data on what people are interested in or what they feel they need. The program is planned and then poorly attended. The educator cannot understand why.

The answer is simple but often not understood. What people say they want is often not what they will commit to! People want many things, but, because they are involved with the many developmental tasks consistent with the life stage they have reached, those are the things to which they will commit. Developmental tasks related to the job, the family, or to some avocational pursuit are what they will commit to. Those tasks are clearly important to them and they will make a concerted effort to achieve them. It is here that the educator should begin.

I believe that goals analysis is the beginning place for assessing educational participation. What is it that people know they are working for and are willing to commit to? When asked, people can most often tell you exactly the reasons why they are doing something. They are striving to reach some specific goal, either immediately or down the road, that will bring some measure of satisfaction to them. They are in control of the situation. They know that by doing certain things they will get what they want. Thus, the motivation for participating in an educational activity is a positive striving to obtain a specific goal that will immediately or in the future bring gratification.

The model presented here stresses that educational planners should begin with assessing goals and then move to understanding the underlying needs states that may explain participation. It assumes that it is easier for people to identify the goals toward which they strive rather than identify the needs that impel them toward these activities. It may be argued that some people are not goal directed and do not strive for much in their lives. That of course is true. However, we are discussing here people who participate in educational activities. Since that obviously takes some concerted and voluntary effort on their part, they are quite different from the non-goal strivers. It is assumed that it is easier for active participants to identify the goals toward which they strive rather than the needs that drove or impelled them into the activity.

Let us summarize the chapter to this point. I have shown that Parsons's instrumental-expressive action orientations within social systems is a useful theoretical construct for explaining how goal gratifications are optimized by individual and collective actions. I have shown that a *needs* → *social system* → *goal gratification* participation model, based on the theoretical constructs of instrumental-expressive need and goal orientations, provides an explanation for why people participate in educational programs. Further, I have indicated that the educational planner should first begin with the goal assessment section of the model and then proceed to the needs assessment section to further clarify the participation patterns. Now it is necessary to show the logical interrelatedness of Parsons's and Londoner's theoretical constructs.

THREE UNDERLYING ASSUMPTIONS

My model and Parsons's model both rest on several similar underlying constructs. First, both models rest on the assumption that in setting goals people are faced with a forced choice among alternative, competing, and desirable choices. The individual actor is in a dilemma because he or she cannot do all things at once. To resolve the dilemma, the individual must decide when to optimize gratifications by achieving either immediate or long-range goals. Resolving the dilemma produces a choice-point: that point at which the actor motivationally makes a total commitment to achieve immediate and/or future goals. This choice-point is of great concern to educational gerontologists, because it is the point at which the individual fully commits psychosocial energies and resources to optimize goal gratifications. At this point the educational gerontologist may see the PLY opt for either immediate (expressive) or delayed (instrumental) goal gratifications by participating in various kinds of educational activities.

Second, both models' constructs require educational gerontologists to shift from a solely front-end analysis (i.e., examining only individual and group needs) to examining goals (those ultimate choices for optimizing personal gratifications) and needs simultaneously. If educational gerontologists can determine what the older adult is committed to achieving, they will discover the kinds of educational activities they will consistently attend.

Third, I have said that educational gerontologists have relied too heavily on perceived expressive needs and not enough on instrumental needs (Londoner, 1971). That is, much planning centered around arts and crafts activities and too few focused on survival programs. The instrumental goals of older adults probably should be analyzed first before comments about either instrumental or expressive needs are postulated. The economic climate of the United States in the late 1980s is such that older adults have great financial burdens. Many of them live on fixed incomes, and their dollars simply do not have the purchasing power they did when these people retired. As costs increase, including major health care expenditures, limited incomes purchase fewer services and have an effect on personal daily living requirements. PLYs are committed to preserving their psychological and physical health and well-being as well as maintaining satisfactory living and social adjustments. Thus, many have survival goals uppermost in mind to help them resolve daily coping problems.

It is true that conflicting data has been collected that shows an inconsistency in the instrumental–expressive dichotomy. At first, several studies showed a preference for instrumental educational activities. Later studies showed preferences for expressive ones. I wonder if the economic well-being of the people sampled was more substantial in the 1970s? The United States experienced serious inflation in the late 1970s and early 1980s. Perhaps PLYs are more likely to prefer expressive educational participation when their economic patterns are more secure and instrumental activities when they are not. If that is the case, then another variable must be added to the paradigm: the social and economic climate at the time of the research. One might also raise the question of the political and economic climate of a country. Would samples of PLYs from predominately socialist countries, wherein most health and living needs are met adequately, indicate difference in the instrumental–expressive dichotomy?

At this writing, just before the 1990s, it seems extremely difficult for many PLYs to meet their basic survival needs and experience a bit of cushion in their lives. If indeed that is true, then it seems more likely that PLYs will respond to activities designed to meet their survival needs and goals rather than to recreational or liberal educational pursuits. Their basic goals seem to be instrumental (i.e., surviving and coping in a less-than-hospitable culture). Consequently, their needs are instrumental because they are committed to instrumental survival goals. Many daily activities may be classified as survival patterns of behavior because these activities optimize their goals, namely, coping meaningfully with life in the best way possible as they interact in society. Thus, the third assumption is that instrumental needs must be examined first.

To summarize this section, it seems to the author that there is a hierarchy of goals that PLYs strive for as they seek goal gratification. Instrumental goals must be examined and dealt with first because PLYs are committed to surviving and are more likely to participate in programs designed to meet these goals. If and when these instrumental goals are responded to adequately, they are then free to pursue recreational and liberal educational activities.

I close this section of the chapter with a note of caution. At least one authority (Havighurst, 1969, p. 62) seems to classify an activity as being inherently instrumental or expressive. This seems to be, however, a misunderstanding of the instrumental expressive orientation classification. It should be remembered that it is the action/behavior of individuals participating in educational programs that is being analyzed and not the activity itself. That is, an educational activity may be both instrumental and expressive simultaneously. The way the actor perceives the educational activity is the key point. Is the activity used for immediate goal gratification (expressive), or is it used for delayed goal gratification (instrumental)?

LITERATURE REVIEW

During the last 15 or so years, a number of doctoral dissertations and masters theses were conducted to determine the educational preferences of PLYs. Many of these employed the instrumental–expressive dichotomy in their instrumentation. This current review is not an exhaustive analysis of these studies; rather, it selectively presents some of the various attempts to show the ways these ideas have been employed to date. Havighurst (1964) and I (Londoner, 1971) are credited for having the seminal conceptualizations. Hiemstra and I were colleagues at the University of Nebraska, Lincoln, and our lively discussions led Hiemstra to conduct the first empirical testing of instrumental and expressive categories of learning. In that study, 86 retired persons, participating in senior citizen center activities or living in residential centers for the aged, responded to a survey questionnaire that contained 12 instrumental activities (competency areas designed for effective mastery of old-age challenges) and 44 expressive activities (experiences designed to increase one's enjoyment of life). A significantly higher preference for instrumental activities was elicited as compared to preferences given for expressive activities. The instrumental type of learning activities included course titles such as "Stretching Your Retirement Dollar," "Wills and Estate Planning," "Nutrition and the Aging Process," and "Medical Care in the Retirement Years." Expressive examples included "Art Appreciation," "Nature Photography," "The Archaeology of Mexico," "Three Black Authors," and "Introduction to Crafts."

Hiemstra (1973) also reported on an examination of these course preferences in terms of various biographical and demographic characteristics. Exploratory null hypotheses of no differences in the types of preferences according to nominal categorization for various characteristics were employed. No statistically significant differences were found in terms of age, gender, or urban versus rural categories. Significance testing did reveal, however, that white-collar workers were less likely than blue-collar workers, and college graduates were less likely than noncollege graduates, to report instrumental course preferences.

Whatley (1974) examined the instrumental and expressive dichotomy by asking (through a questionnaire) gerontologists, adult educators, and people 60 years of age or older to give their perceptions regarding the potential selection of learning activities by older people. She found general consensus among the three groups, with older people making fewer instrumental selections than did the adult educators or gerontologists. She further examined the preference made by the older population and found no significant differences for either instrumental or expressive activities when compared by groupings according to gender, lower versus higher age, urban versus rural residence, and lower versus higher levels of education.

Goodrow (1974) conducted a study related to the instrumental and expressive preferences of PLYs. Employing a random sample of 268 people over the age of 65, a questionnaire with 16 hypothetical instrumental and 16 hypothetical expressive course titles was administered. He found a significant preference for instrumental learning. A further examination of the data revealed that no statistically significant differences existed between the instrumental and expressive preferences; however, within the instrumental preference category, race, sex, and age groups resulted in significant comparisons.

Burkey (1975) examined 40 course titles (20 instrumental and 20 expressive) by asking 243 older church members, all 55 years of age or older, to indicate on a questionnaire their interest toward the learning activities. No differences were found for urban versus rural or small-town categories, lower versus upper age groups, and male versus female classifications. However, people with more than a high school diploma tended to be more expressively oriented in preference than their counterparts. When categories within each type of learning were examined, older people, younger women, and high school graduates selected significantly more expressively oriented activities. For every demographic characteristic, the composite mean for the number of instrumental preferences was significantly greater than for the number of expressive preferences.

Hiemstra (1975) conducted another study employing an interview approach to examine the preferences of 256 randomly selected people over the age of 54. Selections could be made from 16 expressive and 16 instrumental course listings. A significant overall preference for instrumental courses was found. Comparisons according to various demographic or socioeconomic categories revealed that non-white, male, rural, and married people had significantly more instrumental preferences than the counterpart groupings. In addition, the same study used the methodology initially developed by Tough (1971) to determine the number of learning projects actually carried out in one year by the respondents. After the projects were classified as instrumental or expressive, it was found that a significantly higher number of instrumental projects had been carried out. In a comparison according to the demographic groupings, however, only one significant difference was found, namely, that married people carried out more instrumental projects than did single people. Conversely, Bauer (1975) examined 685 people over the age of 55 who participated, or had indicated an interest in participating, in the Seniors on Campus program at North Hennepin Community College in Brooklyn Park, Minnesota. The questionnaire survey showed that the respondents preferred expressive types of classes and activities as compared to instrumental types.

One rather sophisticated doctoral dissertation that centered on the instrumental and expressive scheme was completed by Marcus (1976, 1978). He used a multiple regression analysis on the responses to a questionnaire by 4,000 middle-class participants in educational programs. He established four determinants of instrumental and expressive participation in educational activities for adults. He found that (a) needs, goals, and time orientations were partial determinants of perceived instrumental ability; (b) age, more than any other factor, affected perceived expressive utility; (c) status and being female related more to expressive utility than to perceived instrumental utility; and (d) age was the main discriminant. His findings suggest that PLYs often see expressive utility even in programs classified as instrumental but that they are not necessarily attracted mainly to expressive activities. He further suggested that one's socioeconomic condition is a major variable in the decision to participate or not participate in an educational activity. His data showed that people who had both lower income and status and therefore had current pressing needs were not likely to participate in education to meet those needs. Conversely, PLYs who had high income and status were more likely to participate in education, not because they had any pressing needs, but because they wished to continue their personal growth and perceived education as an enjoyable growth-producing experience. That is to say, in his study PLYs were likely to perceive the education in which they participated as being expressive regardless of the instructional intent. The more advantaged PLYs saw the education as a means of immediate gratification through the enjoyment of intellectual stimulation, social interaction, and interesting leisure time rather than the way to solve more practical coping problems (instrumental orientation).

Peterson (1983), in an excellent book for educational gerontologists, wrote a chapter on the educational needs and wants of PLYs. He made a thorough review of extant literature on the whole field of needs analysis for older people up to that time. In that chapter he drew the distinction between educational needs (the things that professional experts believe PLYs should have) versus educational wants (the stated preferences or desires of the older person). He stated the belief that educational planners have often failed to distinguish between these two variables and have tended to plan programs based on the educational needs and to ignore the educational wants. He saw educational wants as the desires or preferences of older people that rest on the perceived content or skill areas that are pleasurable to them. These programs that are based on wants are often found in community group or institutional settings for the elderly. Peterson did note that some programs have been almost entirely oriented to the older adult's desires and therefore have been greatly criticized by professional educators as being frivolous, or at best, simply social and recreational rather than having any real learning content.

Educational needs are those knowledges, attitudes, values, skills, and understandings that PLYs ought to have, so say the professional experts, even if the older person does not recognize their salience. These needs are generally determined by educational or psychological authorities and theories and are generally alleviated by some sort of educational intervention. Moreover, these educational needs are philosophically consistent with the idealized cultural and social value systems of the United States and especially so with the agency providing the program. Peterson concluded this portion of his chapter by reminding the reader that PLYs vary greatly in their individual characteristics so that it is not possible to generalize needs and wants to all older people. As age cohorts vary demographically over time, so too, must educational planners be prepared to reexamine their assumptions about the needs and wants of these people.

In a brief discussion of the instrumental–expressive dichotomy, Peterson (1983) cited my chapter in the first edition of this book (Londoner, 1978) as falling into the educational wants category of older people because it was based on their gratification and satisfaction levels. Interestingly, just after he had described the instrumental–expressive dichotomy as falling into the wants category, he then indicated that because the concept was clearly based on Parsons's sociological approach to action orientation that the dichotomy really fell into the educational needs category. He further substantiated his position by citing a number of studies already mentioned in this chapter as indication that the instrumental–expressive dichotomy is an expert-based and expert-perceived approach to the needs of PLYs. Because I never made such a distinction between needs and wants, I wonder how it was possible for Peterson to place me on both sides of the fence.

Peterson (1983) then drew some implications from the various studies. He indicated that because there is apparent conflicting evidence about whether PLYs want instrumental or expressive educational activities, the best way to use the dichotomy is to examine subgroups of the older population rather than generalize to the undifferentiated whole. Probably, both can be well received depending upon the specific subpopulation with which one is dealing. That is, expressive education probably draws people who have more education and less pressing coping problems. Instrumental education on the other hand will probably appeal to PLYs with pressing problems and coping needs that require a specific educational intervention. He noted, however, that people in this predicament typically do not participate in educational endeavors.

I believe that Peterson's suggestion to look at specific subgroups of PLYs before planning for either instrumental or expressive programs is insightful. However, as was indicated earlier in this chapter, I believe that many of the contradictory findings were based on the economic instability of the mid-1970s. It may well be that future research must control for the social–economic variable in order to further clarify the instrumental–expressive dichotomy. Indeed, the fate of PLYs who are living in the 1990s and into the 22nd century may well undergo major economic upheavals such that the instrumental learnings may become essential to their survival. One would hope that this is not the case. However, the current political administration has set a somewhat negative climate in Washington, D.C., toward the elderly with constant bickering over whether Medicare and Medicaid will be cut back dramatically in order to help meet a balanced federal budget.

The already considerable research that has been completed on the instrumental–expressive categories of education does not provide conclusive evidence by which educational planners can develop or conduct ideal learning environments for PLYs. As DeCrow (n.d.) has indicated, the dichotomization of educational opportunities into either/or categories has some real drawbacks. However, the apparent preference for instrumental learning opportunities as people age and according to specific demographic cohort subgroupings does provide clues for educational gerontologists to consider. In addition, two fairly broad categories of learning environments should enable program planners and administrators to establish learning environments that contain both instrumental and expressive opportunities.

ANALYSIS AND ASSESSMENT OF NEEDS
AND GOALS

Assessing the goals and needs of adults as a basis for planning educational programs is not an easy task, nor has an abundance of empirical research on goals analysis and needs assessment been carried out. Indeed, if one listens to some practitioners one gets the feeling that many planners feel that it takes too much effort to go through the process. Worse still is the realization that many professional educational planners believe that they know all too well what PLYs need and therefore will plan programs based on their assumptions rather than verifying with the clients themselves. There are two old adages from the world of marketing that bear remembering: "Find a need and fill it" and "A satisfied customer is a repeat customer." In our case, discovering what the goals and needs of PLYs are and then responding to those factors will most likely bring older people back repeatedly to the educational enterprise.

Even a systematic and professional approach is no guarantee that the program will be attended well. For example, Hiemstra and Long (1974) conducted a study and found that the educational needs perceived by a person were not related to the needs that the same person demonstrated through paper-and-pencil testing. An even more frightening finding was reported by Long (1972) in his study of continuing education needs of a professional group. He found no significant relation between what a panel of experts perceived to be the educational needs for the group versus what the same group of professionals felt were their own needs. I found a similar finding when I compared a group of adults attending a public evening school (Londoner, 1972). The ranking of the motivational goals for attending the classes by the adult students were statistically significantly different from the perceived reasons that the teachers and administrators thought those adults would give for participating in the classes.

Assessing the goals and needs of individuals and groups of adults is also plagued by a lack of adequate methodologies and research designs. The survey research design approach using structured mail questionnaires is relatively inexpensive and fairly easy to administer. Its limitations (such as the validity of the responses and, often, the low rate of return), however, raise some legitimate questions concerning the feasibility of generalizing the findings of other groups. The use of advisory councils to determine needs can be time-consuming and often requires considerable training of the council members. Add to this already complex situation the instrumental–expressive categorization scheme, and the program planning process quickly becomes difficult.

McMahon (1970) provided some useful discussion of different types of needs, and Knowles (1970, 1975, 1980) provided some useful discussion of different types of needs assessment strategies. Long (1983) provided an excellent overview of the research findings and definitions related to the broad field of adult education needs assessment up through the mid-1980s. Caffarella (1988) has identified some excellent techniques that educational planners can use. These sources will provide useful background and perhaps some relief from the complexity of the situation. Finally, Apps (1985, pp. 171–188) provided a helpful philosophical overview of the various approaches to needs assessment that currently exist.

Figure 4 is offered as a conceptual scheme to assist the educational gerontologist in determining the goals and needs of PLYs. Expert advice would include information from groups or sources such as an advisory council, a review of related literature, a panel of judges, the findings from research seminars and colloquies, the planner's own expertise, or a third-party consultant. A perception of the goals and needs would usually be in the form of information obtained through a questionnaire, personal interviews, or a panel made up of potential program participants. Goals analysis and needs assessment could be accomplished through demonstration tech-

Needs assessment data: Sources and examples	Type of need
	Instrumental/Expressive
Experts Research reports Panel of judges Interviews Advisory councils Census data Consultants National conferences	
Clients Interviews Survey research "Opinionnaires"	
Educational planners Observations Interviews Questionnaires Advisory committees	

FIGURE 4   Data collection matrix for educational program planning.

niques that could include devices such as paper-and-pencil tests, observational data, performance records, and prior evaluation data. Obviously the model will require considerable testing, research, and refinement before the educational program planner can plug into it every programming or needs assessment effort. The model does, however, provide a basis for discussion and experimentation. The following is a brief description of some simulated use to provide the reader with help in understanding the model.

As one example, the program planner could ask a panel of judges (expert advice) to suggest some preretirement training activities that would help a group of factory workers make the transition to retirement during their last two or three years of employment with a company having a policy of mandatory retirement for people reaching age 65 or 70. The information obtained from the panel would then need to be sifted through the instrumental and expressive screens so that a mixture of programs could be planned for the employees.

A related example can be described by looking at the client group's perceptions of goals and needs in the same situation. A questionnaire could be distributed to the group of workers to elicit their preferences toward a variety of noncredit learning topics. Such information, when screened through the instrumental–expressive categories and perhaps even compared with some demonstration of goals and needs information, could be used to set up some learning experiences that either overlap with or supplement the activities established as a result of the expert advice.

As a final example, an educational planner's observation of the psychosocial environment to establish goals and needs can be employed. The setting is a nursing home for retired school teachers and the program planner is a doctoral student interning in educational gerontology. The program planner had just compiled the results of both personal interviews with the residents and a collection of suggestions from the permanent staff, on the topics of establishing educational and recreational activities. Additionally, over a several-day period, the intern had observed a basic lack of understanding of personal health care related to a fairly confined environment and a general lack of any physical activity. The planner then compiled all of the needs assessment information and, by putting it through both the instrumental and expressive screens, was able to develop a comprehensive educational and recreational program.

As Figure 5 shows, the model can be made three dimensional by using any number of demographic or socioeconomic characteristics to screen the goals and needs or to determine a desired approach for assessing the goals and needs (e.g., male vs. female, blue- vs. white-collar workers, lower vs. higher educational levels, etc.). Additionally, the program planner could employ variables such as the participant's preference for the type of learning activity or could use nominal categories of obstacles or credit versus noncredit preferences as the third dimensional measure.

Clearly, there are some limitations to the model. Implied in the foregoing examples is the suggestion that both instrumental and expressive types of learning activities are necessary. It should be remembered, though, that the actual learning activity is neither instrumental or expressive; the intent of the client makes the activity either instrumental or expressive. Thus, the program planning process appears complicated by such factors in terms of extra time, resources, and analysis requirements. I anticipate, however that as such a model and understanding of instrumental versus expressive categories are both improved, the educational planner will be able to provide learning activities that more broadly meet the needs of PLYs.

THE EDUCATIONAL PLANNER'S RESPONSIBILITY

What is the program planner's responsibility in facilitating a maximum use of available resources and simultaneously meeting the goals and needs of PLYs? Obviously, there is no clear answer to this question. Most educators providing service to older people want to make the best possible programs or learning activities available within given institutional constraints or resource limitations. In addition, most edu-

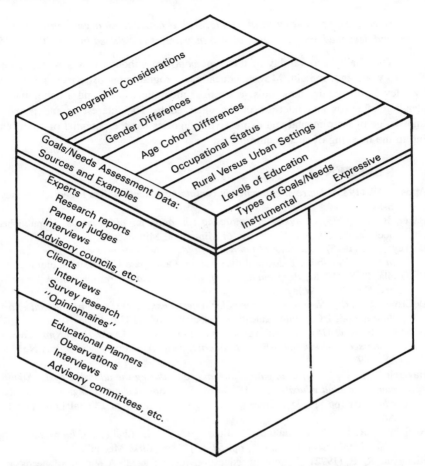

FIGURE 5 Three-dimensional data collection matrix model for educational program planning using the instrumental–expressive categories, sources of goals/needs assessment data, and demographic variables.

cators working with adult learners feel comfortable about facilitating input on wants and interests from prospective participants. Nonetheless, as Moody (1976) suggested:

> *The expectations we bring to an educational experience are regulated and limited by . . . narrowing ideas of what learning is. Institutional inertia reinforces the process until we can conceive of the future only as an expansion or an extension of what we already know . . . . In the evolving field of education for older adults, this describes exactly the situation at the present time. The alternative is to imagine an educational experience from which students would*

*emerge as different kinds of people, with a new and enlarged sense of value
and deepened understanding of who they are as envisioned in stage IV. (p. 15)*

The vitality and validity of that statement, even though it was written more
than 10 years ago, remain. Moving educational programming expertise to a "Stage
IV" level will require new tools, a stronger theoretical base, and a better understanding of needs and interests of the older adult. The interest in and growing
knowledge of instrumental and expressive categories has the potential of contributing to the meaning of such requirements.

REFERENCES

Apps, J. W. (1985). *Improving practice in continuing education.* San Francisco: Jossey-
Bass.
Bauer, B. M. (1975). *A model of continuing education for older adults.* Unpublished
doctoral dissertation, University of Minnesota, Minneapolis.
Burkey, F. T. (1975). *Educational interests of older adult members of Brethren Church
in Ohio.* Unpublished doctoral dissertation, Ohio State University, Columbus.
Caffarella, R. S. (1988). *Program development and evaluation resource book for train-
ers.* New York: Wiley.
DeCrow, R. (n.d.). *New learning for older Americans: An overview of national effort.*
Washington, DC: Adult Education Association of the U.S.A.
Goodrow, B. A. (1974). *The learning needs and interests of the elderly in Knox County,
Tennessee. Dissertation Abstracts International,* (University Microfilms No. 75–
11, 169).
Havighurst, R. J. (1964). *Changing status and roles during the adult life cycle: Signifi-
cance for adult education.* In H. Burns (Ed.), *Sociological backgrounds of adult
education* (pp. 17–38). Chicago: Center for the Study of Liberal Education for
Adults.
Havighurst, R. J. (1969). Adulthood and old age. In R. L. Ebel (Ed.), *Encyclopedia of
educational research* (4th ed., pp. 57–65). New York: Macmillan.
Hiemstra, R. P. (1972). Continuing education for the aged: A survey of needs and
interests of older people. *Adult Education, 22,* 100–109.
Hiemstra, R. P. (1973). Educational planning for older adults: A survey of "expres-
sive" vs. "instrumental" preferences. *International Journal of Aging and Human
Development, 4,* 147–156.
Hiemstra, R. P. (1975). *The older adult and learning.* Lincoln: University of Nebraska.
(ERIC Document Reproduction Service No. CE 006 003)
Hiemstra, R. P., & Long, R. (1974). A survey of "felt" versus "real" needs of physical
therapists. *Adult Education, 24,* 270–279.
Knowles, M. S. (1970). *Self-directed learning: A guide for learners and teachers.* New
York: Association Press.
Knowles, M. S. (1975). *Self-directed learning: A guide for learners and teachers.* New
York: Cambridge Press.
Knowles, M. S. (1980). *The modern practice of adult education.* New York: Association
Press.
Londoner, C. A. (1971). Survival needs of the aged: Implications for program planning.
International Journal of Aging and Human Development, 2, 113–117.

Londoner, C. A. (1972). Perseverance versus non-perseverance patterns among adult high school students. *Adult Education, 22*(3), 179–195.

Londoner, C. A. (1978). Instrumental and expressive education: A basis for needs assessment and planning. In R. H. Sherron & D. B. Lumsden (Eds.), *Introduction to educational gerontology* (2nd ed., pp. 93–110). Washington, DC: Hemisphere.

Long, H. B. (1983). *Adult learning research and practice.* New York: Cambridge University Press.

Long, R. (1972). *Continuing education for physical therapists in Nebraska: A survey of current practices and self expressed needs with recommendations for program development.* Unpublished doctoral dissertation, University of Nebraska, Lincoln.

Marrow, A. J. (1969). *The practical theorist: The life and work of Kurt Lewin.* New York: Columbia University, Teachers College Press.

Marcus, E. E. (1976). *Effects of age, sex, and socioeconomic status on adult education participants' perception of the utility of their participation.* Unpublished doctoral dissertation, University of Chicago.

Marcus, E. E. (1978). Effects of age, sex and status of perception of the utility of educational participation. *Educational Gerontology, 3,* 295–319.

Maslow, A. H. (1954). *Motivation and personality.* New York: Harper & Row.

Moody, H. R. (1976). Philosophical presupposition of education for old age. *Educational Gerontology, 1,* 1–16.

McMahon, E. E. (1970). *Needs—of people and their communities—and the adult educator.* Washington, DC: Adult Education Association of the U.S.A.

Parsons, T. (1964). *The social system.* New York: Free Press. (Original work published 1951).

Peterson, D. A. (1983). *Facilitating education for older learners.* San Francisco: Jossey-Bass.

Tough, A. (1971). *The adult's learning projects* (Research in education series No. 1). Toronto, Canada: Ontario Institute for Studies in Education.

Whatley, L. F. (1974). *Expressive and instrumental educational interests of older adults as perceived by adult educators, gerontologists, and older adults.* Unpublished master's thesis, University of Georgia, Athens.

6

RELIGION AND AGING
AND THE ROLE OF EDUCATION

J. CONRAD GLASS, JR.
North Carolina State University

INTRODUCTION

Of all the important issues facing this nation, perhaps none is more urgent or complex than responding to the changes required by a rapidly changing aging population. This revolutionary development is the result of a medically and technologically advanced society. Old problems have been solved, but new ones have arisen that challenge the imagination and ability of our society to resolve. No other civilization has had such a large number of its population living to such an old age.

Religious institutions, like all major social institutions, are affected by these demographic changes. They must seek to understand the implications that these older people are having and will have on their organizational structures and their programs. Churches and synagogues have a definite responsibility for working with elderly people. Religion and religious institutions are very important to older people. In a survey of religious affiliations conducted by the Princeton Religious Research Center prior to the 1981 White House Conference on Aging, 97% of people 65 years of age and older reported having a religious preference (Letzig, 1987). Palmore (1980) echoed this position when he wrote:

> *Churches and synagogues deserve special consideration because they are the single most pervasive community institution to which the elderly belong. All the other community institutions considered together, including senior citizen centers, clubs for elderly, unions, etc., do not involve as many elders as churches and synagogues. (p. 236)*

Material from *A Ministry to Match the Age* (1984) has been reprinted with the permission of The United Methodist Church, Health and Welfare Ministries Program, New York.

Religious institutions are important to the spiritual well-being of older people. Many older people claim that religion is the most important influence in their lives (Thompson, 1986). They have a higher attendance rate at church than any other age group (Moberg, 1983). For older people, the religious institution is more than a place of worship. It is also a place to meet old friends and a source of help in time of need. It is a proponent of a particular way of life. As a communicator of moral and spiritual values, the religious institution upholds the dignity and value of the life of the older person, as well as enhances the meaning of that life. Churches and synagogues can give strength to older people as they deal with the realities of dying, death, and grief. The religious sector helps translate theological, ethical, and spiritual values into language and practice applicable for secular living (Ellor, Anderson-Ray, & Tobin, 1983; *Executive Summary*, 1981; Thompson, 1986).

Churches and synagogues can and do enable the elderly to remain as active contributors to their community and society and to retain a sense of continuity in their lives. These functions of religious institutions are particularly important to older people because of the many losses they have encountered with advancing age (Tobin, Ellor, & Anderson-Ray, 1986).

Religion is an important force in the lives of the elderly. The elderly tend to have positive attitudes toward religion and religious institutions. Given these facts, it seems strange that so often books that are purported to address various factors related to older adults overlook the area of religion and aging. In the early 1970s, Heenan (1972) called attention to both the general lack and the limited scope of research in the area of religion and aging. Doka (1985–1986) still feels that the study of religion and aging is underresearched. Gerontologists and church professionals have often relied on the rich and valuable resources of the behavioral sciences for understanding the processes of aging and for developing the skills for listening to the elderly. So rich and valuable have these resources been that we have tended to neglect the heritage and traditions of religious faith, which also make a significant contribution to caring for and guiding older people through their life pilgrimage. If we wish to get a holistic picture of older adults, we cannot overlook seeing their life experiences through the eyes of religious faith (Becker, 1986).

In an effort to further the dialogue between gerontologists and the religious sector, this chapter is presented. The role of the religious institution as a vehicle for educating older adults has been missing in past editions of this book. Religious institutions can be and, in many cases, are important providers of educational opportunities for older people. Many gerontologists and adult educators, both outside and inside religious institutions, are not aware of the significant role these institutions have played and can play in educating older adults, not only in matters of the faith, but also in the enrichment of their day-to-day living. In this chapter I will attempt to introduce readers to educational gerontology opportunities within the structure of religious institutions.

I begin discussion with a look at the religious participation patterns of older adults, including some discussion of factors that influence these patterns of participation. Recognizing that it is difficult to plan for the diverse needs of the elderly as if they were one homogeneous group, I attempt to separate the elderly population into several subgroups to facilitate better planning. In order to give some guidelines for present and future work with older adults, I propose several objectives of older adult ministry. The chapter concludes with a discussion of what forms older adult ministry can take and with an examination of the role of education in an aging ministry.

RELIGIOUS INVOLVEMENT OF THE ELDERLY

Over a decade ago, Kuhn wrote: "The percentage of church members over age 60 is at least twice as high as the general population" (1977, pp. 13–14). A Gallup Poll (1987) 10 years later showed that this pattern had not changed. According to this survey, nearly one-fifth of the Protestants are at least 65 years of age, with two-fifths at least 50 years old. Catholics and Jews are somewhat younger, yet at least one-seventh of each of these groups are at least age 65 and a third are 50 or older.

As would be expected, there is variability in the age distribution of the mainline Protestant denominations. About a quarter of the members of the United Methodist, Presbyterian, Episcopal, and the United Church of Christ churches are at least 65 years of age. A sixth of the Baptists are 65 or older, and one-third of the Lutherans are 65 or older. Nearly half of all United Methodists, Presbyterians, Episcopalians, and members of the United Church of Christ are 50 or older (*Aging Society*, 1988; Gallup Poll, 1987). And the United Methodists are predicting that by the year 2000, half of their members will be 60 years of age and older (Custer, 1988). "What all these numbers mean is that aging and the needs of older adults no longer is one of the social issues facing religious communities—*older adults are quickly becoming the congregation as many of us know it*" [italics added] (*Aging Society*, 1988, p. 1). Three-fourths of all older Americans belong to a congregation of one of the three major religious groups. Most older adults are Protestant (70%); nearly one-fourth are Catholic (24%); and 2% are Jewish (Fahey & Lewis, 1984; Payne, 1988).

Older adults support their churches with their attendance. The rate of church and synagogue attendance for older people exceeds that of other age groups (Ellor & Coates, 1986; Hooyman & Kiyak, 1988; Payne, 1984). One study (Princeton Religious Research Center, 1982) has shown that 49% of the people over age 65 attended church in an average week. Another poll (Harris & Associates, 1975) noted that 79% of the elders surveyed had attended a church or synagogue within the past 2 weeks.

Decrease in attendance does occur, however, in the oldest groups of elders, most likely due to increasing physical impairments. The frail elderly who no longer are able to attend religious services have not necessarily abandoned religious life as they understand it. Lacking physical access to public worship services, the frail elderly often seek other expression of their religious faith. This decline in attendance is offset by an increase in religious activities within the home, such as reading the Bible, praying, and listening to religious programs (Doka, 1985–1986; Hendricks & Hendricks, 1986; Karcher & Karcher, 1980; Midel & Vaughan, 1978; Payne, 1988). As Payne has said:

> *Furthermore, the religious role encompasses more than participation in the church; it includes private and everyday religious behavior, as well as the feeling that religion has meaning. Through nonorganizational or daily religious practices, the religious role is a salient factor in the lives of the elderly. For example, the older person whose church attendance is limited by physical and/or social factors associated with the aging process, may at the same time be highly committed—cognitively, emotionally, and morally—to their church. Their faith may be strong, their personal decisions may be made in relationship to the "faith of the church," and their feelings of self-identify with and love and loyalty for the church may remain. (1981, p. 162)*

The fact that older people have higher religious affiliation and participation patterns than do younger people does not necessarily mean that aging church members become more religious as they get older. Such levels of religiosity are probably a continuation of earlier patterns. Those who are over 65 years old today probably joined the church between 1900 and 1940, which was the height of membership and participation in churches in the United States (Karcher & Karcher, 1980; Payne, 1981, 1988). Thus, these older people have continued their memberships in the religious institution, and their faith has remained important to them. Whether such patterns will be true for future cohorts is not yet clear, but at least for the present cohort religion is an important aspect of their lives.

Although religious involvement and church affiliation are high overall in the older population, there are some groups of older adults who rank even higher. Evidence indicates that women are, in general, more religiously involved than men (Gray & Moberg, 1977; Karcher & Karcher, 1980; Jacquet, 1982; Hooyman & Kiyak, 1988; Payne, 1988). More older Protestant and Catholic women have high attendance rates (Payne, 1984), but older Jewish men tend to increase attendance in synagogues (Kahana & Kahana, 1984).

Most blacks are Protestants, and this is true for older blacks as well. The overwhelming majority of blacks appear to be Baptists or Methodists (Payne, 1984). Older blacks report more participation in religious activities and are more likely to attend religious services than are other racial or ethnic groups (Hirsch, Kent, & Silverman, 1972). Regardless of denominational affiliation, older blacks (male and female) are more likely than whites to participate in weekly religious activities (Hooyman & Kiyak, 1988; Payne, 1988; Taylor, 1986). The high esteem afforded the black elderly in the church may partially underlie their positive association with the religious institution (Hooyman & Kiyak, 1988).

In a study comparing Mexican Americans and whites for two time periods (1976 and 1980), Mexican Americans were found to be more religious as measured by church attendance, self-rated religiousness, and private prayer. In addition, these three factors were positively related to the Mexican Americans' life satisfaction (Markides, 1983). Most Hispanics (which includes Mexican Americans) are traditionally Catholic. Only about 4.9% of the Hispanic Americans were 65 or older in the 1980 Census (U.S. Bureau of the Census, 1981). Although whites have 2.5 times the proportion of persons 65 and over than the Hispanics, Hispanics are expected to become the largest minority group in America during the 1980s (Lacayo, 1984). Payne (1988) has called the Hispanic group our future elderly.

Rural dwellers appear to be more religiously involved than their urban counterparts (Auerbach, 1976). Blazer and Palmore (1976) reported that studies over several decades indicate extremely high levels of church membership among the rural elderly. Studies have indicated levels of church membership among rural elderly to be between 90% and 95% (Collier, 1978; Pihlblad & McNamara, 1965; Stojanovic, 1972). These high levels of church membership translate into attendance and participation (Rowles, 1986). Pihlblad and McNamara (1965) found that 71% of the rural elderly in their study were involved in church activities. Collier (1978) reported that 82% of her respondents attended church once a week or more, and 88% attended at least twice a month. Karcher and Karcher have said, "The single most important and trusted institution, outside of the family, in the lives of the rural elderly, is the church" (1980, p. 410). Judging from the literature just cited, this appears to be a true statement for the elderly in general.

SOCIAL AND PSYCHOLOGICAL INFLUENCES OF RELIGION ON THE ELDERLY

Religion seems to have a number of positive social and psychological influences for older people (Karcher & Karcher, 1980; Payne, 1988). Participation in the activities of religious institutions, private religious practice, and beliefs and faith appear to contribute to life satisfaction, personal well-being, an overall sense of comfort, greater personal adjustment to aging, and happiness (Blazer & Palmore, 1976; Gray & Moberg, 1977; Hooyman & Kiyak, 1988; Reynolds & Kalish, 1974; Smith, 1967). Involvement in religion has been found to be a buffer against loneliness and a source of social support, and to offer a sense of feeling worthwhile and protection against change for a number of older people (Blazer & Palmore, 1976; Cheng, 1978; Hadaway & Roof, 1978; Photiadis & Schnabel, 1977).

These various related factors seem to hold for differing racial and ethnic groupings. In fact, they may be accentuated. In a study of four ethnic groups, religion, along with weekly church attendance, was a factor that was three times more important than all others in predicting happiness among older blacks (Reynolds & Kalish, 1974). Religion appears to be very important to life satisfaction and adjustment to later life among black elders (Heisel & Faulkner, 1982; Hooyman & Kiyak, 1988; Payne, 1988; Taylor, 1986; Taylor & Chatters, 1986). Eighty-four percent of older Hispanic people say that religion, next to the family, is very important to their well-being (Gallup Poll, 1987; Payne, 1988). Church attendance, private prayer, and self-rated religiousness appear to be related to the life satisfaction of elderly Mexican Americans (Markides, 1983). Kahana and Kahana (1984) report that, among Jewish groups, Orthodox Jews have a very positive adjustment to old age, and this is attributed to religious and cultural identity with traditional Judaism.

Gray and Moberg (1977), in one of the most comprehensive works on the elderly and the church, indicated that "confronted with all the problems which our society contributes to older people, the elderly individual is often more open to the message of the church than he has ever been before" (p. 37). Although this appears to be particularly true for many categories of the elderly, like those who live in rural areas or for racial and ethnic groups, it seems to be a true statement for older people in general. The religious institution continues to be an important resource to older people in need (Ellor et al., 1983). In a national survey of help-seeking patterns, Veroff, Kulda, and Douvan (1981) found that 45% of people 65 or older who sought help for a personal problem turned to a clergyperson for assistance, followed by 43% who went to a doctor. In addition, the clergy have been identified as "role-related helpers" in informal helping networks (Froland, Pancoast, Chapman, & Kimboko, 1981). Berger and Neuhaus (1977) emphasized the role of the church as a "mediating structure" in their research.

The literature seems to suggest that most older people have a great deal of confidence in their church or synagogue, and the religious institution seems to have a positive influence on older people as they deal with and adjust to their life experiences. It appears that most older people continue to hold a commitment to the religious institution and its beliefs and practices as long as they live. With such an acceptance, the religious institution can touch the lives of today's older people as perhaps no other social institution can.

BARRIERS TO PARTICIPATION

Although older adults, as a group, are actively involved with their churches and synagogues, there are a number of factors that can and do affect the participation of many older people. One of the most important of these barriers is health. As older people continue to live they may have a number of health problems that may prevent them from attending events at their church or synagogue. These health problems may involve the older adults themselves or one of their family members, for whom they are the chief caregivers. One study showed that the major reason older volunteers dropped out of a church-sponsored senior center program was a change in their health or that of a close family member (Payne, 1981). This is probably true for other church-related activities. The health problems may be occasional or long-term in their effect; in any event, older people may be forced to curtail their involvement in church functions.

Many older adults, even with their physical and health problems, might be able to participate in a number of church activities if it were not for the physical barriers imposed by the churches or synagogues. These seniors' physical impairments may range from poor eyesight to blindness, from poor hearing to hearing aids to total deafness, and from simply walking slow to needing walkers or wheelchairs.

Older adults may have trouble seeing or hearing the minister or rabbi, or even getting into the building. The facilities may present major structural barriers to attendance: steps; lack of hand rails, ramps, elevators; slick floors; poor acoustics, lack of an adequate sound system or hearing aids; or lack of toilet facilities to accommodate wheelchairs (Payne, 1981; Fountain, 1986).

Transportation is an important factor that influences the participation of older people in a variety of social activities, including the church (Cutler, 1974; Payne, 1981; Regnier, 1975). Many older people no longer drive or own a car, particularly in advanced old age. Seniors are, therefore, dependent on family or friends for transportation or on the public transportation systems, which may be nonexistent in suburbs, small communities, or rural areas.

The cost of church attendance may be a significant barrier for some older people. The reduction in retirement income or excessive medical expenses may decrease an older person's ability to contribute financially to the church or synagogue. This may be an embarrassment to the older person who has contributed to the church's ministry in years past. Older people may not be able to dress as well as they did at a younger age, which may be a mobility problem as well as an economic one (Moberg, 1962; Payne, 1981). Such inappropriate dress may keep some away from the religious institution.

There are a number of emotional barriers that may affect older adults' participation in church-sponsored activities (Fountain, 1986). These can be related to a number of matters. If older people move to a new community, they may not know anyone in the new church. The order of worship is different. They feel out of place. This can happen even if they do not move away from their old church or synagogue. New members join; old friends die, move away, or become inactive. They are no longer asked to serve on committees. A new member of the clergy comes who is "different" from the previous spiritual leader. The program of the religious institution places so much emphasis on the nuclear family and their needs, and so little is geared to noncouples. Older people with grown children or those who are widowed may feel that there is "nothing there" for them (Payne, 1981). Any or all of these emotional factors can cause older people to feel as if the church or synagogue is different to them. Thus, they become less involved or slowly drop out.

The last barrier that will be mentioned is an attitudinal one. This has to do with the congregation's negative attitudes toward older people. Such attitudes would be reflective of the societal attitudes and standards of the day. So often, older people are not looked to for wisdom, knowledge, and leadership. People within the church or synagogue may be ready to discard older adults as useless, as of little value to the life and ministry of the institution. Pastors or rabbis, as well as lay persons, may share these attitudes. People with such attitudes may not actually impede the membership of older adults, but they certainly would not work hard at assimilating the elderly into the ministry of the congregation (Fountain, 1986). Many elders may perceive these negative attitudes and drop out of the activities of that institution.

There may be other blocks to older adults' participation in the religious institution. However, it appears that any congregation that wishes to relate to older people with a positive ministry must give attention to the health, physical, transportation, emotional, and attitudinal barriers they present to elders. Many of these can be changed.

THE ELDERLY IN THE LOCAL CHURCH OR SYNAGOGUE

Often there is the tendency to speak of older adults as if they are one homogeneous group. A closer look at the older population points up the great diversity among these individuals. It is a mistake to discuss their needs as if they are similar. It is mistake to develop a single program in the church or synagogue to meet the needs of all older adults. One way to avoid this problem is to consider the separate needs of various subgroups of older adults.

Older adults can be categorized into the following groups (Becker, 1986; Ellor & Coates, 1986; Lawson, 1983; Tobin et al., 1986): well-elderly, less-active elderly, homebound elderly, institutionalized elderly, and families of the elderly.

Well-elderly These are the healthy, active, and interested older people who are in relatively good health and live on their own in the community. Their needs have not changed significantly over the past 10 to 15 years. In outlook and attitude these people are middle-aged individuals who have passed their 65th birthday. These are the individuals most like Neugarten's (1974) "young old." Their good health gives them greater potential for independence and for doing those things they wish to do. They have not yet suffered from the illnesses that plague many old people. Most have continuing financial stability. They still have the vigor and ability to fully be a part of the life and ministry of the church or synagogue. It is estimated that 80% of all those over 65 are well-elderly (Tobin et al., 1986).

Less-active Elderly These are those older people who have slowed down physically. They still are vital and alive, but they have certainly slowed down in life. They have limited their activities. This slowing down may be due to factors related to normal aging, or it may be the result of health problems. They are still very functional, but they may not have the stamina or energy they once had. They may not see as well. They may be slower and more careful in walking. They may be reluctant to drive at certain times of day or night. They can be out and about but they have limited their activities.

Homebound Elderly Tobin et al. (1986) have identified several distinct groups within this category. One of these groups is the *temporarily homebound*. This would include those elderly who have had a recent acute illness and are now in the recovery phase. It can include those older people who have a flare-up of a chronic disease. Within time, these individuals generally return to their prior state of health and are no longer homebound.

A second group is the *service shut-in* (Ellor & Coates, 1986; Tobin et al., 1986). This group is difficult to recognize. They are not severely physically disabled. They are homebound for other reasons; mainly, they do not have access to those services that would enable them to remain active within the community. Occasionally, when they do attend church or synagogue, they appear to be doing well physically. When asked, they say that they are doing fine. In reality, they may be quite lonely and feel as if they are removed from the care and concern of the church or synagogue. They may be homebound because they do not drive, or they drive only when the weather is good. They may be homebound because of lack of money to buy adequate clothes or to socialize with friends. Some may be homebound because of emotional reasons, such as prolonged grieving for a loved one. Generally, if services such as transportation or counseling could be provided, these service shut-ins could return to active participation in the community and in the church. Often, these individuals are not recognized as homebound and are not visited; yet they feel that they are unable to participate in community and church activities.

A third category of homebound people is the *chronically sick and bedbound*. These people usually live with a spouse or an adult child, but occasionally they will live alone. They probably have multiple physical and emotional limitations. They may move about the home, but they are limited in their mobility. Others are bound to their beds. These people are easily recognized and usually appear on the shut-in lists of local congregations. They may be called the frail elderly.

One study (Tobin et al., 1986) estimated that, at any one time, about 8% of those 65 or older are homebound, and more than 25% of that group are bedridden. Data from the 1979 and 1980 National Health Interview Survey estimated that about 2.7 million people 65 or older who live in the community need functional assistance from other people for selected personal care or home management activities. It was estimated that 7% of those between 65 and 74, 16% of those between 75 and 84, and 39% of those 85 or older needed such assistance (Feller, 1983; Sherwood & Bernstein, 1986). Those individuals included in these latter data would seem to include those in the homebound category and some in the less-active elderly category. The ability of the vulnerable elderly to live in the community depends as much on the availability of effective helpers and the degree of personal isolation from resources as it does on the individual's own level of personal functioning (Sherwood & Bernstein, 1986).

Institutionalized Elderly   These are those people who live in nursing homes. They comprise about 5% of the over-65 population. It has been estimated, however, that at least one in three older people will spend some period of time during their lifetime living in a nursing home (Vincente, Wiley, & Carrington, 1979). People in this category are usually of advanced age with many health problems. These, too, are the frail elderly. Most people enter a nursing home because of poor physical health. Many have serious degenerative illness. The average age of nursing home residents is nearly 85. More than half of the residents have chronic brain syndrome or mental illness. Only about 10% of these people can perform personal care tasks such as bathing, dressing, toileting, eating, and walking for themselves. The remaining 90% need at least some assistance in performing these daily living tasks. Most of the nursing home residents are without someone who can, for whatever reason, provide for their care; thus the necessity for institutionalized care (Tobin et al., 1986). People in this category can no longer be looked to for active physical participation in life, though many of them do remain mentally active and alert. One must be careful not to characterize this whole group as "senile." Some may be, but many are not. These elderly are frail, but they are frail for a variety of reasons (Becker, 1986).

Families of the Elderly Much of the ministry to older adults is to those individuals who are the homebound and institutionalized elderly. It is often forgotten that the caregivers are homebound because of their responsibilities to the sick elderly. More and more of the caregivers themselves are elderly. They may be spouses or adult children who are 60 or older. Family members of institutionalized older adults have special needs, too. They may feel guilty about having to place their relative in the nursing home. The family may not be able to accept the disabilities of their loved one. It is difficult for many to adjust to the major physical and mental changes that have occurred in a parent or spouse. It hurts to watch the slow decline of one you love. Whatever their age, family members of the homebound or institutionalized elderly need to be recognized as part of older adult ministry. This group is often overlooked.

There are other ways to categorize the many diverse groups of individuals who live within that portion of the life span known as older adulthood. Although the categories proposed here are arbitrary, they do provide an operational base for those desiring to design ministry for and with older people. Basically, these categories are health-related, grouping individuals according to physical conditions. Through the use of such schema, people can be identified according to these categories, and then local churches and synagogues can begin to serve the unique needs of those people within the various groupings with appropriate ministries.

OBJECTIVES OF OLDER ADULT MINISTRY

In order to more effectively respond to the physical, social, and psychological, as well as spiritual, needs of older adults, it seems appropriate that the religious community should give some thought to what objectives or aims it should attempt to meet in its older adult ministry. Clarity on these objectives should help focus the direction of this ministry. A study of the literature (Becker, 1986; *Book of Resolutions*, 1988; Clingan, 1976; Cole, 1981; Miller, 1981; Tobin et al., 1986; Withnall, 1987) has revealed a number of objectives. Realizing that different denominations or local congregations may have different slants and emphases, I still felt it would be helpful to propose some objectives. One overall objective may be to help older people remain a part of their community of faith, to participate in its life and activities, and to make contributions to its ministry and life as fully as possible. More specific objectives of an aging ministry are as follows:

1. To encourage older people to continue giving to society from the wealth of their experience and to remain, up to their potential, active participants in the congregational and community life.
2. To utilize the gifts, skills, and experiences of older people in significant

social roles in the life, work, and mission of the faith community and in the larger societal community.

3. To provide opportunities for older people to continue to participate in the worship, traditions, and celebrations of the faith community.

4. To provide educational opportunities for older people to help them continue to grow in the faith and to see the relevance of theological beliefs to the issues of their life.

5. To train and equip older people for new and continuing roles as leaders or consultants in the life, work, and mission of the faith community and in the community at large no matter where they are or what their condition may be.

6. To help older people affirm their lives, both past and present, and to develop a greater sense of fulfillment in their lives to come.

7. To help members of the faith community to identify the needs and interests of older people in the congregation and in the community and, as a caring community, to give priority to appropriate responses that can best be implemented through the resources of the religious sector.

8. To help the members of the community of faith to accept responsibility for appropriate advocacy roles on behalf of older people.

9. To stimulate the local faith community and higher organizational church structures to cooperate with public and private community agencies and with other faiths in support of more comprehensive and effective policies and programs related to the welfare and dignity of older people.

10. To educate all ages of the faith community for the lifelong process of aging with emphasis on quality of life, understanding among the generations, and personal faith development.

11. To help all ages of the faith community to develop more positive attitudes toward aging and the aged and to understand and value the special uniqueness and worth of aging individuals.

12. To train clergy and laity for ministry to, with, and by older adults.

OLDER ADULT MINISTRY

Having laid out some objectives of older adult ministry, I now turn to what the ministry may look like. Before beginning such a discussion, however, it seems appropriate to remind the reader that older adult ministry is not just ministry *to* or *for* older adults. It is also ministry *by* and *with* older adults. Even with the best intentions, we may do an injustice, and perhaps serious damage, to older people in the church if we only think about ministry to them and for them. We may be contributing to the further isolation, dependence, and devaluing with such a philosophy. We need to be freeing older adults to be their own advocates and leaders. We need them to participate in the decision making, planning, and implementation of older adult ministry to the fullest extent possible. We need their thoughts, planning, and involvement in all aspects of the church's and synagogue's program. We need to be involved in program development and leadership with them, and we need program development and leadership by them. Only a small proportion of the older population are homebound, feeble, and institutionalized. This small group may be the ones we "do for," but then only when it is required. We must remember that older adults may be able to "do for" other older adults. Such a ministry does not always need to be done by younger individuals. Also, we need to remember that even many of those who are being "done for" have special gifts and talents they can give others. Many of us have been ministered to by some of those we thought we were "doing for." The religious community needs to be aware of the distinctions between ministry to or for, with, and by older adults. The church or synagogue needs to be creative in and sensitive to the various aspects of this ministry. Older adults themselves can be helpful in the creativity and sensitivity of ministry.

But what should this ministry look like? What should be its format? The answers to these questions are as many as there are congregations. There are many forms of older adult ministry—some simple, some quite complex. Such ministries depend on the number of older adults in the congregation or in the community; the commitment, knowledge, and creativity of the clergy and laity; the extent of the resources (financial and otherwise) available; facilities; community resources; and so forth. A full discussion of ministry possibilities is beyond the scope of this chapter. All that can be done is to be suggestive. I discuss two ways of conceptualizing older adult ministry. The first of these has to do with conceiving the ministry possibilities under seven general headings (Becker, 1986; Lawson, 1983): worship, study, service, social, personal development, advocate, and referral.

Worship   This has to do with providing experiences for older adults to participate in a ministry of worship. This involves the chance to hear the proclamation of the religious "truths," to praise and commune with one's God, to be involved in the ritual and liturgy of the faith. This may be through corporate or individual worship. It may be realized through the older adult coming or being brought to the church or synagogue. It may be accomplished through taking the worship experience to the older adult.

Study   The importance of continued learning for older adults cannot be overemphasized. Many older adults in our congregations want to continue studying about matters of the faith, to wrestle with many of the issues in their own lives, the community, the nation, and the world, from the faith perspective. Many of these older adults are "old in the faith" as well as chronologically old, but they still feel the need to continue their faith development. They may want to learn how to more effectively deal with their own aging. They may desire to learn about coping with loneliness or the political issues involved in the latest Third World country making the news. No matter how confined they may be, many older adults want opportunities to study.

Service   This category, of course, involves all types of service to and for older people, but it also includes the services by older people to others of all ages. Most adults want to be of service to other human beings, to be of value and worth to somebody or some institution. This includes the homebound and the feeble elderly.

Some ingenuity may be needed, but the church or synagogue needs to help elders discover ways they can contribute to the lives of others. Opportunities for carrying through may need to be developed.

Social All human beings have social needs. They need to be with other people—to develop friendships, to love and be loved. Churches and synagogues may be the vehicles through which older people can socialize with others. This may be through socials, trips, plays, meals, or through visits or telephone calls to the homebound or institutionalized. Opportunities for interaction and sharing with others should be provided.

Personal Development This category of ministry possibilities may cut across the previous four categories. This has to do with the older adult developing the self in ways that are unique to that individual. It is related to developing one's own interests and potential. It relates to Maslow's "self-actualizing" concept. It may involve a study of British short stories or a trip to a local historical site. It may mean recording one's own personal history for one's grandchildren or seeing a professional baseball game. The church or synagogue in ministry may help facilitate this process for some older adults. The possibilities are infinite, and this type of ministry may reach the well-elderly as well as the more limited older adult.

Advocate The church is an advocate when it works to promote the worth, dignity, and rights of older citizens. Helping older people gain a fair share of society's goods or assisting them to gain access to services are advocacy roles the church can fill (Apel, 1986; Barden, 1986; Cole, 1981; Sherwood & Bernstein, 1986; Tobin et al., 1986). When the church is voicing concern to the larger community about issues such as housing for the elderly or crime against older citizens, it is being an advocate. The church can promote continued and new social services and programs for groups of older people. If necessary, when a family is absent or nonexistent, the church may play a direct advocacy role for an individual elderly person. The church or synagogue can act as an intercessor with an agency or agencies to get the support and care needed by that older person. Becker (1986) says the church's advocacy role falls into three categories: the correction of injustice, the positive pursuit of justice, and the prevention of injustice. These seem like good guidelines for a church in thinking of its advocacy functions.

Being an advocate goes beyond the traditional ministries usually associated with older adult programs; however, most religious institutions are concerned with the "whole life" of people, as well as the spiritual life. Rather than attempt to provide many services for which it does not have the resources, the church or synagogue would do better to make sure that the community provides the service, thus the need for an advocacy role.

Referral The church can disseminate information about health, nutrition, and other social services so that the elderly or their caregivers can know where to go for help (Barden, 1986; Karcher & Karcher, 1980; Sherwood & Bernstein, 1986). Because many elderly have positive feelings regarding their church or synagogue, they will be receptive to information that comes from this institution and its representatives, both clergy and laity. The range of social, legal, welfare, community, housing, health, and educational agencies is large in many areas. Most elders are not aware of the wide range of agencies and resources that are available for help. They may not know where to start when help is needed. Many are reluctant to search for such agencies for it smacks at "charity," a negative term when they apply it to themselves. In this situation the church or synagogue has an opportunity for a significant ministry for its older members. The church can provide information and refer elders or their families to the appropriate services. Such a ministry would require someone or some group within the church to become knowledgeable of the available agencies and services.

A second way of conceptualizing older adult ministry has to do with the roles the religious institution can play in the aging network. It means organizing ministry in terms of service functions. Tobin et al. (1986) have proposed that such service falls into four basic groups: providing religious programs, serving as a host, providing pastoral care programs, and providing social services. These services can be organized formally or informally, and may be led either by professionals or lay persons.

Providing Religious Programs This category cuts across the first three headings suggested under the previous schema for conceptualizing older adult ministry: worship, study, and service. This category includes any type of religious program likely to be provided by a religious institution: worship services, study groups on the Bible and other matters of the faith, special holiday programs, service programs of the church or synagogue, and so forth. It also includes any type of service that facilitates the participation of elders in activities sponsored by the church or synagogue, such as transportation, provision of ramps, and hearing aids. Tobin et al. emphasized the importance of these latter services for the religious older adult, and they indicate that these services need to be given just as much priority as the other categories of service.

Serving as a Host This service component may have been included in the first categorizing scheme, but it was not as clearly delineated as in this grouping. This has to do with churches and synagogues becoming hosts to various social service activities—like Meals on Wheels. Many religious buildings remain empty during the week, and the churches or synagogues could offer their facilities to the social service agencies. In this role of host, the religious institution would not be responsible for organizing or managing the program. The church would simply be lending building space to the agency so that it can provide the service.

Providing Pastoral Care Programs These services are usually provided for members of the local congregation, but they can be directed to individual older adults, families, or groups of older people. These services might include home or institutional visiting, telephone reassurance, transportation, and so forth. These are generally "services supplied as needed" and usually do not involve a large number of requests at any one time. Support groups would be under this category. Social events such as fellowship suppers, study events that include topics not normally called "religious study," or peer counseling (like in widow-to-widow groups) would be considered under this category. Many of these pastoral care activities may be close to the type of services provided by social service agencies, yet Tobin et al. (1986) stated that neither the participants nor the religious institution view them as such. These services are seen in the same light as the response of a friend or neighbor. These responses are usually informal services, though, at times, some of the pastoral care services are not long-time involvements. They are provided for a while—until the need or interest subsides—and then they are stopped.

Providing Social Services There may be times when a need in the community causes a church or synagogue to develop a formal social service program. There seems to be no organized program available that addresses that need. Or, there may be services available but the church or synagogue, because of its value structure, may not approve of the type of service or its management system and, therefore, decides to develop its own. Retirement homes and senior centers could be examples. These social service efforts are more formally organized and have a more permanent structure than the pastoral care services mentioned previously. Part of the difference, also, has to do with attitude. More than likely, the participants and the church would view these efforts as social service.

Each church or synagogue will struggle to define its ministry to and with older adults. With few exceptions, most churches and synagogues will not be able to design all the ministries needed by older adults in the congregation or in the community. Yet, the religious institution must be willing to respond to as many as possible of the physical, psychological, social, and spiritual needs of the older people whom they serve. Thinking of ministry in the contexts of worship, study, service, social, personal development, advocacy, and referral, or as providing religious programs, serving as a host for service programs, providing pastoral care programs, or providing social services may be useful frameworks for designing ministry for and with older adults.

THE ROLE OF EDUCATION
IN AGING MINISTRY

Education has a vital role to play in the religious institution's involvement in aging ministry. In a sense, education cuts across every aspect of that ministry—whether in worship, study, service, social, personal development, advocacy, or information and referral, or whether helping the institution to facilitate its providing religious programs, serving as a host, providing pastoral care programs, or providing social services. Education can help people become aware of the need for particular ministries, or it can help people become more skilled in implementing these ministries. Education is a priority for the religious institution concerned about aging ministry. The remainder of this chapter will be devoted to a discussion of three important ways in which education must be involved with aging ministry: education about aging, education of the professional for ministry, and education of the laity for ministry. There are other ways in which the role of education in aging ministry can be approached, but these three are important enough to warrant the remaining space.

Education about Aging

Education about aging is for every age group. It is designed to help people to live through the changes (physically, socially, and psychologically) that occur all through the life span. This perspective assumes that satisfaction in life and fulfillment in the later years depends, to a great extent, upon coping successfully with changes faced in early life and acquiring skills in solving problems and dealing with change. So one aspect of a ministry by, with, and for older people involves educating people of all ages for aging.

This education will involve helping younger and older people to understand and live through the changes within their bodies. It is designed to help young and old to understand and anticipate the role and status changes that occur. It will help people to adjust to the changing relationships with other individuals.

> *Such an education consists of more than giving persons information about the aging process, although that will be part of it. It includes acquainting persons with admirable role models, enabling them to dissolve crude and often inaccurate stereotypes about old age, and stimulating them to change negative attitudes toward the elderly and the later years. It will be cross-sectional inasmuch as programs of particular interest are developed for specific age and interest groups. It will be intergenerational inasmuch as those who are older may share what they have learned with those who are younger and inasmuch as it is important to enable two different generations to learn how to relate to each other positively and live together happily.* (A Ministry to Match, *1984, p. 42*)

From this perspective there would be educational offerings for younger age groups, for older age groups, and for various age groups together. In many instances, care should be given not to give the label of "programs for the elderly" to educational offerings, for many older adults may hesitate to associate with these programs for "old folks." Many educational experiences can bring together the different generations in a common learning experience (Otterness, 1986).

One denomination has delineated some goals of education for aging. These seem appropriate to list. People involved in education for aging would gain

1. *An understanding and acceptance of aging as a God-given process of change and development with which each person must cope at every stage of his or her life.*
2. *A realization that each stage of life in its own way can be as meaningful and as fulfilling as any other.*
3. *A realistic acceptance of aging as a given and a positive and hopeful attitude toward the stages that lie in the future.*
4. *An insight into some of the steps that may be taken to get ready for passage into the next stage, exposure to persons who can provide successful role models, and a commitment to assume responsibility for the making of one's own life and living responsibly with others.*

    5. *A growing understanding and deepening relationship between members of all generations, with older people being given the opportunity to replace lost relationships with those persons who are younger.* (A Ministry to Match, *1984, p. 43)*

Education for aging, as portrayed here, is seen to have several dimensions that may be intertwined with each other in any learning experience:

    1. *Anticipatory socialization* is education which enables persons to look ahead toward some of the changes and challenges they may encounter in the future. This education is designed to help persons gain insights, skills, and knowledge which will equip them to cope more effectively with those changes when they occur. Often this education can acquaint individuals with role models who have been successful in handling the changes and who may guide others through this passage. This dimension of education helps persons rehearse and prepare for the challenges to come. Such topics as the following may be included: preparing for marriage, the empty nest, widowhood, parenting, grandparenting; relating to aging parents, relating to adult children; understanding the changes of aging and their meaning; preretirement planning; and education for a healthy life in my later years.

    2. *Guidance through transitions* is education which enables individuals to learn how to cope while they are actually living through major transitions in life—like separation, divorce, grief, retirement, loss of a spouse, or dying. Persons are helped to understand what they are experiencing, to consider alternative responses, to learn positive coping skills, and to become familiar with positive role models. This dimension of education could include topics similar to these: being single again; living with a chronic disease; living with a dying person; living with my own dying; adjusting to my retirement; community resources available to help with this crisis; accessing community resources; and positive decision making.

    3. *The enhancement of life* is another dimension of education for aging. This is education which enables persons to express their potential more fully, to explore new depths of their personalities, and to understand themselves and others more deeply. This education can help individuals enlarge their world. Enhancement of life education may include such topics as: learning more about our community or State; learning about other cultures; keeping up with national and international issues; acquiring new skills in the arts, crafts, photography; and becoming more familiar with great books, art, or music.

    4. *The reconstruction of life* is education for those persons who have not successfully negotiated the major losses or transitions of life. This is education for those who may need help in putting their lives back together. These persons may be depressed, withdrawn, or burdened down with unresolved grief or unforgiven hurts. Education for these individuals would

attempt to help them understand the dynamics of what they have been through and to put these experiences into some kind of perspective. Efforts would be made to help these persons explore ways to "get on with living." Education for reconstruction of life may consist of a one-to-one relationship with a trained professional or it may involve group sessions led by trained personnel. Topics could involve the following: handling grief; dealing with anger or conflict; starting life again after divorce, after a death; and developing a positive self-image.

5. *The integration of life* is education designed to help persons see and appreciate the "big picture" of their existence, to accept their limits, to assimilate their failures and losses, to grow beyond a preoccupation with themselves, or to get a sense of how their life fits into the context of what has come before and what comes after. This area of education has to do with Erikson's (1963) ideas of ego integrity, or acceptance of one's own life span. Topics for such educational efforts could include such issues as: exploring the meaning and purpose of life; fitting one's life span into the context of one's faith; reminiscing one's life; writing one's autobiography or preparing an oral history for one's family; various issues related to theology or philosophy; and charting one's faith pilgrimage. (*A Ministry to Match*, 1984, pp. 43–46)

The education for aging described here is appropriate, as said before, for people of all ages. And, certainly, ministries for, by, and with older people themselves can fit into these dimensions. Years ago, McClusky (1973) said that education had a role to play in helping older people meet their needs. He identified five areas of needs particularly pertinent to older adults: coping needs, expressive needs, influence needs, contributive needs, and transcendence needs. It seems as if these needs are dealt with in the various dimensions described here. To these areas, the church's educational ministry adds the religious or spiritual dimension that permeates or blankets all aspects of its teaching and learning. All of its teaching is within the context of the belief structure of that faith. Education for aging aims to help people become what the Deity intended them to be—fully human beings of dignity and worth, who hear their "calling," and who live out their destiny.

Education of the Professional for Ministry

Those people in the local churches or synagogues who are most obviously in a strategic position to respond to the many needs of the aged and their families are the religious professionals—the minister, priest, or rabbi; the nun; the religious educator. These individuals have a unique opportunity to be facilitators and enablers of congregational programs of aging ministry. Unfortunately, so often these religious professionals are ill-equipped or apathetic in responding to opportunities for individual and congregational ministries to, with, and by older adults.

Several reasons may account for this reluctance of the professional to be extensively involved in older adult ministry. One may have to do with the professional's own attitudes toward older people and anxieties about the aging process. Professionals are no more likely than anyone else to be comfortable with aging or to be knowledgeable about gerontological issues (Kimble, 1981). Clergy do share some of society's negative attitudes toward older people—but to a lesser degree (Moberg, 1975). They do, however, evaluate older people more negatively than they do younger people (Moberg, 1969; Payne, 1984). Ministers do not seem to mind working with older people, but when asked to compare work with the elderly with involvement with youth and younger adults, the clergy reported they found work with the elderly less enjoyable (Longino & Kitson, 1976).

Other reasons for lack of involvement with older adults may involve negative reactions to visiting in long-term care facilities, negative criticisms about the professional's capabilities and performance from older adults who are not actively involved in the congregation, feelings of helplessness in knowing how to respond to many of the issues facing older people, or congregational pressures to recruit more young people, particularly young couples with children, in order to secure the congregation's survival (Oliver, 1988).

"Over-extended" can be another reason for the professional's reluctance to work with the elderly. This is particularly true for the pastor, rabbi, or religious educator who is the only paid employee in that congregation or work area. Multiple-staff churches can afford to specialize in various areas of ministry, such as with the aged. However, the solo professional has to try to be sensitive to the concerns and needs of the entire congregation. He or she cannot afford to specialize or to give extensive time to one segment of the congregation but must try to serve all of the congregation (Ellor & Coates, 1986; Oliver, 1988).

Most theological education has not prepared professionals to be knowledgeable of, sensitive to, and prepared for ministry for and with older adults. Seminaries, like the rest of society, have tended to give more attention to earlier stages of the life span. Most theological schools will have course work on children, youth, young adults, and maybe middle-aged adults, but little on older adults. Only recently have courses in aging been added to seminary training, and most of these are electives (Kimble, 1981; Oliver, 1988; Payne, 1984; Withnall, 1987). The gerontological content of the existing courses often are not comprehensive enough to equip professionals to work effectively with older adults.

Significant educational programs for clergy and religious educators are demanded if the older adults are to be served. Seminaries need to educate their students for an aging ministry. The American Association of Retired Persons' (AARP) Interreligious Liaison Office has emphasized this need through its publication of *Aging Society: A Challenge to Theological Education* (1988). In this monograph, scholars in eight disciplines (homiletics, New Testament, Old Testament, pastoral care, religious education, practical theology, worship/liturgy, and theology) have written papers on what their discipline has to say about aging and being old in today's society and on how aging information can be integrated into the teaching of that discipline.

There is a need for the church or synagogue professional to be knowledgeable of aging:

> *The utilization of existing research findings and knowledge concerning the processes of aging are extremely valuable to the religious professional. Whether the practitioner is celebrating and proclaiming the value of older persons from the pulpit, providing caring and healing ministries with those who suffer, advocating social change and mission in the larger society, or developing education programs to serve the needs of older persons (and adult children), he or she can extensively use gerontological information collected in a variety of disciplines from a diverse range of perspectives. (Oliver, 1984, p. 100)*

Religious professionals need to integrate theological perspectives and functional ministries in ways that will enhance the quality of living and being for older adults. The theological seminary is the place to start this integration.

Seminary education about aging is a must for the current theological student, but so is continuing education for those professionals who are currently working in congregations and synagogues. They need a better background in the physical, social, and psychological aspects of aging so they can better serve their older constituents. They need suggestions for older adult ministries. They need help in how to develop ministries for, with, and by older people. They may need to develop special skills for counseling older people. Continuing education opportunities need to be provided. These learning experiences could be developed by the seminaries or by the state or national denominational headquarters (Karcher & Karcher, 1980). Local religious professionals are vastly underutilized in terms of older adult ministry. They often are respected and trusted by the older members of the congregation and their families, but they are underequipped for their tasks (Doka, 1985–1986; Karcher & Karcher, 1980). Seminary and other religious educators and denominational leaders would do well to train and cultivate these professionals by offering workshops, programs, retreats, and other continuing education opportunities.

Education of the Laity for Ministry

Important as may be the education of the professional, preparation of the laity for aging ministry is an imperative. So many of the local church or synagogue programs are run and staffed by lay people. For this reason, emphasis needs to be placed on providing these people with training for such ministry. Such training can cover a variety of topics. People may need to be educated regarding the normal changes associated with aging. They may need to understand the different needs of the homebound and institutionalized elderly as compared to the well-elderly and the less-active older people. They may need to improve their communication and listening skills. They may need to learn of various community agencies that have services relevant to the concerns of older people. The laity may need help in learning how to access these services. The laity may need to learn more about some of the injustices inflicted upon various elderly in the community, state, or nation in order to be more effective advocates in the political arena. Lay people may need to gain more positive attitudes themselves regarding older people before they begin a ministry. Congregational members may need to be educated as to how to begin and maintain an older adult ministry. They may need to be sensitized as to how important it is to create an older person's ministry that is by and with, as well as to these elders. Education is involved in all the issues just mentioned.

Education of the laity can involve the training of all age groups for ministry. Children, youth, young adults, and middle-aged adults can all be educated to ministry possibilities. All these groups, within their developmental capabilities, can be involved in ministry. Congregational members may not know how to access and integrate the diverse and rich talent resources of the old and young into the life and ministry of the congregation. Older adults themselves need to be involved in education for ministry. Many older adults have tended to accept passive and less valued roles for older people in the church, as well as the rest of society's life. The lay leaders may need to learn how to continue to involve seniors as contributing participants in the ministry of the church and not just segregate them to older adult ministries. They may need to see older congregational members as planners and implementers as well as recipients of ministry opportunities. They may need to learn possible ways that the shut-ins and institutionalized adults could be "ministers" (Dickerson & Myers, 1988; Ellor & Coates, 1986).

The involvement of the laity in older adult ministries is crucial to the creation and maintenance of these ministries. *Ministry* is not just carried out by pastors, priests, rabbis, and other church professionals. Most faiths emphasize that all people, clergy and lay, are called to be in ministry. "The church's ministry to and with older persons is a ministry of the whole community of believers: young, middle aged and aged—both clergy and lay persons" (Interdenominational Task Force on Aging, 1978, p. 10). The tasks, at times, may differ, but being a believer entails involvement in the ministry of the church or synagogue. Both laity and clergy have unique gifts to offer in a shared ministry. Education has a role to play in the equipping of the laity for their tasks.

CONCLUSION

A religious faith and the religious institution are important to large numbers of today's older adults. The church or synagogue has only begun to recognize its role, its potential in the lives of the elderly. It has only just begun to serve or concern itself about the needs of older individuals. It is becoming increasingly clear that the rising numbers of older adults in the worshiping community need to be recognized, listened to, understood, and provided opportunities to minister to each other, as well as participating in every aspect of the ministry of the church or synagogue. The church's ministry needs to be a ministry for, with, and by older adults.

The church's ministry must be diversified to be relevant to the diversified older population. The needs and potentialities are different for the well-elderly, the less-active elderly, the homebound, and the institutionalized. Families of the elderly must not be forgotten. Ministry will be in many forms: worship, study, service, social, personal development, advocacy, information, and referral. The church may provide religious programs, pastoral care, or social services. The church may cooperate with other churches, denominations, or public agencies in providing services, or it may serve as a host for the work of these agencies.

The importance of education to the older adult ministry cannot be overemphasized: "Education will be a priority, and apathy and ignorance will be a constant threat" (*A Ministry to Match*, 1984, p. 8). There will be no effective ministry without education—whether it is educating older people about sacred or secular matters, educating people of all age groups to anticipate and cope with aspects of aging, educating professionals to work in older adult ministry, or educating laity (both young and old) for a ministry to, with, or by older adults.

Withnall has succinctly summarized what I have been saying in this chapter:

> *It appears that in the future, the churches will have an increasingly important role to play in providing opportunities for older adults to explore their faith using a variety of learning methods; to make the fullest possible use of older members of the congregation in the work of the church which will involve ensuring that church activities are available not just to regular attenders but also to the frail elderly, the housebound and those in residential institutions, ensuring that there are opportunities for inter-generational sharing and caring. There is also a need to consider how education in ageing for the clergy can be achieved and how training programmes for lay people and parish workers at all levels could incorporate such considerations into their curricula. (Withnall, 1987, p. 38)*

Failure by the churches and synagogues to recognize the importance and necessity of older adult ministry is to ignore the spiritual, physical, and psychological well-being of people in the latter part of the life span. Such a practice seems to be contradictory to the belief structures of these faiths—to be unfaithful to the God they claim to serve. Churches and synagogues that fail to be involved with older adult ministry also seem to be ignoring one of the social realities of today—namely, that our churches and synagogues are graying. Churches and synagogues would be wise to pay attention to the words of admonition spoken to one Christian denomination. The statement uses the word *Christians* in one place, but that word can be substituted by the designation for a believer in any particular faith. The thoughts are important for religious institutions of all faiths:

> *Since the vitality of the church will be determined by the vitality of its graying membership, whatever the church does in ministering to the special needs of these members will make of the church's ministry a magnet to draw from its experienced Christians the wealth of knowledge, expertise, skills, behaviors, attitudes, values and beliefs, which age has enabled them to accumulate,*

recycling the abundance of their enriching stores of religious experiences. Failing to do this, the static quality of the church through its membership can put the church on the sidelines, lacking the significance to make a difference in the world which so desperately needs its spiritual dynamics and leadership. (A Ministry to Match, *1984, p. 9*)

REFERENCES

Aging society: A challenge to theological education. (1988). Washington, DC: American Association of Retired Persons.

Apel, M. D. (1986). The attitudes and knowledge of church members and pastors related to older adults and retirement. In M. C. Hendrickson (Ed.), *The role of the church in aging: Vol. 2. Implications for practice and service* (pp. 31–43). New York: Haworth Press.

Auerbach, A. (1976). The elderly in rural areas: Differences in urban areas and implications for practice. In L. Ginsberg (Ed.), *Social work in rural communities* (pp. 99–107). New York: Council on Social Work Education.

Barden, A. K. (1986). Toward new directions for ministry in aging: An overview of issues and concepts. In M. C. Hendrickson (Ed.), *The role of the church in aging: Vol. 1. Implications for policy and action* (pp. 137–150). New York: Haworth Press.

Becker, A. H. (1986). *Ministry with older persons: A guide for clergy and congregations.* Minneapolis, MN: Augsburg.

Berger, P. L., & Neuhaus, R. J. (1977). *To empower people: The role of mediating structures in public policy.* Washington, DC: American Enterprise Institute for Public Policy Research.

Blazer, D., & Palmore, E. (1976). Religion and aging on a longitudinal panel. *The Gerontologist, 16*(1), 82–85.

The book of resolutions of The United Methodist Church: 1988. (1988). Nashville, TN: The United Methodist Publishing House.

Cheng, E. (1978). *The elder Chinese.* San Diego: Campanile Press, 1978.

Clingan, D. F. (1976). *Aging persons in the community of faith.* St. Louis, MO: Christian Board of Publications.

Cole, E. C. (1981). Lay ministries with older adults. In W. C. Clements (Ed.), *Ministry with the aging* (pp. 250–265). New York: Harper & Row.

Collier, C. M. (1978). *A community study of aging and religion among rural Pennsylvania Germans.* Unpublished doctoral dissertation, University of Massachusetts.

Custer, C. E. (1988). Adult ministries. *Interpretation, 32*(7), 33–34.

Cutler, S. J. (1974). The effects of transportation and distance on voluntary association participation among the aged. *International Journal of Aging and Human Development, 5,* 81–94.

Dickerson, B. E., & Meyers, D. R. (1988). The contributory and changing roles of older adults in the church and synagogue. *Educational Gerontology, 14*(4), 303–314.

Doka, K. J. (1985–1986). The church and the elderly: The impact of changing age strata on congregations. *International Journal of Aging and Human Development, 22*(4), 291–300.

Ellor, J. W., & Coates, R. R. (1986). Examining the role of the church in the aging network. In M. C. Hendrickson (Ed.), *The role of the church in aging: Vol. 1. Implications for policy and action* (pp. 99–116). New York: Haworth Press.

Ellor, J. W., Anderson-Ray, S. M., & Tobin, S. S. (1983). The role of the church in services to the elderly. In M. B. Kleiman (Ed.), *Social gerontology* (pp. 119–131). Basel, Switzerland: Karger.

Erikson, E. (1963). *Childhood and society* (2nd ed.). New York: Norton.

Executive summary of technical committee on "Creating an age-integrated society: Implications for spiritual well-being, 1981 White House Conference on Aging." (1981). Washington, DC: Department of Health & Human Services.

Fahey, C. J., & Lewis, M. A. (1984). Catholics. In E. B. Palmore (Ed.), *Handbook on the aged in the United States* (pp.145–154). Westport, CT: Greenwood Press.

Feller, B. (1983). Need for care among noninstitutionalized elderly. In *Health, United States: 1983* (DHHS Publication No. PHS 84-1232). Washington, DC: U.S. Government Printing Office.

Fountain, D. E. (1986). How to assimilate the elderly into your parish: The effects of alienation on church attendance. In M. C. Hendrickson (Ed.), *The role of the church in aging: Vol. 2. Implications for practice and service* (pp. 45–55). New York: Haworth Press.

Froland, C., Pancoast, D. L., Chapman, N. J., & Kimboko, P. J. (1981). *Helping networks and human services.* Beverly Hills, CA: Sage.

Gallup Poll. (1987). *Religion in America* (Rep. No. 259). Princeton, NJ: The Gallup Report.

Gray, R. M., & Moberg, D. O. (1977). *The church and the older person* (2nd ed.). Grand Rapids, MI: William B. Eerdmans.

Hadaway, C. K., & Roof, W. C. (1978, Spring). Religious commitment and the quality of life in American society. *Review of Religious Research, 19,* 295–307.

Harris, L., & Associates. (1975). *The myth and reality of aging in America.* Washington, DC: National Council on the Aging.

Heenan, E. (1972). Sociology of religion and the aged: The empirical lacrenae. *Sociological Quarterly, 9,* 112–116.

Heisel, M. A., & Faulkner, A. O. (1982). Religiosity in an older black population. *The Gerontologist, 22*(4), 354–364.

Hendricks, J., & Hendricks, C. D. (1986). *Aging in mass society: Myths and realities* (3rd ed.). Boston: Little, Brown.

Hirsch, C., Kent, D. P., & Silverman, S. L. (1972). Homogeneity and heterogeneity among low-income Negro and white aged. In D. P. Kent, R. Kaastenbaum, & S. Sherwood (Eds.), *Research planning and action for the elderly: The power and potential of social science* (pp. 484–500). New York: Behavorial Publications.

Hooyman, N. R., & Kiyak, H. A. (1988). *Social gerontology: A multidisciplinary perspective.* Boston: Allyn & Bacon.

Interdenominational Task Force on Aging. (1978). *Aging: A theological perspective.* New York: Author.

Jacquet, C. H. (1982). *Yearbook of American and Canadian churches.* Nashville, TN: Abingdon Press.

Kahana, E., & Kahana, B. (1984). Jews. In E. B. Palmore (Ed.), *Handbook on the aged in the United States* (pp. 115–179). Westport, CT: Greenwood Press.

Karcher, C. J., & Karcher, B. C. (1980). Higher education and religion: Potential partners in service to the rural elderly. *Educational Gerontology, 5*(4), 409–421.

Kimble, M. A. (1981). Education for ministry with the aging. In W. C. Clements (Ed.), *Ministry with the aging* (pp. 209–219). New York: Harper & Row.

Kuhn, M. E. (1977). *Maggie Kuhn on aging.* Philadelphia: Westminster Press.

Lacayo, C. G. (1984). Hispanics. In E. B. Palmore (Ed.), *Handbook of the aged in the United States* (pp. 253–267). Westport, CT: Greenwood Press.

Lawson, R. J. (1983). *Our congregation's ministries with older adults.* Nashville, TN: Discipleship Resources.

Letzig, B. J. (1987). The church as advocate in aging. In M. C. Hendrickson (Ed.), *The role of the church in aging: Vol. 3. Programs and services for seniors* (pp. 1–11). New York: Haworth Press.

Longino, C. F., & Kitson, G. C. (1976). Parish clergy and the aged: Examining stereotypes. *Journal of Gerontology, 31,* 340–345.

Markides, K. S. (1983). Aging, religiosity, and adjustment: A longitudinal analysis. *Journal of Gerontology, 38*(5), 621–626.

McClusky, H. Y. (1973). Education for aging: The scope of the field and the perspectives for the future. In S. Grabowski & W. D. Mason (Eds.), *Learning for aging* (pp. 324–354). Washington, DC: Adult Education Association of the U.S.A.

Midel, C., & Vaughan, C. E. (1978). A multidimensional approach to religiosity and disengagement. *Journal of Gerontology, 33,* 103–108.

Miller, D. E. (1981). Adult religious education and the aging. In W. C. Clements (Ed.), *Ministry with the aging* (pp. 235–249). New York: Harper & Row.

A ministry to match the age. (1984). New York: The United Methodist Church, General Board of Global Ministries, Health & Welfare Ministries Program Department.

Moberg, D. O. (1969). *The attitudes of ministers toward older people.* Unpublished doctoral dissertation, Boston University Graduate School.

Moberg, D. O. (1962). *The church as a social institution.* Englewood Cliffs, NJ: Prentice-Hall.

Moberg, D. O. (1975). Needs felt by clergy for ministries to the aging. *The Gerontologist, 15,* 170–175.

Moberg, D. O. (1983). The ecological fallacy: Concerns for program planners. *Generations, 8*(1), 12–14.

Neugarten, B. L. (1974). Age groups in American society and the rise of the young old. *Annals of the American Academy of Political and Social Science, 415,* 189–198.

Oliver, D. B. (1984). Gerontology in a graduate theological seminary. *Journal of Religion & Aging, 1*(1), 87–101.

Oliver, D. B. (1988). Preparing clergy and professional religious educators to work with older adults. *Educational Gerontology, 14*(4), 315–325.

Otterness, O. G. (1986). Educational opportunities for older adults. In M. C. Hendrickson (Ed.), *The role of the church in aging: Vol. 2. Implications for practice and service* (pp. 87–95). New York: Haworth Press.

Palmore, E. (1980). The social factors in aging. In E. Busse & D. Blazer (Eds.), *Handbook of geriatric psychiatry* (pp. 222–248). New York: Van Nostrand Reinhold.

Payne, B. (1981). Religion and the elderly in today's world. In W. C. Clements (Ed.), *Ministry with the aging* (pp. 153–174). New York: Harper & Row.

Payne, B. (1984). Protestants. In E. B. Palmore (Ed.), *Handbook on the aged in the United States* (pp. 181–198). Westport, CT: Greenwood Press.

Payne, B. (1988). Religious patterns and participation of older adults: A sociological perspective. *Educational Gerontology, 14*(4), 255–267.

Pihlblad, C. T., & McNamara, R. L. (1965). Social adjustments of elderly people in three small towns. In A. M. Rose & W. A. Peterson (Eds.), *Older people and their social world* (pp. 49–73). Philadelphia: Davis.

Photiadis, J. D., & Schnabel, J. F. (1977, Fall). Religion: A persistent institution in a changing Appalachia. *Review of Religious Research, 19*, 32–42.

Princeton Religious Research Center. (1982). *Religion in America.* Princeton, NJ: The Gallup Poll.

Regnier, V. (1975). Neighborhood planning for the urban elderly. In D. S. Woodruff & J. E. Birren (Eds.), *Aging: Scientific perspectives and issues* (pp. 295–312). New York: Van Nostrand.

Reynolds, D., & Kalish, R. (1974). Anticipation of futurity as a foundation of ethnicity and aging. *Journal of Gerontology, 29*, 224–231.

Rowles, G. D. (1986). The rural elderly and the church. In M. C. Hendrickson (Ed.), *The role of the church in aging: Vol. 1. Implications for policy and action* (pp. 79–98). New York: Haworth Press.

Sherwood, S., & Bernstein, E. (1986). Informal care for vulnerable elderly: Suggestions for church involvement. In M. C. Hendrickson (Ed.), *The role of the church in aging: Vol. 1. Implications for policy and action* (pp. 55–67). New York: Haworth Press.

Smith, S. H. (1967). The older rural Negro. In E. G. Youmans (Ed.), *Older rural Americans* (pp. 262–280). Lexington, KY: University of Kentucky Press.

Stojanovic, D. J. (1972). The dissemination of information about medicine to low-income rural residents. *Rural Sociology, 37*, 253–260.

Taylor, R. J. (1986). Religious participation among elderly blacks. *The Gerontologist, 26*(6), 630–636.

Taylor, R. J., & Chatters, L. M. (1986). Church-based informal support among elderly blacks. *The Gerontologist, 26*(6), 637–642.

Thompson, J. E. (1986). Life care ministry: The church as part of the elderly support network. In M. C. Hendrickson (Ed.), *The role of the church in aging: Vol. 2. Implications for practice and service* (pp. 65–76). New York: Haworth Press.

Tobin, S. S., Ellor, J. W., & Anderson-Ray, S. M. (1986). *Enabling the elderly: Religious institutions within the community service system.* Albany: State University of New York Press.

U.S. Bureau of the Census. (1981). *USPO current population reports.* Washington, DC: U.S. Government Printing Office.

Veroff, J., Kulda, R. A., & Douvan, E. (1981). *Mental health in America: Patterns of help-seeking from 1957 to 1976.* New York: Basic Books.

Vincente, L., Wiley, J. A., & Carrington, R. A. (1979). The risk of institutionalization before death. *The Gerontologist, 19*(4), 361–367.

Withnall, A. (1987). The Christian churches and older adults: Research and practice. *Journal of Educational Gerontology, 2*(1), 31–39.

7

INSTRUCTING EXPERIENCED ADULT LEARNERS

CHRISTOPHER BOLTON
University of Oregon

It requires a singularly sensitive instructor to perceive which key opens the door to learning. Most prefer to use a standard key and when the lock does not turn they see no need for self-reproach but refer to the inadequacy of their pupils.

(Belbin & Belbin, 1972, pp. 185–186)

That statement, made some 18 years ago, has never rung more true. Research regarding memory and information processing is beginning to unlock the mysteries of how learning and memory change developmentally as we age. Cognitive psychologists are beginning to explore the unique and developmentally different, but not necessarily declining, learning power elderly people possess (Adams, 1988b). This evolving understanding of older adult learning processes provides those who would involve themselves in instructional endeavors with older learners with a much needed theory base for modifying their teaching methods.

In this chapter I will explore some of the historically promoted beliefs regarding teaching older learners, with a critique of the potential efficacy of each in light of new learning regarding cognitive psychology; I suggest how a learner-centered approach to older adult teaching strategies has the greatest potential for success; and I offer several conceptual notions regarding how older adult education must be altered to ensure greater success in achieving learner-determined outcomes.

WHAT WE KNOW ABOUT INSTRUCTING
OLDER ADULTS

The advent of educational gerontology as a field of study and practice has afforded those at the interface of adult education and gerontology the opportunity to significantly affect the human development potential of education in the third trimester of life. We are often faced with opportunity coupled with frustration in reexamining traditionally held beliefs regarding the adult education process. This is especially true when considering the complexities of instructional strategies for older learners. Our brief experience in this teaching–learning process has been given a fair amount of attention but still represents only a modicum of variation in methods and continues to lack the evaluation research information necessary to validate the efficacy of present methods. Although this may seem unduly critical, the intent is to stimulate the reexamination of our commitment to the practice of employing tried but potentially untrue instructional strategies when designing educational opportunities for older adults.

The available knowledge concerning instruction for older learners is relatively untested. Several writers have cataloged a variety of special problems older learners face. In the development of the field of educational gerontology, several enduring principles of instructing older learners were introduced.

Anderson (1955) cited the heavy reliance older learners placed on past experience as a potential strength in formulating frames of reference and as a hindrance when manifested as learning inflexibility. The Academy for Educational Development (1974) recommended the application of the concepts of *andragogical theory* (the theory of teaching adults that is qualitatively different from theories of teaching young people). Formulated by Knowles (1971) and advanced as a primary instructional theory for older people by Peterson (1984), andragogical theory focuses on relatively independent learning skills that facilitate the development of a learner's ability to achieve personal learning outcomes through informed uses of a variety of resources.

Geist (1968) encouraged a clear presentation style on the part of the instructor with slow pacing and fostering active participation with well-spaced pauses to prevent fatigue. Hand (1973) suggested that the physiological changes that occur in later life dictate the choice of learning environments and dictate the choice of instructional strategies to be employed. DeCrow (n.d.), however, countered with "in real life learning, these intrinsic physiological differences are of little consequence" (p. 57). Others believed that the unique developmental and physiological characteristics of the elderly "as well as their isolated status, as imposed by our society" (Altman, Smith, & Oppenheimer, 1975, p. 3) require special pedagogical methods. van Enckevort (1971) went so far as to suggest that just as there is the study of the aging process, *gerontology,* there should be a theory of teaching elders, *gerontagogics,* and a resulting science of *gerontagology.* Arenberg and Robertson (1974) summarized learning research as follows.

- Older learners can maintain and recall about as much in primary memory as can younger learners; however, when primary memory limits are exceeded, age deficits may occur.
- Fast pace, either for presentation or recall, can handicap an older learner. Thus, self-pacing is highly recommended.
- Information processing skills that facilitate "encoding" for remembering improve the retention abilities of older learners.
- Interference produced by habits and preconceived ideas can be especially troublesome to older adults learning unfamiliar material.
- Retrieving from secondary memory can be difficult for older learners, a natural occurrence with the accumulation of many years of memories.

It should be noted from this summary that the primary outcomes of the teaching and learning process are the traditionally studied recall outcome variables. As cognitive psychologists have recently noted, developmental changes in information processing may require researchers to perceive learning outcomes differently in order to avoid promoting a decrement model associated with aging.

TWO FACTORS THAT AFFECT OLDER ADULT EDUCATION

Individual Differences

To teach middle-aged and older adults, one must understand that individual differences become the predominating aspect of the teaching–learning process (Belbin & Belbin, 1972). It has been stated often that individual differences become more pronounced with advancing age. This fact holds tremendous importance when one approaches the instructional process with this segment of the population. Diversity in educational needs and wants, learning styles, expectations for what is to be learned, the intended use of the learning process, and outcomes makes the task of teaching older adults both difficult and challenging.

Information regarding individual learning (cognitive) styles becomes increasingly important in proportion to learners' ages. Price (1983) pointed out that

> when people learn, they perceive and think. They also interact with resources, methods, and environments. The tendencies and preferences that accrue from this personal experience bring about one's learning style—one's characteristic ways of processing information, feeling, and behaving in learning situations. (p. 49)

Research has begun to affirm that learning style preferences have a great deal to do with learning achievement and satisfaction outcomes.

The differences between older versus younger learners are based more on the learners' experiences than on their ages. A middle-aged person who has been keenly aware of what life has given them can probably reflect on more experience than can the older person who rarely stopped to examine his or her life course. Thus, experience, not age, would seem to be a critical interpreter of how learning is to occur and how effective it will be. Age, as an independent factor, does not have much to do with how older adults learn. There are some age-related changes, however, that do alter the teaching–learning process.

Little research has been done to clearly specify the most applicable strategies for facilitating older adult learning. What has been firmly established is that older adults are able to learn, although in different ways and at different rates with different expectations for both process and outcome. One principle must be reiterated: Older adults can learn, but the way in which they learn will probably be unique.

Life Course and Cohort Effects

Members of one age cohort (people born within a given 5-year period) can differ significantly from members of another age cohort. Two important dimensions of cohort effects bear directly on how one approaches teaching older adults. First, life course variables suggest that people in different stages of life differ, sometimes greatly. People born early in the 20th century were not afforded the early childhood health care presently enjoyed in this country. For a child born in 1900, the average life expectancy was 47 years. In 1986 the average life expectancy was almost 75. Although those who are 70 today certainly survived the critical health concerns of early life, they also were subject to many illnesses that, cumulatively, could suggest diminished health status when compared to people who will be 70 in 2010. Certainly health status has a great deal to do with both participation in learning experiences and the instructional environment that can be, at worst, tolerated.

Common roles held throughout life by today's older adults will also be a significant factor in how we approach instructional designs for them. Some would characterize older people in negative and stereotypical ways, for examples, as being stubborn, rigid, authoritarian, religious, or dogmatic. Many of these characteristics were acquired because of the way they were expected to perform various roles as they matured. For instance, one can imagine the household of the early 1920s, in which children were taught to be seen but not heard, father knew best, discipline was important and sanctions often corporal, and education was simple—the three Rs.

Finally, life expectancy, as a life course variable, can have important implications for planning instructional strategies for older adults. Not only does life expectancy vary between cohorts as a product of previous and present-day health status, but it also has implications for motivating learners. For older individuals some issues related to learning for future utility (sometimes classified as instrumental activities) have less value than do those in which participating in the process of learning and doing becomes paramount (expressive activity).

According to Perlmutter (1983) age deficits in cognitive performance can be linked directly to cohort differences. She suggested that the passage of time is "uniquely experienced by each generation" (p. 234) and that it is this passage of time that becomes a distinct mediator of personal (life-course) experiences. A good example of this factor is the impact of educational experience (attainment) on learning outcomes. Although a person 70 years of age may have experienced 12 years of formal schooling, those experiences have been confounded by historical events since the completion of that education. It thus becomes essential in instructional design to take into account both the amount of education attained and the years since the attainment of that education, plus the events in history that may have interacted with what was learned in the ensuing years.

Few, if any, research projects focusing on the efficacy of instructional strategies for older learners have taken into account the multitude of confounding factors involved in evaluation of outcomes. Thus, in the absence of generalizable data regarding effective instructional strategies, it would seem prudent to rely primarily on methods that emphasize individualization of teaching and learning outcomes.

AUTHORITY-FOCUSED TEACHING METHODS

Methods that reflect a dependence on an external authority source are the most traditional form of pedagogic instruction. These employ concepts familiar to educators versed in school and postsecondary programs. Authority-focused methods encompass a number of factors that aid in the recognition of associated strategies and techniques.

Direction With authority-focused methods, the person responsible for instruction assumes the control or management of the learners' experiences. The learner in turn follows directions explicitly, responds to them when appropriate, and does so in a mandated fashion. Learners are provided all cues for how to behave. Incorrect responses to directives result in negative reinforcement and correct responses are positively reinforced. Often this instructional method is modeled after behaviorist theory, which holds that "Behavior is determined by its consequences. Learning does not occur because behavior has been primed (stimulated); it occurs because behavior, primed or not, is 'reinforced'" (Skinner, 1968, p. 93).

Prescription This factor ignores the possibility of individual learning styles. In a group instructional setting, prescription will usually indicate an attempt to gear the level of instruction toward a presumed middle one-third of learners' abilities. The lower one-third (in ability) are expected to upgrade their skills, whereas the upper one-third are left unchallenged. In an individualized instructional setting, the prescription can more accurately reflect the learner's style and skills, *if they are previously ascertained by the instructor.* As discussed earlier, these individualized, but often prepackaged, approaches fail to really take into account the individual differences produced by life courses and cohort effects.

Authority Dependence Whether the source authority is the professor standing before a class or a computer's cathode ray tube blinking in the student's face, the authority for defining both educational process and content resides with the method.

The curriculum is prescribed, the pertinent facts are preselected, the levels of complexity are predetermined, and the questions and "right" answers are selected by the source authority. Learners act as passive receivers tuned to only one wavelength and are allowed no alternatives. The source authority relies on cognitive (as opposed to affective) content and outcomes.

Efficiency This factor is ensured by the elimination of all but the most rudimentary inputs from learners. Even in the instance of a structured discussion method, efficiency is ensured through the complete control by the authority. Given the high degree of reliance placed in the instructional authority, efficiency is ensured as it directs the input of information, disregards how it is processed, and prescribes output information.

Knowles (1973) described succinctly the conditions that learning and learning skills required when this method is employed. The learner

- is willing to be dependent,
- has respect for authority,
- is learning as a means to an end (instrumental),
- expects a competitive environment,
- listens uncritically,
- retains information,
- takes notes, and
- predicts exam questions.

Critique of Authority-Focused Methods

This description may generate a relatively negative feeling regarding authority-focused instructional methods. We must keep in mind, however, that many, probably most, older adults have experienced only a strict pedagogical instruction process. For many, reliance on a source authority is the only possible means of acquiring the insights they require from a learning experience. They are rendered dependent by virtue of early life experiences and the effects of history. This is not to suggest that older learners cannot learn new ways of learning. Depending on the nature of the subject matter, we might find that elders, embarking on what may be their first attempt at formal education in 40 or 50 years, may derive more benefit and pleasure from an experience that is consistent with their long-held frame of reference regarding how education should be conducted.

The authority-focused methods also reflect what Perry (1970) identified as early "positions" of intellectual development. Perry's contention was that the students' development moved from a world view based in *dualistic* terms, in which the authority held the knowledge of what was right, to a world view based in *relativistic* terms, in which there is really no true authority and nothing is always proven right. As can be seen in the preceding discussion, the implicit assumption of authority-focused methods is one of classifying learners as relatively undeveloped according to Perry's typology.

This approach to instructional design is further compromised for older learners as we gain further insights into how older adults process information. Adams (1988a) suggested that qualitative differences in how older adults process new information recommends the potential for new instructional strategies focused on interpretation prior to memorization. In experiments with retelling short fable stories, cognitive scientists are learning that teaching strategies that focus on verbalization and interpretation may facilitate elders' learning abilities. Although they are still untested by adult instruction researchers, these findings begin to point the way toward development of a unique theory of teaching for elders based upon cognitive science outcomes.

LEARNER-FOCUSED METHODS

In contrast to authority-focused methods, learner-focused methods stress the autonomy of the learner in determining instructional processes. These methods employ a variety of conceptual components, although no one method necessarily employs them all. Learner-focused methods have long held a valued place in schools but have only recently been adapted for use with adults. One underlying notion common to these methods when employed with adults is that they are not typically school oriented. That is, they do not employ the traditional notion of teacher and student, do not require a classroom per se, and do emphasize the restructuring and examination of experiences as a central theme.

Andragogy A fundamental conceptual mechanism associated with autonomy-focused methods is the notion of andragogy. The term *andragogy,* according to Knowles (1975), is derived from the Greek *aner* meaning "the man" and *agogus* meaning "leader of." Thus, andragogy is interpreted as the art and science of teaching adults. The four main assumptions upon which andragogical theory is based are as follows.

1. *Changes in self-concept.* As people mature, their self-concept moves from dependency to self-directedness.
2. *Expanding importance of experience.* As people mature, their expanding base of experience serves as a resource base and as a frame of reference in acquiring new learning.
3. *Learning readiness.* The mature individual is motivated to engage in instrumental and expressive learning experiences voluntarily and with an anticipated developmental outcome.
4. *Learning orientation.* Adult learners tend to orient their learning toward problem solving rather than subject mastery. (Knowles, 1973).

Affective Content Drawn together by a common concern for the "feelings" side of the learning process, methods based on affective content encourage explicit attention to learners' feelings, values, and interpersonal behavior. For Hurst (1980), the affective domain is inseparable from the cognitive in most instances. One might extend Hurst's findings further to suggest that the affective component of "attending" as a prerequisite to higher order learning might be somewhat compromised in older learners as their energies wan and demands on their attention increase. Being cognizant of the affective side of instruction would appear to be most important when facilitating learning by the elderly.

Nondirectiveness   In encouraging nondirectiveness in teaching, Rogers (1969) suggested that "Teaching, in my estimation, is a vastly overrated function" (p. 103). His contention was that, through the use of directive methods, instruction or teaching was not only presumptuous in prescribing content but was also inefficient in communicating that content. His preference was to envision the process as "facilitation of learning" by which one skilled in nondirectiveness could guide learning focused on the learning styles and interests of the individual, again using the adult's wealth of experience as both content and a frame of reference in new learning. Thus, being nondirective really employs a focus on the process of learning. It is derived from an assessed understanding of how a given individual learns most effectively in a satisfying style. It leaves the determination of what is to be learned to the learner. As a result, the facilitator focuses on the climate of the learning experience, acts as a guide to learning resources, becomes a participant in the learning process, and allows the focus of the learning experience to be on whatever has meaning to the learner.

Process Centering   Another way of describing learner-focused methods is through *process centering*. Process-centered instruction emphasizes learners' becoming progressively more sophisticated in the process activity of learning. Described another way, a focus on process is a focus on practice in organizing the information imparted in the learning experience in the manner most useful to the learner. Borton (1970) concluded that the purpose of education "is to produce people who have developed a conscious grasp of the processes through which they themselves grow" (p. 91).

Learner Discovery   The fundamentals of learner-focused methods emphasize learner discovery, with persons responsible for instruction facilitating the process. Often the heuristic nature of these methods leads to trial-and-error situation that invites considerable criticism from proponents of more efficient methods. Although sometimes inefficient, a heuristic element is often felt to produce more meaningful learning experiences. Through the discovery process learners' analyze and extend their abilities to solve problems through individual and group inquiry.

Proaction   Knowles (1973) contended that traditional pedagogy conditioned learners to respond in reaction to stimuli from instructional authorities. He suggested that only by moving any authority to a less "omnipresent" status can proactive initiative on the part of the learner take place. Thus, Knowles suggested that the facilitating conditions of a proactive learning environment include the following:

- intellectual curiosity,
- a spirit of inquiry,
- knowledge of available learning resources,
- a healthy skepticism toward authority,

- knowledge of criteria for testing reliability and validity, and
- commitment to learning as a developmental process.

Knowles also urged the development of learning skills that would allow students to encounter new educational opportunities proactively, including the ability to

- formulate questions answerable by data,
- identify data sources,
- scan quickly written materials,
- test data for reliability and validity, and
- utilize data to answer questions.

Critique of Learner-Focused Methods

Although educational gerontologists have produced few data-based studies of the efficacy of learner-focused methods, there is much to recommend their use with older learners. We have a sufficiently substantiated data base regarding the learning characteristics of elders to suggest that traditional school-oriented instructional approaches will be of value only to a limited subgroup of contemporary elders. Our experiences with these methods is limited and have not been effectively matched with learning outcomes that would optimize their effectiveness. Future instructional intervention research will be required in this matching process to determine when and in what types of learning situations they are most useful.

REDESIGNING ADULT EDUCATION

Throughout the 10 years since the first edition of *Introduction to Educational Gerontology,* a great deal has been learned regarding social and psychological factors associated with aging. In many respects the growing body of knowledge has made the development of specific instructional methods for older learners even more difficult. The ever-changing face of aging, too, has made it nearly impossible to predict with any degree of accuracy, a given instructional model to fit a given learning event for a given age cohort. Given the improbability of prescribing instructional strategies, I conclude that methodology design must become more individualized, more a creative than a technical process, and, probably most important, deschooled. In the remainder of this chapter I discuss several important precepts that contribute to the creative potential in instructional design. These notions suggest more than just *how* to approach teaching older learners; they also suggest *what* older learners need to be able to do to ensure that the developmental processes so dependent on new learning can be accomplished.

Habitual Information Processing

Whether labeled as mindlessness (Langer, 1981), or habituation (Kastenbaum, 1981), or just plain "not paying attention," habitual information processing suggests a characteristic that is hypothesized to limit the ability of some older adults to learn effectively. As Langer (1981) noted: "As an individual's experience with certain situations accumulates, a cognitive structure of the situation is formed" (p. 259). Thus, once we perceive a certain situation as familiar and known, we have the potential for not attending and thus assuming the content and processes of the assumed situation. If we possess a tendency to analyze data and situations based on extensive experience, we may utilize a habitual information processing system as opposed to treating something new as unique. As an opposite, being "mindful" is actively drawing distinctions, consciously making meaning, and classifying new data in unique categories.

Piper and Langer (1986) suggested that "the physical and social environments of the elderly tend to encourage mindlessness" (p. 71). They go on to infer that once an elderly individual begins to process information habitually, a situation similar to Kuyper's and Bengtson's (1973) notion of social breakdown syndrome occurs. In this situation, habitual information processing suggests to those interacting with an elderly person that their competence is diminished. This perception in turn produces responses that reinforce the perceptions of incompetence, which, also in turn, are mindlessly (habitually) accepted by the elder.

Although it is still a relatively untested concept, especially regarding the elderly, the notion of habitual information processing presents a relatively neglected factor that may have a telling effect on facilitating instruction for older learners. Should future research efforts validate the idea, people interested in increasing the efficacy of their older adult instructional strategies will need to be ever alert to the products of habitual information processing. These strategies should

- mindfully pay attention to the potential for automatic processing of information,
- avoid the use of familiar frames of reference that are the basis of habitual processing,
- consider the negative implications of overlearning,
- be attentive to the necessity for creating novel situations, and
- encourage effortful responses in the learning process.

Control and Independence

Probably the ultimate goal of educational interventions for the elderly is to produce the highest level of individual independence possible. In the instance of control-enhancing interventions, knowledge truly becomes power. As McClusky (1974) repeatedly proposed, "margin" results when "power" exceeds "load." McClusky contended that education was the key to maintaining margin as one aged. This use of knowledge as power has been reinforced by social psychologists who study the implications of personal control on feelings of well-being and life satisfaction. As Karuza, Rabinowitz, and Zevon (1986, p. 373) stated: "We argue that one of the critical ingredients determining the form and outcome of help is the implication the help has for the perceived and actual 'control' of the recipient." Because education can be perceived as one form of "helping" interventions, control can be seen as an element in effective instructional strategies. The effectiveness of enhanced personal locus of control has been well documented (e.g., Rodin & Langer, 1977; Schulz & Hanusa, 1978). As in the discussion of learner-focused methods, the notion of control places both the control of, and responsibility for, learning in the hands of the student. It has become important to study the effects that enhanced control may have on the efficacy of instruction focused on empowering elderly individuals through the acquisition of the knowledge essential in sustaining their independence and margin.

Educational Efficacy

According to Knox (1977), a person with a strong belief that education is a means to both coping with aging-related decline and accommodating the developmental opportunities of later life has a "high sense of educational efficacy" (p. 186). For the most part, only those middle-aged and elderly people with a relatively high sense of educational efficacy participate in aging-specific educational activities or accept opportunities to enroll in the traditional school-based curriculum. Without a belief in the value of education in making life richer, fuller, and better, older adults are likely to continue to avoid the typical lifelong learning opportunities designed and marketed just for them.

Rarely do educational program planners consider that elderly adults must be persuaded to believe that educational achievement is possible for them. Most, when recalling their school experiences, may be repelled from traditionally produced and presented adult education fare. Equally rare are the opportunities to encounter the affective barriers to believing that participation in organized classes can produce desirable outcomes. Granted, Tough (1975) and others have demonstrated that surprisingly large numbers of older people have engaged in self-directed learning activities. Self-direction, however, appeals to a relatively select and special group whose interests in learning have already provided a belief in the efficacy of their self-directed study efforts. Again, those who most need education, or at least those who may benefit most, are least likely to be active adult education participants.

Proaction

The value of proaction, according to Knox (1977), is that an "intentional approach to learning" is a critical factor in continuing development as one ages. Proactive self-initiative is described by Knox as being action and goal directed, motivated by hopefulness, and is reflected in aspiration, direction, and assertiveness. A proactive instructional strategy should contribute to the older individual's feelings of self-worth and sense of accomplishment. Proaction, like educational efficacy, stems from the learner's acceptance of a focused, strongly self-initiated action toward achieving a developmental goal. The value placed on self-development and heightened affective states forms the expectation for learning to produce growth and change and begins with the acceptance of personal proaction as a precursor to involvement in learning.

Deschooling Lifelong Learning

"Deschooling society means above all the denial of professional status for the second-oldest profession, namely teaching" (Illich, 1981, p. 99). Although the ideas in this chapter do not necessarily reflect Illich's strong deprecation of schools and "schooling," they do advocate deschooling lifelong learning. This idea reflects what must be assumed to have been relatively "sour" schooling experiences for most elderly cohorts during their formative years. Deschooling is an issue focused on redefining the whole orientation taken to the development of adult learning opportunities—removing any aspect of traditional schooling that might deter older learners from any further consideration of participation.

Deschooling lifelong learning is more than an adoption of proactive, learner-oriented, andragogical techniques. It is completely removing from one's way of thinking any schooling-related methods and, in place of traditional notions, incorporating the knowledge we have gained through social psychological research, in devising interventions that accommodate the learning needs and interests of elderly learners without the accoutrements of the classroom. As Illich noted, "In order to see clearly the alternatives we face, we must first distinguish education from schooling" (p. 95).

Adult Socialization

In studying the role transitions and the concomitant expectations for behavior that occur as mid-life progresses, sociologists have concluded that individuals who anticipate and experience the unknown of aging often lack clear definitions of the behavioral expectations associated with older adulthood (Albrecht & Gift, 1975). The competent performance of the roles only briefly anticipated during middle age becomes one of the mandatory tasks facing the elderly. Although many lifelong education projects have attempted to respond to these developmental tasks, few have had any significant impact when estimating the magnitude of the growing population of elders. It becomes increasingly obvious that although "knowledge is power," in the sense that McClusky's *Theory of Margin* (1974) proposed, most opportunities provided by the educational community are selected by an insignificant minority (U.S. Bureau of the Census, 1985). One explanation for the lack of participation by elderly learners is the notion that schooling-formatted experiences are rejected as being too familiar and unfriendly. Another explanation, again provided by adult socialization specialists, is that to anticipate future roles and to invest in anticipatory socialization, requires an anticipation of futures unknown. As Albrecht and Gift suggested, "individuals often prepare themselves to perform in one world only to find that within a short time the role expectations have changed" (p. 240). Thus, when designing instructional strategies that are responsive to the role transitions anticipated by the elderly, the process of adult socialization, as a social learning endeavor, must be given consideration as the alternative to schooling.

CONCLUSION

I have presented some of the information available regarding how teaching experienced adult learners differs from teaching younger learners. I have discussed a number of factors important in differentiating teaching methods for older learners. Two guiding concepts—life course and cohort effects, and individual differences—provide the basis for additional differentiation among learners of a given generation and between different generations. These guiding concepts are especially important as we discover the magnitude of difference in personality, learning ability, educational attainment, goals, and anticipated outcomes that elderly adults bring to each learning experience. I have presented two alternative instructional models to contrast authority-focused strategies and learner-focused strategies. Although the discussion of the strengths or weaknesses of the two was not necessarily definitive, the discussion does point out the differences that exist between how school-based programs usually operate and how experienced adults become developmentally incompatible with the prevailing instructional philosophy.

In the section devoted to redesigning adult education, I illustrated the many variables that have not, in my opinion, been given sufficient attention in the literature on older adult instruction. Factors such as habitual information processing, the beneficial outcomes of individual control and independence, communicating a strong belief in educational efficacy, and proaction will provide a much-needed theoretical element to our instructional methods. The notion of deschooling lifelong learning, borrowed from Illich, reflects my strong belief that the low level of participation in education by elderly adults is a direct reflection of their disdain for traditional schooling-focused instructional experiences. Alternatives are difficult to propose, given our deeply ingrained experiences both personally and educationally, but there are ways of approaching instructional strategies (e.g., through the use of peer teachers) that remove the pedantic and pedagogical elements of our work.

One intended outcome for the reader of this chapter is an understanding that the design of instructional strategies for all learners, and especially for experienced adult learners, is far more complex than many of us, including me, had expected. Given the growing wealth of information being generated by cognitive and social psychologists regarding learning, thinking, motivational, and experiential aspects of older adult behavior, we are well advised to dismiss dogmatic recommendations as seriously limited and to consider exploring new realms as requisite to the future of instructing experienced adult learners.

REFERENCES

Academy for Educational Development. (1974). *Never too old to learn*. New York: Author.

Adams, C. (1988a). *Cognitive style and aging: The development of a late life metaphoric style*. Paper presented at the meeting of the Western Psychological Association, San Francisco, CA.

Adams, C. (1988b). *Qualitative age differences in narrative processing: A story retold.*

Paper presented at the meeting of the American Psychological Association, Atlanta, GA.

Albrecht, G., & Gift, H. (1975). Adult socialization: Ambiguity and adult life crises. In N. Datan & L. Ginsburg (Eds.), *Life-span developmental psychology: Normative life crises* (pp. 237–252). New York: Academic Press.

Altman, L., Smith, D. C., & Oppenheimer, P. W. (1975). *Education and the older adult* [Mimeograph]. New York: New York City Community College, Institute of Study for Older Adults.

Anderson, J. E. (1955). Teaching and learning. In W. T. Donahue (Ed.), *Education for later maturity* (pp. 60–94). New York: Whiteside.

Arenberg, D. L., & Robertson, E. A. (1974). The older individual as learner. In S. M. Grabowski & W. D. Mason (Eds.), *Learning for aging* (pp. 2–39). Washington, DC: The Adult Education Association of the U.S.A.

Belbin, E., & Belbin, R. M. (1972). *Problems in adult retraining*. London, England: Heinemann.

Borton, T. (1970). *Reach, touch, and teach*. New York: McGraw-Hill.

DeCrow, R. (n.d.). *New learning for older Americans: An overview of national efforts*. Washington, DC: Adult Education Association of the U.S.A.

Geist, H. (1968). *The psychological aspects of the aging process*. St. Louis, MO: Green.

Hand, S. (1973). What it means to teach older adults. In A. Hendrickson (Ed.), *A manual on planning educational programs for older adults* (pp. 86–102). Tallahassee: Florida State University, Department of Adult Education.

Hurst, B. M. (1980). An integrative approach to the hierarchical order of the cognitive and affective domains. *Journal of Educational Psychology, 72*(3), 293–303.

Illich, I. (1981). The alternative to schooling. In J. M. Rich (Ed.), *Innovations in education: Reformers and their critics* (3rd ed.) (pp. 94–103). Boston: Allyn & Bacon.

Karuza, J., Rabinowitz, V. C., & Zevon, M. A. (1986). Implications of control and responsibility on helping the aged. In M. M. Baltes & P. B. Baltes (Eds.), *The psychology of control and aging* (pp. 373–396). Hillsdale, NJ: Erlbaum.

Kastenbaum, R. J. (1981). Habituation as a model of human aging. *International Journal of Aging and Human Development, 12*(3), 159–169.

Knowles, M. S. (1971). *The modern practice of adult education*. New York: Association Press.

Knowles, M. S. (1973). *The adult learner: A neglected species*. Houston, TX: Gulf Publishing.

Knowles, M. S. (1975). *Self-directed learning: A guide for learners and teachers*. New York: Association Press.

Knox, A. B. (1977). *Adult development and learning*. San Francisco: Jossey-Bass.

Kuypers, J. A., & Bengtson, B. L. (1973). Competence and social breakdown: A social-psychological view of aging. *Human Development, 16*(2), 37–49.

Langer, E. J. (1981). Old age: An artifact? In J. L. McGaugh & S. G. Keisler (Eds.), *Biology and aging* (pp. 255–282). New York: Academic Press.

McClusky, H. Y. (1974). Education for aging: The scope of the field and perspectives for the future. In S. M. Grabowski & W. D. Mason (Eds.), *Learning for aging* (pp. 324–355). Washington, DC: Adult Education Association of the U.S.A.

Perlmutter, M. (1983). Learning and memory through adulthood. In M. W. Riley, B. B. Hess, & K. Bond (Eds.), *Aging in society: Selected review of recent research* (pp. 219–241). Hillsdale, NJ: Erlbaum.

Perry, W. G., Jr. (1970). *Forms of intellectual and ethical development in the college years: A scheme.* New York: Holt, Rinehart & Winston.

Peterson, D. A. (1984). *Facilitating education for older learners.* San Francisco: Jossey-Bass.

Piper, A. I., & Langer, E. J. (1986). Aging and mindful control. In M. M. Baltes & P. B. Baltes (Eds.), *The psychology of control and aging* (pp. 71–89). Hillsdale, NJ: Erlbaum.

Price, G. E. (1983). Diagnosing learning styles. In R. M. Smith (Ed.), *Helping adults learn how to learn: New directions for continuing education, 19,* 49–56.

Rodin, J., & Langer, E. J. (1977). Long-term effects of a control-relevant intervention with the institutionalized aged. *Journal of Personality and Social Psychology, 35,* 897–902.

Rogers, C. R. (1969). *Freedom to learn.* Columbus, OH: Merrill.

Schulz, R., & Hanusa, B. H. (1978). Long-term effects of control and predictability-enhancing interventions: Findings and ethical issues. *Journal of Personality and Social Psychology, 36,* 1194–1201.

Skinner, B. F. (1968). *The technology of teaching.* New York: Appleton-Century-Crofts.

Tough, A. (1975). *The adult learning projects.* Toronto, Canada: Ontario Institute for Studies in Education.

U.S. Bureau of the Census. (1985). *Special demographic analysis: CDS-85-1. Education in the United States 1940–1983.* Washington, DC: U.S. Government Printing Office.

van Enckevort, G. (1971). Andragology: A new science [Mimeograph]. Amersfoort, The Netherlands: Nederlands Centrum Vor Volksontwikkeling.

8

UNITING THE GENERATIONS

JOSIE METAL-CORBIN
DAVID E. CORBIN
University of Nebraska at Omaha

To gain continuity in our lives, let us bring together the old—the champions of our past, and the young—our hope for the future, so that we will be a culture growing together.

Steven W. Brummel
President, Elvirita Lewis Foundation

INTRODUCTION

In most instances, Americans live in an age-segregated society in which each generation pursues its own interests and activities. We often lose our perspective on the process of aging or we suffer from a generation gap because of our lack of experience with people of different ages. In order to relate to and understand one another, we need to have contact with one another. In the last several decades there has been research that points to a fragmentation in our society. We have compartmentalized our lives with age-segregated schools, age-segregated housing, age-segregated day-care and long-term care centers, and age-segregated social organizations. The focus on the extended family has shifted to the isolated nuclear family in which extended family ties have been minimized (Newman, 1980; Peacock & Talley, 1984; Pratt, 1984; Tice, 1985; Ventura-Merkel, 1986). Americans have limited their opportunities for interaction between young and old and have diminished the role that their elders once played in passing down traditional stories, customs, and celebrations that served to link the generations and foster a sense of trust, support, nurturance, and pride (Tice, 1982, 1985). The continuity of the family has been dramatically altered.

There is little doubt that economic changes since the late 1940s contributed to the decline of meaningful reciprocal relations between the generations. In many cases, families were separated by divorce or by the demands of a mobile labor force. Children who were separated geographically from their grandparents often gained opinions about older people from youth-oriented media rather than from first-hand experiences. Historically in our society, the elders served as models for the young, as advisers, as spiritual leaders, as guardians of our cultural and historical roots, and as decision makers in the community. Roles and responsibilities within the family and within the community were clearly defined. Children witnessed the life cycle from birth to death and observed their elders coping with major life changes. However, since World War II, the experience of today's children in our society changed drastically from the childhood experiences of those of their parents and grandparents. To cope with this modern family in which there is low expectation of intimacy between the generations, Margaret Mead offered this advice: "The simplest way to give children access to the past and to rapid change is the presence of older people within their immediate community, if not their own grandparents, then someone else's grandparents" (1977, p. 58).

Today, however, we live in a very complex society in which traditional values and roles are changing. There are more and more choices to be made in our cultural, religious, and educational systems, and making those decisions becomes very complicated. With the absence of elders in many families, the youth of today do not have this valuable resource to turn to in times of decision making. Mead stated that "the continuity of all cultures depends on the living presence of at least three generations" (1970, p. 3).

Some experts are predicting a new kind of class warfare between the generations. According to Beck (1988, p. 10) "the nation's elderly are under attack for having too much money, wielding too much political clout, taking an unfair share of federal tax dollars and leaching money from a hard-pressed younger generation." Fairlie (1988), in his controversial article in *The New Republic*, questioned many of today's entitlements for America's elders, but at the same time he acknowledged that "If this two-way transmission [between generations] ceases, both the young and the elderly suffer" (p. 20). Fairlie also noted that Americans still do not accept aging and that many older Americans separate themselves from younger generations.

There are no young where they live, no children, no bawling infants, no working, productive men or women. These [retirement] communities frequently advertise the fact that they are "adults-only." They live reflections of themselves. They are set apart, no longer a piece with any larger society, with no obligations. (1988, p. 21)

Even when older people live in the community at-large and they want contact with other generations, they can suffer from the separation of the generations. If families remain separated over a sustained period, the elders may develop feelings of rejection and loneliness because of their lack of involvement in family activities. They may feel disenfranchised and socially alienated from others. If you add to this the loss of work roles upon retirement, then there is a strong perception of purposelessness and lack of role delineation. All generations lose when there is this lack of interaction among generations (Newman, 1980).

Not all is negative in terms of the current status of intergenerational activities. There is evidence to indicate that the modern family does care for its elder members as well as it did in the "good old days." Some would postulate that the isolated nuclear family that was expected to emerge with the modernization of our society never really predominated. Instead, the trend seems to be the emergence of the three- and four-generation family in which members provide more care to parents over much longer periods of time than they did when elders made up only 4% of the population and the life expectancy was 47 years. Today's families provide a significant proportion of the social, emotional, and physical health care for its elders (Hooyman & Kiyak, 1988). Indeed, evidence within the last few years indicates that there is an increasing trend toward traditional interdependence within the family structure.

Secunda (1984) pointed out that it is the middle generation that is faced more and more with the care of their elderly parents who may be suffering with poor health or lack of financial resources. As the over-65 generation continues to grow, the phenomenon of aging parents living with their children becomes more widespread in our society. Different generations living in the same house can wreak havoc on a family, presenting moral dilemmas and possible conflict. Does this present a threat to the integrity of relationships between generations? Secunda observed that a century ago, there was not a potential power struggle between the generations within the family as the seniority was maintained by the elder parent as he or she owned the land and because age was venerated. Today, in the modern family, the middle generation is more likely to have the "power of the purse." Because Medicaid requires that older people cannot receive benefits until they have depleted their own resources, middle-age children sometimes strip their parents of their assets in order to enable them to qualify for Medicaid. This can certainly set the stage for mounting tension between family members.

Notwithstanding all these difficult issues, Abrams (1986) found that the middle generation is making space in their lives to care for older people in the family. This "sandwich generation" is establishing a pattern of mutual support and compassionate caregiving within the family for future generations to follow. They are reestablishing intergenerational bonds at a time in our society when there is an increasing trend toward the four-generation family. An important distinction is to determine whether the motivation for care for and about family elders has become paternalistic or duty-oriented and whether this caregiving extends to intergenerational exchanges outside the family structure. The ever-increasing numbers of today's older population are not likely to agree to being powerless and segregated from society. If service to country by youth through the Peace Corps and Volunteers in Service to America (VISTA) was admired for its idealism in the 1960s and 1970s, then there is no reason why idealistic service projects among older adults should not garner the same respect without the pejorative notions that "it keeps them busy" or "it gives them something to do." In addition, retirement should not be seen as a devaluation but rather as a changing of priorities. Personhood encompasses much more than the worker role, and retirement can give people the chance to emphasize other aspects of their lives and to pass this knowledge on to their juniors. Retirement also affords older adults the opportunity to learn new skills and to grow intellectually.

It is important to remember that the majority of retirement-age people live in their own mortgage-free homes and that most prefer privacy and independence rather than burdening their children. In fact, older people are often the ones who must assume major responsibilities in multigenerational families as they are asked to care for grandchildren at a time in their lives when they planned to recreate and reduce personal demands on their time. Of course, some elders may welcome an opportunity to be involved and be included in parenting responsibilities, but for many, these requests may cause resentment and frustration (Secunda, 1984). According to Ventura-Merkel (1986), the establishment of intergenerational programs within a community can provide natural solutions for the many problems facing the middle generation as they try to care for their dependent children as well as their aging parents. Indeed, all generations may benefit from intergenerational programs.

There are diverse ways in which older and younger people can share in mutually beneficial exchange. Pratt (1986) categorized intergenerational programs in schools as follows.

1. Programs in which older adults provide services to younger people.
2. Programs in which young people serve older people.
3. Programs that involve older people and younger people in activities that provide a service to the community or are mutually beneficial.
4. Programs that sponsor conferences or retreats between teenagers and retired people.
5. Programs that use the arts as common ground for linking the generations.

To this list we would add another category:

6. Programs that involve older adults with undergraduate and graduate students in higher education.

RATIONALE FOR AND BENEFITS OF INTERGENERATIONAL PROGRAMS

The National Council on the Aging defines intergenerational programs as "activities or programs that increase cooperation, interaction or exchange between any two generations. It involves the sharing of skills, knowledge or experience between old and young" (Thorp, 1985, p. 3). Intergenerational programs have many formats, including those located in day-care centers, public schools, universities, senior citizen centers, nursing homes, places of worship, clubs, businesses, and government. The common thread that is found in intergenerational programs, regardless of format, is that all generations involved are mutually benefiting from the program. They are sharing in meeting the needs of one another.

Newman (1980) listed some of the developmental needs that have historically provided a base for kinship among the generations. All generations have a need to develop self-esteem, feel a connection to the past and the future, feel competent, and identify their role in our society. Intergenerational programs can help to meet these needs and to give emotional and psychological support to each generation.

There are many obvious benefits and therapeutic values that are inherent in intergenerational activities and that appear to occur at both ends of the age continuum. Intergenerational programs bring older adults and younger people together for common activities and service and create opportunities for the different generations to enrich each other's lives. Both generations are given meaningful roles that help develop a sense of personal worth. They provide an environment that encourages the natural acceptance of a person from a different age group. They foster harmony among the generations and have the potential for reducing anger, prejudices, fears, and distrust. Stereotypical perceptions of one another may be changed.

Newman (1985a) found that the experience of older volunteers in intergenerational programs in schools has a positive effect on their life satisfaction. In another study, Newman (1985b) found that students with one or two years of contact with older people in their classroom have more positive increases in their attitudes toward their elders than do pupils without this type of contact. Corbin, Kagan, and Metal-Corbin (1987) found that children began to perceive older participants in active rather than passive terms after involvement in an intergenerational program in an elementary school. Participants (aged 13–18) in a 4-H Club showed improved attitudes toward older people after involvement in an intergenerational program (Glass & Trent, 1980). Preschoolers who had the greatest contact with older family members performed age-discrimination tasks more accurately (Sheehan, 1978). Contact with active older people in a school setting was a contributing factor in the formation of positive attitudes toward their elders (Caspi, 1984; Rosencranz & McNevin, 1969; Seefeldt, Jantz, Galper, & Serock, 1977). In a one-year follow-up study of an intergenerational program about aging that was conducted in an elementary school, the student participants who were engaged in the experimental program were judged (by experts in gerontology) to be significantly more positive toward aging than was a comparison group in the same school (Corbin, Metal-Corbin, & Barg, 1989).

There is not a wealth of information on the intergenerational classroom in higher education or the older adult as a college student. The research in this area, however, does support the concept that an intergenerational classroom experience will result in positive outcomes. Beattie (1974) pointed out that elders can serve as mentors, tutors, and educators. MacLean and Marcus (1981) viewed the exchange of knowledge of experiences between generations as a way of bridging the generation gap. Versen (1986) concluded that senior adults enrolled in the college classroom help to break down the stereotypes of aging held by the younger generations and assist in providing "an integrative function in the students' cognitive development" (p. 427). Undergraduate students who lived with grandparents or great grandparents showed more positive attitudes toward older people than did those without this type of contact (Bekker & Taylor, 1966).

Whether in schools, colleges, or universities, intergenerational programs are cost effective and may provide the power needed to help more people live healthier and fuller lives (Thorp, 1985). Through the sharing of public resources for all ages, they can encourage intergenerational equity. Ventura-Merkel (1986) pointed to the mutual beneficial exchange that can occur in health care, education, and service providing. Intergenerational programs can create linkages that close the gaps that formal social service programs and families are unable to provide. They promote partnerships among different community organizations, and they help to connect some of the disparate parts of the service provider system in the areas of tutoring, respite care, household chores, and meal provision. Thorp (1985) stated that intergenerational programs contribute to a renewed sense of community wherein people acknowledge their interdependence with others, begin to work together, and promote the well-being of the entire community. Intergenerational programs help to unite various factions of the community, fostering a sense of cooperation and discouraging a feeling of competition. They can facilitate a renewed sense of involvement and commitment to one's school, organization, or community.

Not all the research, however, shows positive outcomes of intergenerational programs. Auerbach and Levenson (1977) reported that the effect on the attitudes of 60 undergraduates who had older people as classmates showed significant negative shifts from pre- to post-test scores. Immorlica (1980) found that as intergenerational interaction between older volunteers and 120 elementary school children increased, the more unfavorable the children's attitudes toward the elderly became. Corbin et al. (1987) found that children's global affective perceptions of older adults grew less positive as an intergenerational program in the school progressed, but the children and the older adults did interact more. It was hypothesized that five sessions of questions encouraging the students to make closer observations may have cued the students to search for physical and psychological differences.

It has been suggested by Auerbach and Levenson (1977), Versen (1986), and Seefeldt (1987) that Amir's (1969) research on contact between ethnic groups may be applicable to studies concerning intergenerational contact. In Amir's review of the research regarding the effects of intergroup contact, he found that contact between various ethnic groups did not always result in the development of positive attitudinal changes. Mere contact between diverse groups is not enough to generate positive outcomes. One of the conditions that can increase prejudice between two groups is the element of competition. Auerbach and Levenson (1977) reported that students involved in an undergraduate intergenerational classroom experience had significantly more negative attitudes toward the older students. They postulated that competition over contact with the instructors and competition over grades were contributing factors. This sense of competition is not restricted to only intergenerational programs in higher education. Tice (1985) warned that in order to secure the future of intergenerational programming at all levels, we must not apply competitive strategies. Rather, cooperation must be emphasized, with each generation becoming mentors for and providing encouragement for one another.

Of course, part of the reason for conflicting research findings in the area of intergenerational education is that the research methodologies, samples, statistical analyses, and types of programs differed considerably among the different studies.

To ensure more positive outcomes there are many things, other than the elimination of competition, that can be done to increase the chances of having a successful intergenerational program. These suggestions are discussed in the following sections of this chapter.

DEVELOPMENT OF FORMAL INTERGENERATIONAL PROGRAMS

Since the late 1960s there has been a movement to create intergenerational experiences involving the young and old. In 1965, the Foster Grandparent Program (FGP) set the stage for linking the generations in mutually beneficial programs by bringing together, lonely, aging people with children who had special needs. Shortly thereafter, the Retired Senior Volunteer Program (RSVP) recruited older volunteers to go into the schools as tutors. In addition, a few model cross-age programs were funded by grant monies from the Administration on Aging (Tice, 1985). In 1976, the Elvirita Lewis Foundation (ELF) created the first Intergenerational Child Care Center. ELF is a nonprofit, public interest operating foundation representing the view that older people are a significant national resource that can help alleviate many community problems. ELF operates intergenerational child care projects and publishes a variety of materials, including a guide for older volunteers working in child care centers.

The American Association of Retired Persons (AARP) has also been a champion of the intergenerational movement in this country. Its motto is "To Serve, Not To Be Served" and its projects focus on service with elders, by elders, and to elders. AARP encourages intergenerational activities as an effective way to replace negative stereotypes with positive, healthy attitudes about growing older. AARP has established many programs that are designed to help students appreciate the concerns, skills, and lifestyles of older Americans. Since 1977, their Book Purchase Project has sparked activities to encourage teenagers and others to "travel the generations" by reading books that carry meaningful messages about old age. Through the Book Purchase Project, local AARP chapters and state and local Retired Teachers' Association units select and buy books on aging for local secondary schools and community libraries.

AARP also sponsors the "Growing Up—Growing Older" project. This is a film and discussion program that was designed to help children ages 9–11 years to develop positive attitudes toward aging by portraying the friendships that can exist between the young and the old. Another program integrating the generations is the "Youth Conferences with Older Americans" project. It provides an opportunity for secondary school students to learn about aging and to discuss issues of importance to all generations (AARP, 1984).

Until 1980, statistical information on the types and numbers of ongoing intergenerational programs in the United States was quite limited. In 1980, ACTION, the federal volunteer agency for RSVP, FGP, and VISTA established a Clearinghouse on Intergenerational Programs and Issues through its RSVP of Dane County,

Wisconsin Chapter. The outcome of this national survey of ACTION programs was four newsletters that were disseminated to all delegates to the 1981 White House Conference on Aging. "Intergenerational Clearinghouse on Programs and Issues" continues to be published as a quarterly newsletter that provides information on intergenerational programs and solicits articles and bibliographic information.

A politically active group that has spearheaded many intergenerational programs and issues is the Gray Panthers. In 1970, the Gray Panthers was founded by social activist Maggie Kuhn and five friends who envisioned a society in which old and young would share in our country's abundance. Their philosophy is that "the old and the young in our society have much to contribute to make our society more just and human, and that we need to reinforce each other in our goals, our strategy, and our action" (Gray Panthers, 1972). One of their major concerns deals with the reformation of the American education system so that it includes programs and opportunities for people of all age groups.

The National Council on the Aging (NCOA) has developed an array of intergenerational programs ranging from education for illiterate elders (Literacy Education for the Elderly Program), to matching older volunteers with chronically ill and disabled children (Family Friends), to finding jobs for disabled youth with help from older volunteers (Team Work). In 1986, NCOA and the Child Welfare League of America co-founded Generations United (GU): A National Coalition on Intergenerational Issues and Programs. By 1988, GU had expanded to include 110 national organizations whose goal is to act as a catalyst in the creation of national public policies and programs to assist people of all ages. GU is committed to searching for creative options that will bring together talents and resources across the generations in order to meet the shared needs and to provide solutions to problems that are unique to different age groups ("Think Intergenerationally," 1987).

In 1985, Tice reported that intergenerational programs could be found in all 50 states as evidenced by responses to questionnaires sent to state officials by New Age, Inc., a Center in Support of Intergenerational Education. The impetus for many of these programs is more increasingly being provided by dedicated individuals working in educational settings and in health and human service areas. During her tenure as U.S. Commissioner on Aging (1981–1984), Lennie-Marie P. Tolliver challenged individuals and communities across the nation to find new, untried approaches for increasing interaction among the generations. She stressed the importance of building bridges between the generations as longevity is increasing and four-generation families are becoming the norm in American Society (Struntz, 1985). Many individuals and communities have heeded the call. There are intergenerational orchestras, drama groups, dance companies, exercise groups, tutors, and caregivers all over the country.

Indeed, the last decade has seen a surge of intergenerational programs that are quite diverse in nature. To assist individuals, agencies, and organizations in their efforts to develop, implement, and promote age-integrated programs, several national resource centers have emerged. Descriptions of three intergenerational resource centers and some of the programs they offer are provided here.

Center for Intergenerational Learning
Temple University Institute on Aging
206 University Services Building
Philadelphia, PA 19122
(215) 787-6970
Director: Nancy Z. Henkin

This nonprofit organization is committed to fostering cooperation and exchange among people of different generations. Since 1980, the Center has developed programs that involve youth and elders in a variety of programs that promote interdependence across the generations. The Center for Intergenerational Learning also serves as a clearinghouse for information concerning intergenerational programming. Its resource library includes written materials profiling intergenerational programs, curricula on aging, research studies, evaluation tools, and public policy position papers. Other resources include video and slide-tape presentations, program development guides, intergenerational activity handbooks, program directories, and a quarterly newsletter.

The following are some of the model projects in intergenerational programming that have been developed in response to community needs and concerns.

- *Project LEIF (Learning English through Intergenerational Friendship)* pairs college-age volunteers with elderly refugees to tutor English as a second language. This program has become a national model and is replicated in four cities across the United States.
- *Full Circle Intergenerational Theater Troupe* is a performing ensemble of elders and teens who have skills in improvisational theater and develop skills that focus on issues that affect people as they move through the various stages of life.
- *ECHO (Elders and Children Helping each Other)* is designed to link elders who wish to become employed as child care workers with children in child care centers throughout the Philadelphia area.
- *Time Out* is a special program that links college students with families of frail elders. Students have the opportunity for part-time employment as respite workers and elders receive supervision and companionship.
- *S.O.S. (Sharing Our Skills)* unites retired tradespeople with vocational school students. The elder volunteers assist classroom teachers and guide students in career development.

The Center for Intergenerational Learning also provides training and consultation. The Center assists educators, human service practitioners, senior citizen center directors, child care providers, corporate managers, health care providers, or anyone who is concerned about improving the quality of life for young and old. The following programs focus on training and consultation.

- *Linking Lifetimes* is a program designed to integrate older adults and students in intergenerational programming at a neighborhood level.

- *Partners in Time* is a program designed to stimulate the development of intergenerational programs in religious settings.
- *Intergenerational Mitzvah Corps* focuses on facilitating program leaders in the development of cross-age activities in Jewish organizations, schools, agencies, and synagogues.
- *Delaware Valley Intergenerational Network (DELVIN)* promotes collaborative program planning and resource sharing among five county organizations representing human service and education networks.
- *Intergenerational Learning Retreat* has convened every summer since 1980. It is a five-day residential learning retreat designed to break down myths and stereotypes about aging and to foster understanding across the generations.
- *Across Ages* is a community-based organization that was an outgrowth of the first intergenerational retreat. It sponsors workshops, seminars, and community service projects.

Generations Together
811 William Pitt Union
University of Pittsburgh
(412) 624-5470
Director: Sally Newman

Generations Together of the University of Pittsburgh's Center for Social and Urban Research was established in 1978. Its purposes are as follows: (a) to reach out to the community and develop intergenerational programs that promote growth and understanding between young and older people, (b) to develop programs that facilitate linkages among human service agencies, (c) to conduct research on the effect of these programs, and (d) to disseminate information, both locally and nationally, on the research and development of intergenerational programs. Generations Together shares its expertise and experience with other professionals through conferences, community presentations, training packets, workshops, manuals, curricula materials, publications, and its nationally distributed newsletter, *Exchange*. The research conducted by Generations Together focuses on the impact of its intergenerational programs on the participating children, youth, and older adults. For the youth, the research investigates the effect of cross-age programs on their academic and social growth and on their attitudes toward aging. For the older adults, the research examines the impact of intergenerational programs on their well-being, life satisfaction, and on their attitudes toward children and youth.

The following are some of the innovative projects that illustrate the variety of outreach programs that have been pioneered by Generations Together.

- *Senior Citizen School Volunteer Program* is designed to provide opportunities for older people to serve as resources in classrooms in their community's schools.

- *Artist Resource Program* fosters an interchange of knowledge, skills, and appreciation between the generations by bringing together artists, teachers, and students in meaningful ongoing art experiences.
- *Providers of Intergenerational Child Care* trains and places older adults in jobs as child care aides.
- *Youth in Service to Elders* involves students who volunteer to provide service to elders in the community. It links students between the ages of 14 and 22 with frail homebound or institutionalized older people.

In addition to offering these programs, Generations Together is constantly evolving extensions of these basic program models. Some of these unique program developments involve at-risk youth from families in crisis, children with special needs, and latchkey children with active and frail elders from diverse ethnic, socioeconomic and racial backgrounds.

Understanding Aging, Inc.
Center for Understanding Aging
Framingham State College
Framingham, MA 01701
Director: Fran Pratt

The Center for Understanding Aging is the headquarters for Understanding Aging, Inc., a nonprofit organization supported by a national membership, by grants from foundations and government agencies, and by friends and sponsors. Understanding Aging, Inc., founded in 1983, had its origins in the Teaching and Learning About Aging (TLA) project. Project TLA, begun in 1979, focused on elementary and secondary educators. Understanding Aging, Inc. has enlarged the scope of that audience to include professionals from the biological and social sciences, gerontology, arts and humanities, health and human services, clergy, media, and all levels of education. The goals of this organization are as follows: (a) to educate the public about issues of aging, (b) to dispel myths about aging and old age, and (c) to encourage interaction and cooperation between generations. Understanding Aging, Inc. seeks to reverse patterns of agism and to build a social environment in our society wherein people of all ages can live together. This mandate is carried out through the following services and programs:

- *Consultation.* The staff and members are available to consult with individuals and groups needing assistance in planning or developing aging education or intergenerational activities.
- *Presentations.* A broad range of presentation services are available. Contracts are individually negotiated and designed to meet the needs of the client for short- or long-term services such as conference presentations, workshops, and staff development programs. Typical clients have included business and industry, libraries, service agencies, school districts, professional groups, colleges, churches, and civic organizations.

- *Information.* The Center individually responds to requests for information and assistance received by mail and telephone. Requests should be as specific as possible, especially when sent by mail. Small donations to cover the cost of responding (such as postage or photocopying) are appreciated, but not required.
- *Resource Center.* The Center contains hundreds of print and audio-visual resources for aging education and intergenerational programming.
- *Publications.* All publications of the TLA are now available from the Center for Understanding Aging. Publications include teacher resources and curriculum materials for a broad range of subjects in elementary and secondary schools.

A periodic newsletter, *Linkages,* provides updates on new publications, services, conferences, workshops, and other news relating to aging education and intergenerational programming.

Other Resource Centers

- Community Education Center on Aging
  2723 Foxcroft Road, Suite 211
  Little Rock, AR 72207

- Wisconsin Positive Youth Development Initiative Inc.
  30 W. Mifflin Street, Suite 310
  Madison, WI 53703

- New Age, Inc.
  1212 Roosevelt
  Ann Arbor, MI 48104

- Intergenerational Clearinghouse
  Retired Senior Volunteer Program of Dane County, Inc.
  540 W. Olin Avenue
  Madison, WI 53715

IMPLICATIONS FOR PLANNING, IMPLEMENTING, AND MAINTAINING INTERGENERATIONAL PROGRAMS

Newman (1986) outlined the necessary steps for developing a successful intergenerational program regardless of the setting or population involved. Before any formal planning begins, the agency initiating the program should conduct a needs assessment to identify the specific needs of the agency. After the needs are defined, then a partner agency should be chosen. At this point, planning may begin. The following five steps for planning should be employed:

1. Involve key decision makers from the beginning, and obtain a formal endorsement of the program from them.

2. Outline the goals and objectives of the program that address the needs of the collaborating agencies.
3. Meet with the community and agency leaders who can become resources to the program.
4. Prepare a written plan detailing the procedures, activities, and time line for the implementation of the program.
5. Delineate the roles and responsibilities of the participating agencies.

Once these steps are completed, recruitment of the participants and orientation and training of the staff and participants should typically occur. Tice (1985) stressed the importance of recruiting not only people of diverse ages but also people with multicultural diversity and people with different levels of achievement. Intergenerational programs offer excellent opportunities for generations to share the integrity of who they are.

Seefeldt, Jantz, Serock, and Bredekamp (1982) addressed the importance of including an educational component when training staff and participants. They pointed out that it is important to educate each generation about the other. It makes sense then to conduct an orientation for all participants before the generations are integrated in a cross-age program. To ensure the program's future success, Newman (1986) urged that maintenance and support activities such as scheduled events and public relations activities are crucial to the program's effectiveness and for reinforcing participants and staff members.

Tice (1985) suggested that organizations not only develop a written history of their program but also that each elder be invited to share his or her own history with the younger participants. These efforts not only can serve to strengthen the older person's identity but also create an awareness of the past, present, and future for the younger generation. Another consideration for successful cross-age program planning and implementation is an ongoing and end-of-the-year evaluation process that assesses the goals of the program, its effectiveness, and its impact on all the generations involved.

In her findings on contact between the generations, Seefeldt (1987) made the following recommendations for planning and designing intergenerational programs.

1. Protect the prestige of both young and old. Involve the elders in the planning of the activities, allowing them to select their role in the program.
2. Limit frustration for both adults and children by clearly identifying the parameters of their roles and the policies and procedures of the school or program. Baggett (1981) found that in an educational setting, teachers need to examine their attitudes toward aging and to be sensitized to the capabilities and limitations of older volunteers so that older adults are not stereotyped and automatically forced into the usual role of tutor to the children.
3. Plan time for the elders to have on-the-job training, to receive feedback from staff, and to meet with one another. These strategies will allow for interaction between the generations that has integrity and is functional.

4. Ensure that contact between the generations is intimate, pleasant, and rewarding by planning one-to-one contact. Recognizing the contribution of
the elders to the program through monetary reward or media coverage can
enhance the prestige of all generations involved.

STRATEGIES FOR THE FUTURE

In order to improve intergenerational relationships and encourage the implementation of intergenerational programs, we need to dispel the belief that cross-age
programs are only one-way avenues benefiting only one generation. Brahce (1980)
noted that the following strategies implemented at the local, state, national, and
international level may help to overcome this problem.

- Encourage youth and senior organizations to exchange opinions and strive
to find cooperative ways to overcome negative images of one another.
- Challenge the communications media to assist in changing the stereotyped
images of both young and old.
- Promote intergenerational linkages among such groups as the Girl Scouts,
Boy Scouts, 4-H Clubs, and so forth.
- Actively seek ways to effect changes in public policy by forming community political action groups. Examples of this on the national level are the
Intergenerational Library Literacy Act (H.R. 5486) and recent amendments
to the Older Americans' Act, which emphasizes intergenerational programs.
- Explore ways to involve policy makers, doctors, lawyers, and others from
public and private domains to ensure leadership roles in developing intergenerational sharing and pooling of resources.

Nishi-Strattner and Myers concluded that

*Intergenerational programs both within and outside the school setting, may
serve to facilitate educating young persons, may provide needed companionship for older people, may provide emotional and psychological support for
both generations, and may help teach children that growing old need not be a
frightening or hopeless experience. (Nishi-Strattner & Myers, 1983, p. 396)*

Newman (1980) pointed to some significant trends that may in the future help to
reunite the generations. The U.S. Department of Labor projected that American
families may not be as mobile in the next decade because of concerns for conserving
energy. Businesses and industries may focus on maintaining and expanding local
sites rather than encouraging geographic expansion. This may reduce the necessity
of separating generations of families. Newman's (1980) projections indicated that
elders are moving back from the sun belt areas to their hometowns and that many
recent college graduates are seeking jobs closer to their family's roots.

Baggett (1981) described the public education system as a prime environment for examining society's attitudes and stereotypes toward the elderly and for providing interventions such as intergenerational programs to challenge them (Fig. 1). The schools have always had a crucial role in transmitting the values and ethics that form children's behaviors and attitudes about aging. Schools have contributed to the isolation of the generations with their emphasis on peer relations. Often teachers and parents are misinformed about the process of aging and inadvertently reinforce negative feelings toward older people.

In 1981, Davis and Westbrook reported that there was limited use of curricula on aging by classroom teachers and that few schools provided opportunities for contact with people of different ages. However, since the early 1980s, school administrators and educators are becoming more aware of the educational implications of the age distribution of our citizens. With the ever-increasing ratio of older to younger people, administrators and educators are recognizing the importance of preparing young people to take a look at their lives over the entire life continuum in order to develop a more positive outlook on their future.

Wass, Fillmore, and Ward (1981) suggested that the majority of teachers would be more willing to include aging in the curriculum if the schools properly prepared them by providing inservice education and access to teaching and resource materials. Berkson and Griggs (1986) encouraged school counselors to assume a major role in aging education by collaborating with teachers in the planning, implementation, and evaluation of intergenerational programs. Hooyman and Kiyak (1988) emphasized that school personnel not only must present a curriculum on aging but also must create a learning environment in which students have an opportunity to interact with different types of elders so that they can understand variations in the aging process. Davis and Westbrook (1981) observed that without this interactive dialogue, children may never learn to question the stereotypes they have about growing older.

In 1986, Pratt observed that one of the most rapidly growing movements in education was in the area of intergenerational programming. Because aging is an interdisciplinary topic, it can be effectively woven into the curriculum without the addition of new courses or new faculty. Aging education can be integrated into language arts, social science studies, health education, dance, art, music, physical education, science, and home economics (Bottum, Metal-Corbin, & Corbin, 1985; Corbin et al., 1989; Leviton & Santa Maria, 1979; Metal-Corbin, 1983; Metal-Corbin, Corbin, & Barker, 1988).

Many educational institutions across the country have used the arts as the common ground for uniting the generations (Langdon & Metal-Corbin, 1988; Langdon, Metal-Corbin, & Greenblatt, 1986; Manheimer, 1986; Metal-Corbin & Foltz, 1985; Pratt, 1986; Romberger, 1988; Scollon & Metal-Corbin, 1983; Scollon, Metal-Corbin, & Foltz, 1985). Other programs in places of worship (Adams, 1988) and community centers (Caplow-Lindner & Harpaz, 1988; Lerman, 1984) have used dance and music to help participants gain a better understanding and a deeper appreciation of their shared religious, ethnic, and national heritage.

FIGURE 1   A three generation exercise class. Photograph by Bob Whitmore.

Henig (1988) reported on the intangible benefits that schools receive from intergenerational programs. Children are exposed to good role models of aging adults and have the opportunity to develop a cadre of friends from another generation. At the same time, the older people become informed about the inner workings of the school and are more likely to vote for school board issues because of their personal involvement in the educational process. Auerbach and Levenson (1977) predicted that the university classroom would increasingly become an arena for a great deal of intergenerational contact. Universities would benefit financially from the increased enrollment of the older population and older students would benefit by improved physical and emotional health.

Beattie (1974) suggested that there is a critical need for all students in gerontology to work with older people not only in classes and laboratories on campus but also in a variety of community settings. It is imperative that students learn to relate to well elders as well as impaired elders. Beattie proposed that gerontology program administrators need to invest in the well-being and lives of older people in the community by providing linkages between the academic setting and society-at-large and to also invest in faculty emeriti addressing the needs of retired faculty.

It is apparent that intergenerational programs offer great promise for the future. If they are properly planned, implemented, and evaluated, they can greatly enrich the lives of young and old. The consequences of not getting involved in intergenerational programs might be an ever-widening schism in the generation gap that will contribute to a class warfare among the generations. The intergenerational programs that are already operating show us that we can avoid these problems and that indeed we can build intergenerational ties that are stronger than ever.

REFERENCES

Abrams, R. S. (1986). Intergenerational caregiving: A new twist to an old tradition. *Perspective on Aging, 15*(6), 19–21.

Adams, D. (1988). Dance for older adults in a worship setting. In R. K. Beal & S. Berryman-Miller (Eds.), *Dance for the older adult: Focus on dance XI* (pp. 126–127). Reston, VA: American Alliance for Health, Physical Education, Recreation and Dance.

American Association of Retired Persons. (1984). Hand in hand: Intergenerational activities unite young and old. In *Community programs idea book: A volunteer's guide*. Washington, DC: AARP Publications.

Amir, Y. (1969). Contact hypothesis in ethnic relations. *Psychological Bulletin, 71*(5), 319–342.

Auerbach, D., & Levenson, R. (1977). Second impressions: Attitude change in college studies toward the elderly. *Gerontologist, 17*(4), 362–366.

Baggett, S. (1981). Attitudinal consequences of older adult volunteers in the public school setting. *Educational Gerontology, 7*(1), 21–31.

Beattie, W. M. (1974). Gerontology curricula: Multidisciplinary frameworks, interdisciplinary structures, and disciplinary depth. *Gerontologist, 14*(6), 545–549.

Beck, J. (1988, December 5). Generational jealousies begin to flare. *Omaha World Herald,* p. 10.

Bekker, K. D., & Taylor, C. (1966). Attitudes toward the aged in a multi-generational sample. *Journal of Gerontology, 16,* 115–118.

Berkson, J., & Griggs, S. (1986). An intergenerational program at a middle school. *The School Counselor, 34*(2), 140–143.

Bottum, D. (Director/Producer), Metal-Corbin, J. (Project Director), & Corbin, D. E. (Writer/Narrator). (1985). *Age doesn't matter: Weaving dance and aging into a fifth grade curriculum* [Videotape]. Omaha, NE: University of Nebraska at Omaha Television.

Brahce, C. (1980). Intergenerational linkage: An emerging field for policy formulation and funding. *Grants Magazine, 3,* 169–175.

Caplow-Lindner, E., & Harpaz, L. (1988). A moving experience: Young children and older adults. In R. K. Beal & S. Berryman-Miller (Eds.), *Dance for the older adult: Focus on dance XI* (pp. 128–132). Reston, VA: American Association for Health, Physical Education, Recreation and Dance.

Caspi, A. (1984). Contact hypothesis and inter-age attitudes: A field study of cross-age contact. *Social Psychology Quarterly, 47,* 74–80.

Corbin, D. E., Kagan, D., & Metal-Corbin, J. (1987). A content analysis of an intergenerational unit on aging in a sixth grade classroom. *Educational Gerontology, 13*(5), 403–410.

Corbin, D. E., Metal-Corbin, J., & Barg, C. (1989). Teaching about aging in the elementary school: A one-year follow-up. *Educational Gerontology, 15,* 103–109.

Davis, R. H., & Westbrook, G. J. (1981). Intergenerational dialogues: A tested educational program for children. *Educational Gerontology, 7,* 383–396.

Fairlie, H. (1988, March). Talkin' 'bout my generation. *The New Republic*, pp. 19–22.

Glass, J. C., & Trent, C. (1980). Changing a ninth-graders' attitude toward older persons. *Research on Aging, 2*(4), 199–512.

Gray Panthers. (1972). *Age and youth in action* [Brochure]. Philadelphia, PA: Author.

Henig, R. M. (1988, July/August). Forging ties that ignore age. *AARP Bulletin*, pp. 8–9.

Hooyman, N., & Kiyak, H. A. (1988). *Social gerontology: A multidisciplinary perspective*. Boston: Allyn & Bacon.

Immorlica, A. G. (1980). The effect of intergenerational contact on children's perceptions of old people. (Doctoral dissertation, University of Southern California). *Dissertation Abstracts International, 40*, 56218.

Langdon, J. (Producer/Director), & Metal-Corbin, J. (Choreographer). (1988). *A good age: A collection of dances for women over fifty-five* [Videotape]. Omaha, NE: University of Nebraska at Omaha Television.

Langdon, J. (Producer/Director), Metal-Corbin, J. (Director/Choreographer), & Greenblatt, D. (Composer). (1986). *Out of the shadow, into the light* [Videotape]. Omaha, NE: University of Nebraska at Omaha Television.

Lerman, L. (1984). *Teaching dance to senior adults*. Springfield, IL: Charles C Thomas.

Leviton, D., & Santa Maria, L. (1979). The adults' health and developmental program: Descriptive and evaluative data. *Gerontology, 19*(6), 534–543.

MacLean, M. J., & Marcus, L. (1981). The role of senior consultants in a course on aging. *Educational Gerontology, 6*(2–3), 241–250.

Manheimer, R. (1986). Common ground for generations through arts and humanities. *Perspective on Aging, 15*, 15–17.

Mead, M. (1970). *Culture and commitment*. Garden City, NY: Natural History Press/Doubleday.

Mead, M. (1977, March). Grandparents as educators. *The Saturday Evening Post*, pp. 54–59.

Metal-Corbin, J. (1983). Shared movement programs: College students and older adults. *Journal of Physical Education, Recreation and Dance, 54*(5), 46, 50.

Metal-Corbin, J., Corbin, D. E., & Barker, G. (1988). Age doesn't matter: Weaving dance and aging into a fifth grade curriculum. In R. K. Beal & S. Berryman-Miller (Eds.), *Dance for the older adult: Focus on dance XI* (pp. 88–96). Reston, VA: American Alliance for Health, Physical Education, Recreation and Dance.

Metal-Corbin, J., & Foltz, R. (1985). All my grandmothers could sing: An interdisciplinary and intergenerational choreographic work. *Journal of Physical Education, Recreation and Dance, 55*(9), 52–55.

Newman, S. (1980, September). *Rationale for linking the generations*. Statement presented at the National Council on the Aging Mini-Conference, Athens, GA.

Newman, S. (1985a, July). *The impact of the school volunteering experience on the life satisfaction of senior citizens*. Paper presented at the 13th International Congress of Gerontology, New York, NY.

Newman, S. (1985b). The impact of intergenerational programs on children's growth and on older persons' life satisfaction. In K. A. Struntz & S. Reville (Eds.), *Growing together: An intergenerational sourcebook* (pp. 22–24). Washington, DC: American Association of Retired Persons.

Newman, S. (1986). Sharing skills, experience key to interaction between young and old. *Perspective on Aging, 15,* 6–7, 9.

Nishi-Strattner, M., & Myers, J. (1983). Attitudes toward the elderly: An intergenerational examination. *Educational Gerontology, 9*(5–6), 389–397.

Peacock, E. W., & Talley, W. M. (1984). Intergenerational contact: A way to counteract ageism. *Educational Gerontology, 10,* 13–24.

Pratt, F. (1984, August/September). Teaching today's kids—tomorrow's elders. *Aging,* 19–26.

Pratt, F. (1986). Aging education aim to prepare youth for long life. *Perspective on Aging, 15*(6), 4–5, 27.

Romberger, M. (1988). Arts across the generations. *Intergenerational Clearinghouse, 6*(1), 1.

Rosencranz, H. A., & McNevin, T. E. (1969). A factor analysis of attitudes toward the aged. *Gerontologist, 3,* 71–77.

Scollon, W. (Director/Producer), & Metal-Corbin, J. (Project Director). (1983). *Old friends: An intergenerational approach to dance* [Videotape]. Omaha, NE: University of Nebraska at Omaha Television.

Scollon, W. (Producer/Director), Metal-Corbin, J. (Director/Choreographer), & Foltz, R. (Composer). (1985). *All my grandmothers could sing* [Videotape]. Omaha, NE: University of Nebraska at Omaha Television.

Secunda, V. (1984). *By youth possessed.* Indianapolis: Bobbs-Merrill.

Seefeldt, C. (1987). Intergenerational programs: Making them work. *Childhood Education, 64*(1), 14–19.

Seefeldt, C., Jantz, R. K., Galper, A., & Serock, K. (1977). *Children's attitudes toward the elderly: Curriculum implementation* (Final Report). College Park, MD: University of Maryland.

Seefeldt, A., Jantz, R., Serock, K., & Bredekamp, S. (1982). Elderly persons' attitudes toward children. *Educational Gerontology, 8*(5), 493–505.

Sheehan, R. (1978). Young children's contact with the elderly. *Journal of Gerontology, 33,* 567–574.

Struntz, K. A., & Reville, S. (Eds.). (1985). *Growing together: An intergenerational sourcebook.* Washington, DC: American Association of Retired Persons.

Think intergenerationally. (1987, April). *Generations United: Newsline,* p. 4.

Thorp, K. (Ed.). (1985). *Intergenerational programs: A resource for community renewal.* Madison, WI: Wisconsin Positive Youth Development Initiative, Inc.

Tice, C. H. (1982). A gift from the older generation: Continuity. *Children Today, 11*(5), 2–6.

Tice, C. H. (1985). Perspectives on intergenerational initiatives: Past, present and future. *Children Today, 14*(5), 6–10.

Ventura-Merkel, C. (1986). Perspectives on intergenerational issues and programs. *Perspective on Aging, 15*(6), 2, 13.

Versen, G. (1986). Senior adults in the undergraduate classroom. *Educational Gerontology, 12,* 417–428.

Wass, H., Fillmore, D., & Ward, L. (1981). Education about aging: A rationale. *Educational Gerontology, 7*(4), 355–361.

9

EVALUATION OF EDUCATIONAL PROGRAMS IN SOCIAL GERONTOLOGY

THOMAS A. RICH

University of South Florida

Several recent reviews of evaluation in education point to both the need for and the problems of application of current methodologies (Phi Delta Kappa National Study Committee on Evaluation, 1971; Perloff, Perloff, & Sussna, 1976). In Perloff et al. (1976), some of the anxieties and resistances to evaluation as well as some of the technical problems are discussed. They point out that

> *Since program evaluation is still clearly in its infancy as a field of study and is yet to achieve the cohesion and the tautness expected in the multidiscipline field let alone a unitary discipline, it would be presumptuous, prodigal and even disruptive to wrap up the field in a neat package, pontificating upon its past and prescribing its future. (p. 587)*

Pfeiffer (1972) also pointed out that it is well known that it is difficult to evaluate training programs in medical schools, nursing schools, or other types of institutions; but he indicates a need for evaluation to be made. In other references, the lack of funding for evaluation is also cited as a frequent problem. In the literature examined, evaluations of educational programs, such as educational gerontology, are more noted for discussions of the difficulties involved than of workable methods.

In this chapter, I undertake a discussion of goals and objectives, as these are the primary basis for setting up an evaluation schema. Who sets these goals and what the priorities become is a topic of concern. Research necessary for understanding the background of existing programs, consumer needs, and projections of needs is an integral part of goal and objective setting. Descriptions of target populations, specific objectives for measurement, implementation steps, methods of measurement, methods of feedback to existing and new programs, and evaluation of the product of the programs are also a part of the present concern. My recommendations are very basic, but they represent a beginning.

GROWTH PROBLEMS:
ACADEMIC AND FEDERAL ISSUES

Examination and development of evaluative procedures in gerontological education and training programs go beyond academic exercises in accountability and have serious implications for the survival of the field. With some important exceptions, as noted in Kushner and Bunch (1967), today's education and training programs are the offspring of the Older Americans Act of 1965, which created the Administration on Aging. To a lesser extent, the National Institute of Child Health and Human Development has also influenced program development. The national recognition of the increasing magnitude of the problems of older people, both in numbers and in substantive issues to be dealt with, helped bring about this mid-1960s birth of academic programs. Their future growth and development face many uncertainties and the infant mortality rate may be high.

Several factors contribute to the problems of survival of educational programs throughout the country. Many of today's new programs born in the 1960s and early 1970s benefited from the educational boom in which many people felt, despite reports to the contrary (Mayhew, 1970), that higher education could expand indefinitely. Increasing faculty size, turning out more Ph.D.s, and continuing growth were seen as inevitable. Labor-force reports such as those by the Carnegie Commission and by professional societies all seemed to be ignored until we turned the corner on 1970 and, indeed, even until a little later when the country began to experience the combined effects of recession and inflation. Educational institutions suddenly moved into a period of retrenchment. This change is generally observable across the country; all programs are being systematically examined by a variety of means of evaluation and measures of accountability to determine which ones should be provided where, or whether they should be provided at all. In the last five years of growth, with expansion in areas of service delivery, research, and teaching, programs have been sharply curtailed by economic realities.

In view of this upward surge in the 1960s and retrenchment in the 1970s, the role of the federal government is interesting and complex in that its capacity or desire for leadership in the field of gerontology seems to have diminished. The early promise was for continuing funding and for the development of an academic discipline that was new and that offered something to a neglected segment of our population. That promise now seems to have become diffused by lower federal priorities that have resulted in a retreat into the issuing of uncertain guidelines and into decreasing allocations for training, research, and demonstration throughout the states. Although the

National Institute of Aging (NIA) may rectify this situation through increased research funds, present federal policies, though not clear enough to be criticized adequately, appear to lead gerontology futher into uncertainty by continuing to give priority to seeding new programs all over the country at undergraduate and graduate levels and in a variety of training settings. At a time when there is such fierce competition for dollars from established disciplines within universities and colleges, th.s dilution of programs can only lead to further confusion and disorganization in the field. In sum, it appears that federal policy is based on seeding new programs, which, in effect, create an ever-widening pool of underfunded programs. New programs cannot properly be staffed in many settings, and short-term training, although useful for professionals who have some related background, will never supplant the need for more fully trained workers in all areas of gerontology.

I have set out to provide the rationale for evaluation in the policy area in gerontology. It is true that we have sufficient professional and disciplinary demands for evaluation for quality education and perhaps this should be enough. For a fledging discipline, however, fathered by serious advocates of the field of gerontology (Tibbitts and others) and now caught in its middle childhood between the whimsical parenting of uncertain leadership in Washington and the stern disciplinarian of academic retrenchment, we are potentially in crisis. The strength in the field of gerontology is presently in the disciplines associated with it. The methodology of those disciplines and the gerontological content are sufficient, if marshaled together, for a careful development of the field, keeping national educational priorities (not synonymous with federal priorities) in mind. Funding priorities indirectly set the program objectives that are necessary for evaluation.

In this chapter, I make recommendations that will allow those who agree to build upon them and those who disagree to provide better alternatives. The issues must be faced and the answers that are arrived at by concerned persons in the field will ultimately be useful to all. In my review of the potential for evaluation that now exists, the following areas are discussed:

Background issues related to evaluation processes
The development of a national consultative body
Utilization of a case history approach
A measurable objectives approach
Job analysis and worker development studies
Follow-up evaluation of graduates
Consumer studies: quality of service and satisfaction

Considering the age of the field, it is certainly premature to attempt to impose stringent accountability requirements on the variety of new programs inasmuch as they are usually still developing their objectives or goals, staffing, population to be reached, or functions of the students. We do need, however, to provide specific and formal guidelines useful to academic administrators in budget-minded university and college settings throughout the country in developing new programs. Evaluation should provide a basis for decision making, for program monitoring through feedback, and finally, for assessing the impact of training on the consumer.

BACKGROUND ISSUES IN GERONTOLOGY

Despite the problems, in many ways the growth of education in gerontology has been phenomenal in recent years. Several landmark publications document this growth and the issues of concern to the field. A brief backward look at where the field has been may help illuminate the issues of today. In 1967, a committee of the section on psychological and social sciences of the Gerontological Society published their report, *Graduate Education in Aging within the Social Sciences.* Its issues are still with us, paraphrased from Kushner and Webber (1967) as follows:

1. Gerontological training as single discipline, multidiscipline, or both
2. Workforce needs present and projected to solve problems of the aged
3. Issues on breadth or specialization of training
4. An emphasis on incorporating social gerontology as an area of specialization within the established social science disciplines
5. Consideration of training in social gerontology as an independent discipline
6. Specialized training for professional services
7. Kinds of research facilities
8. A review of current status of education in social gerontology, with models examined

In each issue, questions yet to be answered are raised: How to train whom for what about what in which setting to serve whom?

The next major review of the state of the art in education and training was the 1971 White House Conference on Aging statement *Training—Background and Issues,* by Birren, Gribbin, and Woodruff (1971). They noted that, while compared to the 1960s, growth has been rapid, "from evidence presented in this report that in relation to surveyed and demonstrated need, the amount of training and education activities in the field is astonishingly low" (p. 1). Thus we see an apparent, rapid growth in training far outdistanced by current and projected increases in the proportion of older people in our society.

The issues emerging from this background paper (Birren, Gribbin, & Woodruff, 1971) were:

1. *Given, that manpower development in aging is lagging seriously behind the proven need, should responsibility for the development of a more vigorous national plan and continuing surveillance of training be lodged in a single Federal agency created for the purpose? Or, should funds be made available to several Federal agencies for the support of manpower training in accordance with their individual perceptions of needs, as at present?*

2. *Should policy formation and planning for manpower training in aging be the sole responsibility of government agencies having statutory responsibility for programs and services for older people? Or should these functions be shared with nongovernmental groups such as scientific and professional organization and organizations of older and retired persons?*

3. *Should the major focus and priority be placed on doctoral-level training for teaching and research? Or, should equal or greater priority be placed on short- and long-term training of professional and semiprofessional personnel for planning and delivery of services to the older population?*

4. *Should there be developed regional university-based multidisciplinary training centers in gerontology? Or, should research and training be fostered in a wide range of colleges and universities in individual departments or multidisciplinary programs in gerontology?*

5. *Is the need for personnel especially trained for serving the older population and for teaching and research critical enough to call for continued or increased Federal and State government financial support? Or, should educational institutions at all levels build training for work in aging into their programs and look to their established sources (State appropriations, tutition, gifts, and foundations) for support?*

6. *In allocating funds for support and recruitment of personnel to be trained in aging, should priority be given to young persons yet to make a career commitment? Or, should the major focus be on providing knowledge and skills in aging to persons who have had work experience in other areas or who may have retired? (pp. 73–78)*

Many of these issues are similar to the ones cited earlier. The major new ingredient is the concern about locus of responsibility for planning and development, government or nongovernment support, and sources of support.

By 1974, the White House conference issues remained unresolved and the new ones had risen. The 1974 *Gerontologist* devoted part of one issue to "The Real World and the Ivory Tower: Dialectics of Professional Training, Education, and Delivery of Services to Elderly Persons." Beattie (1974) introduced a set of propositions with implications for evaluation. The propositions are offered as suggestive for those who wish to develop programs in gerontology. They are:

1. *That the development of gerontological programs for research, education and training, and practice must be carried out within the context of the changes occurring within higher education itself and the societal forces which impinge on higher education.*

2. *That the status of gerontology in higher education is similar to the status of older persons in the society—low in visibility, low in prestige, and low in recognition and rewards.*

3. *That gerontology is related, with varying degrees of identity and intensity, to all disciplines—scientific and humanistic—and professions.*

4. *That a conceptual-philosophical framework is essential for determining administrative and curricula goals and strategies and for the clarification of research, teaching, and service responsibilities and priorities.*

5. *That administrative strategies and understandings in regard to a multidisciplinary setting for interdisciplinary linkages and disciplinary depth are essential if we are to move beyond isolated unidimensional course offerings to substantial commitments of resources—faculty, facilities, and fiscal—for the development of gerontological programs relevant to academic and societal needs.*

6. *That one or two faculty committed and working in the area of gerontology does not constitute a gerontological program. Rather, the goal should be to work toward a critical mass of faculty within and among academic units.*

7. *That there is need for all students, regardless of career goal—research, education and training, or service (and these goals are not dichotomous)—to have, in addition to the class-laboratory cognitive learning of the campus, affective learning with older persons in a variety of community settings. The goal is for students to know, relate to, and learn from and with the "well" aged, as well as the "impaired" aged.*

8. *That the elderly have important contributions to make on the campus and in the classroom and should: (1) be envisioned as colleagues and contributors; (2) have access to the resources of higher education—students, faculty, administration, and facilities—to meet their own needs and identities in pursuit of lifetime learning, new careers, and in the formulation of life goals; and, (3) contribute to academic programs as mentors, tutors, and educators in their own right.*

9. *That students of all ages have a participatory role and contributions to make to the design of their learning and the institutional curricula arrangements vis-a-vis gerontology.*

10. *That academic institutions offering work in gerontology must be willing to invest and give of themselves in affecting the well-being and lives of older persons in the larger society.*[1]

From three perspectives, Kushner and Bunch (1967), Birren, Gribbin, and Woodruff (1971), Beattie (1974), I have drawn issues that share great commonalities and suggest questions for evaluation. Where possible, the common issues are dealt with in the body of this chapter in the context of suggestions for approaches to evaluation. A common theme of several basic unanswered questions is found in all three documents reviewed; it has been put in the form of questions common to the documents and combined and summarized as follows.

Who Should Do the Planning and Set Priorities for Program Development in Gerontology?

A critical mass of personnel and resources in gerontology exists in higher education and should be mobilized to do definitive planning and set priorities for the field. An input system from active programs should be developed so that the widest possible range of information is available for decision making and disseminating such decisions. Moreover, the decision-making power of active programs should be greatly enlarged. It was appalling to me as a professional gerontologist to sit at a recent meeting of the Association for Gerontology in Higher Education and speculate with a group of other training-program directors concerning the potential directions in which a federal agency might point us in the coming year. At the same time, a meeting was going on to tell us in the business of education, training, and research in the social and behavioral sciences, which directions and priorities would be set by another agency. The fact that higher education gave up its initiative for the sake of money some years ago does not mean that we could not become leaders rather than followers in the search for new ideas and new programs.

If a unit in a higher education system asked whether it should have a program in gerontology, we should be available to help answer that question. Not all would ask and not all would care to hear the answer, but the fact that professional guidance and counsel is available would be appreciated by many. This would contrast sharply with the present approach, which is largely that of meeting the guidlines for a new contract from the Administration on Aging, guidelines set by unknown faces and reviewed by the same unknown faces.

[1]Copyright 1974 by The Gerontological Society. Reprinted by permission. From "Gerontology Curricula: Multidisciplinary Frameworks, Interdisciplinary Structures, and Disciplinary Depth" by Walter M. Beattie, Jr., *The Gerontologist*, Volume 14, No. 6, 1974, pp. 545–548.

What Are the Workforce Needs
and Who Determines Them?

Some years ago the regional Office on Aging in Atlanta conducted a workforce study and found that there was indeed a need for knowledge and training in the field of aging (Smyth & Cole, 1963). We must keep in mind, however, that if such a study had been done ten years ago and had asked how many people were seeking a master's in gerontology, we would never have started any programming because the answer would have been zero. We are in a position of creating a workforce need, to provide services that have never been provided, from an educated base that has never existed. There are enough graduates from a variety of training programs in gerontology presently working in the field so that more sophisticated job analysis and workforce studies could be conducted today. We need better job analysis of the kinds of functions being served by the graduates of our programs and appropriate change in programming where necessary.

Barriers to employment still exist in the field of gerontology, and many major agencies such as the Veterans Administration do not recognize a master's degree in gerontology. Many state merit systems or civil service systems have not incorporated training and education in gerontology into jobs that are related to the field of aging, although some accept them in lieu of, perhaps, a master of social work. These barriers need to be an active target in every state and in the federal government. The Administration on Aging, the very agency that has funded most of the training, has never made any real effort, to my knowledge, to require that their programs be operated by people trained in the field of aging.

What Kinds of Academic Structures
Should Be Supported?

A quick tally of my own information and a look at the Association for Gerontology in Higher Education (AGHE) *National Directory of Education Programs in Gerontology* reveal something over 35 different names under which gerontology programs are being offered. This diversity probably leads to considerable confusion among students who wish to get training in gerontology and encounter everything from an elderly services program to an all-university gerontology center to an institute to a human life center.

The continuous review and updating of the status of available programs throughout the nation would be most useful as a planning device. At present, based on the AGHE catalog, the structure appears to be something like the following:

1. Single-course offerings, either in gerontology or within disciplines that assist students with the following goals:
   a. Understanding the life cycle
   b. Changing attitudes concerning aging

    c. Acquiring elective credit in general education
    d. Developing career interest
2. Core concentration of courses, wherein several courses relating to gerontology are found grouped together, usually called "gerontology," that assist
students with the following goals:
    a. Understanding the life cycle
    b. Changing attitudes
    c. Acquiring elective credits or fulfilling minors
    d. Developing career interests and getting work-related training, such as an
       associate of arts program for nurses' aids, community aids, or recrea-
       tion workers
3. Bachelor of arts in gerontology; assists students with the same goals as
listed above and, in addition, with:
    a. Providing a career entry level for jobs
    b. Serving as a ladder for further graduate study
4. Master of arts in gerontology or in other disciplines such as sociology,
psychology, economics, or political science with provision for doctoral level
study
5. M.A. in gerontology—considered a terminal service degree
6. Ph.D. in a discipline, with gerontology or developmental specialty
7. Other college or community programs that are primarily service

As the field matures a more functional classification system will emerge. The
listing provided, however, is illustrative of the present state of development.

    At this point, the word *center* seems to be the key, and almost every
college has its own center of gerontology. The centers range from well-
developed and structured programs to one person who has named herself or
himself a center. They range from centers resembling the partial vacuum
found in the center of a tornado; to centers that gather together all
age-related activities on a campus, list them in a brochure, and call the result a
center; to those performing multidisciplinary and multifaceted roles both
within the university community and the community at large. There are
enough different kinds of institutional structures existing now so that we
could make some professional comparisons of their strengths and weaknesses
in terms of general program objectives.

Where Should the Emphasis
Be Placed in the Career Ladder?

    All of the steps on the academic career ladder, from the associate of arts
to the bachelor of arts to the masters of arts to the Ph.D, and also
intermediate steps with certificates and specialty degrees, are developing. The
issue is whether or how we encourage and assist, and in what ways, the
development of this career ladder. Many students begin with an associate of

arts degree, are trained as nursing aides, home health care technicians, mental health service technicians, or a whole range of other titles, and may or may not work actively in the field. What will their next step be, to the bachelor of arts or to a master's or PhD? Some programs clearly should be assisted in helping develop training programs appropriate for serving their own areas or regions. Others may have the resources and ability to train workers who might be useful or employable anywhere in the nation and at a different career-ladder level.

What Are the Relative Merits of Short-term and Long-term Training?

Research on the impact on knowledge, attitude, and practice of short-term and long-term training would greatly assist in providing data to answer the question. Meanwhile we probably will continue to train and educate on the basis of individual biases. To some, short-term training is a way of widening the pool of undertrained workers, and to others, long-term training is a way of making junior academicians who do not understand practice in the field. Neither view needs to be correct. We can clearly question, however, whether the limited federal dollars should be split down the middle for short-term and long-term training. The priority may actually be misplaced because long-term training is needed to produce people with bachelors' and masters' degrees in gerontology to staff programs in agencies for the aging. Given a base or background in gerontology to start with, short-term training in agency management, budgeting, grant preparation, public relations, and many of the other tasks that are necessary in the field becomes meaningful. On the other hand, using short-term training (and it's usually very short and on someone else's terms) to effectively bring about knowledge, attitude, and practice changes in someone who is not trained at all in the field is probably a waste of time and money, although it looks good on paper.

What Should Be the Relative Contributions of Teaching, Research, and Service from Academic Settings?

We often separate these three categories for the sake of faculty evaluation and sometimes for the sake of requesting outside funds to help operate a program. In fact, as most people in the academic world know, they are mutually complementary and virtually inseparable. Universities differ greatly in their capacity to do basic research and often, because of their location, to do service. Guidelines and advice from other institutions involved in the multifaceted roles could be helpful in getting institutions to set priorities. The choices are sometimes simple yet difficult in that the question may be Should I spend the time to teach one more course in introductory gerontology, or take the same time to develop an evaluation plan for a community aging program, or make some other direct service contribution?

What are the Advantages and Disadvantages of the Trend of Role Reversal Whereby the Federal Establishment Asks the Questions and Universities Scramble to Find Answers?

My phrasing of the question reveals my bias. Meeting short deadlines for short-range answers drains creative thought about the real issues in aging. Some of the government's contracts, model projects, and request for proposals may result in better utilization of current knowledge, but the new knowledge gap widens.

RECOMMENDATIONS

Develop a National, Consultative Body

If this is to be accomplished, some changes in the current approach to programming must take place in gerontology. First, a separation of academic status from Washington is necessary. Budgeting, priority setting, research direction, and planning have been done without adequate representation of the concerned publics—us. How is this to be accomplished? The most obvious vehicle is the Association for Gerontology in Higher Education in association with the Gerontological Society and other groups such as the First National Congress on Education in Gerontology; together, they might carry out the development and implementation of an adequate evaluation model.

If this proposal were accepted and the Association for Gerontology in Higher Education or some other body of scholars developed an interest in carrying out these objectives, what would they do in relation to program planning and evaluation in gerontology? I would suggest the following:

1. Establish a planning committee to project population change and its implications for workforce needs and social policy over the next 20 years, on a national, regional, and local basis.
2. Provide consultation, at cost only, to the wide range of institutions contemplating gerontology programs to help them analyze resources within area needs, national needs, staffing needs, and development of clear program goals. This would be consultative and not restrictive.
3. Provide consultation to existing programs on the direction for future growth and development.
4. Develop a curriculum-exchange center so that the best possible teaching materials would be available.

5. Establish relationships with foundations and other private sources of funds.
6. Provide input to AOA; NIA; National Institute of Mental Health; and regional, state, and area offices on aging.

Use a Case History Approach

In addition to developing a consultative body to provide the myriad kinds of inputs that would be helpful to a program, it could be of great value to develop case histories of existing programs sampled from the various types found around the country. A format should be developed that would include kind of sanction provided for a program at what levels in the university and system, kind of administrative structure, nature and sources of funding, and a year-by-year accounting of progress. Although such a case history would follow a general outline, it would also allow for the idiosyncratic differences that exist in programs to be shared and so provide many answers to problems presented daily by people attempting to begin programs.

The issues go further than those listed above in that the relationship of the university structure with the outside community should be explored. The use, composition, and function of advisory or policy-making bodies is of continuing interest in this area. Case histories could be useful here, too.

The determination and development of new curricula based on program goals and objectives and how they are accomplished need to be shared. Many of the inquiries received concerning program development say simply, "We are starting a new program in gerontology and need materials. Can you help us?" From a collection of perhaps 20 case histories, many of the kinds of questions and answers posed by people considering starting programs could be answered, many of the pitfalls could be avoided, and a sharing could take place that would be healthy and useful for a young discipline trying to set its own directions and goals.

Take a Measurable Objectives Approach

All programs should, with some guidance, be able to set measurable objectives in concrete terms. These can range from reaching certain kinds of students to offering certain numbers of courses to certain numbers of graduates in long-term training programs. At the same time, short-term training programs would offer more immediate feedback both on change in direct, day-to-day working skills and in evaluations of further need for training.

A number of models for program evaluation exist, although few have worked effectively in the field of education. In the area of nonformal education, which has received considerable interest in the last few years, the knowledge, attitude, practice, and effectiveness (KAPE) model seems to be one worthy of discussion in the total process of evaluation of educational programs in social gerontology. By utilizing this model, a simple, skeleton outline can be developed so that first levels of knowledge and expected change based on the kind of input being provided are identified. Next, levels of attitude and expected change based on the kind of input being provided are identified. Then, an attempt is made to identify behavior changes, again based on the kind of knowledge and attitude data provided. Last, effectiveness measures are provided to demonstrate whether the practices that are observed are truly more effective and more useful than those seen before.

Provide Funds for Job Analysis

To determine the nature and quality of training in aging that is required to fill jobs in public and private agencies, and then to convert these findings into programmatic changes, job analysis is needed. Planning should be based on projections of changes in workforce needs for the aging population over the next 20 years and should not rely only on current problems. The need for continual planning for dealing with today's problems and for projecting needs for future service-delivery systems is critical.

Systematically Follow Up Graduates

Students who have graduated from an associate of arts, bachelor's, or graduate program should be followed up nationally to find out if they are filling places in the job market as needed. Studies of their concerns and interests and the services they provide should be conducted. Such feedback would help develop a reliable bank of workforce information and, in addition, expand the boundaries of work inasmuch as many students show initiative and innovativeness in ways far beyond program aspirations and fit their training into new settings and new services. As long as we remember that the students are likely to know more than we have taught them and therefore to utilize this information in effective ways, we have a reliable source of new data. Yearly follow-up of graduates in gerontology at the University of South Florida, for example, reveals high employment in age-related positions as well as suggestions for program revision.

Plan Consumer-Service-and-Satisfaction Follow-ups

Working with agencies, again public and private, to determine levels of consumer service and satisfaction would be useful for providing feedback in a formal way. A study of graduates with training in aging, with level of training controlled, to determine how they are employed should be carried out in relation to quality of service.

Measuring consumer satisfaction from older clients would be a useful index of services provided. The only danger here is that all resources cannot be devoted to dealing with today's problems; many must instead be devoted to program-planning and prevention aspects so that better services will be developed for people not yet in the older age category. It might well be that proper reconsideration of priorities would place emphasis on prevention services to people in the middle years at least equal to the emphasis on services to people in the older years, where most resources have been concentrated.

SUMMARY

In this chapter, I have examined and reviewed some of the paper issues that have influenced the development of gerontology over the past decade. I have treated the growth of the field of gerontology from the perspective of social policy, from the views of members of the profession of gerontology, and by consideration of the special conditions placed on the field by its emergence at a time of national and academic retrenchment. The development and application of evaluation procedures in gerontological education and training is necessary for its continued growth and development. The rigor of the evaluation required reflects a time of accountability in our society. Other, more established disciplines are just now beginning to be questioned, and new ones must meet the standards of proof of need.

In setting educationally and socially appropriate goals for education in gerontology, we provide the basis for the measurement of effectiveness and in turn a justification for the existence of the field. In this world of finite resources, priorities will, I hope, be set based on the data that we provide and not on historical precedent or whims of the federal or educational bureaucracy.

Although the technology of evaluation may be viewed as both in its infancy and in a state of disorder, there are evaluation approaches that can be applied to many of the pressing problems concerning the field. In this chapter, I have suggested six different approaches; and they provide different ways of appraising programs, from the use of outside, consultative bodies to the development of meaningful measures of goals, objectives, and products of the program. None of the approaches requires great expenditures of dollars, and all could be applied immediately to most areas of programming in gerontology. Certainly, more clear-cut communication links between guideline makers, funding sources, program planners, and program operators could be established with minimum funding and modest goodwill. The very process of evaluation becomes less disorderly if it is applied to the stage appropriate to the field. We are still gathering data and need interchange of descriptive information about current programs.

In today's growth and confusion in the field, there is the real opportunity for advancement to a discipline of gerontology. All of the evaluation approaches discussed have considerable potential for adding information about where we are and should be going in the field. If we apply ourselves to the problem of evaluation of the developing gerontological programs of education, research, and service; we will have more knowledge about the impact of gerontological programs on this nation than that available to any other educational program.

REFERENCES

Association for Gerontology in Higher Education. (1976). *National directory of education programs in education.* Draft Edition, University of Wisconsin, Madison.

Baker, E. L., & Popham, W. J. (1973). *Expanding dimensions of instructional objectives.* Englewood Cliffs, NJ: Prentice-Hall.

Beattie, W. M., Jr. (1974). Gerontology curricula: Multidisciplinary frameworks, interdisciplinary structures, and disciplinary depth. *The Gerontologist, 14,* 545–548.

Birren, J. E., Gribbin, K., & Woodruff, D. S. (1971). *Training—Background and issues.* Washington, DC: White House Conference on Aging.

Blummon, P. D. (1971). *Behavioral objectives: Teachers success through student performance.* Chicago: Science Research.

Elias, M. F. (1974). Symposium—The real world and the ivory tower: Dialectics of professional training, education and delivery of services to older persons. *The Gerontologist, 14,* 525–553.

Kushner, R. E., & Bunch, M. (Eds.). (1967). *Graduate education in aging within the social sciences.* Ann Arbor: University of Michigan.

Kushner, R. E., & Webber, I. L. (1967). Summary. In R. E. Kushner & M. Bunch (Eds.), *Graduate education in aging within the social sciences* (pp. 110–112). Ann Arbor: University of Michigan.

Mayhew, L. B. (1970). *Graduate and professional education, 1980.* New York: McGraw-Hill.

Perloff, R., Perloff, E., & Sussna, E. (1976). Program evaluation. In M. Rosenzweig & L. Porter (Eds.), *Annual Review of Psychology, 27,* 569–590.

Pfeiffer, E. (1972). Translating aging research into training: Getting the job done systematically. In *Training needs for services to the elderly* (pp. 1–18). Atlanta, GA: Southern Regional Education Board.

Phi Delta Kappa National Study Committee on Evaluation. (1971). *Educational evaluation/decision making.* Itasca, IL: F. E. Peacock.

Popham, W. J., & Baker, E. L. (1970). *Planning an instructional sequence.* Englewood Cliffs, NJ: Prentice-Hall.

Smyth, V. M., & Cole, W. E. (1963). A regional assessment of personnel and training needs. In J. C. Dixon (Ed.), *Continuing education in the late years.* Gainesville: University of Florida Press.

Yeager, J. L., & Robertson, E. A. (1974). Academic planning in higher education. *Management Forum, 3*(7), 1–4.

10

CAREER EDUCATION FOR THE PREPARATION OF PRACTITIONERS IN GERONTOLOGY, WITH SPECIAL REFERENCE TO ADULT EDUCATORS

MARGARET E. HARTFORD*
University of Southern California

The inclusion of content on aging in the curricula of career education in the human services becomes increasingly imperative, if we accept the premise, based on a demographic prediction of population trends, that practically all workers being educated today for the human services will spend some part of their careers in practice with or in behalf of older adults. An increasing proportion of workers will specialize in the field of aging, in developing or working in new service areas directly related to older adults. Career education in this chapter refers to the preparation of nurses, adult educators, primary and secondary teachers, medical doctors, dentists, public administrators, librarians, social workers, lawyers, occupational therapists, recreation workers, clergy, planners and architects, public health administrators, business administrators, and others who work directly for or in behalf of the human services.

Consideration is given in this chapter to some of the rationale, educational design, and curricular aspects of content on aging for all students in the human services and for those students specializing in services particular to the field of aging. Note is taken of career education at the community college level, the baccalaureate level, and the master's level of professional education. The students in professional education today show no age boundaries. They may be young adults in the late teens or 20s, in their initial educational preparation; second-career people in their 30s to their 50s; and third-career or retired people from their mid-50s to their 70s, preparing for professional work with their peers. It is not the intent in this chapter to neglect doctoral studies, in which much of the basic research on gerontology

Professor emeritus.

takes place, but rather to focus more sharply on professional education, which in most of the human services is centered at the undergraduate and first-graduate levels.

With the decreasing birth rate, lower mortality rates, and newer methods of prolonging human vigor and productivity both through disease control and through greater understanding of the circulatory, respiratory, digestive and endocrine systems, a new, more vigorous, and potentially more involved older population is emerging. It is a population that may spend almost as long out of the work force in retirement as it spent working, if present employment practices and attitudes continue. The implications for economics, social relationships, life-styles, health services, housing, and for various other education, welfare, and health programs begin to open up new horizons.

Siegal and O'Leary (1973) predict that the population of the United States will become stationary very early in the twenty-first century. Once the population has stabilized, it will rapidly begin to get proportionately older, provided the birth rate stays the same and the mortality rate decreases. When the young students of today reach the prime of their careers in 15 or 20 years, it may be predicted that a vast proportion of their practice will be with or about older adults and their families, in social policy and planning, in individual care, education, support, and counseling. The aged will no longer be the exception or the recipients of marginal services but will become central to many services. It is imperative that such a predictable population shift and consequent need for services be anticipated today with a preventive, epidemiological approach. Planning, development, and program design should be undertaken now and in the immediate years ahead to establish the necessary approaches, programs, and services. Today's students should be as well prepared as possible with knowledge about aging, should develop skill in working with and in behalf of older adults, and should develop a philosophy and an attitudinal set that encourages enlightened engagement in appropriate practice. They must also develop skills in divergent thinking in order to find new solutions to both old and newly emergent problems.

The thesis put forth by the futurists, including Alvin Toffler in his book *The Eco-spasm Report* (1975), is that the society must seek new approaches to the social changes that are occurring: in occupations, where white-collar jobs have outnumbered blue-collar jobs; in family life-styles, in which old patterns no longer serve the needs of much of the population, particularly those of older adults; and in geographic and social changes and the mobility of a highly transient society in which people must make or break old relationships and build new ones with things, places, people, and organizations at an ever more rapid pace. Preparing students in the human services for work with and in behalf of older adults and for the creation of new programs and services as yet undreamed of is, without a doubt, part of the wave of the future. Not only do the demographic predictions for the years ahead suggest changes in types of services, but the social changes in the economy, in family life-styles, in employment patterns, in retirement and leisure patterns, in population transiency and mobility, and in the rapid obsolescence of things, customs, problem solutions, and relationships—all these social changes combine to shake the very core of our culture, our socialization process, and the ways we have learned to cope with life about us. Our generation is affected, as are those who came before and come after us. Although we hold onto the fundamentals of our foundations, our beliefs, our knowledge, and the science that has emerged from our cultural heritage; we may at the same time find ourselves at the epicenter of so much cultural and social shaking that, if we do not have the flexibility to bounce and rock with the tremors, we may crumble because of a rigid tenacity that does not permit response to change. For students to be not just prepared for the present, but to be responsive to, even be leaders of the future, career education must take into account the rapidly changing future and the population trends and accompanying social needs of a society that is growing older.

The demand for flexibility may lead us to look at newer modes of curriculum development, new styles of teaching, and new arrangements of available knowledge. The intent is that graduates who become professional workers in the human services will have in-depth mastery of the content of an array of social problems as well as the mastery of technical skills in several modes of intervention in individual and group approaches to education, therapy, and growth of individuals, families, and other small groups. Students should also learn some administration and management, some planning and program development, some coordination and collaboration of services, and some community organization and change. Graduates in the human services specializing in gerontology may need both administrative skills and the capacity to work directly with older adults.

It is evident that professional practitioners—especially educators, health practitioners, social workers, and others who are used to working directly with individuals and families—must learn to find the sources of support not only for funding but also for the organization of citizen support, for the formation of boards and councils, for the preparation of proposals for the development of programs and the location of funds, for determining the nature of policy issues, and for seeking out the laws and regulations supporting certain types of programs. This administrative knowledge and skill must accompany the capacity for program design, curriculum development, and teaching or practitioner skill.

Some educators in professions have been concerned that students in their brief, professional education programs might not be able to master all of these skills nor the necessary range of knowledge of the many kinds of social problems. True, in no field do students master a professional practice in an educational program; rather, they are exposed to options; and they are given an opportunity to try their skills; and they may develop a beginning competence in assessing situations, making judgments, and acting deliberately in a variety of modalities. Real mastery, however, comes with time. Students should be exposed to the potential for growth in many areas of approach. Mastery, in the futurists terms, may be a capacity for the flexibility needed to transfer knowledge and technical skill from one situation to another. Professional education sets the frame of reference, develops the attitudes, teaches the basic skills, provides, we hope, the base on which the graduates grow and develop their own styles and capacities. This is the framework within which the following educational designs in curriculum development and the models for preparing human-services practitioners to work with and in behalf of older adults have been developed.

THE CHANGING FUTURE

As we seek new ways to work with the issues in gerontology that are emerging in our society and as we find new ways to view life with a new focus, we will prepare students for these changes and for a flexibility in the face of future conditions. Toffler (1975) predicts, for instance, that full employment most probably will never mean the return to highly industrialized labor force; rather it will take place through an expanding development of new service jobs, especially those involved in providing more adequately for the elderly. New kinds of jobs in new types of programs will be emerging, as the nature of the social problems associated with an increased older population becomes clear. Thus we may find a larger and somewhat different group of students seeking professional or career education. They will not only need to be educated for providing the services now available, but they will also need to be stimulated to create new and imaginative approaches toward the newly emerging aging population, which has experienced a different history and has a different set of social and educational needs from the aging population that preceded it.

For example, in viewing the trend toward age segregation that has characterized retirement homes, public housing for seniors, and nursing homes for the elderly, Margaret Mead (*Los Angeles Times,* May 4, 1975) suggests that we need to find a way to have a mixed society in which grandparents live down the block—not in the house, but a short distance away—and therefore can provide a place for the teenager to run away to for 24 hours. Fifty years go, when there was less mobility and transience, and when fewer of our grandparents lived into their 80s, 90s, and 100s, some of us had the opportunity to live with or near our grandparents. Today, in most of the country, the grandparents are either back in the community from which the family moved, or in Florida or Arizona, or in a retirement community, senior apartment complex, or nursing home where they cannot have overnight guests. They may be on the other side of town, but they are probably on the other side of the country. If we could have mixed communities, as Mead suggests,

"Grandma could come over and house sit for the plumber for the several days it may take him to arrive." To carry the idea a little further, in the mixed society, the son or the daughter or the in-laws can take grandparents who can no longer drive shopping, to the doctor, to the bank, or to the club, without either generation having to give up their privacy or their independence.

How Human Services Education
Must Adapt

From where we are today, however, such a society will necessitate a different approach to social problem analysis, program planning, and service delivery. It would also have to emerge from a different set of social values than are present today, either about aging or in the self-fulling prophecy that has captured the older adults themselves—the work ethic, role definition by productivity, the youth culture, the nuclear-family life-style, or the obsolescence of the old. Professional education in the human services will have to preface its skills training with some value modification in students to parallel that which must come in society. Social planners and social philosophers may need to work on encouraging and facilitating age-integrated communities and family life-styles as well as age-integrated classrooms and activities. We may, in fact, need busing of older adults to educational programs so that they may be integrated within the classes and programs.

Professional education for the human services, therefore, must have a heavy component on philosophy, values, and value changes related to aging and agism. Not only should there be curriculum content and educational experiences designed to affect the students' attitudes, but students also need to be prepared with the methodological approaches with which to change attitudes about age in individuals and in the society as a whole. They will need to be prepared to help older adults to avoid being caught up in the self-fulling prophecy that has caused some of them to believe in the stereotypes about aging and to thus behave in such a way as to further perpetuate these false ideas. Mixing age groups in the classroom is one helpful way to work on this matter.

Two examples of the programatic aspects that future adult educators must be able to consider are: (1) senior-adult educational programs in which social relationships, finding new peers, and gaining a sense of adequacy are *as* important as learning the subject matter, and (2) assistance and preparation for new careers after 60 and developing competency in them. Adult educators will also begin developing educational programs for residents of nursing homes whose bodies may be limited but whose minds can respond to education and learning; who may suffer physical limitations from strokes, Parkinson's, or other disabilities, but who also have the potential to keep learning and enjoying the life about them. Activity of this type has only begun in very limited amounts and holds a tremendous potential.

Shifting Composition
of Student Bodies

If we follow the predictions of the futurists and again look at population trends, we may see a shift in the composition of the student bodies of professional schools. People seeking career education, especially in work with and in behalf of older adults, may have somewhat different characteristics than in the past. Already we see signs of this shift in the young people who want to vocationalize their college education at the community college or baccalaureate level. They want a solid academic education, but they want occupational or job-related content and experience also. Some of these students are attracted to the field of practice with older adults because they have found a challenge in conditions they have observed in nursing homes or old, residential hotels in the central city, crowded with lonely and isolated old people; they have visited grandparents in segregated, retirement communities with plush surroundings and equipment and have seen the overeager participants frantically trying to find things to do to keep busy; or they have worked in senior centers where there is need for some organization and direction for self-developed activities. Young people with these experiences are seeking professional education to enhance their skill to work in these kinds of positions and to facilitate the development of social relationships in people who have lost mates, peers, occupations, or meaningful connections. Adult educational programs are a way for older people to achieve new social relationships and new roles as well as preventing their disengagement, isolation, and obsolescence in the rapidly changing society.

A second segment of students who indicate interest in the practice of social gerontology are middle-aged adults, in their 30s to their 50s seeking second careers. They are frequently people with some life experiences that equip them for service careers. They are seeking professional education at all three levels: community college, baccalaureate, and master's. Some of them are disenchanted with their business dealings. Others have become obsolete in aerospace, industry, automotive manufacturing, insurance, real estate, public education, or the military. Some are homemakers whose families are old enough to allow them to be away from home all day or who wish to define themselves with a service type of vocational activity. These second-career students see in the field of aging an opportunity for a new professional activity, and they know they are needed. Many of these people have also experienced the responsibility for an older relative, at home, in a nursing home, or in another part of the country, and are convinced that society has not come up with adequate services. They are seeking new education to prepare themselves for employment opportunities in the field of aging.

As educators, we are discovering that the motivation, interest, learning capacity, demands, and expectations of second-career students are somewhat different from those of young adults just preparing for their first work experience. Education designed for second-career students must make use of what they already know, must rearrange knowledge and values, must teach new skills, and may have a heavy component of attitude change. It must also take into account the threatening nature of midstream shifts and the consequent possibility of expressions of anxiety, but it will also be rewarded by the rapid acceleration toward learning once middle-aged students have pulled themselves together and found new direction.

The third category of students is older people themselves. Some who have been retired for several years wish to prepare themselves to work professionaly with their own peers, not only on a volunteer basis, but within the workforce, providing services for older adults, in health, welfare, education, or social services; in recreation, volunteerism, nutrition, nursing care, housing, or social relationships.

In light of the evidence regarding job placement and career opportunities for people in their later years, if we accept these students, we may also need to accept some responsibility for placing them or at least, once they have completed their work, for getting them in contact with potential employers. We need to be more innovative in developing career education opportunities to prepare older adults to become human-services workers— gerontologists themselves—who design programs, develop services, administer organizations, and teach courses for their peers, not only on a volunteer basis but on a regular, professional level.

There are many examples of older people who have gained or retained leadership in the arts, in professions, and in politics; we also see leadership emerging among the older adults in the field of aging. We need only look at the Senior Community Service Project program, administered by the Department of Labor via several of the organizations for older adults, including the American Association of Retired Persons/National Retired Teachers Association (AARP/NRTA) and the National Council on Aging (NCOA), in which retired professsionals are employed to design, develop, and expand a program to find employment opportunities for people over 55. Most of the administrative staff of this program were employed after retirement from full careers in other professions. Consider Ethel Percy Andrus who designed and launched the NRTA and later the AARP after she retired as a school principal. She founded an organization that pioneered in obtaining benefits for older adults in insurance, housing, travel, recreation, education, and legislation. Consider Maggie Kuhn who organized the Gray Panthers, a major advocacy organization, after her retirement from traditional human services; Ollie Randall of the NCOA who continues to fly about the country speaking brilliantly to conferences and conventions; or Arthur Flemming who continued as commissioner on aging in his later years. Look at the many highly paid executive consultants and workshop leaders in agencies for the aged who have retired from the YMCA, welfare councils, or community chests. Many people now retiring, early or later, have indicated an interest and have enrolled in formal educational preparation for turning to new careers in social gerontology, social services in aging, and adult education geared to older students.

Surely in education for the professions, where we understand engagement, mastery, independence, and the importance of a personal contribution to the welfare of others as a means of keeping involved; we should be the first to engage people in an educational process to work in their own behalf and that of their peers. We should lead the way in dropping age barriers to education, employment, and program development and in recognizing the contributions to their peers of people over 60. This may mean modification both in age criteria for admission to professional schools and in tuition requirements. It also means access to scholarships and student loans that now have age cutoff points. There is enough evidence now from research on brain cells, on memory, on continued learning capacity, and on motivation to counteract the old stereotypes about the ability of people to continue to learn throughout life, provided there is motivation and the opportunity to do so. Content and curriculum on aging is an ideal and natural spot in human-services education for those older adults who are interested, are motivated, and have the capacity to engage in the rigors of study. What we know about andragogy (the education of adults), which makes use of peer teaching of each other based on the knowledge acquired through life experience and previous study, is particularly applicable to second- and third-career students. Perhaps we need to develop a new class of education called *geragogy,* "education of and by the old." Geragogy, if such should exist, would consist of education that includes a high component of self-pacesetting, social interaction and relationships, activity to maximize involvement, use of the talents of each individual, and continuous learning.

Objectives

From the rationale for career education that includes gerontology and an exploration of the types of students and their motivation to enter careers in gerontology, the educational objectives begin to emerge:

1. To provide *all* students in education for the human services with some exposure to course content related to gerontology and some practical field experience in working with or in behalf of older adults
2. To provide *some* students with expertise, or a specialization, in working with and in behalf of older students
3. On the basis of the predictions of the future regarding the social, health, and educational needs of older adults, to include philosophical and attitudinal content regarding the meaning of aging and its implications for older adults in the society
4. To integrate content on the specific needs of older adults with content on children; adolescents; early adulthood; and special social

problem areas such as delinquency, drugs, education, housing, mental retardation, race and ethnicity, family relationships, alcoholism, mental health, health care, and recreation inasmuch as all of these areas touch upon one or another apsect of the problems of the older population

5. To establish a teaching style that leads students to a flexibility in their approach to practice that will make it possible for all practitioners to transfer knowledge and practice skills from one modality and content area to another and to provide a potential for more future practice with and in behalf of older adults

CURRICULUM DESIGN FOR THE FUTURE

In considering curricular design, each department, program, or school generates for itself the general component parts of knowledge, skill, and value that are peculiar to its context, region, or particular leadership and educational approach. There continues to be debate about:

Life span approaches to human behavior versus a systems approach
Developmental versus behaviorist theory of human functioning
Social problems versus intervention modality approaches to teaching practice or methods
Historical versus existential approaches to social policy
Theoretical versus experiential teaching of knowledge

It is more appropriate here to consider more specifically the content that students need to know and what they need to be able to do to work with older adults.

Content

Social Policy All human-services practitioners should know (1) the provisions of the Social Security Act and its amendments; (2) the Older Americans Act, the services provided through each of its titles, and the local services of any given geographical area that have been funded as a result of the act; and (3) the Medicare provisions and the procedures for taking advantage of them. Students should know how to go about discovering and locating all of the services for older adults that exist in any given community. They should be familiar with state licensing of nursing homes and other institutional facilities. They should know the educational provisions for older adults within their areas; for example, community colleges, boards of education, universities and colleges, community centers, and private clubs and forums. They should understand the working of probate court as it relates to the elderly. They need some grounding in legal procedures and the resources for legal protection of the elderly. They should know about the senior volunteer programs, the employment programs for senior adults, and the various adult educational programs geared to retired adults. They need to be aware of special consumer affairs and citizen protection programs that serve as resources for older people.

Specialists in gerontology may need a great deal more knowledge on public social policy and may want a good grasp of the history of services for the elderly and some grasp of the economic and demographic factors that affect them. Specialists also need to be able to analyze existing laws and regulations and to begin to develop some know-how about changing inadequate laws and regulations. Whether this content is taught in a general social policy course or in an age-specific course will depend on the context, the resources, and the total program.

Human Behavior and Social Environment Whereas knowledge of the biology and physiology of aging, the psychology of aging, and the sociology of aging are important theoretical bases, especially at the undergraduate level, even more important are the relationships between health and nutrition; e.g., the effect of diet on digestion, circulation, and respiration, and the relationship of all of these to mood, mental health, thinking, and problem-solving capacity. Knowledge of the relationship of exercise to depression, relaxation, sleep, nutrition, and the capacity for gratifying interpersonal relationships is important. All of these factors are also interrelated with isolation, alienation, social relationships, self-image, territoriality, and social functioning.

Curriculum content in aging should have meaning in the career education program at the applied level, as research findings are translated from understanding of concepts into program development, service design and delivery, legislative provisions, and economic support. The scientific knowledge is preliminary; the applied biopsychosocial sciences are at another level that would constitute the real heart of career education. Such teaching may require a new kind of teacher in career education who can develop the *theories of the middle range,* that is, applied theories for practice.

From the generalized knowledge about aging to be integrated with practice, there can be taken specific knowledge applicable to populations in double jeopardy; e.g., the aged poor, aged blacks, aged Chicanos, aged Asian people, who face double discrimination and double liability. The healthy elderly, who face certain role changes and economic, status, and place losses, comprise a different segment of society from the frail or ill elderly. Part of the educational aspect of the human-behavior and social-environment content should be an understanding of the various subsections of the aged population, by age, health, and sex differentials; by socioeconomic, racial and ethnic, generational, and regional differences; and by historical experiences.

Practice Skills Graduates who will work specifically in the field of aging will need to be taught a mixture of intervention modalities, or practice skills. Whereas they need to be able to use individual and group methods for working with older adults and their relatives, they also need skill in program planning, development, and administration. Experts in social gerontology will discover that the demands for new and innovative services to meet the emerging needs of older adults will require the most imaginative use of knowledge and skills for developing services and programs. Students, therefore, must have some theory and experience in practice that will provide them with alternative modes of problem solving to use once they have assessed the given conditions. In fact, social gerontologists should be able to engage many potential clients in their own assessment and design of programs and plans for themselves.

As practitioners who use the findings of social and biological research in designing programs and delivery services, they may realize, for instance, that many programs discriminate against racial and ethnic minorities. Consider the emerging facts that the average life expectancy for black men is 60 and for black women is 62; yet all blacks who are employed pay into a Social Security plan from which less than 50% of them will benefit (Jackson, 1974)). Consider the fact that, at any one moment, no more than approximately one million, or 5–10%, of the aged are in any kind of institutions for health care; yet the health-care service provisions of Medicare, for instance, are available only for hospital services or attendance of a doctor. Ethal Shanus (Shanus & Sussman, 1976) has estimated that about two million people over 70 are confined to their homes by health problems, but never have the services of a doctor, hence never benefiting from Medicare. Provisions for home health care, home medical attention, and home nursing care are lacking in many areas and not given programmatic support (Shanus & Sussman, 1976). These kinds of factors become policy issues of concern to human-services workers in their planning as well as in their work with older adults and their families. The students should be helped to recognize findings of research such as those that show effects on larger numbers of older adults; and they should learn how to find ways to translate the findings into services. Some political sophistication is also essential for workers as they recognize the need for new laws, bills, regulations, court orders, and licensing, and as they gain access to lawmakers. Human-service workers specializing in gerontology should gain credibility and influence through their practice in the real world of specific problems of older adults and their relatives and through the application of their analyses of social and biological research.

Thus all workers in gerontology need some knowledge of individual and group methods for working with individuals, families, and unrelated groups; and in program development, design, administration, planning, community development and organization, and social and environmental planning. Workers whose emphasis may be on individual work will nonetheless find that they need some social and community skills. Workers whose emphasis is on legislative action, community organization, or work with systems will also need some firsthand knowledge and skill in working with individual old people and their relatives. Thus, all workers' education should include knowledge and practice at the micro and macro levels of programs and service delivery.

Philosophy and Beliefs Human-services students must confront their own attitudes that are products of a culture that rewards youth and productive work. They may be *agist* without realizing it, so subtle is the tendency to patronize, sentimentalize, or reject old people. They must also acknowledge some responsibility for changing the attitudes of those about them, none the least of whom may be older adults themselves who have come to believe stereotypes about themselves as a self-fulfilling prophecy. They must come to terms with the meaning of life and of death and learn to help others with these values and realities. They must view the aged person as one with a life to live, with the capacity to function even with pervasive illness and disease, with a thrust toward physical and mental health despite some deterioration. When death is inevitable, they must be able to help the person and the family to face and handle their emotions, their beliefs, and the reality of death. They must deal with the tendency to sentimentalize and be overprotective of older adults; they must not encourage dependency where independence may be important; yet they must support dependency where it is indicated. These attitudes, this philosophy, and these capacities come, not just through books, lectures, and discussions, but also through interaction with people who are experiencing these crises. Thus a good emphasis on gerontology in career education means some direct contact with older people within the services that are being studied.

Research Workers in gerontology must be knowledgeable consumers of research. They need their own beginning mastery of research methodology and statistics, scientific method, problem analysis and research design, and the appropriate types of research methodology for the study of social problems and the evaluation of programs. Most particularly, they need enough knowledge to read and to make use of authoritative research in gerontology in order to translate the findings into programmatic development. They need to be able to see researchable questions and problems in their practice in order to suggest studies for the scientists, even if they are not in a position to do research themselves.

Levels

So how does all of this translate into curriculum at the various levels of education, and with various models of learning and teaching? Surely the students at all levels need the fundamental knowledge of the aging person and the interrelatedness of the bio–psycho–social developments and dysfunctions. In fact, a time may come soon when a course in gerontology, a multidisciplinary, multiprofessional approach to understanding the aging, may appear as an elective or a requirement in primary, secondary, and higher education programs for general public consumption; right along with basic English, languages, social studies or sociology, psychology, biology, chemistry, physics, and math. The content of this course will prove crucial to the understanding of life and living. At the community college level, this fundamental knowledge may be in the form of an overview with preparation to practice as an associate, as a paraprofessional aide, or as a health or social assistant. At the baccalaureate level, it may be descriptive and provide a sound academic knowledge as preparation either for further graduate study, or for entry jobs in practice of recreation, adult education, health care, technical assistance, or social services. For all students at the master's level, there should be (1) considerable searching out of primary data from research; (2) the integration of the data into some comprehensive view of aging and its effects on the people, and, in the process, (3) the acquisition of the ability to transfer knowledge from one situation to another. Those who would specialize in aging would go into greater depth with some of the major studies, their findings, and the implications for work with older adults and their families.

Summary

All students, from community college to master's level, should have basic knowledge of the Social Security Act and its amendments, the Medicare provisions, and the Older Americans Act. The specialists will need to know how to process applications for Social Security and Medicare, a special skill in itself. They will also need knowledge both of ways of acquiring funds for programs and of the existence of local programs developed from the Older Americans Act. The specialists will also need familiarity with state laws covering nursing homes, institutions, and health plans. The undergraduates need familiarty; the graduates need experience in conceptualizing such provisions into services and programs.

Some of the content on values, philosophy, and beliefs; on specific skills translated for work with older adults and their relatives; on knowledge of the basic legal provisions for older adults; and on biopsychosocial development should be in curricula for all human-services workers. Some examples of research related to aging should permeate all of professional education. The specialists in gerontology need additional, elective courses to go into depth in human behavior theory as it relates to aging, services for aging, working with older adults, and programs and social policy related to the elderly. The undergraduate programs should have basic knowledge and some practice with older adults. Master's-level students should have knowledge and research integrated with some practice with older adults and their families and some practice at the administrative and planning levels of practice in programs for older adults.

THE FUTURE BEGINS NOW

As we look to the future, then, we can anticipate that in the human services of health, welfare, and education, more attention will need to be paid to education for designing programs, establishing services, and working directly with older adults. The demographers and the futurists give us the message. If we look around us now, however, we will see that already there is a large population of unserved, or inadequately or inappropriately served, older men and women. Responsibility for the preparation for careers in the development of innovative and imaginative services rests to a large degree with the educators at both the undergraduate and graduate levels. Somehow we must spark our students to become excited about developing the new frontier of social gerontology.

REFERENCES

Eisele, F. (Ed.). (1974, September). Political consequences of aging. *The Annals*.

Harris, L., & Associates. (1975). *The myth and reality of aging in America*. Washington, DC: National Council on the Aging.

Jackson, J. J. (1974, September). NCBA, black aged and politics. *The Annals*, p. 415.

Shanus, E., & Sussman, M. B. (1976). *The elderly, the family and bureaucracy*. Durham, NC: Duke University Press.

Siegal, J., & O'Leary, W. (1973). Some demographic aspects of aging in the United States. In *Current Population Reports* (Special Reports, Series P. 23, No. 43). p. 6, Washington, DC: Government Printing Office.

Toffler, A. (1975). *The eco-spasm report*. New York: Bantam.

Woodruff, D. S., & Birren, J. E. (Eds.). (1975). *Aging: Scientific perspectives and social issues*. New York: D. Van Nostrand.

11

CREATIVE BEHAVIOR AND EDUCATION: AN AVENUE FOR LIFE–SPAN DEVELOPMENT

JOY H. DOHR
MARGARET PORTILLO
University of Wisconsin at Madison

Living for me is creative action; I am unsatisfied with simply existing. I can't help it—it is part of my makeup. I want to know every moment how I can refine and intensify my relation with the world, and every moment make some definite contribution.

Ansel Adams

INTRODUCTION

Growth in maturity and wisdom, life course adaptation and integration, productivity, and sustained purpose in life are all concerns for optimal aging. A case has been made for the necessity of understanding life-span patterns that enhance such outcomes (Ward, 1984). Developments in gerontology have given new meanings to the reality of mature adulthood, and these developments require new approaches in research and in education. But what domains contribute to optimal aging, and how can we develop programs that stimulate such well-being?

The premise of this chapter is that creative activity through educational offerings maintain and enhance lifelong development. Although we assume that creativeness is a human capacity that may be studied in a variety of content areas, our discussion is directed toward creative, expressive, productivity. Writing, visual arts, design, music, and drama are no less important to older adults than they are to younger people. Research in creativity and aging is beginning to warrant more attention in an area that has focused almost exclusively on the earlier part of life.

In order to explore avenues to optimal aging within a context of education and creative activity, we must step back and examine existing interrelationships among these constructs. Are there compatible underlying assumptions between frameworks of life-span development and creativeness? What developmental components are involved? How might a conceptual framework, uniting perspectives on creativity and human development, be useful for educators interested in promoting optimal aging? How can programs be structured to respond to both subjective and objective aspects of creative activity? Finally, what knowledge is gained for the field by examining the topic of creativeness in older adults? In fact, might not creative productivity be an index of well-being in aging?

Research on life-span productivity alone logically supports creative activity. Productivity studies most often focus on employment, volunteer work, and household work (Kahn, 1986). Whereas findings show age-related declines in employment and volunteer work patterns, declines are not noted in household work. What surfaces for our consideration is not so much specific content areas or thresholds and valleys of production, but the conceptualization of a public versus private sphere of activity. In educational gerontology, an activity that spans both private and public spheres would seem to be desirable for community life and aging networks. We suggest that creative activity does span both spheres. Evidence shows that creative activity can yield social benefits of public recognition, increased family interest, social networking, and product dissemination. Psychological benefits such as thought stimulation, goal setting, enhanced self-esteem, and perceived improvement of health have also been noted (Dohr & Forbess, 1986; Greenberg, 1987; Hoffman, Greenberg, & Fitzner, 1980). Thus manifest creative production would appear to encourage an expressive exchange or communication between the adult and larger community in addition to stimulating learning and self-discovery.

Although creative behavior has typically been understood in a psychological realm, more recent writings take a social–psychological perspective on manifest creativity (Amabile, 1983; Simonton, 1977). Furthermore, Amabile has been concerned with the paucity of empirical research regarding specific social factors that influence creativity. Dohr (1984; Dohr & Forbess, 1986) has argued that additional meaning is gained when aesthetic perspectives are combined with social–psychological views. The study of creativity is often criticized because of its interdisciplinary nature and its dynamic and experiential character. Creativity, development, and education may all be viewed as processes as well as products. Therefore, converging on a common meaning is difficult. Creative activity and education alike must stand scrutiny from internal and external viewpoints. In order to address these issues, we first present a framework that incorporates four components of creativeness: person, process, product, and perceiver. We then discuss the interdependence among the components and their relations to personal and social development. Interest in clarifying a sense of time and place has not only been recognized in gerontology, but is also called for in design domains. We conclude with a discussion of program development issues.

AN INTEGRATIVE FRAMEWORK FOR CREATIVENESS AND AGING

Creativeness is not a unidimensional concept. The explanation that creativity is a construct of personality, product, process, and environment has gained wide acceptance and use in literature, and many publications offer excellent reviews of creativity (e.g., Davis, 1986). Motivational interest, thinking, making, and evaluative appreciation are all involved in creativity (Gardner, 1982; Gruber, 1981; Taylor, 1971). These complexities multiply when one examines creativity in the context of aging. Concerns have been voiced about cohort effects (Alpaugh & Birren, 1977; Alpaugh, Parham, Cole, & Birren, 1982); how creativity is defined and measured (Romaniuk & Romaniuk, 1981; Romaniuk, Romaniuk, Sprecher, & Cones, 1984); and the need for social as well as psychological interpretations of creativity (Dohr & Forbess, 1986).

In order to better understand creative behavior in aging, we developed a framework that originated from aesthetic design by Boyd (1976). Boyd outlined a relation among person, product, and perceiver/community. We extended this notion to structure meaning and interrelationships of the previously cited psychological, social, and aesthetic components of creative activity. Only after applying this three-part equation in Dohr's studies of manifestly creative older adults, did the integrative framework for creative development and productivity begin to emerge (see Figure 1). Five basic tenets support any one of the creative components (e.g. person, process, product, or perceiver). These tenets are appropriate to domain-specific questions in art and design and are compatible with developmental theory in aging.

First, creative action as supported by research in creativity and experiential reports is a three-way communication endeavor—not a two-way exchange. A creative person initiates and expresses ideas in a product. In turn, the product communicates objective and subjective imagery that allows evaluation by the same person in a new role of perceiver or by other members of a community. To focus on an isolated aspect of this trilogy denies the complexity of the whole and their needed relationships. Although one may control for parts in examining questions about a component or relationships, interpretations and applications are derived from the complete association.

Second, multiple perspectives are used in analyzing creative behavior in aging. The ability to take a social–psychological perspective, a cultural perspective, and an aesthetic perspective logically and empirically follows the three components. Movement and associations from psychological to aesthetic to social meanings occur in both vertical and horizontal directions of the framework. Thus, a systems approach is needed in order to more fully understand wholistic meanings (Ainsworth-Land, 1982; Taylor, 1974a, 1974b). Each perspective provides essential questions and allows for in-depth analysis. For example, *aesthetic* might first conjure up an interpretation of

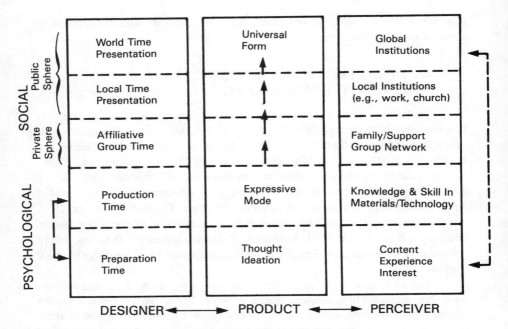

FIGURE 1 Integrative, Associative Framework for Creativity in Aging.

surface image or noninstrumental features of a product. However, *aesthetic* has multiple definitions: It may mean "in content and composition of form," "in intellectual and emotional interests," "in stimulation of human sensibilities" (Dohr, 1984; Kerr, 1978). These three meanings might open considerations of aesthetic interpretations of lifetime development. Applying Kerr's thesis to social policy for older adults, an aesthetic perspective would serve as a handmaiden for social change. "Social and environmental policies should serve persons' needs for meaningful design and for experiences that enhance aesthetic sensitivities in their lives" (Dohr, 1984, p. 594).

Third, the transformation of meaning in the creative association occurs in time and place. (Time is represented in a vertical direction, and place in the horizontal direction.) The progression of tenets leads to creative behavior found in "times" of planning, making or producing, and presenting or marketing (Morita, Reingold, & Shimomura, 1986). The importance of time and place has been further supported by research with older creative adults (Alpaugh et al., 1982; Dohr & Forbess, 1986; Dohr & Portillo, 1986a; 1986b). The following references to time have been consistently documented: time to think and play with ideas, time to make (experimenting with materials and techniques), and time to share (presentation of product that moves among levels of private and public spheres). As will be discussed further, our understanding of adults' personal, subjective meanings of time and of social normative and historical times are central to our framework.

Place suggests the locus of the world of older and adults and the values of their products. It is more than a physical setting. The criteria and location for presenting creative work have social and cultural importance to the adult. This tenet helps to explain why work might be viewed as creative in one place and not in another. It also suggests why a product may move across realms for appreciation, changing its association with the creator. It also helps us conceive why creative productivity may allow an older person "ageless" activity (Coberly, McCormick, & Updike, 1984). As one older writer stated, "When I write, I'm no longer an older woman, but another human being sharing my observations, thoughts, and emotions with another." This has similarities to Mircea Eliade's statement that artists suspend traditional time through the act of making (cited in Apostlos-Cappadona, 1988). Thus a social function of using chronological age to categorize an individual or their work is removed. (A general discussion of social expectations surrounding chronological age have been discussed by Neugarten, 1977, 1979.)

Fourth, creative activity in aging involves a balance of self-reliance and interdependence. Self-support is complemented by social support. This is a tenet not only necessary in making a creative product, but also essential for older creative adults and their communities. In Western societies, the creative spirit is often represented as rugged and fully independent—the deviant or individual stands alone against the norm. Yet the previous tenets assist in seeing that creative activity, either through people or through their products, at some point also has an interdependent character. The very definition of bringing two unlike things together into a new whole or entity that has value or beauty (Alpaugh & Birren, 1977), provides for both independent and interdependent needs. Time to prepare, believe, and make takes self-reliance. Receiving and sharing ideas, and performance, require interdependency. What varies again is the extent to which it is shared and in what context the presenting occurs. Such a balance needs mutual understanding, strengthened by individual energy and spirit.

Finally, recognition of creative behavior in aging should incorporate mature creativeness. As was previously discussed, creativity is a construct not singular in meaning or operation. It is observed at different levels of thought, product types, and settings of presentation ranging from the self to the larger world market. Robinson (1921) presented a development in thought that ranged from a reverie—a spontaneous type of thought—to a practical and functional thought, to creative thought that incorporated contemplation and reflection. Ainsworth-Land (1982) also presented similar levels in a framework on imaging and creative thought. More recently, this approach was reinforced by findings that showed that manifestly creative older adults were more reflective, contemplative, intense, resourceful, and adventurous than were peers not involved in creative activity (Dohr & Forbess, 1986). Yet this contemplative quality is often missed or neglected in the more divergent process explanations of creativity that emphasize spontaneity of ideas. This tenet accentuates the evaluative, thoughtful dimension of creativity action, as well as free association, fluency, and flexibility of ideas that have generated more use in creative technique, inventions, and education.

As we discuss the relations among components from a perspective of life-span development and well-being, the framework's tenets provide the structure for identifying key issues. Discussion of personality development identifies issues of continuity and change as well as objective and subjective realities. A second perspective of product development surrounds an interplay of two issues important to well-being—a purposeful activity and the persons-mode of expression in product form. Thus productivity (product and activity) becomes intertwined with social–psychological issues of continuity and change and time elements.

The third perspective of a social dimension presents five contexts for sharing or performance. Evaluative responses assume social roles involved in transformation of person through ideas and the creative product itself. In this dimension, comparative images surface about oneself or the product against the general human condition. Thus benefits, frustrations, satisfaction, dissatisfaction, and competency of older people engaged in creative activity may be expressed.

DEFINITIONS OF CREATIVITY: PERSON, PROCESS, AND PRODUCT

Without spending too much time on definitions, we think that a brief review is necessary for later discussion. Is creativity synonymous with imagination, divergent thinking, spontaneity, productivity, originality, or innovation (Ainsworth-Land, 1982; Rothenberg & Hausman, 1976)? How has it been defined? *Creative personality* has often been defined in terms of mental health. Psychoanalytic interpretations often surrounded issues of unconscious processes and conflict resolution. Currently, mild mood swings have been purported to facilitate the production phase of creativity (Kinney, cited in Coleman, 1988). Maslow's (1968) humanistic approach defined creativeness as "the universal heritage of every human being that is born, and which seems to co-vary with psychological health" (p. 135). He also distinguished between special talent creativeness and self-actualizing creativeness.

Others were intrigued with the process of creating. An early influential account described the creative process through the stages of preparation, incubation, illumination, and verification (Wallas, 1926). An analogy was also drawn from hypotheses testing in which creativity was believed to include identifying a problem, forming and testing hypotheses, and communicating the results (Torrance, 1976). Another approach focused on one part of the process, Eureka—the "aha" feeling of enlightenment, also called the "nascent moment" (Council of Scholars, 1981). The forming of new associations was also identified as important (Mednick, 1962).

Others concentrated on the creative product's originality and value (Parnes et al., 1976; Rothenberg & Hausman, 1976). Amabile (1983) put it well, "A product or response will be judged as creative to the extent that (a) it is both novel and appropriate, useful, correct, or a valuable response to the task at hand, and (b) that task is heuristic rather than algorithmic" (p. 33). In the following section, the creative person, process, and product are not viewed as mutually exclusive entities but are integrated within our framework of private and public spheres, and personal and sociocultural times. These views are fewer in number, but are directed toward optimal aging.

TIMEFRAMES OF DEVELOPMENT

The cliche "you're only as old as you feel" underscores that chronological time or number of birthdays does not predict the biological, psychological, or social state of an individual (Ward, 1984). The fact that these dimensions of aging run on different timeframes has important implications for creativeness, as well as lifelong development.

An individual lifetime runs on chronological age, social time runs according to sociocultural norms, and historical time runs by the characterization of significant past events (Clausen, 1986). Others would add a subjective timeframe of self-perceived development to this scheme (Ryff, 1984). For more than a decade, Ryff and her associates have used a phenomenological orientation to study personality processes. Her primary question is whether adults interpret their own aging process in a manner proposed by the theories of Erikson, Buhler, Jung, and the concept of interiority described by Neugarten. Although self-perceived personality change was supported on a variety of measures, the clearest patterns were obtained for Erikson's dimensions of generativity and integrity. Finally, the control scales of abasement, impulsivity, and order consistently showed self-perceived stability. The findings indicate that older adults see both change and stability in themselves.

Returning to the subjective timeframe, personal meaning is given to time.

One thinks of oneself in the present in terms of where one has been and what one has become. The adult has a built-in dimension of thought that is the present-relative-to-the-past, and it is the blending of past and present that constitutes psychological reality. (Neugarten, 1979, pp. 892–893)

In our scheme, private and public spheres would be added as contexts for creative activities and products. Expectations, purposes, and roles assigned to the participant and product may differ from sphere to sphere. We learn about the world through subjective and objective views. "Society has objective reality by the processes of institutionalization and . . . has subjective reality by the process of internalization and socialization" (Ryff, 1986, pp. 41–42).

Likewise, creativity has objective and subjective components that run on various timeframes. In the private spheres, we see how time is needed for thinking, producing, and presenting. The actors in this sphere include the individual and intimate social identity groups such as the family and support networks. Thus, we see the role of subjective time in the private sphere. Extending creativeness into the public sphere involves institutional structures that provide values and norms. Standards for acceptance are institutionally defined. Productivity is apparent in different levels of presentation—the larger world, subcultures, or institutions—for example, in the work place, community centers, or church (for a thorough discussion of the developmental applications of systems theory, see Bronfenbrenner, 1977). In this larger sphere, social and historical time are more prominent.

THE PUBLIC SPHERE

Whereas development may occur throughout the framework, public sphere activity is associated with different levels of external recognition. We call more noted achievement *world time*. Other creative productivity that has a presentation component, without such extended recognition, is identified as public *local time*. In world time, whereas the product is critically acclaimed and perceivers are experts or general public, the literature on creativity and gerontology often focuses on the eminent person. For example, older creative superstars are often cited to combat negative stereotypes of aging:

> *Many of our greatest statesmen, scientists, educators, and scholars have functioned into old age: John XXIII was chosen Pope at 77; Golda Meir became prime minister of Israel at 71; Pablo Picasso executed three series of drawings between 85 and 90; and Frank Lloyd Wright completed New York's Guggenheim Museum at 89. (Ward, 1984, p. 38)*

In this place and time, a type of stellar creativity is exhibited—a creativity that permeates all aspects of the individual's life (Davis, 1986). Moreover, entire books have been devoted to late life creativity of people, with an emphasis on the traits of these world-time individuals (e.g., Musterberg, 1983).

A well-written synthesis of research and anecdote, *The Ulyssean Adult: Creativity in the Middle and Later Years,* describes those individuals who have been exceptionally creative in old age (McLeish, 1976). The emphasis on great achievement remains true to the creative person approach; however, McLeish advocated recognizing creativity in the general population. In this case, the Ulyssean adult is characterized as having a sense of adventure, openness of mind, curiosity, resourcefulness, courage, and acceptance. Development is shown to have occurred in old age or has been maintained over the life span. Although this account is uplifting, it does little to describe how creative abilities might be developed (Baldwin, Colangelo, & Dettman, 1984). Amabile's work (1983) also supports Baldwin et al.'s claim. Although world-time creativity is valued by society, a down side to innovation is often present for the individual who may become immersed in their creativity at the expense of healthy personal relationships and a fully functioning life (Coleman, 1988). A conflict may arise between wanting to contribute something significant of oneself and taking pleasure in one's everyday experience.

Who is creative remains the mainstay of this approach. In the study of the creative person, traits of the acknowledged creative genius are investigated. The basic core of self—personality—remains stable over time. The creative person is associated with confidence, energy, and risk-taking (Davis, 1986). Most of the work is closely linked with general personality theory, either stressing unconscious and preconscious processes or self-actualization and well-being (Rothenberg & Hausman, 1976). Although theorists such as Maslow viewed creativity as more than the gift of genius, the emphasis on personality structure may have contributed to a predominant image that separates "those who have it" from "those who don't."

"Designer. Inventor. Architect. Genius. Leonardo da Vinci. Our new tradition, in the West, has been to believe that creativeness is a matter for gifted individuals and that an 'ordinary person,' or group cannot do anything new" (Jones, 1981, p. 47). Although we think this might be an overstatement, misconceptions and barriers to participation in creative activities may be created when solely applying the gifted person explanations.

Early *process-centered work* analyzed life-span patterns of creative achievement (e.g., Dennis, 1956; Lehman, 1953). Eminent creative individuals were studied in disciplines ranging from science to the arts. Although some interdisciplinary differences appeared, the general trend indicated that productivity peaked early in adulthood and subsequently declined. This research has been cited frequently to support age-related declines in creativity. As Romaniuk (1978) noted

> *Perhaps the saddest misunderstanding of this research is the implication that the capacity to be creative declines with age. Although this is never stated explicitly (Lehman himself points out that age cannot be regarded as causing anything), the repeated citation of these data in general readings on aging . . . contributes to the general impression that as one reaches older age, the ability to be creative wanes. (p. 64)*

Sociological perspectives also yield insight into the public sphere's sense of time and place. As stated, networks, organizations, and institutions help define these spheres. Becker (1982) provided insights into the structuring of high-level "art worlds," and Clignet (1985) addressed underlying dynamics that contribute to the restructuring of such institutions. A sociological interpretation of the creative personality emphasizes the individual's connection with the art community. For instance, we often overlook the large social support network needed in the marketing and promotion of an artist (Becker, 1982). The "solitary Titan" laboring alone without the backing of a social support system is often a myth (Council of Scholars, 1981).

Those who examine creative social development in the public sphere have noted personal as well as social, world or local time. As Clignet stated, "Artistic careers evolve within two distinct types of time: The time of the individual and the time of his or her surroundings" (1985, p. 99). This helps explain why some artists might be ahead of their time. What are the sociocultural expectations and synchronies of time suggested by Clignet? Do any age differences emerge in public sphere analysis? Younger, unestablished creators have less at stake when challenging existing norms. They are less committed to a style or approach. Moreover, if their work does not make a dramatic statement, they risk being passed over, going unnoticed, or not gaining admission into the art world. On the other hand, for older artists who have gained a reputation, changing directions in their work may jeopardize their critical acclaim and loyal following.

As has been emphasized throughout this chapter, context is fundamental for establishing parameters of meaning. To be creative necessitates having a norm

(Council of Scholars, 1981) to contrast against. However, any deviation from the status quo should not be interpreted as being creative by default. A component of worth or value is central to many of the definitions of creativity (Rothenburg & Hausman, 1976). This issue has often been skirted. Value judgments in creativity are thought to be idiosyncratic, thus not reliable or valid. But qualitative and quantitative methods exist to systematically examine this phenomenon. Because creative precedence and standards set in public spheres often provide a yardstick for measuring creative achievement, the position of value must be better addressed and understood. Our framework may assist this need. Although much can be learned from studying world-time activity, educational gerontologists interested in programming probably are more interested in the general population of older adults.

THE PRIVATE SPHERE

When attention shifts to a general population, we find a difference in how creativity is defined and researched. The creative process assumes central importance. *How* people create is the issue generating the majority of current empirical research in the field. Creative personality has generally been studied through descriptive techniques; in contrast, the process orientation has been historically committed to the quantitative measurement of creative abilities. This was especially true in the attempt to disentangle creative processes from global intelligence (Kogan, 1973).

Guilford's (1967) extensive work in creative process identified significant factors and set the stage for the divergent thinking approach. His work stimulated others such as Torrance who developed popular creativity instruments measuring fluency, flexibility, originality, and elaboration of ideas. Although Torrance's tests are widely used, their reliability and validity for older adults have been questioned (Romaniuk & Romaniuk, 1981). Similar concerns have been raised by Engelman (1981). Amabile has also argued that objective assessment of creativity is insufficient and recommended her consensual assessment technique.

The purpose of many process-oriented studies was twofold: to identify creative abilities in later life, and to investigate any age-related changes in the creative process. Often creativity was assumed to represent a capacity to be fully developed. One study by Alpaugh and Birren (1977) assessed the creative abilities of 111 teachers who ranged in age from 20 to 83 years. Creativity was assessed by divergent-thinking tests and the preference for complexity.[1] No age differences were exhibited in intelligence; however, age-related declines on the creativity measures were noted. These findings also add credence to the age decrement model, although the authors of that model do acknowledge that cohort effects or insensitive instrumentation may have influenced the outcome.

---

[1]Preference for complexity measured by the Welsh-Barron Art Scale is believed to be associated with the creativity, although Dohr and Forbess have raised concerns regarding confusion with aesthetic measurement. The scale is also used in experimental aesthetics.

Another direction in process-oriented research was toward investigating the relation between affect and creativity (Janquish & Ripple, 1981). Using an adult life-span framework, researchers examined cognitive–creative abilities (divergent thinking) and self-esteem. This research was influenced by an earlier study (Coppersmith, 1967, cited in Janquish & Ripple, 1981) that identified a positive linear relation between self-esteem and divergent thinking in adolescents. This relationship may be of special interest in later adulthood if negative social views on aging influence older people's feelings of self-worth. Therefore, lowered self-esteem, rather than declines in creative capacity, may contribute to purported age decrements.

Janquish and Ripple used a cross-sectional research design with 4 age groups in a total sample of 218 adults: young adults (18–25 years), adults (26–39 years), middle adults (40–60 years), and older adults (61–84 years). Divergent thinking (fluency, flexibility, and originality) and self-esteem were assessed. The findings showed that all three younger groups were significantly more fluent on the divergent thinking test than were the older adults. Flexibility measures showed young adults and middle adults to be significantly more flexible than were older adults. On this measure, there were no significant differences between adults and older adults. In terms of originality, fewer significant differences emerged between age groups. The middle adults were the only group exhibiting more originality than the older adults. Overall, the middle-aged adults out-performed all the other groups. Comparisons on self-esteem portrayed adults and middle adults as higher in self-esteem than were older adults. It was suggested that developmental change in older adulthood gives priority to quality rather than quantity of divergent responses. This might further be supported by other results suggesting that older individuals become more reflective with increasing life experience.

How creativity is viewed, as a quantitative or qualitative variable, has direct consequences for the measurement approach taken (Romaniuk & Romaniuk, 1981). These researchers further suggested that if creativity is viewed as changing quantitatively with age, a single test with age-appropriate forms would be recommended. In contrast, if creativity is assumed to be qualitative, then a single test would not be appropriate. Defining and assessing the different stages of creativity across the life course would be essential. The Romaniuks also advised a "grass roots" approach to measurement whereby "persons in different age and cohort groups perceive and define creativity" (p. 377).

Although self-esteem appears to be associated with divergent thinking in the Janquish and Ripple study, the pattern is not clear in the two younger adult groups in which no significant relationships were identified. In middle and older adulthood, self-esteem and divergent thinking were positively associated. In order to advance this merging of creative thought and affect, Janquish and Ripple called for future investigations emphasizing, "the importance of self perceptions to the psychological functioning of the older adult" (p. 117). Additionally, perhaps older people, as well as those of all ages, need to define their perception of self-esteem. Self-esteem may hold different meanings for adolescents, young adults, middle-aged adults, and older adults. Nevertheless, this research advances the cognitive–creative process approach to include affect.

Crosson and Robertson-Tchabo (1983) criticized the two studies previously described (Alpaugh & Birren, 1977; Janquish & Ripple, 1981) because they did not account for the subjects' past creative history. Combining process and product views, Crosson and Robertson-Tchabo examined preference for complexity in 271 manifestly creative women, ages 23–87. They questioned whether age differences would be present in these creatively productive women. Women artists and writers were defined as creative if they consistently attempted to exhibit or publish their work. No significant negative correlations with age were present. However, age-related declines in preference for complexity were found in the comparison group. The findings did not distinguish artists from writers. In fact, this may support a common underlying process that transcends the creative mode. Two explanations were given for the findings: Preference for complexity is fundamental to the creative personality, and creative abilities that are "exercised" are maintained into old age. The authors also recommended studying creative older adults' adaptation to sensory losses that often accompany the aging process. Further research was also encouraged on a larger issue relating creativity to optimal aging issues and life-span satisfaction.

A later study of Alpaugh et al. (1982) integrated creative process and product approach with adult life-span concerns. Sixty-one women were divided into a young (26–38 years) and old group (60–83 years). The subjects completed an open-ended creative writing exercise and took divergent thinking tests and an intelligence measure. Subjects' stories were scored on creativity by expert raters. Both quantitative and qualitative measures supported declines in creativity with age. Alpaugh et al. did note, however, large intragroup heterogeneity. In fact, an 83-year-old woman received the second highest creativity score. Finally, an argument was made for a qualitative shift in cognitive abilities between younger and older adulthood. Alpaugh et al. acknowledged a limitation inherent to many studies of creativity in controlled settings: Motivation, interests, and activities that play such a vital role in creativity are not addressed.

Several other researchers have attempted to develop workshops to enhance creative thinking in older people. Engleman (1981) conducted a six-week program for older adult women. Creative thinking abilities as measured by the Torrance tests did not show any significant improvements, but qualitative data from the instructor's journal and class evaluations indicated worthwhile benefits. Romaniuk (1978) also set up a training workshop that did not appear to produce changes in creative thinking abilities. However, creative attitudes were modified, and several interesting ideas on the assessment of creativity in old age (e.g., creative lifeline curve) were developed through this study.

Romaniuk and her colleagues (Romaniuk, 1978; Romaniuk et al., 1984) systematically examined self-perceived attitudes and levels of creativity across the life span through retrospective, concurrent, and prospective measures. Using several measures, adults plotted their creativity lifeline and gave descriptions of creative peaks and definitions of their creative productivity. Analysis of the timelines revealed that perceived creative peaks were typically represented by concrete products and activities rather than by abstract abilities. Early peaks were associated with more public career meaning; later peaks were linked with family, suggesting private sphere meaning. Given Romaniuk's findings and definition of creativity, Dohr and Forbess (1986) concluded that a creative aesthetic framework, rather than the frequently used cognitive perspective (Alpaugh et al., 1982) was more appropriate for understanding the creative development in aging.

Analyzing the lifeline graphs, Dohr and Forbess found three profiles of the creatively active older adults—consistent, up-early/up-late, and rising types. The up-early/up-late profile was the most frequently observed pattern. Career and family involvement were significant social factors tied with creative peaks in Dohr's work, similar to those Romaniuk found. The consistent types adapted their creative activity by changing lifestyles and environments to accommodate to their interests. Two rising types were identified: those who showed gradual development in creative interest and those who showed sharp increases in creative activity around middle age. The study identified a sense of self-growth or creative maturity and that different contextual meanings accrued with time.

Continued statistical analyses of why the consistent profile differed from the up-early/up-late profile has resulted in a model of creativeness that is supported by the theories of Gruber (1981), Feldman (1980), and Gardner (1982). Gruber stated that creative development is dependent upon coincidence of genetic, familial, motivational, and cultural factors. In the recent study, combination of three systems appear to be significant in predicting the difference in creative activity patterns: personality ↔ internal motivation, social environment ↔ family interest and career flexibility, and knowledge ↔ mode. These systems provide the bases for mature creativeness (Dohr, 1988; in press).

The preceding discussion indicates that perceptions of decline, stability, and growth of creative trajectories exist. The variations in constancy and change suggest that further discussion is needed. It would appear that creative productivity can be conceptualized through both constancy and change. Furthermore, both may be represented within the same individual. This interplay between constancy and change is often evident throughout the life span and in the pattern types just discussed. Sometimes a surface change in interests disguises underlying constancy. The psychologist, Heider's, childhood fascination with art resurfaced when he chose his thesis topic on visual perception (Rappoport, 1985). Sometimes a broad repertory of creative activities is present in people's lives; other times a single talent is developed over years of experience. The former case represents change, whereas the latter shows greater continuity. Yet both types may exhibit creative productivity. Thus, the study of creative development and personality have underlying issues that not only complement each other but also must be considered together for knowledge in educational gerontology to expand.

PURPOSEFUL PRODUCT

Purpose

As we change our emphasis in the framework to product and to considering the social–psychological nature of older people, two essential issues surface. The first is the relation between the adult and the manifestation of thought, feelings, or experience. This manifestation has been described as being "purpose driven." The purpose in turn gives meaning and inspires the process of making that occurs on a timeline (Nadler, 1981). Apostlos-Cappadona, writing about Mircea Eliade, stated that "a major work is distinguished by an intensity of inspiration and an overwhelming sense of personal vision" (1988, p. xi). The product—a major work—is emphasized. Although the author was writing about the work of an acclaimed scholar, the source of intensity and personal vision has similarities to significant attributes perceived by older participants in creative arts programs (Dohr & Forbess, 1986). Whereas "major work" appears to implicate world time, underlying characteristics of intensity, inspiration, vision, and commitment are observed across spheres. This subjective interest of the person becomes stated in the more objective sense of *product purpose*. The shaping, energy, and imaging of purpose are distinguishing features for study through the product. Subjective meets objective.

Ansel Adam's quote, prefacing this chapter, also reinforces this purposeful drive in the words "refine," "intensify my relation," and "make some contribution." We recognize multiple purposes—for making, experiencing, and appreciating. People's experience and knowledge, and their sense of beauty and imagination, are made apparent to themselves and to others through productivity. In this sense creative action blends with the subjective and objective meaning in life described in Ryff's work.

For educational gerontologists, the construct of purpose, however, has been researched extensively under the guise of several meanings, terms, or phrases. We refer to purpose-in-life. We study motivation as one's underlying drive and energy. We do need assessments in trying to identify motivational orientations and rationales for participation in programs and content interests. We provide goals and objectives for our institutions, ourselves, and learners as we develop programs. How do these various explanations fit within a context of creative productivity in aging? A trajectory of "purpose" levels begins to emerge if we focus on creative making, or product.

In considering a global, life-course meaning, Frankl's (1962) writings are insightful. He spoke of three overarching value positions affecting purpose-in-life: experiential, creative making, and attitudinal choice. Attitudinal value is viewed as a base choice of humans and is thus given overriding consideration. However, we suggest that the three are transactional for product emphases. And one may enter the cycle at any point, whereby the other two will be enhanced. People might argue that a given attitude is needed for creative making. This ability to make in turn influences how life is experienced, thus reinforcing the attitude that brought about manifest expression and satisfaction in the first place. In the cases of some creative people, this appears to be supported. However, we have also observed older individuals who enter creative activity programs, such as creative writing or painting, at another person's suggestion rather than at their own initiative. Once there, they are stimulated and assisted by the instructor and other peers, actively reexperiencing a situation, idea, or feeling through creative making and socialization. An insight is revealed, and they describe changes in their attitude and self-motivation (Dohr, in press).

An extrinsic–intrinsic character of purpose or motivation is apparent in this discussion. Maslow, in his early discussion of motivation on the creation of art (1954), differentiated between the goal to communicate and the goal of expression. He described communication as the need to arouse emotion, to show someone else and, to do something, and he saw such a need as being motivated. Expression was viewed as an *intra*personal goal and nonmotivated. "The fact that expression may have unforeseen *inter*personal effects, is a secondary gain and beside the initial point" (Maslow, 1954, p. 297). It would seem, however, that communication and expression are both purpose oriented; the difference lies in kind, not in whether one is motivated or not. Communication is more concrete (i.e., to arouse emotion, to show someone else) and requires external exchange, whereas expression has a more abstract quality and has intrinsic overtones or motivations.

Literature on creative production and extrinsic–intrinsic motivation points up differences. Creativity research involving tasks that are heuristic (or ill-defined) and consensual ratings of product showed that an intrinsically motivated state were conducive to creative products, whereas extrinsic motivations were detrimental (Amabile, 1983). Amabile noted, however, "That although it appears that extrinsic constraints can be detrimental to creativity, there are individuals who appear to produce consistently creative work under clear and salient extrinsic constraints" (p. 67). Although we recognize that Amabile has shifted meaning somewhat from task motivation to task constraint factors, our research of adult consistent types who were creatively productive across the life span, regardless of life stressors, does support her work.

In another study with younger adults, Amabile reported that external constraints made tasks seem like work, thus decreasing the students' satisfaction and creativity. In light of the role that life activity plays, we ask the following question.

If some older adults are shown to be threatened by leisure rather than welcoming it, or their level of participation in creative arts programs is more cautious, such as production-line types (Bloom, 1980), then could extrinsic motivations be beneficial to their creative production? At least in initial entry and guidance, until the person experiences the growth of their own involvement.

Our work with thought structuring of college students in design arts demonstrated domain-specific development in thought. The developmental transitions were similar to Perry's model (1970), where dualistic thought shifts to multiplicity of ideas without commitment, to a relativism in thought with commitment (Portillo & Dohr, in press). This change in commitment suggests intrinsic purposes. A developmental structuring of thought in design arts is similar to an aesthetic expressive stage, identified by Eisner (1965) and discussed by Bloom (1980). In this stage, the challenge that a beginner finds inhibiting serves to motivate the mature creative adult toward a new curiosity or need to find and express order.

Mode

Mode is the organization of words, figures, symbols, sounds, or even social "actors and setting" that give manifest meaning to one's purpose. We have presented distinctions of single-talent and self-actualization types, and comparisons of creativity in writers, musicians, artists, and scientists. The single-talent type exhibits creativity through a product, whereas a self-actualization type is characterized as a person who creates to integrate aspects of self. Therefore, it is useful for discussion, comparison, and application to clearly identify the modes in which a person creates.

By considering mode, one can gain an objective understanding of creativeness. Aesthetic knowledge is an objective resource to the educator and older producer. Furthermore, manifested products themselves allow us to count, to compare against a standard or expectation of quality. We can examine the product for its originality—where it would be placed in a curve if compared to a quantity of other similar products. We are able to critique the extent to which an objective, a desired outcome, is achieved. We are able to discuss its aesthetic, functional, or useless value. Even as artists and designers, we may train ourselves to develop a given disinterestedness that gives an objectivity similar to that of a scientist examining a phenomenon. Objective characteristics of product have been referred to as the technical factors of production (Amabile, 1983) and may have both quantitative and qualitative references.

From this perspective, we appreciate that some modes require different skill training and may be more or less developed at various life stages and places. Furthermore the time required to produce in different modes warrants different interpretations. For example, older adults and educators in creative writing classes might produce prose or poetry realizing a whole and changes in their work more quickly than would, for example, adults working on a large-scale, textile mural that requires a longer time before a whole is viewed and a final critique contemplated. In examining the product, older adults interested in selecting their life-span mode of creative expression and in strengthening their expression might explore the nature of the mode related to their previous creative interests and preferred modes.

Research with children, young adults, and older adults has shown that a propensity toward a given mode is established early in life. In fact, we suggest that people's sense of what is interesting and the way in which they choose to work or spend leisure time may stem from aesthetic sensibilities. Older writers significantly reported English, literature, or language-related content as being their favorite subjects in school or early life. They liked words. Visual artists and craftspersons, although less clearly, expressed preference for manipulating physical materials (Dohr & Forbess, 1986). An older woman who expressed that she did not see herself as "creative" in things, did describe herself as "cultivating friends" and "blending different people" in establishing a social group. Although the older adult might report that the creative activity was a new endeavor for them—"It's my first painting or creative writing class" or "No, I've never done this before"—an underlying mode appeared to be consistent with preferences in early life. Thus, a poetic form, an intellectual involvement, and a stimulation in sensing—whether visual, sound, textural, or social motion—are woven together in the mode.

When considering objective, technical factors and the underlying nature of creative activity modes, the evaluative and presentation needs of the activity should be taken into account. In studies with younger populations, as previously reported, Amabile (1983) found that task expectations influenced creativity scores. However, when comparing groups on the technical factors, expectations were not detrimental to success. Extrinsic expectation appeared to influence participants' sense of freedom subjectively, but not objective concerns.

Subtle distinctions, clarified through the framework, can be made when discussing creative activity and evaluation. It is important for individuals to understand when they are in a preparation time, when they are in a making time, and when they are in a presentation time. In each case the evaluative criteria might shift, the role of critique changes, and the type of evaluator role changes. For example, a puppeteer reported that she never let others see her puppets when she was working on their costumes and paint or when she was practicing with them. An older man, who was enrolled in a painting class, reported, "We really go at it when we critique each others' work. It pushes you to think more." This class evaluation was viewed as formative, in a supportive manner. Afterward the paintings were exhibited at a local bank, where other standards came into play.

The nature of creative activity suggests that the presentation or performance dimension is an important consideration for programmers and individual producers. In fact, to some older adults, participation is deterred if a sharing is not viewed as possible (i.e., "Why should I do the activity; I don't have anyone to give it to"). However, if the presentation time is collective or built into the program in some way, such as a final class reception, then an individual may engage in a larger social experience. A fullness of the experience is needed.

THE ROLE OF SOCIAL EXCHANGE

We have established the older person's role as artist or designer with social-psychological and aesthetic needs. We have looked at the nature of their product as being purpose-guided and as being produced in a given mode or form. At this point in the framework, the role of the perceiver comes into play; a response or expectation also has a role in creative activity. Although we have reviewed social expectations of producers and for product, we have not yet shown that the social dimension of the perceiver's role has important implications for creative action. The social dimension involves knowledge concerning similar forms or products and the skill level of the adult and the context of his or her involvement—in other words, the social transactions of persons and products. Although we recognize that the benefits of creative arts activities may occur and transcend the context (Clignet, 1985), if assessment of one's work and oneself compared to others is involved, then the benefits of creative activities become tied to the perceiver's role. Five dimensions of social relationships are important for consideration when examining creative action and life-span development.

Collective Social Categorizing

The first social dimension is collective social categorizing. We must be sensitive to how the collective view of society, and of older adults themselves, toward older adulthood can influence creative action. This collective view offers images that may serve to assist or deter individuals from activity. These images may be based in myth, stereotype, or generalized knowledge. As educational gerontologists, we continually seek understanding of the truth and beauty of aging in order to replace myths and stereotypes that hinder development. For example, if creative action is always equated with famous people and if expectation of creativeness is not true to one's context, then, as research shows, creativity is deterred. Attitudes such as "Oh, I can't do that," or "I don't have the same resources to do that," or "Why would I even try?" could prevail, and a sense of freedom to explore or play is lost. In contrast, if individuals "see" different views, some in a cultural sense, some in the context of work, leisure, family, church, senior centers, or one's own personhood, then several alternatives are available from which to choose and in turn contribute to views of aging. The bases by which a collective view toward aging and creative action is reinforced or is changed may be provided by the following social-role exchanges.

Mentors

A social dimension of person-to-person exchange regarding creative productivity has been shown to be important across the life span (Amabile, 1983). The single person serves as a mentor and encourages another individual when others might not. Data comparing creative individuals who participated in community programs to those who did not participate in programs revealed that the latter group often cited a specific person with whom they exchanged letters or who encouraged their activity. This finding is similar to findings from earlier research or anecdotes on creativity that cite a mentor relationship as often being present. Relationships between learners and instructors and between learners and fellow class members were also noted to be important for creative productivity in program settings.

Support Groups

A third dimension is the individual-to-group relationship. In this case, the appreciation of the class or group's ideas, their struggles, their work, and their critiques were cited as being stimulating to an individual's creative productivity. Knowledge and encouragement come from several people rather than from one mentor. The opportunity to assess one's skill level compared to others is present, and more important, the sharing of interests is reinforced. In this case the purpose of comparison is not always to assess achievement; it may also stimulate thought and allow appreciation of human abilities in general. Listening to the voice of a fellow classmate reading a story was cited as being inspirational. Other people related amazement that a single idea of childhood dwelling could result in so many different images and richness of material. Such appreciation shows an aesthetic conception of an enlarged sense of older being. The achievement, so important to public-sphere recognition, gives way to personal inspired vision. "Our quilting is beautiful; I simply love it and do it to do it. I'd die without it." When achievement did result, and one member of a group was externally rewarded, other members also reported a sense of pride and accomplishment. The work became "our" work.

Inner Voices

What on the surface might not appear appropriate as a social dimension to creative action is a frequently overlooked relationship that our work and findings lead us to address. The person-to-object dimension appears to have social meaning to some individuals. For example, one older painter called her work her "friends." A writer described conversations with a fictional character as she structured her prose. Visual thinking development for quilters and other visual artists required them to change roles from designer to evaluator during the making process. Active shifts in thought perspectives were reported. Reflective thought and exchange through keeping a diary or filing design ideas or images take on a social, conversational nature, although the conversation may be with the inanimate product. The social value to the individual may not be any less important for his or her satisfaction and creative development. In fact, the creativity exercise of talking to and taking the perspective of an inanimate object, such as a garbage can or a pencil, as a way of changing and freeing one's mind-set has been shown to reinforce this concept of the social value of the inner voice (Davis, 1986).

Product as Social Tie

As the product leaves the individual person, it also may become a social tie to the larger community. In other words, the product or image speaks to the larger audience without the originator's physical presence, yet a spiritual presence is felt or understood. Thus we circle back to the first collective dimension where society says, "This is what creative action from our older members is." Through a person-to-person concrete association, through opportunities of a person-to-group association, through a person-to-product association that in turn becomes a social expression-to-larger-community association, we experience new meanings in creative action and aging.

EDUCATIONAL INTERPRETATIONS—CONCERNS FOR PLANNING PROGRAMS

In interpreting and applying the framework and interdependent constructs to educational settings, we do not presume to give you solutions to follow, nor do we address planning phases such as activity or instructional plans, elevation, administration, and so forth. Rather, we present key issues through the framework by which you may assess existing programs or develop new ones while viewing creativeness as an avenue for development. Through the very evolution of the framework, issues of creative thought and production over the life span have been identified. These have either been derived from or analytically tested against other research and experiential reports. Therefore, the abstraction of parts synthesized through the framework should provide some confidence in moving ahead to program considerations. Using the framework and tenets as a planning tool may assist toward achieving optimal aging outcomes.

By beginning with the component of product, educational gerontologists can examine with different emphases the purpose and mode or content through a subjective–objective interplay. The inherent nature of creative arts programs in the broad sense and purposeful meaning sought by adults in later years elicits several considerations as we plan and offer programs. Creative activity has been discussed as ill-defined problem solving (see Simon, 1984) or heuristic in nature (Amabile), each suggesting that a direct path to development, or a recipe for production or imitation, is not present. However, Morita et al. (1986) stated that creative productivity might be considered to be adaptive in some respects and leap-oriented in others. This distinction is helpful in discussing creative activity whereby an individual might be refining parts of their work rather than initiating entire, wholistic, new forms. We have seen that creative activity is also experiential—thus necessitating the involvement, commitment, and action of individuals. Furthermore, the response component of the framework suggests the need for presentation or performance planning that is different from that designed for other domain-specific content.

By encompassing person-product-perceiver and community communication, program developers can visualize and respond to participants as being producers and creators, not just as learners for receiving information or reproducers (Taylor & Sacks, 1981). The participants, at whatever expressive or skill level, offer resources for channeling thoughts, feelings, and imagination and making them accessible to others. This enriches their own self-discovery and the community's as well. The ideas and thoughts in planning, in making, and in sharing provide a cycle that underscores the strong subjective–objective relationship of personality, product meaning, and social values and knowledge. This suggests that as we plan and examine the components of our programs (content, setting, learner, educator), we must understand the balance of objective criteria that are needed with subjective experience.

In doing so, the purpose that guides programs and creative production is clarified. A creative activity program that would focus only on subjective needs, without objective criteria, has a different purpose. For example, if a program is developed in creative writing and its purpose is fundamentally to discover one's feelings through keeping a journal, then the objective nature of thematic structure, criteria of standards in form, and critical examination of other writings might potentially be excluded. The program might end up being viewed as a personality development seminar rather than a creative writing program because emphasis in purpose is on the person, not the product. This is not necessarily negative, nor are we denying that writing skill could be realized as a by-product. We simply recognize that the educational direction is different. Similarly, if a creative activity class is objective in emphasis, has only informational content, and teaches technique-oriented skills, then the inspiration and development for self-discovery and integration of the self might be excluded. The expressive nature is overshadowed by functional concerns.

Although they are viewed as benefits of creative programs, therapy, health, personality, past reminiscences, or activity for activity's sake are not the focus. To deliver a creative activity program with such emphases risks undermining the value of the product to the person. In such instances, the product simply becomes a vehicle for other purposes. Thus the performance or presentation component is weakened, and response and appreciation of the product changes. Older adults in such cases could end up perceiving themselves as being noncreative or as being nonproducers because the concept of product purpose never surrounded manifested productivity. The product purpose in such cases would emphasize personality or community activity. Thus, aging outcomes of new consciousness, integration, productivity, and self-esteem potentially are missed or experienced by chance. Another consequence might be that once the activity as therapy is completed, the adult no longer feels the need to continue because creative productivity for its own sake has not been valued. We as educators and gerontologists therefore are partners in giving meaning and value to programs.

An aesthetic view, as well as psychological and social views, is encompassed in thought and product structuring through planning, preparation, production, and evaluative operations. Creative activity needs three foci: (a) content—thematic ideas to be explored and expressed; (b) skill and competency in expression to give order and meaning for discovery, and (c) a contextual understanding for reflection on the universal nature of both idea and form. Hoffman et al. (1980), who have done extensive work in arts education and aging, stated these as program goals of personality and social exchange, critical thinking about creative art, and basic art (or content) knowledge.

Understanding the various concepts of time also may prove helpful. An awareness that time in some cases may be suspended in creative expression as individuality becomes incorporated with universal humanness may suggest new program thrusts. Everyday experiences in creative activity serve as sources to be viewed in uncommon ways, thus time applications change. Chronological time is less important than personal subjective time, and social time. Biological time changes suggest skill or scope adaptation. Equally, it helps to consider the social time of program participants from a cultural perspective to understand potential conflicts in values and meaning. Further ideas on time to think and plan, time to make, and time to present also can assist the educator in establishing criteria for phases. Thus adult learners see shifts in activity and their own expectations. Not all production during program sessions need be intended for final presentation. Thus short exercises may help build toward ideas, skills, and final form developments. This approach may be particularly helpful in cases in which older adults' time of involvement is limited.

These time concepts and components may also suggest to the adult program planner that a creative activity program in senior centers and sites be approached from a multiple program or modular concept. With an overview of a given creative activity, a module might be offered on developing ideas and experiences for expression. A concurrent or subsequent module could focus on skills and the nature of a mode; another module could focus on contextual meaning or comparative material and culturally related knowledge. Finally, a presentation or marketing of work would follow. Flexibility in programs could be realized because cross-modal and intergenerational participants would participate in these various productivity modules and timeframes. Currently, creative programs are structured around expressive modes or techniques (e.g., creative writing, photography, or woodworking). The creative process stages are incorporated and tied to the topic. A potential limitation with this organizing practice is that an adult's stereotypes or social expectations for the mode may be incorrect, and participation or new discovery may be missed.

The social exchange roles highlight educators' considerations of instructional methods and techniques. Might a mentor program be more appropriate than a group program for some learners and at some times? How could both be shared? Are there components, times, and modes of interest allowing shifts to be made with more ease between public and private spheres through home video viewing or call-in programs? The social place concepts for creative production may also assist the programmer and older adult producer to understand developmental or natural aging shifts and the ways to change or maintain productivity depending upon the desires of the individual.

CONCLUSION

We began the chapter with a description of issues of well-being in aging that are developmental in nature. Successful aging may bring about many changes and requires a flexibility to adapt and grow. In the face of change, how do we create an agenda for balancing losses and potentials? To meet expressive, intellectual, and social needs, older people must actively seek out a supportive yet challenging environment. Education in creative activities should strive to provide such a stimulating milieu.

In order to do so, we have offered a framework that evolved from the interplay of research findings and theories in creativity, adult education in the arts and design, and adult development. In past research, dimensions of creativity have often been presented without an overall context. Although life-course development and well-being may be enhanced by creative activity, our understanding of creativeness is clarified and expanded through examining it from a developmental perspective. The creative personality approach excluded the everyday older person, whereas the cognitive process approach focused on the everyday person but lacked contextual or ecological validity for mature adulthood. Each approach has its strengths but does not reflect the complexity of the construct or often acknowledge limits in its application. A multifaceted assessment of creativeness and aging must be recognized. By using the framework, several outcomes may be realized.

First, if integration is desirable in both creativity and aging, the framework's integrative structure allows us to better visualize the weaving together and influence of various parts. For example, interiority as a characteristic of maturity may be manifested in external form. Thus, rather than viewing it negatively as a closing-in on the self with a creative thrust, it could become supportive to growth and health, increasing esteem and life satisfaction. The subjective–objective phenomenon of aging also is better visualized within all domains, and the public and private sphere transitions may be addressed. This helps us better analyze and understand age patterns of decrement, stability, and up-down-up and rising types.

Second, if continued or new productivity is desired, we again see reinforcement of the same subjective–objective theme. Through the external product and social presentation, internalized ideas are transformed. We repeatedly put forth personal, social, and aesthetic sensitivity needs that come together in creative activity education. Productivity may be a celebration of maturity as well as achievement.

Third, we suggested that creative expression and education sustain a purpose in life because they are purpose-driven phenomena with value and social worth. Evaluative choices are exercised, and new possibilities of arrangement are elicited. The communicative social dimensions of mentor roles, social support groups, inner-voice exchange, and product social ties may vary in emphasis and quantity, but they do bring forth images of influences on creativeness and its collective reality in aging.

Finally, applied value of theoretical explanations rest with educational gerontologists for advancing their own work. Thus, the true test for this chapter is whether the concepts might be used in programs for seniors advancing their well-being. Toward this end, we have shared suggestions for developing programs.

REFERENCES

Ainsworth-Land, V. (1982). Imaging and creativity: An integrating perspective. *Journal of Creative Behavior, 16,* 5–28.

Alpaugh, P. K., & Birren, J. E. (1977). Variables affecting creative contributions across the adult life span. *Human Development, 20,* 240–248.

Alpaugh, P. K., Parham, I. A., Cole, K. D., & Birren, J. E. (1982). Creativity in adulthood and old age: An exploratory study. *Educational Gerontology, 8,* 101–116.

Amabile, T. M. (1983). *The social psychology of creativity.* New York: Springer-Verlag.

Apostlos-Cappadona, D. (1988). *Symbolism, the sacred, and the arts: Mircea Eliade.* New York: Crossroad.

Baldwin, C. B., Colangelo, N., & Dettmann, D. F. (1984). Perspectives of creativity throughout the life span. *The Creative Child and Adult Quarterly, 4*(1), 9–17.

Becker, H. (1982). *Art worlds.* Berkeley: University of California Press.

Bloom, L. P. R. (1980). Toward an understanding of lifelong growth and participation in visual arts production. In Hoffman, Greenberg, & Fitzner (Eds.), *Life-*

long learning and the visual arts. Reston, VA: National Art Education Association.

Boyd, V. T. (1976). *Valuing of the material environment: A conceptual model of object value.* Unpublished doctoral dissertation, Michigan State University, East Lansing.

Bronfenbrenner, U. (1977). Toward an experimental ecology of human development. *American Psychologist, 32*(7), 513–531.

Clausen, J. A. (1986). *Sociology of the life course.* Englewood Cliffs, NJ: Prentice-Hall.

Clignet, R. (1985). *The structure of artistic revolutions.* Philadelphia: University of Pennsylvania Press.

Coberly, L. M., McCormick, J., & Updike, K. (1984). *Writers have no age: Creative writing with older adults.* New York: Hawthorne Press.

Coleman, D. (1988). New index illuminates creativity in daily life. *New York Times,* September 13, pp. 17, 24.

Council of Scholars. (1981). *Creativity: A continuing inventory of knowledge.* Washington, DC: Library of Congress.

Crosson, C. W., & Robertson-Tchabo, E. A. (1983). Age and preference for complexity among manifestly creative women. *Human Development, 26,* 149–155.

Davis, G. A. (1986). *Creativity is forever.* Dubuque, IA: Kendall/Hunt.

Dennis, W. (1956). Age and achievement: A critique. *Journal of Gerontology, 11,* 331–333.

Dohr, J. H. (1984). An aesthetic perspective for family issues. *Family Relations, 33*(4), 593–596.

Dohr, J. H., & Forbess, L. (1986). Creativity, arts, and profiles of aging: A reexamination. *Educational Gerontology, 12,* 123–138.

Dohr, J. H., & Portillo, M. B. (1986b, November). *Place and time: Variables of creativeness over the life span.* Paper presented at the meeting of the Gerontological Society of America, Chicago, IL.

Dohr, J. H., & Portillo, M. B. (1986a). Life span development and the creative design process. *Forum, 1,* 9–11.

Dohr, J. H. (1988). *Mature creativeness.* Paper presented at the meeting of the American Society on Aging, San Diego, CA.

Dohr, J. H. (In press). Mature creativeness: A differentiating pattern in adult development. *The Creative Child and Adult Quarterly.*

Eisner, E. W. (1965). A typology of creative behavior in the visual arts. *American Educational Research Journal, 2,* 125–136.

Engleman, M. (1981). The response of older women to a creative problem solving program. *Educational Gerontology, 6,* 165–173.

Feldman, D. (1980). *Beyond universals in cognitive development.* Norwood, NJ: Ablex.

Frankl, V. E. (1962). *Man's search for meaning.* New York: Simon & Schuster.

Gardner, H. (1982). *Art, mind, a brain: A cognitive approach to creativity.* New York: Basic Books.

Greenberg, P. (1987). *Visual arts and older people: Developing quality programs.* Springfield, IL: Charles C Thomas.

Gruber, H. (1981). *Darwin on man* (2nd ed.). Chicago: University of Chicago Press.

Guilford, J. P. (1967). *The nature of human intelligence.* New York: McGraw-Hill.

Hoffman, D. H., Greenberg, P., & Fitzner, D. H. (Eds.). (1980). *Lifelong learning and the visual arts: A book of readings*. Reston, VA: National Art Education Association.

Janquish, G. A., & Ripple, R. E. (1981). Cognitive creative abilities and self-esteem across the adult life span. *Human Development, 24,* 110–119.

Jones, J. C. (1981). *Design methods: Seeds of human futures*. Chichester, England: Wiley & Sons.

Kahn, R. L. (1986). *Productive behavior and well-being*. Paper presented at the meeting of the Gerontological Society of America, Chicago, IL.

Kerr, D. (1978). Aesthetic policy. *Journal of Aesthetic Education, 12*(1), 5–22.

Kogan, N. (1973). Creativity and cognitive style: A life-span perspective. In P. B. Baltes & K. W. Schaie (Eds.), *Life span developmental psychology: Personality and socialization* (pp. 145–178). New York: Academic Press.

Lehman, H. C. (1953). *Age and achievement*. Princeton, NJ: Princeton University Press.

Maslow, A. (1954). *Motivation and personality*. New York: Harper & Row.

Maslow, A. (1968). *Toward a psychology of being* (2nd ed.). New York: D Van Nostrand.

McLeish, J. A. (1976). *The Ulyssean adult: Creativity in the middle and later years*. New York: McGraw-Hill.

Mednick, S. A. (1962). The associative basis of the creative process. *Psychological Review, 69,* 220–232.

Morita, A., Reingold, E. M., & Shimomura, M. (1986). *Made in Japan*. New York: Dutton.

Musterberg, H. (1983). *The crown of life: Artistic creativity in old age*. New York: Harcourt Brace Jovanovich.

Nadler, G. (1981). *The planning and design approach*. New York: Wiley.

Neugarten, B. L. (1977). Personality and aging. In J. E. Birren & K. W. Schaie (Eds.), *Handbook of the psychology of aging* (pp. 626–649). New York: Van Nostrand Reinhold.

Neugarten, B. L. (1979). Time, age and the life cycles. *American Journal of Psychiatry, 136,* 887–894.

Parnes, S. J., Noller, R. B., & Biondi, A. M. (1976). *Guide to creative action*. New York: Schribner's.

Perry, W. (1970). *Forms of intellectual and ethical development in the college years*. New York: Jossey-Bass.

Portillo, M. B., & Dohr, J. H. (In press). Design education: On the road toward thought development. *Design Studies*.

Rappoport, L. (1985). Scholarly creativity and the poetry of human development: The life of Fritz Heider. *Human Development, 28,* 131–140.

Robinson, J. H. (1921). *The mind in the making*. New York: Harper & Brothers.

Romaniuk, J. G. (1978). *Training creativity in the elderly: An examination of attitudes, self-perception, and ability*. Unpublished doctoral dissertation, University of Wisconsin, Madison.

Romaniuk, J. G., & Romaniuk, M. (1981). Creativity across the life span: A measurement perspective. *Human Development, 24,* 366–381.

Romaniuk, J. G., Romaniuk, M., Sprecher, P. L., & Cones, J. H. (1984). Assessing self-perceived creativity across the life span: A comparison of younger and older adults. *Journal of Creative Behavior, 17*(4), 274.

Rothenberg, A. (1976). The process of janusian thinking in creativity. In A. Rothenberg & C. Hausman (Eds.), *The creativity question* (pp. 311–327). Durham, NC: Duke University Press.

Ryff, C. D. (1984). Personality development from the inside: The subjective experience of change in adulthood and aging. In P. B. Baltes & O. B. Brim, Jr. (Eds.), *Life-span development and behavior,* (vol. 6, pp. 245–279). New York: Academic Press.

Ryff, C. D. (1986). The subjective construction of self and society: An agenda for life-span research. In V. W. Marshall (Ed.), *Later life: The social psychology of aging* (pp. 33–74). Beverly Hills, CA: Sage.

Simon, H. A. (1984). The structure of ill-structured problems. In N. Cross (Ed.), *Developments in design methodology* (pp. 145–166). Chichester, England: Wiley & Sons.

Simonton, D. K. (1977). Eminence, creativity, and geography marginality: A recursive structural equation model. *Journal of Personality and Social Psychology, 35,* 805–816.

Taylor, C. W., & Sacks, D. (1981). Facilitating lifetime creative processes: A think piece. *Gifted Child Creativity, 25*(3), 116–118.

Taylor, I. A. (1971). A transactional approach to creativity and its implications for education. *Journal of Creative Behavior, 5*(3), 190–198.

Taylor, I. A. (1974a). The measurement of creative transactualization: A scale to measure behavioral disposition to creativity. *Journal of Creative Behavior, 8,* 114–115.

Taylor, I. A. (1974b). Patterns of creativity and aging. In E. Pfeiffer, (Ed.), *Successful aging: A conference report* (pp. 113–117). Durham, NC: Duke University Press.

Torrance, E. P. (1976). Education and creativity. In A. Rothenberg & C. Hausmann (Eds.), *The creativity question* (pp. 217–227). Durham, NC: Duke University Press.

Wallas, G. (1926). *The art of thought.* New York: Harcourt Brace & World.

Ward, R. A. (1984). *The aging experience: An introduction to social gerontology.* New York: Harper & Row.

12

THE POLITICAL ECONOMY OF HIGHER EDUCATION FOR OLDER LEARNERS

University of Massachusetts at Boston

INTRODUCTION

As early as the late 1800s, social scientists such as Emile Durkheim sought to examine the role of education in society. It was not until the 1940s, however, that rigorous scholarly research was conducted on the function of education in the larger society. This work was conducted concerning issues in public schools (both elementary and secondary), in private schools, and in higher education.

Two of the questions that have preoccupied scholars concerned with the societal role of schools and that have relevance to this chapter include "How do schools function in allocating persons and resources to various social classes and positions in society?" and "How are subcultural struggles for equality and supremacy, integration and pluralism influenced by educational processes?" (Brookover & Erickson, 1975). An extensive literature exists on each of these questions, with different theoretical schools regarding the unintended outcomes of educational activities. We are concerned here, however, with a relatively narrow subset of questions regarding policies and programs as they affect learners 60 years old and older in higher education and their consequences for the political economy of higher education.

Education for our older citizens means many different things to different people. To some educators, *older learners* means nontraditional students who are in their 30s and 40s, often working at paying jobs and in need of further study and credentialing. In this chapter, however, older learners refers to individuals who are 60 years old or older. Also, the term *education* for older people may mean many different kinds of learning opportunities, ranging from those that lead to a formal degree to informal self-learning. To help describe and differentiate the different

227

kinds of educational opportunities available to older people, Bass (1986) has grouped them into six different areas, as follows.

1. Educational programs designed to assist with the transition to retirement. The focus of such educational programs is on planning for retirement and retirement itself. Generally these programs include information on financial planning, the use of leisure time, and making the psychological adjustment to the change in role.

2. Educational programs the primary purpose of which is to provide personal enrichment and exposure to the arts and sciences. Often such courses and programs are offered by a continuing education division of a university, a community school, an adult education center, or an organization that specializes in travel/social educational programs for older learners (such as Elderhostel), or they can be arranged on a space-available basis in a degree-granting institution. In fact, more than two-thirds of all colleges and universities sponsor such opportunities for older citizens with reduced rates or tuition waived. Approximately half of the state public higher education institutions have tuition waiver policies (Timmerman, 1985). Students in these educational programs would be described in the literature as expressive learners, interested in learning for the sake of learning itself.

3. Educational programs that emphasize personal planning and management. These might include classes in budgeting, nutrition, exercise, language skills, health care, and the like. These programs can be offered in a school or college building, but frequently are offered at off-campus locations such as a library, elderly housing units, a congregate meal site, or a senior center.

4. Educational programs designed to provide individual physical therapy or memory retention techniques to respond to the special needs of the frail elder. These specialized programs are conducted by professionals in the allied health professions often in conjunction with a university research team, medical school, or community health center.

5. Educational programs designed to help the elder and his or her family cope with the terminal stage of life. Such programs are offered under the auspices of a religious organization or a ministry for the elderly, by hospice organizations, or by community organizations.

6. Educational programs designed to provide professional certification to enable older people to enter or reenter the primary, secondary, or voluntary labor markets. These credentialing programs in university or college settings are generally available for older people on a space-available, tuition waiver basis. In a few instances, higher education settings have developed special degree-granting programs designed to attract older learners.

Of the many types of learning opportunities available to older learners, the most popular are those programs that are offered on a noncredit basis for personal enrichment by special programs or continuing education centers (Covey, 1980; Hiemstra, 1976; Hooper & March, 1978). Despite tuition waiver policies, participation of older people as degree- or certificate-seeking students within traditional university or college settings remains very low (Kingston, 1982).

The fact that few older people seek or are involved in career-oriented degree or certificate programs is perplexing. After all, one thinks, the retired have the time to attend college. Just as scholars have examined the larger societal purposes, intended and not, that schools have played concerning access to education for minority groups and women, should we not ask if age segregation—the fact that students in colleges and universities are primarily young—serves some larger societal purpose? What are the political and economic implications of expanding access to higher education for older people? Are arguments for access to higher education by age similar in principle to those arguments made for access by race and gender? These are some of the questions explored in this chapter.

SOCIOLOGICAL THEORIES OF SCHOOLING

Sociologists have generated numerous theories about the role that schools play in society. In his comprehensive work, *The Limits and Possibilities of Schooling,* Hurn (1985) has organized these theories into two distinct perspectives concerning the school's role in modern society. The first theoretical point of view is what he refers to as the "functional paradigm." In the most basic terms, it refers to those theorists who argue that schools provide two basic functions for society. The first is the provision of equal opportunity; the school is a rational mechanism by which the best and the brightest can rise to the top. The vision here is of a meritocracy in which ability and merit are determining factors in success, in direct contrast to the notion that economic and social success are achieved by prescribed characteristics such as family background. The egalitarian notion remains among functionalists that if you are good at what you do and you are successful in school, you can "pull yourself up by your bootstraps" (Ryan, 1971) and assimilate into any social class regardless of the circumstances of birth.

The second function of the school in society, say the functionalists, is that it plays a primary role in providing the technical training and transmission of knowledge essential for the kind of skilled work force necessary for expansion of the economy. It is the school setting that provides the educational preparation, the technical skills, and the normative behavior appropriate for sustained economic growth in an increasingly technological society. Both industry and government are helped in developing credentials, standards, and competencies to match the skills needed in the workplace. Through the transmission of knowledge, the school filters and identifies those individuals who are best suited to the demands of employers and consumers. According to the functionalist perspective, this second function is related to the first function in that those positions in the work force for which schools serve as the gatekeepers are, therefore, available to all based on merit.

In 1976, Bowles and Gintis presented a different theoretical perspective on the function of schools in society, now regarded as conflict theory. In their book, *Schooling in Capitalist America,* they argued that the evidence indicates that the school is the very institution that perpetuates inequality and reinforces among the poor and vulnerable feelings of inferiority and inadequacy. When one looks at the institution of schooling, one must look at it in the context of the economy, they say.

Their thesis is that schools are designed to maintain the status quo, to provide education and training that reflect a certain class bias and values that in turn can be instruments of domination and oppression. Educational outcomes indicate that the children of the elite and wealthy remain in positions of power and influence as a result of the schooling process, and the children of the poor and minorities remain outside of the political and economic system. Schools as gatekeepers select, distinguish, and reward those individuals who have qualities most nearly like existing leaders, and they do not reward those who are different.

This radical departure from the functionalist egalitarian perspective is based on findings that reveal a dramatic differential in student educational and career outcomes for low-income groups or racial minorities. Bowles and Gintis (1976) postulated that this differential must be related to the norms and attitudes of the school itself. Indeed, the school may be a path out of poverty for a unique few, but for most who do not subscribe to its prevailing culture and rule, it becomes an institution that slowly tracks them out of the mainstream. The school is the instrument that excludes and separates them from others. Those whose cultural traditions concerning competition and cooperation differ from the prevailing culture, those who speak other languages or English dialects, those who look or behave differently, and those with nontypical values can be labeled, tracked, and frightened by the schooling process. Rather than being an environment that fosters learning and social mobility, the school becomes for them a painful setting that reinforces feelings of inferiority and insecurity.

It is this institution, which caters to and rewards a select few for the benefits of the larger society and ignores or criticizes so many others to their detriment, that Bowles and Gintis described as "school." Although students in the United States reflect very different cultures and values, the school itself maintains standards and normative structures that change very slowly over time. And these standards and normative structures are determined outside of the school to serve larger social and economic agendas of a select, self-serving few.

THEORETICAL PERSPECTIVES ABOUT OLDER LEARNERS

The Functionalist Perspective

If we accept the theoretical position of the functionalists that schools are egalitarian institutions, then how would we interpret the role that older people play in higher education in contrast to younger students? Based on this theoretical point of view, one could argue that older people are not evident in large numbers in higher education because their numbers are a rational allocation based on the status and role of the aged. That is, older people have reached a time in their lives when the pressures and demands of being a student involved in higher education is no longer viewed as desirable. Although 90% of elders in the United States who are 65 years and older have not gone to college or have not completed an undergraduate degree, the completion of a degree is not the prevailing requirement for participation in the labor force or in achieving social status. Furthermore, we know that 86% of men 65 and older are no longer in the full-time work force and nearly 94% of women 65 and older are not part of the labor force (U.S. Department of Labor, 1987). Based on such a profile, one could assume that higher education is of limited value.

On the other hand, according to this perspective, younger people by virtue of their age are more motivated and able to provide the leadership needed for the future. Education is a form of investment in the future; societal costs for educational opportunity are returned by its beneficiaries after many years of contribution to the workplace and economy. A subgroup of functionalists subscribe to the notion of human capital theory. Based on this perspective, education is an investment that increases the individual's human capital over time. It has been argued that cognitive training and skill development for a sophisticated technical economy is best assigned to the young who can fulfill roles as experts in a changing workplace.

Juster (1975) stated

Individuals begin life with a certain amount of potential capital in the form of genetic endowment; they add to that capital throughout early childhood, school years, and the early working years; and they suffer deterioration or depreciation of the capital as their learning or training becomes outmoded or obsolescent. (p. 8)

According to this thinking, older people are therefore less needed and less able to take on ever-changing technical roles; they are encouraged to take on the role of depreciated economic capital by retiring from the work environment. It is consistent with this position, however, that older people have access to education that is designed for cultural enrichment, but education designed for participation in the economic marketplace is incongruent with the rational societal role and function of the aged.

The foregoing analysis may sound a bit harsh about the role of older people, but the functionalist theorists actually have a very pragmatic and positive outlook. They would argue that if older people want to go to schools, they can enroll. There are no rules or regulations barring older people from attending degree-granting programs, and, if older people have the ability and motivation, they can earn degrees. The opportunity exists for their participation. If they want to attend school at an advanced age to receive the credentials needed for certain occupations, all they need do is apply. Actual evidence of age discrimination upon application to colleges and universities has not been significantly proven. Furthermore, they would argue that society has placed a high value on lifelong learning by establishing tuition waivers for older learners. This incentive, not available to younger learners, should further make it possible for older people to go back to school. The low numbers of those who participate in these programs, therefore, is an indication of market forces and the significance ascribed to higher education by older learners.

The Conflict Perspective

The conflict theorists would look at the outcome of a small number of older people in higher education from a very different perspective. They would argue that a primary function of schools is to reinforce the status quo or the current economic distribution of rewards and status as defined by those with power and influence. The college or university helps foster attitudes and behaviors that allow large numbers of people to accept the way things are. Young people going to the university are un-likely to ask why are there so few older people in their classes: A predominance of younger people in most colleges and universities is the norm and the expectation. Yet, because so few older people have college degrees but do have flexible time afforded by reduced employment, it seems that older people would be a good poten-tial market for higher education.

Conflict theorists would further point out that if colleges and universities were to change their age profiles and engage older learners, such a flood of highly trained older people could have a significant impact on the work force, employment, and the current distribution of resources. Newly skilled older people would be put into conflict with emerging younger graduates for potential occupations. And even if the older students were not all interested in employment, based on the extensive experi-ence they bring to their studies, they would seek and demand changes in the way training programs are designed and the way university policies are carried out. Such a policy of engaging older people in higher education would trigger numerous changes that could alter or influence the current configuration of power and author-ity.

Conflict theorists believe that ours is a conflict-ridden society in which differ-ent groups compete for scarce resources—the school being one of them. Certain groups bring better skills and resources into the conflict, ensuring that the poor, people of color, and those who are different in some way are fighting a battle that they are not likely to win. A belief in equal opportunity hides the underlying fact that the youth of privileged groups have advantages over other groups. The values and priorities of the schools reflect the values and priorities of a capitalistic order in modern society, an order that, for the most part, views labor as a commodity that depreciates with age. Older, less-skilled workers are eventually abandoned in favor of younger, highly skilled workers. Finally, the colleges and universities reinforce these inequalities rather than redress them.

Based on this perspective, schools at all levels simply reinforce the larger societal values. Older people are not a valued resource in the current economic scheme and as a result are not likely to be embraced by higher education. Those colleges and universities catering to nontraditional students are viewed by their contemporary institutions as being somewhat less rigorous and prestigious than those focusing on the fast-track, high grades, high SAT scores, and athletic youth. The presence of older people in large numbers would be dysfunctional from the viewpoint of the economic status quo. A significant increase in the pool of talented and credentialed older people could destabilize the current distribution of power.

Thus, conflict theorists argue that from a vested interest perspective college and university administrators can offer only the illusion of equal opportunity in higher education—older people are not equally or fairly represented because that is not in the interest of the controlling social classes. Access will remain tokenistic; those older people who enroll will be doing so in settings ambivalent to their special needs and oriented to the values and needs of younger students. Any major effort to provide supports and programs that would truly involve older students in higher education will be met with resistance, as this assistance would begin to shift the distribution of power and influence and the allocation of resources in higher education.

Although the outcomes are the same whether one describes the participation of older people in higher education as a functionalist or conflict theorist, the perspective is quite different. For the functionalist theorist, the outcome is the result of a fair and equitable process of merit and rational order. The conflict theorist believes the outcome is part of an unfair and elitist manipulation of the social and economic order in a capitalist society. In either case, older people are not major participants in higher education and, from a societal point of view, are not likely to be in the near future.

EQUAL OPPORTUNITY AND ACCESS

Despite some limited participation of older people in higher education, it is argued that the current profile of the student population does not meet our social goal of equity. In the literature, *equal opportunity* initially meant the right of all groups to attend publicly supported educational programs. But since the mid-1970s, the term actually has been used to refer to equality of results (Hurn, 1985). This is a dramatically different perspective. In the earlier instance, providing opportunities for minority groups to apply to higher education sufficiently met the institution's social obligation. Under current thinking, the institution is obligated to affirmatively attract and maintain minority and disadvantaged students. Offering the option of attending an institution of higher education to a variety of groups is not the same as affirmatively ensuring their equal treatment once they are admitted. Equal opportunity has been stretched to mean not just that all can apply, but also that the institution will make some accommodation so that those who bring a different set of experiences, culture, or preparation to the institution will be given an equal chance for success based on their own intellectual merit.

This principle, of course, applies to older people as well as others. As Moody (1987–1988) pointed out, simply making the current higher education programs more available to older people is not really providing access. If access means attending an institution where the older person is an anomaly, where pedagogical techniques are insensitive to the knowledge of adults, where class schedules and class locations are inconvenient, or where the elder feels out of place, then access becomes a superficiality. Access is not merely the right of the nontraditional learner to attend, but the responsiveness of the institution in meeting the needs of those students. When that is achieved, it is then and only then that older people will be interested in taking advantage of the opportunities of higher education. If having equal opportunity means that older people are free to apply to an environment that requires substantial social or psychological adjustment, an environment that is designed for younger learners without the experiences of a lifetime, then that opportunity is not inclusive but remains exclusive and untapped. "Equal opportunity" in this case becomes a hollow phrase without real meaning.

Yet, looking around the United States, we see few colleges and universities that have redefined their programs, reallocated resources, shifted their pedagogy, and offered activities that respond to older people's needs. The few experimental or innovative programs are unique, and even among these pioneering programs, few are providing direct access to the more expensive career-related degree programs. Whether we accept the theoretical position of the functionalists—that older people attend colleges and universities in small numbers because that is the outcome of a rational and fair process—or we accept the conflict theorist position—that older people are excluded as a way of maintaining the current distribution of power and resources—it seems that, in either case, older people are viewed as less valuable for training or retraining for positions in the marketplace than are younger students. This perception of the declining value of older people in the work force is one that is well documented in the literature, despite numerous studies to the contrary and the relatively recent introduction of retirement as a concept (Doering, Rhodes, & Schuster, 1983; Peterson, 1988; U. S. Senate, 1985).

THE ECONOMIC ROLE OF OLDER PEOPLE IN THE WORK FORCE

The idea of retirement being related to a worker's age is a relatively recent phenomenon in industrialized nations (Blank, 1982). Graebner noted in his book, *A History of Retirement,* that in the 1828 edition of Webster's *American Dictionary* the definition of the word *retirement* is not specifically identified with the elderly. In fact, at the turn of the century when Sir William Osler discussed "the uselessness of men above sixty years of age," substantial debate and critical arguments were sparked in defense of older workers (cited in Graebner, 1980). It was not until the depression of the 1930s when employment was scarce that the concept of retirement would be linked to Social Security to become a dominant ideology for those over 65 (Morris & Bass, 1988).

For the most part, prior to the development of Social Security, older people worked until they chose to stop or could work no longer. Undoubtedly, there may have been differing views on the capacity of older workers, but few older people had been required to leave the workplace before that time. They had a role and purpose in the economy, the same as a younger worker (Morris & Bass, 1988). But Graebner (1980) pointed out that as the American economy shifted from a predominantly agrarian mode to a corporate mode, so too did its view of older workers shift. In a newly competitive environment with a priority for efficiency in the work and with too many workers, it was thought that by having older people retire, room would be made for newer, more productive workers. These new workers would bring new ideas to improve productivity and profitability. Also, this would allow employers to substitute aging workers with younger workers at lower salary scales. Retirement, in short, was viewed as a requirement for the effective growth of a robust corporate America. Graebner noted that as the mode of work changed during the early 20th century, so did the prevailing view of the role of older people. By the 1930s economists, management experts, medical leaders, and politicians had begun to reconsider the traditional role of older people in the workplace.

The Social Security Act of 1935 was the landmark legislation that dramatically changed the country's view of older people (Olsen, 1982). The Act provided economic security for old age and at the same time removed them from the work force (Schulz, 1988). Associated with the new status of being retired was an emerging social attitude about the role and capacity of the elderly. Never popular among the elderly, mandatory retirement became something that older people had to accept and learn to adjust to (Graebner, 1980).

In the 1970s, advocates of the elderly came to question the concept of forced retirement in sectors where safety or security were not at stake. After all, they said, should not ability be the best determinant of when an individual should retire? The elimination of mandatory retirement may be the inevitable outcome, because acceptance was never won. But the beginnings of the abolition of forced retirement have not slowed the movement of older people to retire (U.S. Senate, 1987–1988). Nor has it fostered new economic roles or retraining for older workers (Moody, 1987–1988). Although the requirement to leave the work force has been eliminated, the social changes associated with new roles for the elderly have not as yet occurred.

The Effect of Nonparticipation of Older People

The economy of the 1980s and that projected for the 1990s reflects a very different diversification than did the economy of the middle of the 20th century. Rather than relying on an industrial base for growth, the economy has turned to the service industries (Bluestone & Harrison, 1982). Labor has become less physically intensive and more technical in orientation. Rather than having large surpluses of labor, as in the 1930s, in selected areas we now face labor shortages. And so just as the definition of retirement changed 50 years ago to meet the changing needs of the economy, so too can it change now to adapt to current economic needs. Retirement is purely a social phenomenon, institutionalized in capitalistic societies to respond to economic conditions (Phillipson, 1983). It is not based on individual performance nor on the biological condition of older workers (Graebner, 1980; Guillemard, 1983).

Given the changes in the economy over the past several decades and the increased life expectancy of the elderly, to what extent does the social institution of retirement best serve it? And within that context, what role does education play in providing access to the job market for older people? Chen (1987) has argued that the elderly can be viewed as a major economic asset rather than as a liability. With a shrinking work force caused by demographic shifts, older people become a major asset in terms of the work force. Table 1 shows the numbers of both elderly (65 years and older) and young (0 to 17 years), and the combined total of those two groups, who have been or must in the future be supported by each 100 persons of working age. In addition, the table provides a profile of the changes in the ratio of potential supporters to the youth population as well as the ratio of the potential supporters to the elderly population. These ratios are projected over a 100-year period from 1940 to 2040.

As is demonstrated in this table, this measure does provide some direction as to the number of workers available in the work force to support a dependent population. As Chen stated, "When the number of potential supporters relative to potential dependents declines, society may need to call upon the old to remain in or re-enter the workforce in order to provide a labor resource" (1987, p. 414). The continued participation of older people in the labor force can provide the state with additional tax revenue and can reduce the outflow of funds from Social Security.

Schulz (1988) indicated that older workers do have some problems competing in the marketplace. On the average, older workers have less formal education, they have a greater risk of chronic illness, and generally they have less work flexibility because of their seniority, pay scales, or work rules. Yet numerous carefully conducted studies indicate that there is no real difference in performance between younger and older workers (Sparrow, 1986). Other researchers have summarized the literature (Robinson, Coberly, & Paul, 1985) by stating that there are wide differences among individual workers in productivity, and that declines related to aging workers can be seen in certain physically demanding industries. In some industries, however, older workers are actually more productive than younger workers. In areas such as "creativity, flexibility, facility of information processing, absenteeism, accident rates, and turnover," older workers scored better than younger workers (Robinson et al., 1985). At one time, to remove less productive, redundant, older people from the work force was perceived to enhance the economy. Now, however,

TABLE 1 Young, Elderly, and Total of Those Needing Support by the Working Population: 1940–2040 (per 100 persons of working age)

Year	Elderly (65 + years)	Young (0–17 years)	Total
1940	10.9	51.9	62.8
1960	16.8	65.1	82.0
1980	18.6	45.8	64.4
2000	21.1	40.7	61.8
2020	28.7	36.9	65.6
2040	37.9	36.7	74.6

Note. From "America in Transition: An Aging Society" by C. M. Taeuber, 1983, *Current Population Report* (Series P-23, No. 128). Washington, DC: U.S. Government Printing Office. Adapted by permission.

the voluntary loss of able older workers from the work force through retirement may, in fact, reduce productivity and expedite issues of labor shortages.

THE ECONOMIC ROLE
OF FORMAL EDUCATION

As discussed earlier, the current cohort of older people is less formally educated than are younger people. Because of economic circumstances and social roles, educational opportunities were formerly available to far fewer individuals, particularly, choices were few for women and minorities. As a result, individuals who may have enormous potential have not had the same opportunities for higher education and its enrichment, and for the specialized career training now available at colleges and universities. The implications of having limited credentials in an increasingly credentialed society has been a barrier for the current cohort of older people. With access to, but limited inclusiveness for, older people in higher education, many have had to accept roles assigned to workers without college degrees. Phillipson (1983) stated that

> the capitalist mode of production not only leads to unequal incomes which contribute to poverty in retirement, but by limiting the access of workers to education throughout their lives and institutionalising the division between manual and mental labour, creates tensions and contradictions in the way workers experience retirement. (pp. 135–136)

Given that both employment and education have been rationed resources among the elderly, and that education serves as one of the gatekeepers to economic and social standing, it may be understandable why older people occupy a lower social status in our society. Walker (1983) argued that the dependency of many elderly is caused by a "structurally enforced inferior social and economic status in relation to the working population" (p. 144). If, however, the social invention of retirement no longer best serves our economic needs, and if education is an important resource in gaining employment mobility and status, then how can educational opportunities be made more available to an older population?

Perhaps one of the most evident things about the older population is its diversity in experiences, interests, and preparation—economically or socially—for aging (Schulz, 1988; Walker, 1983). For some, retirement is a time of leisure and pleasure. For others, aging poses new economic burdens and stresses. Burdens caused by inadequate income in old age are particularly acute for older women and people of color (Commonwealth Fund Commission, 1987; Palmer & Gould, 1986; Reischauer, 1985).

Through years of discrimination in the workplace, women and minorities historically have been paid less than white men. In fact, 80% of all women workers are concentrated in only 20 of the 420 job categories identified by the U. S. Department of Labor. These positions are generally characterized as having relatively low earnings, little job mobility, limited job security, and few fringe benefits (Minkler & Stone, 1985). Furthermore, women are more likely to experience interrupted careers as a consequence of child-rearing. The combined result for them is smaller Social Security checks, smaller savings for retirement, and often no pension plan. Also, because of their longer life span, women are more likely than men to become single and poor in the course of their lives. Women are also more likely than men to be placed in a caregiving role for an elderly relative, distancing them further from the regiments of work. For older women of color, the economic problems are even greater. Frequently referred to as individuals of "double jeopardy" or "multiple hazard" (Schulz, 1988), older minority women represent the poorest segment of American society (Minkler & Stone, 1985).

Despite economic gains for most groups of elders, the incidence of poverty for older women who live alone is projected to continue to rise slightly through the next 30 years (Commonwealth Fund Commission, 1987). As these poor older women often lack formal educational training beyond high school, higher education that provides training for careers for older people is one way to respond to America's need for skilled workers and at the same time arrest a lifetime of economic hardship. Certainly not all older people will qualify for entrance to college, but, given that 90% of the current cohort of elders have not gone to college or have not completed an undergraduate degree, surely some will have college potential.

To attract and retain older students in higher education will require resources and approaches not currently available in most colleges and universities. Just as we have learned that providing access for minority students requires ongoing supportive services, or that access for disabled students requires adaptation of the physical environment, so too we see that the involvement of older students requires some adaptation of the college setting.

ADAPTING HIGHER EDUCATION
TO THE OLDER LEARNER

Since the early 1970s, colleges in the United States have experimented with various educational approaches for students of nontraditional ages. In most cases programs were designed for working people in their 30s and 40s. Institutions such as Alverno College, the College of Human Services, Union College, and the College of Public and Community Service at the University of Massachusetts at Boston have been in the forefront in attracting adult students (Taylor, 1976). Competency-based education, for which specific written performance standards and criteria were developed as objective measures of the material needed to be demonstrated, became institutionalized as a pedagogical approach responsive to these students. The competency statements allowed students with prior experiences on the job and in the home to demonstrate ability or competence in specific areas without always having to take a course to do so. Such a system provided increased flexibility in earning college credits for adults who already had acquired some of the content and skills needed for an undergraduate degree.

In most of these programs, which actively sought to attract 30- to 40-year-old adults, grading was deemphasized, and, in its place, written evaluations were instituted. These two changes, no grading and alternatives to classroom learning through the competency system, forced changes in authority and the role of the faculty member and in the allocation of resources on campus (Taylor, 1976). Monies for supportive reading and writing programs became more important, and evening and weekend classes became more important to accommodate working students. Access to day care was essential for older students. And, as the faculty began to work with adult students—students who brought a world of experience to the classroom—the relationships between teacher and student evolved and changed.

Much as these changes in the structure and teaching have accommodated one sector of nontraditional students and provided them with access to degree-granting higher education programs, so too must changes take place in the structure and teaching to attract and retain older learners. Such changes in the distribution of resources in higher education, however, pose political questions the answers to which are influenced by the political economy of older learners.

CONCLUSION

At the center of an assessment of the political economy of older learners is society's perceived value of their contribution as producers in the economy. The prevailing scale of the economic value of elders is decidedly tipped toward older people as consumers rather than as producers. As Estes (1979) has argued in *The Aging Enterprise,* the political economy of older people has been based on their value in developing or expanding industries that profit from their dependence. If this is the prevailing notion of the economic utility of the aged in a capitalistic society, the political economy of investing in the education and training of those in their later years will not be viewed as a high priority. That is a low value in an abstract hierarchy of priorities.

In terms of the original and central question posed by scholars over the last several decades as to how schools function in allocating people and resources to various social classes and positions in society, one must comment that at this time institutions of higher education reflect, rather than seek to change, the stratification and role of the aged in society. In answer to the second question, regarding how subcultural struggles for equality and supremacy are influenced by the educational process for the aged, at this time, it must be stated that higher education's role is marginal. This is not to say that institutions of higher education cannot or will not play a major role in the redistribution of the social and economic standing of the elderly, but that at present the prevailing needs of the economy do not force a rethinking of the needs of older learners.

From a practical viewpoint, higher education is sensitive and reactive to the market conditions and needs of the economy and the work force. Rather than shifting priorities, power, and structural arrangements merely to accommodate a nontraditional student population, colleges and universities will need both forces that push them externally and forces that pull them internally to consider reassessing the political economy of older learners.

In the foreseeable future, the economy's need for skilled older workers will be decidedly different than it is today. Demographic trends and economic indicators all point to a need to reconsider retirement and the economic role of older people (Sandell, 1988). But without these macroeconomic shifts and the concurrent restructuring of educational opportunities, older learners in higher education will remain as occasional partners in youth-oriented institutions, or they will be segregated in specialized continuing education programs or tracked into even more cultural enrichment programs, rather than being integrated into the educational mainstream with a full complement of academic resources and career opportunities. Institutional change does not come easily to higher education. Without a substantial rethinking of the political economy of the aged as learners and producers, this change is not likely to occur.

REFERENCES

Bass, S. (1986). Matching educational opportunities with the able elderly. *Lifelong Learning: An Omnibus of Practice and Research, 9*(5), 4–7.

Blank, R. C. (1982). A changing worklife and retirement pattern: An historical perspective. In M. Morrison (Ed.), *Economics of aging: The future of retirement* (pp. 1–60). New York: Van Nostrand Reinhold.

Bluestone, B., & Harrison, B. (1982). *The industrialization of America.* New York: Basic Books.

Bowles, S., & Gintis, H. (1976). *Schooling in capitalist America.* New York: Basic Books.

Brookover, W. B., & Erickson, E. L. (1975). *Sociology of education.* Homewood, IL: Dorsey Press.

Chen, Y-P. (1987). Making assets of tomorrow's elderly. *The Gerontologist, 27,* 410–416.

Commonwealth Fund Commission on Elderly People Living Alone. (1987). *Old, alone and poor: A plan for reducing poverty among elderly people living alone.* Baltimore, MD: Author.

Covey, H. C. (1980). An exploratory study of the acquisition of a college student role by elder people. *The Gerontologist, 2,* 173–181.

Doering, M., & Rhodes, C. R., & Schuster, M. (1983). *The aging worker.* Beverly Hills, CA: Sage.

Estes, C. (1979). *The aging enterprise.* San Francisco: Jossey-Bass.

Graebner, W. (1980). *A history of retirement.* New Haven, CT: Yale University Press.

Guillemard, A-M. (1983). Introduction. In A-M. Guillemard (Ed.), *Old age and the welfare state* (pp. 3–18). Beverly Hills, CA: Sage.

Hiemstra, R. (1976). Older adult learning: Instrumental and expressive categories. *Educational Gerontology, 1,* 227–236.

Hooper, J. O., & March, G. B. (1978). A study of older students attending university classes. *Educational Gerontology, 3,* 321–330.

Hurn, C. J. (1985). *The limits and possibilities of schooling.* Boston: Allyn & Bacon.

Juster, T. (Ed.). (1975). *Education, income, and human behavior.* New York: McGraw-Hill.

Kingston, S. J. (1982). The senior citizen as college student. *Educational Gerontology, 8,* 43–52.

Minkler, M., & Stone, R. (1985). The feminization of poverty of older women. *The Gerontologist, 28,* 351–357.

Moody, H. R. (1987–1988). Why worry about education for older adults? *Generations, 12*(2), 5–9.

Morris, R., & Bass, S. (1988). Toward a new paradigm about work and age. In R. Morris & S. Bass (Eds.), *Retirement reconsidered: Economic and social roles for older people* (pp. 3–14). New York: Springer.

Olsen, L. K. (1982). *The political economy of aging.* New York: Columbia University Press.

Palmer, J. L., & Gould, S. G. (1986). Economic consequences of population aging. In A. Pifer & L. Bronte (Eds.), *Our aging society* (pp. 367–390). New York: Norton.

Peterson, D. (1988). The older worker: Myths and realities. In R. Morris & S. Bass (Eds.), *Retirement reconsidered: Economic and social roles for older people* (pp. 116–128). New York: Springer.

Phillipson, C. (1983). The state, the economy and retirement. In A-M. Guillemard (Ed.), *Old age and the welfare state* (pp. 127–142). Beverly Hills, CA: Sage.

Reischauer, R. D. (1985, July 18). *Retirement income security.* Hearings before the Subcommittee on Social Security and the Subcommittee on Oversight of the Committee of Ways and Means, U.S. House of Representatives, Serial No. 99-50.

Robinson, P., Coberly, S., & Paul, C. E. (1985). Work and retirement. In R. Binstock & E. Shanas (Eds.), *Handbook on aging and the social sciences* (2nd ed.) (pp. 527–537). New York: Van Nostrand Reinhold.

Ryan, W. (1971). *Blaming the victim.* New York: Random House.

Sandell, S. (1988). The labor force by the year 2000 and employment policy for older workers. In R. Morris & S. Bass (Eds.), *Retirement reconsidered: Economic and social roles for older people* (pp. 107–115). New York: Springer.

Schulz, J. (1988). *The economics of aging.* Dover, MA: Auburn House.

Sparrow, P. R. (1986). Job performance among older workers. *Aging International, 13*(2), 5–6.

Taeuber, C. M. (1983). America in transition: An aging society. *Current population reports* (Series P-23, No. 128). Washington, DC: U.S. Government Printing Office.

Taylor, C. (1976). *Planning an urban experimental college: CPCS.* Doctoral dissertation, Rutgers University, NJ.

Timmerman, S. (1985). Options in aging education for developing institutions. *AGHE Exchange, 8*(4), 1–2.

U.S. Department of Labor, Bureau of Labor Statistics. (1987). *Employment and earnings.* Washington, DC: U.S. Government Printing Office.

U.S. Senate, Special Committee on Aging. (1985). *Personnel practices for an aging workforce: Private-sector examples.* Washington, DC: Government Printing Office.

U.S. Senate, Special Committee on Aging. (1987–1988). *Aging America: Trends and projections.* Washington, DC: U.S. Government Printing Office.

Walker, A. (1983). Social policy and elderly people in Great Britain: The construction of dependent social and economic status in old age. In A-M. Guillemard (Ed.), *Old age and the welfare state* (pp. 143–168). Beverly Hills, CA: Sage.

13

MODELS OF COGNITIVE FUNCTIONING IN THE OLDER ADULT: RESEARCH NEEDS IN EDUCATIONAL GERONTOLOGY

GISELA LABOUVIE-VIEF
Wayne State University

Recent demands for extending educational opportunities to the later phases of the life cycle have created new and unprecedented needs for educators, who are consequently searching for data and theory to answer their questions as they attempt to design sound, specialized programs for older learners. It is my purpose in this chapter to explore some possible answers from my perspective as a psychologist interested in life-span developmental processes. On the one hand, given the interdisciplinary nature of the problem, my perspective may well be somewhat limited; on the other hand, such a life-span view may also serve to broaden our understanding of the problem. A primary focus on processes of development may force us to examine any answers, not merely from the vantage point of how currently available research can be translated into classroom applications, but also with the superordinate goal in mind of understanding all those interactions of elderly people with each other, with other strata of society, and even with researchers, and of understanding as well the ways in which those interactions may serve to enhance or dampen cognitive competence in later life.

The main thesis of this chapter may at first sound overly pessimistic, but I hope it may help to delineate more sharply the research needs in learning, intelligence, and cognitive processes in later life. According to this thesis, the emerging emphasis on growth, change, and education in later life has caught the theoretician as much by surprise as it did the practitioner. Both have been socialized into an outlook on late adulthood that has its roots in a static conceptualization of the needs and capabilities of the older adult. Both have come to expect adulthood to be the achievement of a static level of maturity and the endpoint, rather than the continuation, of education. As a result, we are now observing a curious mismatch between theory and social reality: whereas much of our theory appears to document the frailties and limitations of old age, this picture is already being denied by many elderly who are searching for avenues toward continued growth.

The rapid changes in our society, of which this mismatch is but one indication, have created, among theorists concerned with the developmental capacities of adults, a growing disenchantment with the available body of theoretical constructs, research methodologies, and even content issues, all of which appear better suited to the past than to the present, let alone the future. As a result, the time-worn and comfortable assumptions that we have held about the abilities of the older individual are eroding, and we are beginning to expose a new view of adult development that is opening up new interpretations, new avenues of research, and new goals as they relate to education in later life.

In this chapter, therefore, I am not attempting to derive prescriptive statements about the education of older people from what at present appears to be an accepted body of knowledge about the intellectual and cognitive capabilities of the aging individual. Toffler (1974) has recently argued that goals and policies relating to education must spring from images about the future. To search for answers in the past is merely to adopt a timeless view of development in which yesterday predicts today and in which tomorrow is only more of today. Such a view is bound to yield obsolete research findings, for phenomena are changing at a faster rate than researchers are able to provide useful data about them. In line with this position, I am less concerned with clear answers than with raising questions, less with knowledge as a static goal than with knowledge as a process and a potentiality.

IDEALISM IN ADULT
DEVELOPMENTAL THEORY

At first sight, the problem of isolating those issues and questions that are particularly deserving of research attention in the future may appear simple enough; we might elect simply to survey issues on the basis of some assessment of empirical needs. The problem is not quite so straightforward, however. This is so because, for those trained in a particular discipline, interesting research problems are not defined merely by current needs (e.g., the educational needs of older populations); rather, many of those research problems appear to involve a time dimension that is more easily grasped from a historic perspective. Any scientific discipline tends to evolve a specialized language, a certain way of looking at reality, that may often appear to be somewhat removed from real-life applications. Indeed, it is often this language system that not only reformulates important real-life issues, but also generates new corollary issues that, although they may be highly challenging to the community of scientists, are often rather removed from any immediate, practical import.

The point just raised is of some importance because, contrary to widespread popular opinion, the activity of researchers does not merely amount to constructing a faithful copy of "things as they are." Rather, it is our own ways of conceptualizing, interpreting, and looking at things that determine the way they appear in the first place. This is why merely recording currently known findings in the area of adult cognitive functioning may not be particularly useful in elucidating what we need to know. Instead, we need to go one step further here and consider why, in the past, certain questions have been deemed more worthwhile of research attention than others, why certain interpretations have been favored, and why, as a result, many current views of adulthood are slanted toward a picture that is not necessarily complete, convincing, or valid.

Idealistic Views of Development

The traditional view of how our knowledge of certain empirical givens originates has been to assert that this knowledge derives from a careful recording of reality. Knowledge, in this view, is not seen to be potentially contaminated by more pragmatic considerations such as its usefulness or its compatibility with a certain ideological position, but is thought, rather, to be somehow defined, independent of human existence, in an a priori sense. This view is expressed in Plato's theory of innate ideas, which has exerted a powerful influence on Western philosophy of science and serves as a model for many current ways of conceptualizing the process of development. It was Plato's assertion that the concepts, truths, and laws known to humans were not merely a somewhat whimsical construction by human minds, but rather reflected a system of laws and truths inherent in the universe. Development from birth to maturity could thus in many ways be likened to a "rediscovery" of those innate ideas, and the most mature level of development—the age of reason—would therefore be the time in a persons's life-span at which these universal truths could be understood with a relatively high degree of faithfulness. Thus, the end of development is thought to be fixed a priori by some ideal conception of maturity, and as a result, views of development deriving from the Platonic system may be called *idealistic* (Labouvie-Vief & Chandler, 1978; Riegel, 1975).

To be sure, the particular basis, according to which the ideal outcome of development was fixed, has varied throughout the course of the centuries (*see*, for example, Muuss, 1975). Thus, in medieval systems, maturity was a state of knowledge of principles revealed to humans from God, whereas more recent theories have opted for a more evolutionary view according to which "mature" criteria represent the highest evolutionary accomplishment of which humans are capable. Whatever the basis, however, the resulting views of development all fit one general pattern. As development is thought to be realized in some fixed goal or end state, it is thought to be teleologically oriented toward this final stage of maturity. Just as this mature state is given a priori, so also is the route along which individuals move as they mature: growth is thought to proceed in a unilinear fashion, moving through a series of imperfect, preliminary stages until the ultimate, ideal stage is realized. As development is thus conceptualized in terms of ideal end states that are realized via a universal development pathway, the ensuing notion of development acquires prescriptive overtones; that is, it serves as a standard against which to judge variations in the rate of progression and final achievements of development. What is "normal" in development, consequently, is judged, not by pragmatic criteria, but by idealistic standards.

Although still popular in development psychology, similar idealistic notions have largely been abandoned in contemporary philosophy. The danger inherent in idealistic positions, as pointed out by several writers (e.g., Barrett, 1962; Habermas, 1971), is that they may easily confuse descriptive and normative aspects of a science. Thus, recording and observing the course of development often becomes equivalent to theorizing about it: The resulting patterns of development are assumed to be indicative of one, universal, organic process of development that is not substantially altered if examined from other perspectives, for example, from those of other subcultural groups, other cultures, or other periods of history. Such a position easily entails the danger of ruling diversity in development out of court. More recent views, in fact, have emphasized that what appears to be a relatively firm objective truth from the perspective of idealism, often may be contaminated by particular biases, interests, and time-bound conceptions that are not objective by any means.

The position that research findings and accepted "truths" of a science are only relative to particular ideological contexts from which they emerge has quite profound implications for our current evaluation of what is known about adult development. In line with others (e.g., Buss, 1975; Gergen, 1973; Giorgi, 1971), I maintain that much of what is currently accepted about the capacities of older people must be taken with a bit of caution, as it is likely to reflect not inevitable psychological processes, but cultural norms that need to be reexamined on the basis of their particular historical-ideological context.

Prevalent Conceptualizations of Adult Intelligence

Before discussing more specifically some of the pitfalls that idealistic notions of development may entail, it may be useful to present a brief synopsis of current conceptualizations of adult intelligence, together with a discussion of how their idealistic slant may have resulted in a somewhat prejudicial account of what older people can do. As argued previously (e.g., Baltes & Labouvie, 1973; Labouvie-Vief & Chandler, 1978), the notion underlying much of life-span cognitive theory is one that has proven to be a useful working assumption primarily when discussing development from infancy to adolescence. According to this notion, intellectual development displays distinctive features of growth (e.g., Flavell, 1970): it is thought to be relatively momentous, universal, and irreversible. This uniform, normal growth pattern is usually attributed to the constraining principles of biological-maturational growth; it does not discount the role of experience in intellectual development, however. Experience is thought to operate in concert with the constraining process of biological growth. Thus, although experience may introduce a source of variation, uniformity of growth is nevertheless virtually guaranteed, and the resulting deviations from an idealistically conceived developmental path are attributed to differential tempos of development.

The conviction that childhood development follows highly universal pathways and is characterized by rather dramatic transformations from stage to stage may have created a bias in theoreticians of adult development to primarily attend to similar, eye-catching phenomena in late life. Thus, much of current theorizing about life-span cognition can be seen as an effort to isolate what one might call "true," "normal," and universal components of aging, which are contrasted with those processes of development not held to be intrinsic to aging. This dualistic system of normal and extrinsic factors of aging has provided a framework for what, in reality, is a highly diverse pattern of both improvements and deterioration in tasks of intellectual competence throughout adulthood and old age.

The empirical data on intellectual change after maturity have been extensively summarized elsewhere (e.g., Baltes & Labouvie, 1973; Botwinick, 1967, 1973; Horn, 1976; Jarvik & Cohen, 1973), and a brief summary will suffice at this point. Those functions that appear to be least sensitive to the passage of time are, in general, those thought to reflect the effects of lifelong learning. Thus, cognitive tests that assess an individual's accumulation of verbal skills and general information, or tasks of learning, memory, and problem solving that are well embedded in a matrix of meaning, are those typically found to improve throughout adulthood and well into old age. On the other hand, tests relating to the perception of relationships among abstract symbols (e.g., geometric shapes), to the integration of new and complex material, or to the effective use of information under conditions of time restriction and in highly abstract contexts are the kinds of tests on which older adults tend to do much more poorly than their younger counterparts.

On an empirical level, this differential pattern of growth and decline has been substantiated across literally hundreds of research studies, and it must therefore be accepted as a rather sound finding of the geropsychological literature. What is less convincing, however, is the theoretical interpretation it has received. It has often been thought that the abstract, more *age-sensitive* (Botwinick, 1967) measures are particularly telling of a presumed, primary universal component of aging. Specifically, it has been proposed that these more abstract performances are particularly well integrated with biological-maturational processes and that their decline is tied to "loss and degeneration of the psychological (particularly neurological) substratum, as produced either by (or both by) catabolic maturational changes or (and) irreversible damage brought on by illness and injuries" (Horn, 1976, p. 463). In contrast, the cognitive, *age-insensitive*, functions were usually thought to be less telling of such sweeping and universal aging processes. Rather, they are usually said to reflect the effects of lifelong information accumulation and the overlearning of well-established habits and, therefore, have not been of as much interest to many developmental psychologists because they are viewed as distractions from the truly dramatic effects of advanced age on cognitive functioning.

Thus, we see that the rather dramatic picture of childhood cognitive changes is, in essence, continued throughout the rest of the life-span. Aging processes, like earlier developmental changes, are thought to display the characteristics of universality and irreversibility; although, unlike growth processes, they are regressive rather than progressive. But we also see that this continuity of theoretical interpretation along the age continuum is bought at a certain expense: "True" aging no longer is universally expressed across the total range of behaviors. In fact, it appears only if one becomes rather selective in the definition of what are valid criteria of true aging. Whether or not one is willing to underwrite traditional interpretations of adult cognitive functioning, as a consequence, depends upon whether one feels this selectivity is an asset or a fateful limitation of one's view.

The latter opinion has been expressed in a number of recent writings that despite the rather overwhelming case against cognitive competence in later life, have opted for a more positive view by questioning the heavy decremental emphasis in traditional theories of intellectual aging. Decrement, according to these interpretations, is not necessarily a reality of adult cognitive functioning; it may result from the fact that current models of life-span intellectual functioning contain a number of unquestioned and untested assumptions and from the fact that the interpretations, as a consequence, may be based upon biased methodologies and unduly narrow measures of cognitive performance.

At the crux of the emerging, competing interpretations is the recognition that generalizations from empirical data often tend to confuse descriptive and normative aspects. That there *is* a relationship between increasing age and decreasing competence on tests of speeded, abstract performance certainly is descriptively accurate. What is less certain, however, is that this empirical fact can be construed to represent a theoretical law, or the prescriptive, idealistic conclusion that such a relationship *ought* to exist. This questionable "is" to "ought" (Kohlberg, 1971) reference, in fact, has formed the basis for several equally fateful assumptions, which are discussed more fully throughout the remainder of this chapter.

The first of these assumptions relates to the presumptive organizing principles of development, which are seen to reflect the epigenetic unfolding of biological-maturational capacities. This maturational bias has not only resulted in a tendency to biologize the aging process on the basis of quite inadequate evidence, but—with its corollary assumption of the irreversibility of such changes—has also led to a too-ready acceptance of the view that whatever apparent decrement was demonstrated reflected the result of a universal, irreversible process of deterioration. A second assumption is that development is universal and therefore transcends boundaries of history, culture, and locale; as a consequence, the potential transitoriness of what appeared to be relatively inevitable aging changes has not been sufficiently subjected to critical test. A third assumption, recently reevaluated, relates to the presumed teleological end goal of development. Although it is probably true that any developmental analysis ought to presuppose a rather thorough conceptualization of its end point, it is also true, however, that most theories of cognitive development may have located this "final" stage at a rather early point in the life-span. As a result, the achievements of adults and older people are rarely assessed against age-appropriate standards, but more often against those of adolescents and youth who may be involved in wrapping up the final stages of their formal education. By this comparison standard, the achievements of adults and elderly individuals often have appeared static at best, amateurish at worst. Finally, as it was believed that all of behavior is ultimately governed by the same set of universal, maturational principles, there has been an implicit tendency to think that the particular behavior under study did not really matter. In contrast, I think that this assumption, rather than guaranteeing truly universal insights about the learning of the elderly, has encouraged criterion measures of learning and cognition that may be best suited to the relatively lifeless, meaningless context of a laboratory and at least suited to the concrete, day-to-day demands adults encounter.

PSYCHOBIOLOGICAL MATURATION AND COGNITION IN THE ELDERLY

Although the notion that cognitive development grows and declines under the control of physical maturation carries much intuitive appeal, this assumption is, in actuality, supported by a minimum of empirical evidence. It is, rather, most usually an explanatory hypothesis thought to subsume two major sets of observations. First, as already pointed out, developmental changes, at least those from childhood to adulthood, often appear to be both universal and dramatic: "Cognitive changes during childhood have a specific set of 'morpho genetic' properties that presumably stem from the biological-maturational growth process underlying these changes: Thus, childhood cognitive modifications are largely inevitable, momentous, directional, uniform, and irreversible" (Flavell, 1970, p. 247). Second, this organismic maturational hypothesis appeared to provide an adequate explanatory framework for the large body of empirical data on the decline of abstract cognitive functioning alluded to in the previous section.

What evidence, then, is there for the supposition that the same kind of organismic maturational control applies to postmaturational development? As Baltes and Labouvie (1973; *see also* Labouvie-Vief, 1976) have pointed out, the presumed causal connectedness between maturational changes and certain cognitive functions has rarely been subject to any rigorous empirical tests. Often, for instance, studies that have claimed to support an association between symptoms of biological and psychological deterioration have actually inferred both from behavioral data such as tests of intellectual and memory functions; thus, they merely attest to the fact that cognitive decline on one set of psychological measures is often predictive of decline on others. Also, many studies have merely conjectured that cognitive decline must be caused by biological decline, supporting their arguments by pointing to the many instances in which aging and biological deterioration are correlated. To find evidence of psychological decline in one sample of elderly people and to find indexes of biological deterioration in other, independent samples does not really permit a causal connection of the two sets of syndromes to be made. Even if both were found to be correlated across the same set of subjects, one cannot infer causal dependencies, as it is not clear which set of changes causes which.

In most cases, therefore, the notion of psychobiological maturation is used as a hypothesis that in actuality, refers to a host of unspecified processes presumed to be organic and biological (Baltes & Labouvie, 1973; Denney & Wright, 1975). It is important, as a consequence, to clearly differentiate between the changes for which there are unmistakable organic antecedents, and those changes that show considerable covariation with other factors (i.e., environmental and sociological factors).

Biological Antecedents

If examined from a more stringent perspective, in fact, the notion that biological decline inevitably brings about cognitive decrement in later life appears to have rather restricted validity. Much recent evidence, for instance, points to the conclusion that neither decline in cognitive functions nor biological decrement are normally distributed within the population of the elderly but are instead indicators of conditions of pathology, poor health, and/or nearness to death (Birren, 1970). Thus, strong relationships between biological indicators and cognitive performance are usually found only in those elderly subjects who may already show signs of failing health, such as people with elevated blood pressure (Eisdorfer & Wilkie, 1973) or institutionalized elderly subjects who suffer from various neuropsychiatric disorders (Obrist, Busse, Eisdorfer, & Kleemeier, 1962; Wang, 1973). In contrast, two major studies observed no such correlation. In one of these, (Birren, Butler, Greenhouse, Sokoloff, & Yarrow, 1963), a sample of exceptionally healthy elderly men was subjected to a variety of medical and psychological assessments, and the number of significant biobehavior relationships in this sample proved to be negligible. In a second, more representative study, Hertzog, Gribbin, and Schaie (1975) in a 14-year longitudinal study sought to isolate physical health antecedents of cognitive declines. Although there were indexes of such health problems as hypertension and arteriosclerotic disease, none of these were correlated with the declines that appeared in some subjects. Hence, it now appears that no significant portion of variance in intellectual behavior may be accounted for by readily demonstrated maturational change *as long as* subjects are in reasonably good health and/or living in the community.

Conversely, where cognitive and biological changes occur together, they may both be indicative of major health changes that eventually lead to natural death. Thus, several researchers have conducted large-scale, longitudinal studies in which it was possible, as subjects died out of the research population, to retrospectively examine cognitive changes, not as a function of chronological age, but of distance from death (Eisdorfer & Wilkie, 1973; Jarvik, 1973; Palmore & Cleveland, 1976; Riegel & Riegel, 1972). Once the reference point was changed in this way, most of the elderly appeared to exhibit, throughout their adult life-spans, a remarkably stable level of intellectual functioning; it was only in the few years preceding death that major cognitive declines became apparent, which usually were accompanied by arteriovascular and cerebrovascular disease. Thus again, the conclusion is suggested that cognitive impairment is not so much a universal concomitant of advancing age as of impending death. This conclusion would suggest, of course, that great care must be taken in the selection of these samples of elderly subjects from which one wishes to draw generalizations concerning a "normal" aging process—a precaution that has not been observed by many researchers who, under the pressures of time and economic restrictions, may have relied on captive populations of elderly subjects who tend to represent the lower, more frail spectrum of the total population of the elderly.

In light of the difficulty in establishing powerful biocognitive relationships in relatively healthy, normal samples of elderly subjects, the frequent explanation of adult cognitive decrement in terms of progressive neural impairment is being challenged for a major portion of the adult life-span. Birren (1963), in this context, has argued for the possibility of a discontinuous relationship between physiological indexes and cognitive behavior. According to this *discontinuity* hypothesis, physiological factors account for variability in behavior only if they reach critical abnormal ranges, as they will in individuals suffering pathology or approaching death. As long as they stay within a normal range, physiological conditions provide a necessary basis for behavior, but they become determining and sufficient causes only when healthy limits are exceeded. If they are not, there appears to be little evidence to point to the notion of universal biologically based cognitive declines; thus, the assumption of unidirectional (biology → behavior) cause–effect sequences may be a highly problematic one and should be rejected in favor of more complex, interactive models (*see also* Flavell, 1970; Reese, 1973; Woodruff, 1973, 1975).

If health may not constitute such a powerful explanatory variable—at least as long as health is measured by such relatively crude parameters as the absence or presence of pathology—what, then, may be the causes of cognitive decline in later life? Many such causes, I think may lie in defeating life-styles and environmental conditions that may be detrimental to high-level cognitive functioning. This is not to say, however, that such causes may not have a biological component or concomitant. Some researchers, for instance, have conjectured that such life-style factors as physical exercise habits—rather than aging, per se—may be predictive of cognitive declines. Botwinick and Thompson (1971) have suggested that age differences in psychomotor speed may be related to poor exercise habits rather than to age. Lack of physical exercise has similarly been implicated in the decline of measures of abstract intelligence (Barry, Steinmetz, Page, & Rodahl, 1966; Powell & Pohndorf, 1971). In another study (Woodruff, 1973, 1975), it was suggested that slow behavior in the elderly, together with its biological mediator (brain-wave slowing), might be a result of certain learning experiences rather than an inevitable consequence of advanced age.

It is important to stress that the above arguments and data are not to be construed as a rejection of the role of biological factors in the cognitive performance of older subjects. To do so, in fact, would be shortsighted and violate the intuitive conviction of most behavioral scientists that behavioral expressions must in some way have a physical counterpart. They do suggest, however, that the role of biology in much of past research on the aging process has been conceptualized in altogether too simplistic a fashion, in that often biological decrement was accepted as an a priori given out of which behavioral decrement would, in some automatic and inevitable sense, naturally follow. What is more likely, instead, is that both biological and psychological changes may often be a result of certain conditions of life, and in this sense, are more intricately and interactively related (Woodruff, 1975). What these conditions are, of course, remains to be shown by future research. I can, however, suggest some that may be particularly fruitful candidates for research attention. I have already alluded to the role of habits of physical exercise. Other important sets of factors might relate to nutritional and dietary practices, to preventive health practices, and, as I argue later, to even more "psychological" habits geared toward the maintenance of effective coping styles.

Behavioral Plasticity

If one opts for a less inevitable relationship between advancing age and cognitive performance, it is also natural to pose the question of whether cognitive declines, in those cases where they do occur, are really a sign of some irreversible, deteriorative process. In the past, many studies suggested this interpretation; more recently, however, considerable interest has mounted in examining whether it has been premature to conceive of the elderly individual's cognitive performance as something beyond adaptive control. To examine this issue, a number of researchers have introduced systematic variations into the conditions under which cognitive performance was assessed and then observed the effects of such treatments on subsequent cognitive performance.

I have already remarked on interventions that may take place on a more biological level, and several authors have indeed reported positive results on indicators of cognitive functioning as a function of either physical exercise (Barry et al., 1966; Powell, 1974) or biofeedback training (Woodruff, 1975). What is of particular significance about these studies is that they have utilized measures of abstract reasoning or speeded performance—those indexes that have, in the past, been linked with "normal," age-related, biological deterioration. Similarly, comparable measures were found to respond quite favorably to more psychological interventions as well. In one study (Hoyer, Labouvie, & Baltes, 1973), for instance, it was hypothesized that the often-reported low levels of functioning on highly speeded tests might reflect the elderly person's lack of experience with such tasks. Consequently, a sample of elderly women received some training on three tests of psychomotor speed. Despite the brevity of the training program, which consisted of two 30-minute sessions, subjects were found to significantly improve their speeds.

In another study (Labouvie-Vief & Gonda, 1976), elderly subjects received training in the particular strategies that are helpful in solving abstract cognitive problems. It was believed that, as a function of either lack of experience or heightened apprehension, older people might engage in a variety of behaviors that are irrelevant and even detrimental to the solutions of such tasks (e.g., not systematically scanning all components of an item or repeatedly asserting that one is not "clever" enough to figure an item out). More helpful behaviors were modeled for the subjects, who subsequently improved their performances, not only on the same tasks, but also on related ones. Moreover, this positive training effect could still be demonstrated two weeks after initial training—an unlikely result if one favors a simple biological-decrement interpretation. Similar results have also been reported in a series of other studies (Denney, 1974; Hornblum & Overton, 1976; Ismael & Labouvie-Vief, 1976; Mergler & Hoyer, 1975; Panicucci & Labouvie-Vief, 1975; Plemons, Willis, & Baltes, 1975), and further research has suggested that poor cognitive performance may be the result of the older person's greater susceptibility to fatigue (Furry & Baltes, 1973), raised anxiety level (Eisdorfer, Nowlin, & Wilkie, 1971), or reluctance to merely guess when not sure (Birkhill & Schaie, 1975)—a strategy automatically adopted by any younger person who knows the advantage of guessing in such tasks.

What are the implications of these studies for future research? In a sense, it is easiest to state the implications at a very general level. I believe that, despite all the evidence that might cause the case for a severe cognitive deficit to appear open and shut, more recent studies would suggest that the case deserves serious reevaluation. Often, relatively fateful conclusions concerning the older adult's adaptability have been resolved on the basis of fairly superficial examination, usually relying on single-occasion, one-shot assessments. The ready tendency of older people to respond favorably to a variety of helpful interventions, however, suggests that this weighty conclusion is a most unfortunate one. It often seems, indeed, that what older people do at first in tasks of learning and cognition is a rather invalid indicator of what they *can* do, given the right kinds of supports and conditions. At present, of course, we know little about what exactly those conditions are, although some of them are discussed more fully in a later section. To discover the various factors that might aid in the optimization of cognitive adaptability and continued learning, therefore, presents a tremendous challenge to future generations of researchers.

SOCIOHISTORICAL CONTEXT AND ADULT INTELLIGENCE

Much of the evidence reviewed in the previous section certainly is difficult to reconcile with the assumption that cognitive behavior in adults and older people is bound to decline as a function of some species-specific, epigenetic developmental program. Whatever this program might be, we find evidence to suggest that the resulting trajectories are not so inevitably fixed, but may be significantly altered under the influence of certain external and situational indexes. Indeed, it is my conviction that more situational variables are of much greater importance than has traditionally been conceded; and, as I demonstrate in this section, this likelihood has a tremendous number of exciting implications for further research on the education of older people.

Historical Time

I have argued that much of the somewhat negative and fatalistic outlook on adult intelligence may have been a result of a view of development that was relatively static and fixed and that this bias appears to have caused a certain degree of methodological oblivion on the part of many researchers concerned with the intellectual competence of older adults. This same oblivion is also reflected in the use of the very paradigm that developmental psychologists have long deemed appropriate to the study of ontogenetic change. As such research is usually carved out of a cross-section of subjects of varying ages obtained at one particular historical date, the assumption that the resulting age-group differences reflect nothing but the effects of development on behavior carries with it the implicit conviction that neither the particular historical point at which a study was done, nor the widely different historical strata in which different subjects were born and raised, must really be a matter of deep concern to theoreticians of development and aging.

As originally pointed out by Kuhlen (1963), Schaie (1965), and Baltes (1968), however, the idealistic notion that development can be assessed with the use of what Proshansky (1976) has called "time-less" cross-sectional designs contains serious difficulties. Their argument is perhaps most intuitively grasped by citing evidence, not from the area of intellectual development, but of age-related changes in physical development. Although this aspect of development is truly universal in the sense that adolescents of all cultures and historical times pass through the growth acceleration accompanying puberty, it is also known that this pattern varies somewhat across cultural groups and historical times (Tanner, 1972). Thus, the final, adult height achieved at the end of pubescence, over the course of the last two decades or so, has increased at the rate of about one inch per generation. As a consequence, if one were to take a cross-section of adults originating from different generations, one would observe an age-related decrease in height; a decrease that does not reflect developmental *change* over one's adult life-span, however, but results from generation-related growth acceleration that has differentially affected each of the generations in the study population.

Similarly, as in any cross-sectional study in which subjects differ, not only in age, but in their birth years as well, the resulting "age" differences may actually reflect either developmental or historical change, or they may be a compound of both. This argument, almost self-evident if such behaviors as sex-role conceptualizations or political attitudes are under consideration, still has, for many, an almost heretical ring when applied to something as immutable as intelligence. Yet, if appropriate designs are implemented (Nesselroade, Schaie, & Baltes, 1972; Schaie, Labouvie, & Buech, 1973), it is invariably found that intraindividual, longitudinal changes in people of the same age (originating from the same cohort) are minor as each cohort maintains a stable performance level through periods as long as 14 years. Thus, the sharp drops so typically found in cross-sectional gradients are an artifact. They do not assess age change at all, but rather, pronounced differences in the performance levels of successive cohorts. Consequently, it is not in relation to their own younger days that the aged can be described as deficient, but only in relation to younger, better educated populations.

Thus, as Nesselroade and Baltes (1974) have argued, we see that a quite distorted picture of the process of development may be the result of the use of designs based upon an essentially ahistoric idea of ontogenesis that ultimately is rooted in the idea of idealistically predetermined developmental outcomes. Instead, the existence of generation-related differences in behavior forces one's attention to the fact that development does not merely unfold in a cultural-historical vacuum; it is inextricably interwoven with a particular sociohistorical context.

Intelligence and the Social Context of Aging

We conclude, then, that what is "normal" and presumably universal in development may often be a relative matter in that is rather futile to talk about development without consideration of the influence of a particular sociocultural milieu. As a result, it is also more compelling to look at the often-reported, age-related ups and downs of cognitive development not so much as an inevitable, preprogrammed course of cognitive growth and decline, but as something that is fashioned by the particular growth-generating or growth-attenuating experiences that adult and aging individuals are encountering. This conclusion restates, in fact, the proposition cited earlier that throughout adulthood—and in the view of other authors (e.g., Baer, 1973; Gewirtz, 1969; Nesselroade & Baltes, 1974), throughout the total *process* of development—it may be variables related to one's social context rather than to one's age that account for the particular developmental gradients obtained. Rather than relying on quasi-biological arguments, such a viewpoint suggests that one consider a variety of change-producing experiences throughout adult life. Whether they be called societal "prods and brakes" (Neugarten and Datan, 1973), "changing reinforcement systems" (Labouvie-Vief, Hoyer, Baltes, & Baltes, 1974; Lindsley, 1964), or "normative life crises" (Datan & Ginsberg, 1975), such experiences, then, ought to be viewed as the catalysts that activate cognitive change.

Such an interpretation has extremely important implications for theory and research on adult and elderly populations. Consider, first, the now-accepted finding that throughout most of adulthood intellectual development is characterized by stability rather than by change. On the one hand, one might take this as a somewhat uninteresting, though encouraging, indication of the fact that most of adulthood is a rather static period. On the other hand, one might wish to doubt this apparent peacefulness and argue that what appears to be stability is merely a somewhat artifactual result of the likely fact that most, significant, adult experiences (e.g., establishment of a career, marriage, parenthood) are rather poorly ordered along an age continuum, so that the stable picture might just be the result of the smoothing out, by averaging, of individual developmental pathways that actually display considerable warps. If this were true, it would be much more fruitful to examine adulthood changes in cognition, not as a function of chronological age, but as a function of the temporal distance from one or another of these life crises. As similar research based on younger populations has suggested (*see* Bayley, 1970; Bloom, 1964), the apparent placidity of adult intellectual change might easily break up into a fascinating pattern of highs and lows if research subjects were grouped according to shared life experiences rather than according to age.

This same interpretation may also shed new light on what does appear to be rather universal developmental progression. If universality is sought, not in age, but in certain invariant context-behavior relationships, then apparent universality in developmental progression may be seen to reflect the fact that a particular context, or change in context, is the function of certain social policies. Such policies (e.g., entrance into school, college, or retirement) may be age graded due to particular economic and political conditions, but may not really reflect any inherent developmental capacities that are often presumed to be the primary cause of social policy decisions based on chronological age.

On a concrete level, therefore, it is rather interesting to observe that probably the only adult life crisis that is highly correlated with chronological age is that of retirement; and it is indeed entirely possible that retirement, not aging, is a major cause of the ubiquitous decline in cognitive functioning found after the age of 60 years. Indeed, this hypothesis has been suggested by a number of recent reinterpretations drawing on social-ecological models for cognitive decrement in later life (Baltes & Labouvie, 1973; Labouvie-Vief et al., 1974). Thus, as many authors believe that the present social context of retirement creates many problems of personal and social adjustment, so many also believe that the particular social climate in which many, perhaps a majority, of elderly people live is one that discourages those competence-related behaviors that are relevant to effective intellectual functioning (Labouvie-Vief et al., 1974; Lindsley, 1964).

At present, there is little research that directly examines such a sociocultural hypothesis of declining cognitive competence in old age. I am not aware of any research that—as in the domain of social adjustment and levels of social activity (e.g., Bengtson, 1973; Maas & Kuypers, 1974)—follows people into retirement in temporal sequence and examines their cognitive behavior as they establish their different patterns of adjustment to retirement. There are, however, more indirect indications of the fact that such a hypothesis is, indeed, a highly fruitful one.

I have already summarized studies that suggest that cognitive "deficit" in the elderly may be a rather transitory and situation-bound phenomenon that responds readily to a variety of situation-related manipulations and interventions. This fact itself suggests that cognitive behavior is not so inevitably linked to biological deficit, but may result from the particular scheduling of rewards and reinforcements that elderly people experience (e.g., Labouvie-Vief et al., 1974). But in what ways could it be said that changing reward contingencies produce, as it were, cognitive incompetence? Several authors have remarked on this issue and pointed out possible mechanisms.

First, old age appears to be the target of a variety of negative stereotypes. If compared to other periods of the life cycle, old age is often viewed as a time of dependency, frailty, and decrement (e.g., Bennett & Eckman, 1973; Nardi, 1973). Indeed, few positive labels appear to be associated with the process of aging in either the lay or scientific communities. Thus, the elderly may often be unjustifiably treated as "sick." They may be discouraged from exercising their skills because to do so may either create problems within the current economic structure or interfere with efficient (if not to the same degree humanistically oriented) institutional administration. The detrimental consequences of expectations rooted in the sick role of the elderly were dramatically demonstrated in a study by MacDonald and Butler

(1974), who found institutionalized elderly subjects who were wheelchair bound but showed no organic deficit to proscribe their walking. When encouraged to walk and attended to while walking, these patients showed immediate "recovery," and their walking or not walking appeared to depend entirely on whether or not they were encouraged to do so. In a similar vein, it is also likely that many older people are conveniently pushed into a social niche in which they are deprived of their independence and of decision making, and in which, as a consequence, their competence is either not reinforced or negatively reinforced (Labouvie-Vief et al., 1974).

Second, in addition to relatively active discouragement of intellectual competence, the life situation of many older people further exacerbates their sense of being unable to cope effectively. What little anticipatory socialization toward old age does exist in our society appears to encourage older people to have the negative expectations surrounding aging well internalized. Thus, their self-concepts are often unduly poor, as was demonstrated in a study by Ismael and Labouvie-Vief (1976) in which elderly women and men significantly improved their cognitive performances after receiving a "social support" treatment aimed at rectifying some of the negative stereotypes concerning cognition in old age.

Third, there are also many personal crises older people may encounter that may corrode their sense of efficacy, such as crises related to failing health, loss of loved ones, social isolation, and similar personal traumata. On a somewhat suggestive level, Seligman (1975) has argued that both of these factors—i.e., the more cognitive aspect of labeling oneself as ineffective, and the more direct one of being overwhelmed with personal and social losses without simultaneous social supports—may precipitate a state in older people that is characterized by an intense sense of loss of control and helplessness and that strongly interferes with their ability to function effectively in a variety of cognitive situations. Indeed, in a 14-year longitudinal study by Schaie and Gribbin (1975), it was found that social isolation was the life-style indicator most strongly predictive of intellectual losses.

CRITERIA OF DEVELOPMENT AND MATURITY

Despite the more optimistic posture contained in the previous sections, however, our idealistic dilemma would be only incompletely resolved if we were to stop at this point. We might wish to rush and examine all imaginable context effects, whether "natural" or of human origin, on the cognitive functioning of the older individual. To do so effectively, however, we need to face a particularly tricky problem dormant in idealistic conceptions of development: how to measure the criterion behavior of adult cognition in the first place.

Adult-appropriate versus
Youth-centered Criteria

As already noted earlier in this chapter, one's view of what constitute acceptable criteria of cognitively "mature" behavior is intricately interwoven with one's particular theory of development in general. With very few exceptions, current theories of cognitive development culminate in a concept of maturity that not only is rather context free, but also tends to be located in that period of one's life-span in which one is extensively involved in the process of formal education. Thus, those measures of learning, cognition, and intelligence available to us tend to be derived from theories that speak to adolescent and young-adult subjects and/or are specifically constructed for the purpose of evaluating and predicting academic achievement in young people. If evaluated against such youth-centered criteria, adult behavior often appears to be a rather amateurish attempt to behave like the young. It may be questioned, however, if such a pejorative view is really necessary and inevitable.

The contention that adulthood should not be evaluated against now-prevalent criteria of cognitive growth may seem farfetched at first sight. It certainly appears to violate all the evidence that points to the conclusions that (1) development is directed toward the perfection of exactly those kinds of performances I have mentioned thus far in this chapter, and (2) the progression toward this goal so readily appears to conform to and to occur with such universal regularity as to preclude any doubt that these acquisitions might not be of utmost, universal significance. Nevertheless, as Hamlyn (1971) has argued, the peacefulness of this unilinear view is, ultimately, more a result of the conceptual selectivity of scientists than of the existence of clear, inevitable laws. What appears as a universal teleology (and thus as self-evident and inevitable) is ultimately based upon an a priori selected, to-be-explained, mature form of behavior, and specific theories are constructed to teleogically explain exactly that behavior. In so doing, many other possible goals and behaviors are deselected from the realm of theoretically interesting phenomena. Indeed, Hamlyn argues, if one were to examine cognitive development from a less idealistic, more empirical perspective, one could point to many instances in which the course of cognitive growth defies any unilinear view and in which inconsistencies, detours, and blind alleys, discarded for the sake of a more elegant view, are exposed. Such inconsistency is a relative matter, however, and may become much more meaningful if examined from a somewhat different perspective.

The question of what is to constitute an acceptable end point of development—and thus what is to define an appropriate criterion of mature, adult behavior—has been discussed much more in the literature on cognitive anthropology (e.g., Cole & Scribner, 1974) than in that on adult development.

A number of recent writings in cognitive anthropology have suggested that the ways in which we have come to conceptualize development and maturity are not necessarily universal; rather, what appears universal to the Western thinker may actually reflect the particular value system and cultural pace to which Western societies are accustomed (Berger & Luckmann, 1966). That is, forms of behavior that appear intuitively necessary and important from a narrow cultural perspective, may not be of similar importance from the vantage point of other cultures. Hence, it may be inappropriate to examine any cultural (or age) group through the narrow experiential framework derived within another cultural (or age) group (e.g., Buck-Morss, 1975; Cole & Scribner, 1974). In other words, according to this rationale, one must entertain the possibility that individuals who appear deficient according to the measurement criteria that are applied to them are deficient only in *relation to those standards* but might perform much more adequately if more appropriate standards were applied.

How plausible is it to apply the same argument to the elderly? At present, to be sure, firm evidence is rather lacking, and I wish to raise possibilities for future research rather than to defend a posture that is to be understood as a "fact." With this caution in mind, I nevertheless point to a few research results that may suggest that the hypothesis that older adults are put at an undue disadvantage by established research procedures is, at least, not an unreasonable one.

It has often been argued, for instance, that the cognitive behavior of children shows striking similarities to that of elderly subjects (e.g., Denney, 1974; Papalia, 1972), a fact that has been taken to mean that the elderly person is "childlike," "primitive," "unsophisticated," or otherwise deficient in her or his approach to cognitive tasks. Such an interpretation is sometimes based, however, on rather superficial similarities. In research on the classification of behavior in subjects of widely varying age levels, for instance, it has been reported that young children and older adults tend to group on the basis of complementariness rather than conventional class relations (e.g., Denney, 1974; Denney & Wright, 1975). As Kogan (1974) has pointed out, however, there are also striking differences between the performance of each of these age groups. In his research, elderly individuals also produced categories that were more inclusive and hence might be called more abstract. Thus, the first criterion (basis of classification) might suggest "deficit" in the elderly, whereas the second (inclusiveness of categories) would lead one to conclude the opposite. Certainly, such a state of affairs suggests that the diverse differences between younger and older subjects are not always captured by a decremental hypothesis, and, as a consequence, it would be of value to take a more careful, less biased look at many ways in which performance differences between young and old subjects may arise.

Indeed, other authors have gone even further and argued that current conceptualizations of "mature" cognition may in actuality describe forms of cognitive behavior that are but a preliminary stage. Riegel (1973), for instance, has proposed that the stage of formal operational cognition quite inconsistently captures the cognitive activity of mature adults, which he believes is directed at the creation and tolerant coexistence of inconsistency rather than at its removal. Arlin (1975) has similarly provided suggestive results in support of the hypothesis that currently available theories of cognitive development do not properly concern themselves with the creative, problem-generating activities of adults. Thus, it is certainly fair to state that too little research has been directed at spelling out the possible strengths of the older learner. In contrast, I believe that the imposition of youth-centered standards on older adults will often automatically yield results in line with a deficit view of cognitive functioning—a deficit that may, however, sometimes have its root in a certain degree of egocentric interpretation of research data rather than in the research subjects themselves.

Ecologically Valid Criteria

A final problem inherent in idealistic models of adult cognitive functioning is related to the one just discussed and similarly may form a potential starting point for future research into the education of the elderly. It is an implicit conviction of idealistically oriented theories that ultimately all development follows the same path, although this path may be most easily recognized if one focuses on a few selected instances that are particularly telling. As already discussed, the measures thought particularly revealing have tended to be those of abstract cognitive functioning, that is, of the ability to manipulate abstract symbols and material of low meaning. The point to be considered here is that this conviction, in actuality, may have created a widening gap between what are considered important theoretical concepts and what are the realities of day-to-day cognitive performance.

The last decade or so has witnessed a proliferation of writings (e.g., Buss, 1975; McClelland, 1973; Proshansky, 1970, 1976) reassessing psychological theory in the light of what Proshansky (1970) has called "phenomenon legitimacy," that is, the ability of theories to generate predictions about real-life outcomes. In this view, many theories may have sacrificed scope and relevance for internal consistency and promoted criteria of cognition and intelligence that are relatively overspecialized, tautological, and validated by their fit to theory rather than to reality.

Despite the widespread use of intelligence tests and related cognitive measures in life-span research, for instance, the notion that such tests predict important life outcomes within a life-span framework has rarely been subjected to any critical tests. To be sure, the correlation, mentioned earlier, of cognitive measures with social status, education, health, age, and mortality has connoted to many (e.g., Kohlberg, LaCrosse, & Ricks, 1970; Jensen, 1973) that such tests indeed measure what they are to measure: a person's ability to adapt to life's demands. Such an interpretation is not so inevitable, however, as pointed out by McClelland (1973). As long as these tests are based on individuals from widely divergent social strata, such correlations may be a rather tautological consequence in a society in which opportunities are stratified along class and age lines. If the association is examined within more homogeneous groups, measures of intelligence often fail to predict life outcomes (McClelland, 1973). Nevertheless, such indexes have attained the rather autonomous status of some ultimate criterion, as exemplified in Borings's famous tautology that "intelligence is what intelligence tests measure." Indeed the assumed superiority of cognitive measures over relevant behavioral samples is so widespread a phenomenon that, to this date, there is no research available examining the ecological validity of measures of cognitive functioning from a life-span perspective.

The question of ecological validity is not merely of importance from the perspective of whether or not cognitive research can be applied outside of highly controlled laboratory settings (Botwinick, 1973; Jenkins, 1974); it may also throw a new light on what are "good" measures as judged by other criteria. Because the validity of cognitive measures tends to be evaluated primarily on the basis of measurement and theoretical considerations, most current cognitive indexes tend to encourage samples of achievement of extreme specialization. Insensitivity to situational variability tends to be required, both from psychometric (McClelland, 1973) and developmental-theoretical considerations (Kohlberg, 1971; Wohlwill, 1973). In contrast to this view, McClelland (1973) has argued that situational *sensitivity* should be made the sine qua non of validity considerations; that is, tests should be constructed in such a way that scores *change* as a person grows in experience, wisdom, and the ability to successfully cope with life's problems.

From this perspective, the consistent finding that age differences are augmented on tasks of high abstractness and low meaning—far from attesting to their validity as indicators of powerful developmental dimensions—rather raises doubts concerning their validity. In the absence of clearly demonstrated real-world correlates, statements about levels of cognitive-structural complexity may be quite misleading. On the contrary, age functions may change in a most decisive manner if tasks are devised that are high on both meaning and abstractness (Arenberg, 1968; Fozard & Poon, 1976).

Thus, there is a need to attempt to redefine what are important cognitive skills related to life outcomes in the elderly. Whereas research on "abstract" cognitive skills abounds, for instance, there is almost no available documentation of such important outcomes as communication skills, response delay, ego development, and the abstraction of meaning from verbal and written communication. Research in this area, I believe, has been too widely guided by a priori assumptions; a healthy pendulum swing in the opposite direction is needed, with careful naturalistic and ethological mapping of relevant cognitive skills.

CONCLUSION

In sum, I have argued that much of what we now know about the educability of older adults is in need of revision. Research in this area has tended to derive its assumptions, predictions, and interpretations, via deduction, from idealistic, maturational, youth-centered models of cognitive functioning. It is, as a result, excessively biased in favor of decremental interpretations that tend to foster doubt about the feasibility and value of education in later life.

In contrast, my position is that many pessimistic interpretations of the past are far from inevitable and necessary and that the intellectual potential of the older person is, to this date, essentially unexplored. To some, this might be a position lacking in objectivity, particularly as it is at variance with a vast body of research on the cognitive abilities of older adults. It must be reiterated, however, that it is the opinion of many philosophers and scientists (e.g., Buss, 1975; Habermas, 1971) that the role of objectivity in science may have been somewhat misunderstood in the past. Thus, objectivity in the conduct of research and in the gathering and interpretation of data is a sine qua non of scientific activity; it does not, however, render objective those prescientific assumptions that have suggested the phenomena to be studied and the hypotheses about their conduct in the first place. Objectivity of this latter kind is achieved, rather, by attempting to broaden one's viewpoints. Therefore, I have intended this chapter to serve as a heuristic and to generate alternate viewpoints that are intended, not as the erection of a new dogma, but rather as guidelines for research that I deem particularly important in counteracting a context of hopelessness about the elderly individual's cognitive status.

I suggest that researchers direct their attention to the investigation of variables that are unique and representative of aging behavior, thus concentrating efforts on the potentially progressive aspects of adult cognitive development (Labouvie-Vief & Chandler, 1978; Schaie, 1976). For example, wisdom (Alpaugh, Renner, & Birren, 1976), personal control and mid-life crises (Brim, 1974a, 1974b), and adult coping with professional inter- and intrapersonal stress (Coelho, Hamburg, & Adams, 1974; Lowenthal & Chiriboga, 1973) are all representative of research efforts aimed at issues particularly relevant to adulthood and late maturity. Accordingly, a stronger emphasis on contextual and experiential factors in the explication of aging behavior is needed.

REFERENCES

Alpaugh, P. K., Renner, V. J., & Birren, J. W. (1976). Age and creativity: Implications for education and teachers. *Educational Gerontology, 1,* 17–40.

Arenberg, D. (1968). Concept problem solving in young and old adults. *Journal of Gerontology, 23,* 279–282.

Arlin, P. K. (1975). Cognitive development in adulthood: A fifth stage? *Developmental Psychology, 11,* 602–606.

Baer, D. M. (1973). The control of the developmental process: Why wait? In J. R. Nesselroade & H. W. Reese (Eds.), *Life-span developmental psychology: Methodological issues.* New York: Academic.

Baltes, P. B. (1968). Longitudinal and cross-sectional sequences in the study of age and generation effects. *Human Development, 11,* 145–171.

Baltes, P. B., & Labouvie, G. V. (1973). Adult development of intellectual performance: Description, explanation, and modification. In C. Eisdorfer & M. P. Lawton (Eds.), *The psychology of adult development and aging.* Washington, DC: American Psychological Association.

Baltes, P. B., & Willis, S. L. (1976). Toward psychological theories of aging. In J. E. Birren & K. W. Schaie (Eds.), *Handbook on psychology of aging.* New York: Van Nostrand-Reinhold.

Barrett, W. (1962). The twentieth century in its philosophy. In W. Barrett & H. D. Aiken (Eds.), *Philosophy in the twentieth century.* New York: Harper.

Barry, A. J., Steinmetz, J. R., Page, H. F., & Rodahl, K. (1966). The effects of physical conditioning on older individuals: II. Motor performance and cognitive function. *Journal of Gerontology, 21,* 182–191.

Bayley, N. (1970). Development of mental abilities. In P. H. Mussen (Ed.), *Carmichael's manual of child psychology.* New York: Wiley.

Bengston, V. L. (1973). *The social psychology of aging.* Indianapolis, IN: Bobbs-Merrill.

Bennett, R., & Eckman, J. (1973). Attitudes toward aging. In C. Eisdorfer & M. P. Lawton (Eds.), *The psychology of adult development and aging.* Washington, DC: American Psychological Association.

Berger, P. L., & Luckmann, T. (1966). *The social construction of reality.* Garden City, NY: Doubleday.

Birkhill, W. R., & Schaie, K. W. (1975). The effect of differential reinforcement of cautiousness in intellectual performance among the elderly. *Journal of Gerontology, 30,* 578–583.

Birren, J. E. (1963). Psychophysiological relations. In J. E. Birren, R. N. Butler, S. W. Greenhouse, L. Sokoloff, & M. R. Yarrow (Eds.), *Human aging: A biological and behavioral study.* Washington, DC: U.S. Government Printing Office.

Birren, J. E. (1970). Toward an experimental psychology of aging. *American Psychologist, 25,* 124–135.

Birren, J. E., Butler, R. W., Greenhouse, S. W., Sokoloff, L., & Yarrow, M. R. (Eds.). (1963). *Human aging: A biological and behavioral study.* Washington, DC: U.S. Government Printing Office.

Bloom, B. S. (1964). *Stability and change in human characteristics.* New York: Wiley.

Botwinick, J. (1967). *Cognitive processes in maturity and old age.* New York: Springer.

Botwinick, J. (1973). *Aging and behavior.* New York: Springer.

Botwinick, J., & Thompson, L. W. (1971). Cardiac functioning and reaction time in relation to age. *Journal of Genetic Psychology, 119,* 127–132.

Brim, O. G., Jr. (1974a). *The sense of personal control over one's life.* Unpublished manuscript, Foundation of Child Development, New York.

Brim, O. G., Jr. (1974b). *Selected theories of the male mid-life crisis: A comparative analysis.* Unpublished manuscript, Foundation of Child Development, New York.

Buck-Morss, S. (1975). Socio-economic bias in Piaget's theory and its implications for cross-cultural studies. *Human Development, 18,* 35–49.

Buss, A. R. (1975). The emerging field of the sociology of psychological knowledge. *American Psychologist, 30,* 988–1002.

Coelho, G. V., Hamburg, D. A., & Adams, J. E. (Eds.) (1974). *Coping and adaptation.* New York: Basic Books.

Cole, M., & Scribner, S. (1974). *Culture and thought: A psychological introduction.* New York: Wiley.

Datan, N., & Ginsberg, L. H. (Eds.) (1975). *Life-span developmental psychology: Normative life crises.* New York: Academic.

Denney, N. W. (1974). Classification abilities in the elderly. *Journal of Gerontology, 29,* 309–314.

Denney, N. W., & Wright, J. C. (1975, April). *Cognitive changes during the adult years: Implications for developmental theory and research.* Paper presented at the biannual meeting of the Society for Research in Child Development, Denver, CO.

Dohrenwend, B. S., & Dohrenwend, B. P. (Eds.) (1974). *Stressful life events.* New York: Wiley.

Eisdorfer, C., Nowlin, J., & Wilkie, F. (1971). Improvement of learning by modification of autonomous nervous system activity. *Science, 170,* 1327–1328.

Eisdorfer, C., & Wilkie, F. (1973). Intellectual changes with advancing age. In L. F. Jarvik, C. Eisdorfer, & J. C. Blum (Eds.), *Intellectual functioning in adults.* New York: Springer.

Flavell, J. H. (1970). Cognitive changes in adulthood. In P. B. Baltes & L. R. Goulet (Eds.), *Life-span developmental psychology,* New York: Academic.

Fozard, J. L., & Poon, L. W. (1976, October). *Age-related differences in long-term memory for pictures.* Paper presented at the annual meeting of the Gerontological Society, New York.

Furry, C. A., & Baltes, P. B. The effect of age differences in ability-extraneous variables on the assessment of intelligence in children, adults and the elderly. *Journal of Gerontology, 28,* 73–80.

Gergen, K. J. (1973). Social psychology as history. *Journal of Personality and Social Psychology, 26,* 309–320.

Gewirtz, J. L. (1969). Mechanisms of social learning: Some roles of stimulation and behavior in early human development. In D. A. Goslin (Ed.), *Handbook of socialization theory and research.* Chicago: Rand McNally.

Giorgi, A. (1971). Phenomenology and experimental psychology. In A. Giorgi, W. F. Fischer, & R. Von Eckartsberg (Eds.), *Duquesne studies in phenomenological psychology* (Vol. 1). Pittsburgh, PA: Duquesne University Press.

Habermas, J. (1971). *Knowledge and human interests.* Boston: Beacon.

Hamlyn, D. W. (1971). Epistemology and conceptual development. In T. Mischel (Ed.), *Cognitive development and epistemology.* New York: Academic.

Hertzog, C., Gribbin, K., & Schaie, K. W. (1975, October). *The influence of cardiovascular disease and hypertension on intellectual stability.* Paper presented at the annual meeting of the Gerontological Society, Louisville, KY.

Horn, J. L. (1976). Human abilities: A review of research and theory in the early 1970's. *Annual Review of Psychology, 27,* 437–485.

Hornblum, J. N., & Overton, W. F. (1976). Area and volume conservation among the elderly: Assessment and training. *Developmental Psychology, 12,* 68–74.

Hoyer, W. J., Labouvie, G. V., & Baltes, P. B. (1973). Modification of response speed deficits and intellectual performance in the elderly. *Human Development, 16,* 233–242.

Ismael, M., & Labouvie-Vief, G. (1976). *Self-concept and intellectual performance in the elderly.* Unpublished manuscript, University of Wisconsin, Madison.

Jarvik, L. F. (1973). Discussion: Patterns of intellectual functioning in the later years. In L. F. Jarvik, C. Eisdorfer, & J. C. Blum (Eds.), *Intellectual functioning in adults.* New York: Springer.

Jarvik, L. F., & Cohen, D. (1973). A biobehavioral approach to intellectual changes with aging. In C. Eisdorfer & M. P. Lawton (Eds.), *The psychology of adult development and aging.* Washington, DC: American Psychological Association.

Jenkins, J. J. (1974). Remember the old theory of memory? Well forget it! *American Psychologist, 29,* 789–795.

Jensen, A. R. (1973). *Educability and group differences.* New York: Harper.

Kogan, N. (1974). Categorizing and conceptualizing styles in younger and older adults. *Human Development, 17,* 218–230.

Kohlberg, L. (1971). From is to ought: How to commit the naturalistic fallacy and get away with it in the study of moral development. In T. Mischel (Ed.), *Cognitive development and epistemology.* New York: Academic.

Kohlberg, L., LaCrosse, J., & Ricks, D. (1970). The predictability of adult mental health from childhood behavior. In B. Wolman (Ed.), *Handbook of child psychopathology.* New York: McGraw-Hill.

Kuhlen, R. G. (1963). Age and intelligence: The significance of cultural change in longitudinal vs. cross-sectional findings. *Vita Humana, 6,* 113–124.

Labouvie-Vief, G. (1976). Towards optimizing cognitive competence in older adults. *Educational Gerontology, 1,* 75–92.

Labouvie-Vief, G., & Chandler, M. J. (1978). Cognitive development and life-span developmental theory: Idealistic vs. contextual perspectives. In P. B. Baltes (Ed.), *Life-span development and behavior.* New York: Academic.

Labouvie-Vief, G., & Gonda, J. N. (1976). Cognitive strategy training and intellectual performance in the elderly. *Journal of Gerontology, 31,* 327–332.

Labouvie-Vief, G., Hoyer, W. J., Baltes, M. M., & Baltes, P. B. (1974). Operant analysis of intellectual behavior in old age. *Human Development, 17,* 259–272.

Lindsley, O. R. (1964). Geriatric behavioral prosthetics. In R. Kastenbaum (Ed.), *New thoughts on old age.* New York: Springer.

Lowenthal, M. R., & Chiriboga, D. (1973). Social stress and adaptation. In C. Eisdorfer & M. P. Lawton (Eds.), *The psychology of adult development and aging.* Washington, DC: American Psychological Association.

Maas, H. S., & Kuypers, J. A. (1974). *From thirty to seventy.* San Francisco: Jossey-Bass.

MacDonald, M. L., & Butler, A. K. (1974). Reversal of helplessness: Producing walking behavior in wheel chair residents using behavior modification procedures. *Journal of Gerontology, 29,* 97–101.

McClelland, D. C. (1973). Testing for competence rather than for "intelligence." *American Psychologist, 28,* 1–14.

Mergler, N. L., & Hoyer, W. J. (1975, October). *Cognitive performance of elderly adults as a function of strategy training and non-contingent social praise.* Paper presented at the annual meeting of the Gerontological Society, Louisville, KY.

Muuss, R. E. (1975). *Theories of adolescence* (3rd ed.). New York: Random House.

Nardi, A. H. (1973). Person-perception research and the perception of life-span development. In P. B. Baltes & K. W. Schaie (Eds.), *Life-span developmental psychology: Personality and socialization.* New York: Academic.

Nesselroade, J. R., & Baltes, P. B. (1974). Adolescent personality development and historical change: 1970–1972. *Monographs of the Society for Research in Child Development, 39*(1).

Nesselroade, J. R., Schaie, K. W., & Baltes, P. B. (1972). Ontogenetic and generational components of structural and quantitative change in adult cognitive behavior. *Journal of Gerontology, 27,* 222–228.

Neugarten, B. L., & Datan, N. (1973). Sociological perspectives on the life cycle. In P. B. Baltes & K. W. Schaie (Eds.), *Life-span developmental psychology: Personality and socialization.* New York: Academic.

Obrist, W. D., Busse, E. W., Eisdorfer, C., & Kleemeier, R. W. (1962). Relation of the electroencephalogram to intellectual function in senescence. *Journal of Gerontology, 17,* 197–206.

Palmore, E., & Cleveland, W. (1976). Aging, terminal decline, and terminal drop. *Journal of Gerontology, 31,* 76–81.

Panicucci, C., & Labouvie-Vief, G. (1975, October). *Effect of training on inductive reasoning behavior.* Paper presented at the annual meeting of the Gerontological Society, Louisville, KY.

Papalia, D. (1972). The status of several conservation abilities across the life-span. *Human Development, 15,* 229–243.

Plemons, J. K., Willis, S. L., & Baltes, P. B. (1973, October). *Challenging the theory of fluid intelligence: A training approach.* Paper presented at the annual meeting of the Gerontological Society, Louisville, KY.

Powell, R. R. (1974). Psychological effects of exercise therapy upon institutionalized geriatric mental patients. *Journal of Gerontology, 29,* 157–161.

Powell, R. R., & Pohndorf, R. H. (1971). Comparison of adult exercisers and nonexercisers on fluid intelligence and selected physiological variables. *Research Quarterly, 42,* 70–77.

Proshansky, H. M. (1970). Methodology in environmental psychology: Problems and issues. *Human Factors, 14,* 451–460.

Proshansky, H. M. (1976). Environmental psychology and the real world. *American Psychologist, 31,* 303–310.

Reese, H. W. (1973). Life-span models of memory. *Gerontologist, 13,* 472–478.

Riegel, K. F. (1973). Dialectic operations: The final period of cognitive development. *Human Development, 16,* 346–370.

Riegel, K. F. (1975). From traits and equilibrium towards developmental dialectics. In W. Arnold (Ed.), *Nebraska Symposium on Motivation.* Lincoln: University of Nebraska Press.

Riegel, K. F., & Riegel, R. M. (1972). Development, drop, and death. *Developmental Psychology, 6,* 306–319.

Schaie, K. W. (1965). A general model for the study of developmental problems. *Psychological Bulletin, 64,* 92–107.

Schaie, K. W. (1977). Toward a stage theory of adult development. *International Journal of Aging and Human Development, 8*(2), 129–138.

Schaie, K. W., & Gribbin, K. (1975, July). *The impact of environmental complexity upon adult cognitive development*. Paper presented at the 3rd biennial conference of the International Society for the Study of Behavioral Development, Guildford, England.

Schaie, K. W., Labouvie, G. V., & Buech, B. U. (1973). Generational vs. cohort-specific differences in adult cognitive functioning: A fourteen-year study of independent samples. *Developmental Psychology, 9,* 151–166.

Seligman, M. E. P. (1975). *Helplessness.* San Francisco: W. H. Freeman.

Tanner, J. M. (1972). Sequence, tempo, and individual variation in growth and development of boys and girls aged twelve to sixteen. In J. Kagan & R. Coles (Eds.), *Twelve to sixteen: Early adolescence.* New York: W. W. Norton & Company.

Toffler, A. (1974). (Ed.). *Learning for tomorrow.* New York: Random House.

Wang, H. S. (1973). Cerebral correlates of intellectual functioning in senescence. In L. F. Jarvik, C. Eisdorfer, & J. C. Blum (Eds.), *Intellectual functioning in adults.* New York: Springer.

Wohlwill, J. F. (1973). *The study of behavioral development.* New York: Academic.

Woodruff, D. S. (1973). The usefulness of the life-span approach for the psychophysiology of aging. *Gerontologist, 13,* 467, 472.

Woodruff, D. S. (1975). A physiological perspective on the psychology of aging. In J. E. Birren & D. S. Woodruff (Eds.), *Aging: Scientific perspectives and social issues.* New York: D. Van Nostrand.

14

LEADERSHIP TRAINING
FOR RETIREMENT EDUCATION

CARL I. BRAHCE*
WOODROW W. HUNTER*

University of Michigan

Like aging itself, retirement may be studied as a complex process having multiple meanings for the individual. Viewed most simply as a change over time from a working role to a nonworking role, retirement seems to have a noticeable impact upon all other positions held by retirees as well as upon all of their relationships with others (Sussman, 1972). This phenomenon is usually associated, in our industrialized society, with negative connotations that are primarily due to the preoccupation in the United States with the work role. "Retirement is a demotion in the work system. For most individuals it means a sharp reduction in income. Less income may result in inability to meet behavioral expectations in a group or organization. The consequence is a change in status."[1]

Although the factors relating to the retirement process are complex, research studies indicate the importance of economic and health variables. Research on social-psychological factors shows that both men and women who tend to work longer have higher income levels, higher positions in the occupational structure, and higher education attainments. It also shows that, in our work-oriented society, the older person who works is, over time, more likely to feel useful than the person who retires (Streib & Schneider, 1971, p. 159).

Research findings raise theoretical questions about the process of retirement and its impact on the individual. These questions, in turn, present considerations and choices for the retirement educator. Glamser (1976) investigated the factors relating to a positive attitude toward retirement among older, male, industrial workers and concluded that:

---

[1] Reprinted from Gordon F. Streib and Clement J. Schneider, S.J.: *Retirement in American Society*, p. 159. © Copyright 1971 by Cornell University. Used by permission of Cornell University Press.

Retired.

Workers who can realistically expect a positive retirement experience in terms of finances, friends, social activity, and level of preparedness were likely to have a positive attitude toward retirement .... The worker's appraisal of his present situation and the kind of experience he expects to encounter in retirement was much more important than the meaning of work per se. (p. 107)

In the Scripps Foundation studies in retirement, Atchley (1971) found that although retirement did result in loss of a sense of involvement, this was not related to the other self-concept variables of optimism and autonomy. Differences in adjustment to retirement were found according to occupational status, with upper white-collar jobs oriented around symbols, middle-status jobs oriented around people, and semiskilled jobs oriented around things. He concluded that there is no concrete evidence that retirement per se has a negative influence on the quality of one's life. Atchley (1971) suggests that as retirement becomes more an expected part of the life cycle, work may be seen as a temporary phase of life rather than as the dominant life function for many people.

Usefulness has a significant effect on the individual's ability to adjust to the changing impact of retirement during the time intervals—usually 10 to 20 years—before death. The years after retirement, for both the individual and the spouse, are marked by continuing changes. Roles in later maturity would ideally involve anticipatory socialization, inasmuch as workers often know the exact time at which they will retire. Many older people, however, delay in making plans. Traditionally, educational institutions are not as concerned about socialization for new roles in later life as in earlier periods of the life cycle (Streib & Schneider, 1971).

Learning to be retired is an unusual kind of adult socialization because it exposes individuals to a kind of double jeopardy. Not only do older people have to learn roles that are new to them, but the roles themselves are new, and consequently not well defined in the social repertory of most industrial societies. The increasingly long period between the loss of a social maturity that is derived from a work world and the physical decline of old age has created a new retired state in the social life cycle. Without the help of specialized agents to teach them about these changing social roles of retirement, older people frequently seek informal ways to clarify roles with their peers (Ross, 1974).

The French author, Simone de Beauvoir (1972), derides the societal treatment of the retired in our culture: "The worker is condemned to idleness much earlier than he was formerly .... The idleness forced upon the aged is not something that necessarily happens in the course of nature, but it is the consequence of a deliberate social choice" (pp. 223, 232).

In their transcultural study, Doris and David Jonas (1973, p. 107) learned that only in a few roles, such as the papacy, heads of other religions, and senates of the world, do the elderly still hold positions of leadership. In the practice of medicine, many prefer younger physicians, and teaching is succumbing to youth and technology. The old yield to compulsory retirement to assure the vigor of new blood in the conduct of offices and to permit the promotion of younger aspirants for power and influence. In all other areas of daily life, our elders have become, or are rapidly becoming, functionless.

Researchers of the Cornell retirement study (Streib & Schneider, 1971) observed that it is not enough to view retirement in terms of new roles in a changing industrial society. Not only is the retirement process something with negative or positive impact on the individual, but it also may have favorable or unfavorable consequences for the operation of organizations, institutional structures like the economy, and the society itself. An important conclusion of the Cornell study has implications for the retirement educator as well as the sociologist: the higher the individual's educational and professional status, the more positive attitudes and the more resources that individual has available in coping with the changing circumstances of retirement. The unskilled and uneducated are the least prepared and have the least personal, economic, and social resources with which to meet life's challenges upon retirement.

The increasing body of knowledge about the retirement process has implications for the education of retired people, and correspondingly, for the training of professionals who would be engaged in planning and carrying out education programs. First, both psychological and social factors can be critical in how well men and women adjust to aging. The ingredients of satisfactory old age are: a stable relationship with the immediate and extended family, purposeful activity, and a sense of one's own value. These qualities are aptly illustrated by Esther Hunt More of Hickory, North Carolina. An elementary school teacher for 40 years, she was named Mother of the Year in 1970, and she was the first black woman to register and vote in her county. After her children were graduated from college, she studied at Columbia University, earned her master's degree at the age of 64, and went on to teach mentally retarded children (Jonas & Jonas, 1973).

Second, there is a questioning of the very basis of the whole concept of retirement. To date, the attempts of governmental agencies and those who are responsible for formulating policies to improve the lot of the elderly have been concentrating on improving the conditions that now exist. Such actions promote, rather than decrease, dependency, and they do nothing to help retirees fill their time constructively. "It is ironic that those members of such panels who themselves are elderly, whether they are physicians, sociologists, or politicians, advocate such things—and forget that the reason for their own well-being and physical fitness is precisely that they are active and purposeful."[2]

[2] From *Young till We Die* by Doris Jonas and David Jonas. New York: Coward, McCann & Geoghegan, 1973, p. 164. Copyright 1973 by David Orr. Reprinted by permission.

Third, some earlier assumptions about work and retirement require careful analysis and new theoretical applications. In a study of older men and women to learn about social and psychological differences between men and women in later life, Atchley (1976) controlled for age, marital status, education, and income adequacy. His findings contradict some earlier assumptions that work is not a primary role for women who work. Women in his sample reported difficulty in getting used to retirement more often than did men. Whereas men often responded to aging in terms of how it affected their relation to the social system, women neither accepted social aging nor tried to fend it off by continued engagement; instead, they responded to aging with high levels of psychological stress. Atchley notes that it is possible that differences observed in his study may *not* be the same for upcoming cohorts of older people.

Fourth, the impact of retirement is a continuing, complicated process, affecting older people in different ways and with varying degrees of force. It is not likely to diminish in importance as industrialized societies like our own confront the increasing growth of technology. Retirement education has concerned itself primarily with helping individuals and their spouses understand and adjust to the changes retirement brings to their normal workaday worlds. Gerontologists need not only to be concerned with preparation for retirement, but even more urgently, to determine the educational needs of men and women throughout the later years following retirement. A major question for the retirement educator is: What can the system of education do to train professionals to provide meaningful and helpful education programs for the elderly during the extensive postretirement years?

To place this discussion of retirement in perspective requires an overview of the past and current roles of institutions in retirement education.

HISTORIC DEVELOPMENTS
IN EDUCATION FOR THE ELDERLY

The first major development was the historic enactment of the Older Americans Act of 1965, which established the Administration on Aging and provided for funding for training and research. Although total appropriations to carry out community programs to provide services to older Americans totaled only $7.5 million during 1966, the action to provide services in the field of aging in recognition of diverse needs of older men and women was consequential. The act recognized the need for training and research by giving universities and colleges the funding to begin what has become a significant new direction in higher education in the United States, not only serving older people, but also extending educational gerontology, workforce training, and multidisciplinary graduate programs, as well as research, both empirical and applied, crossing many fronts.

Appropriations increased steadily in subsequent years, with the 1972 total being $101.7 million. More than one million older people were served by over 1,500 community projects funded under Title III, the services including those for independent living, group and home-delivered meals, community programs involving older volunteers, transportation, and health and health-related services (United States Senate, 1973). The 93rd Congress enacted the Older Americans Comprehensive Services Amendments of 1973 to strengthen and improve the Older Americans Act. The Administration on Aging was reorganized within the U.S. Department of Health, Education, and Welfare; the Federal Council on the Aging was created, as well as a National Information and Resource Clearinghouse for the Aging. The commissioner on aging was authorized to make grants to the states for special library and education programs for the elderly, to conduct research in the field of aging, and to make grants and contracts for training personnel for programs for the aging, including the establishment of multidisciplinary centers of gerontology (United States Senate, 1973).

The second major development was the creation of a new dimension—community service—to the two-year junior college. During the 1960s, as the states determined to meet an unprecedented demand to educate youth, community colleges were established to extend post-secondary education to every citizen. During the accelerated movement in education, 500 community colleges were created. Junior colleges became community centered, i.e., within commuting distance for most people (Gleazer, 1974). At the same time, the social turbulence of the 1960s brought about the development of community services departments in these two-year institutions. Aided by the catalyst of federal funds, these emerging departments began to serve special community groups—including senior citizens—and their identified needs. It was a fortunate circumstance for the elderly, who were suddenly recognized in the public sectors as neglected citizens requiring support services.

Those 65 or older were also identified as target populations most in need of education following the enactment of the Older Americans Act in the middle of the decade. Colleges, which were filled with young people, began offering a variety of educational programs to specific community groups including the aged. A variety of formats, or delivery systems, emerged under the community services structure: short courses, seminars, lectures, short-term workforce-training programs, recreational programs, extension center courses, social-action programs, and community development institutes (Myron, Huber, & Sweeney, 1971). The position of continuing education director was reshaped into the role of dean of community services charged with the responsibility for making college resources available to all groups and citizens in the college community district.

A third significant development was the 1971 White House Conference on Aging. Delegates, who represented public and private institutions and whose interests spanned many fields of study and endeavor, developed and recommended policies that, in many cases, led to important improvements in the quality of life of older people (*Toward a National Policy,* 1973, pp. 1–8). In his address to education section delegates, Howard Y. McClusky (1973) observed that education should be regarded as a program category to which all other aspects of living in the later years should be related. He said education for older people is an investment by society in resource development, that older people have experience and special assets that the society needs for the cultivation of its health and well-being. He singled out the community colleges and community schools for promise of "superior achievement in education for aging" (McClusky, 1973, pp. 5–6).

A fourth development provided timely leadership and stimulation to community and two-year college administrators just at the time that they were recognizing an educational imperative to serve their older constituents. The Administration on Aging, in 1971, awarded a two-year grant to the American Association of Community and Junior Colleges (AACJC). This grant provided funds to AACJS to work with the nation's 1,100 community and junior colleges as well as with technical institutes. The objective was to develop an awareness of the needs of older Americans and to explore ways in which these community-oriented institutions might contribute to an improvement in the quality of life of the nation's elderly population.

The timing also was significant in another way. As Arthur S. Flemming, commissioner on aging, noted:

> *It is gratifying that community college recognition of this new field of social action as an opportunity for extending its services parallels a basic objective of the Administration on Aging, namely, that of fostering the establishment of a network of state and area agencies on aging charged with planning, conducting, and expanding services for older people throughout the country. (p. 3)*

The 1971 White House Conference on Aging underscores the directions taken by Andrew S. Korim, director of the AACJC aging project, in rallying colleges throughout the nation to extend learning opportunities to older people, to seek cooperative development of programs with area agencies on aging and community organizations, and to improve workforce training for the field of aging.

A fifth development occurred when community service and continuing education programs at several community colleges specifically sought out the older learner under such federal funding as Title I of the Higher Education Act of 1965 and Title III of the Older Americans Act of 1965. These grants greatly accelerated program development by providing for a coordinator or part-time program director to design and implement courses for older men and women. New community colleges, already expanding their education programs to adults through community service departments, recognized the potentials of a new student population—the older American. College programmers did not believe that society should declare statutory senility upon the 20 million Americans 65 or older.

Community services directors found that retirees were responsive to a variety of offerings. At North Hennepin Community College, Brooklyn Park, Minnesota, most of the programs were in the area of self-development or direct services to senior citizens. Popular classes included trimnastics, psychology, dancing, painting, public speaking, creative writing, films, rap sessions with students, defensive driving, and senior power (Bauer, 1973).

Innovative programs involved not only community agencies, but also local television stations, as colleges extended their resources and sought answers to problems of the elderly in their districts. Vincennes University, Indiana, first organized a 13-week television series with experts discussing community issues including problems of the elderly. Following this, senior citizens were encouraged to enroll for credit courses with tuition discounts and permitted to attend academic classes by paying low audit fees. The institution then obtained a Title III grant from the Indiana Commission on Aging and Aged to conduct a six-county project called Community Development for the Aged. Later, the university became designated as an area agency on aging and received a state grant to become the training and resource agency for southwestern Indiana for the staffs of area agencies on aging in that quarter of the state (Bottenfield, 1974).

Kirkwood Community College in Cedar Rapids, Iowa, developed an extensive program for the elderly that utilized elderly volunteers and specialists to provide a variety of services to older people: a speakers bureau of senior citizens, instructor aides, student tutors and advisors, recreational and leisure-time activities involving college students and staff, extensive preretirement programs, a resource library, and a seven-county-area senior citizen monthly newspaper with a 40,000 circulation (Feller, 1973).

Other community colleges were able to begin programming for senior adults under state grants for developing community services. For example, Schoolcraft Community College, Livonia, Michigan, in 1971, became the first institution in that state to provide a full-time coordinator of programs for older people.

These historic developments led to an unparalleled acceleration of educational efforts on behalf of the nation's older population. Not since the millions of returning World War II veterans took advantage of the GI bill and swept into colleges and universities had these institutions faced the challenge of a new constituency.

An emerging trend that appears to be growing stronger every day must now be added to the list of significant events. This is the assumption on the part of a vigorous, active, older population of positive roles in voluntary service, in contributing to the development and well being of adult children and grandchildren, the learner role, as it becomes increasingly recognized that continuing education is essential to meeting the demands and aspirations of longer life, and in extended roles as advocates and lobbyists, political leaders, conference participants, and members of program advisory groups. (Tibbits, 1978).

Other developments that are worth noting relate to the continuing recognition by responsible educators, legislators and policy makers, and philanthropic leaders of foundations that it is practical as well as humane to encourage useful, active and productive roles for the elderly.

A report titled, Older Americans: An Untapped Resource (1979), points out that both the private and public sectors have taken the initiative in launching projects designed to demonstrate that older persons have both the desire and the capacity to become involved in new career or otherwise furthering their collective value to the economic and social life of the nation. Private sector programs include the American Association of Retired Persons; National Retired Teachers Association; National Association of Retired Federal Employees; National Association for the Spanish Speaking Elderly; National Center on the Black Aged, Inc.; National Council on the Aging, Inc.; National Council of Senior Citizens; National Farmers Union; and the National Indian Council on Aging. The Edna McConnell Clark Foundation invested $10,000,000 in projects over a period of five years that was designed to show how the services of older persons could be better utilized. The Federal agency, ACTION, has supported paid and volunteer programs such as the Retired Senior Volunteer Program, Foster Grandparents, and Senior Companions. The U.S. Administration on Aging, through its network of State and Area Agencies on Aging, has financed projects to help older persons serve as volunteers or paid workers.

The American Association of Community and Junior Colleges assumed another leadership role in extending career opportunities to the elderly. Assisted by the Edna McConnell Clark Foundation, the Association developed a special Older Americans Program to encourage member colleges to take community leadership in assisting older people, both before and after retirement, to prepare themselves for further careers.

Program directors of older adult projects and college presidents agreed that for higher education to be accessible to older adults, the following factors (Older Americans Are a Resource, 1980) were required:

College and trustee endorsement of community based education
Expressed commitment by community college presidents
Innovative and resourceful older adult program directors
Use of instructional and counselling techniques appropriate for mature learners
College outreach activities
Senior citizen advisement in program development
External courses and simplified registration.

THE ROLE OF INSTITUTIONS

Colleges Recognize Need for Training

It is not surprising that many of the two-year colleges suddenly found that they were unprepared to extend their programs to the elderly. Most of the community services directors and coordinators of adult education programs had no training in gerontology. The Institute of Gerontology, affiliated with the University of Michigan and Wayne State University, became the first to recognize the developing thrust of community college programming and services to older constituents. This recognition followed earlier programs under the leadership of Wilma T. Donahue to meet the workforce shortage in the field of aging. In 1967, 29 adults, including community college faculty, were graduated from a crash-implemented training program, which served as a model for training professional and technical personnel, under a grant from the U.S. Administration on Aging. Under AOA Title V funding to train specialists in aging, the Institute of Gerontology began, in 1972, to develop a comprehensive program of in-service training for community service directors of community colleges, and to effect a statewide effort at education programming for older people. The Institute staff provided several kinds of consultation:

1. on conducting community surveys
2. on discovering community leaders among older people
3. on assessing existing programs and services for the elderly
4. on writing proposals and designing programs or working with college faculty in the disciplines of nursing, sociology, psychology, and other social sciences
5. on introducing gerontological content in existing courses
6. on designing new curricula in aging

Consortium projects were developed in cooperation with the Michigan Community College Community Services Association.

The Institute of Gerontology offered a summer institute program to extend its training facilities to personnel of colleges and other institutions serving the elderly. A course in community college teaching and programming in aging was developed. Participants attended from various institutions representing many states, and resource leaders from colleges responded eagerly from as far away as Hawaii.

Training Roles of the University

Retirement education began in this country in the spring of 1948 when Clark Tibbitts offered the first course for older people at the University of

Michigan. Shortly thereafter, Wilma T. Donahue and Woodrow W. Hunter adapted Tibbitt's course for older people *before* retirement (Tibbitts, 1948).

Today, the emphasis of most universities in gerontology education is on graduate instruction or career training rather than on the training of professionals who are in a position to develop pre- and postretirement education programs for older people. Starting with the Older Americans Act of 1965 (and continuing with the Older Americans Comprehensive Services Amendments of 1973), grants have been made to help initiate, expand, or strengthen research and instructional programs with a primary emphasis on social, economic, and professional services. Seven career and job areas of training were identified: national, state, and community planning; personnel for retirement housing; senior-center personnel; specialists in aging; faculty institutes on aging; semiprofessional and technical personnel; and volunteer leaders (Donahue, 1967, p. 85).

Most of these areas fall in the purview of university instruction. In March 1966, the Administration on Aging awarded a grant under Title V to the University of Georgia for a one-year project designed to equip university and college faculties throughout the seven-state region with the information and knowledge needed to provide gerontological instruction. The timing was fortuitous; universities were ready to respond to the need for a large number of qualified professional personnel and the availability of training moneys. Within 13 months after the first grant was awarded, programs at 16 more universities were funded (Donahue, 1967, p. 86). These included the University of Michigan, which became the base along with Wayne State University, for the first institute of gerontology in a university setting created by state statute.

The university may be said to have both direct and indirect roles in leadership training for retirement education. Although some overlap may occur, direct responsibilities include: the planning and offering of short-term courses, seminars, workshops, and institutes to education personnel, including administrators, program coordinators, and faculty; research in the design of new curricula for the aged; research on the problem areas of aging that relate to program development and service to the elderly; and graduate instruction to train professionals in the areas of education, administration, and service delivery to older people.

The university's indirect training roles encompass consultative services to professional people who are actively engaged in programming for the elderly or in community organization work, mostly at the community colleges; collaborative efforts to establish consortia with other universities, community and junior colleges, and private institutions in the interest of cooperative programming or improving educational opportunities; and resource development including the preparation of bibliographies, instructional materials, and teaching aids.

The variety of subjects and target participants suggests that leadership training in retirement education is multidisciplinary and, at the same time, broad enough in curriculum content to interest professional workers in many service areas. Tibbitts (1967) identified four categories of professional personnel that would be required to create the environment and provide the services needed by the older population: (1) direct providers of services; (2) planners, administrators, and program directors; (3) researchers; and (4) teaching faculty (p. 58).

The increasing scope of training to serve gerontology's rapidly accelerating service area as the needs of the elderly become the focus of education and service bears out Tibbitt's (1967) statement: "Again, there are no estimates of the numbers of faculty personnel required for teaching gerontology either to those who will prepare for work in the professions or in research or to those who are to train these teachers" (p. 58).

University-College Linkage

In his work, *Older Americans and Community Colleges: A Guide for Program Implementation,* AACJC aging project director Andrew Korim (1974) suggests that colleges take the initiative in establishing links with universities in order to obtain needed services and to influence programming development: "University centers of gerontology are a valuable resource regarding research on aging and the needs of the elderly, and centers can assist the two-year institutions by providing personnel and graduate student internships" (p. 101).

Centers that have been of value to community colleges include those at the University of California, Duke University, the University of Nebraska, the University of Oregon, Pennsylvania State University, and Syracuse University, as well as at the University of Michigan. Korim expects college-university relationships to expand in the future as two-year colleges increase their services in the field of aging. Two examples may be cited to illustrate how expanding university pursuits in research and education can stimulate 2-year institutions to offer programs for retired people. The first concerns an Institute of Gerontology research project on older drivers, which began in 1974. Under joint sponsorship of the NRTA/AARP Andrus Foundation, the Michigan Office of Highway Safety Planning, and the National Highway Traffic Safety Administration of the U.S. Department of Transportation, this research resulted in the development of an older driver refresher course. Age-related changes likely to affect driving behavior of older people were studied and incorporated in the training program, which will be tested at various community colleges. The ultimate application to curriculum will involve the training of college administrators and driver education teachers as well as the older people themselves.

In the second example, in cooperation with four community colleges in the Detroit metropolitan area, a 2-year research project, titled "Development of Post-Retirement Education Models with a Community College Consortium on Aging," was launched by the Institute of Gerontology on July 1, 1974. The objective was to design, implement, and evaluate, drawing upon resources of the four colleges, postretirement education programs that would be directed to poor, ethnic, single, and institutionalized populations of retired people. This project was one of 11 community service and continuing education projects funded under Title I of the Higher Education Act. A series of instructional videotape and tape-slide presentations was developed to provide information to administrators and faculty of 2-year institutions interested in assisting the elderly constituents in their districts to successfully meet the changes occurring in their lives. The presentations include: the rationale and importance of education for retirees, methodologies and strategies in teaching older adults, and administrative processes in designing and offering programs to retirees. Faculty who were participating in the project supplied the answers and cross-fertilization of ideas that were obtained in response to the university-sponsored workshops. The data were then analyzed and corroborated with field research before being translated into instructional materials. Throughout the project, a teamwork approach proved beneficial in bringing the university and college staffs together to address problems.

The implications are clear: (1) the university's role in research is crucial to the design and implementation of programs offered by colleges directly to retired people; (2) knowledge obtained from research, both theoretical and practical, can and should be utilized for training educators and providing them with the theoretical as well as the applied systems; (3) the growth of knowledge through university research efforts can be effectively translated into programmatic actions, and this is possible only with the cooperative understanding and involvement of faculty and administrative staff of other institutions, in this case, 2-year colleges.

The value of research to administrators may be illustrated by a study of free and reduced tuition policies for older adult students at community, junior, and technical colleges. The research project of the Older Americans Program, AACJC, was carried out by Loretta J. Butcher, Research Fellow, Gerontological Society. Among her findings, Butcher learned that there are important differences in state policy. Only two states with highest percentages of older adults have passed tuition waiver legislation on a state-wide basis regulating the two year colleges, Arkansas and South Dakota. Some states have policies that waive tuition for older adults but prohibit institutions from including these waivers in the computation for state funding. A number of states have policies with a space available restriction. Butcher found that such policies have been legislated or established to appeal to an age group in our population that is increasing in size and power, while actually providing financial assistance for very few older adult learners. States that waive tuition for both credit and non-credit courses, and indicate that they will fund both types of courses, seem to have made a positive commitment to aid the older student (Butcher, 1980).

A similar finding resulted from a statewide study of Michigan colleges to learn what impact curtailed funding would have on policies, priorities and programs for seniors. The study found that commitment to serve older adults as evidenced by continuing to provide courses despite financial hardship is more important than policy and that more sensitivity to community resources may provide the motivation to circumvent the circumstances of curtailed funding. (Brahce & Prokop, 1980).

Communication Exchange

In a growing, changing field like gerontology, it is essential to keep the communication lines open between universities and colleges and the other community agencies involved in programming for retired people. As personnel in the field experience different situations imposed by social and institutional changes, these can be communicated to university faculty who are responsive to these patterns. Therefore, faculty should be involved in research and program development projects whenever possible. In addition, community agencies and civic groups may occasionally call upon faculty for assistance in providing new information or interpreting advances in scientific theory and knowledge for the practitioner and citizen.

TRAINING RETIREMENT EDUCATORS
Identifying the Needs

It is perhaps axiomatic that the first requirement in training educators to program for the retirement years is to help them understand the needs of the retired people themselves. Among the needs identified by gerontologists are income, health and nutrition, housing, transportation, consumer protection, employment, retirement roles and activities, education, and spiritual well-being (Myran, Huber, & Sweeney, 1971, pp. 4-9).

McClusky (1975) has also identified five categories of educational needs with programmatic relevance. The first are *coping* needs. They must be satisfied in order for adequate social adjustment, psychological health, and physical well-being to continue. They take priority over all other needs and may be termed survival needs. They are most urgent for the aged poor and the isolated ethnic populations living in deteriorating cities or in isolated rural environments. Education responses have been short-term sessions providing knowledgeable resource persons to give the elderly useful information that can be important for survival itself. Community police officers, for example, can provide useful hints about self-protection, or social security personnel can interpret the latest policies.

The second category is *expressive* needs, the needs for involvement in activities for the sake of the pleasure the activity gives. Educational responses could be providing courses in personal interest areas such as genealogy, current affairs, or improving skills in a hobby.

The third category is *contributive* needs, the needs of older people to give. They desire to contribute something acceptable to others and to the community. These needs can be easily met through volunteer programs such as foster grandparent or retired senior volunteers. Older people can also satisfy this kind of need by working as volunteers in a college, aiding teachers or administrators. McClusky believes older people represent a reservoir of wisdom and experience that society needs but has not yet learned to exploit.

The fourth need category is *influence*. As we get older, we have a need to exert greater influence on the circumstances of our community, our society, and the world around us. According to McClusky, this kind of need is actually the need to affect the direction and quality of life. Educational programs that are intellectual and that open new dimensions of service in political activity and community leadership may meet these needs.

The need for *transcendence* is the fifth category and is manifested during the later years by the need to become something better than one has been, to achieve a sense of fulfillment in the later years. This kind of need may well be satisfied as a by-product of the gratification of another need. It has to do with ego satisfaction and is an introspective attainment that can be reached only in the mature years of life (pp. 330–338).

Defining the Task

The second requirement in training educators is to translate the real, life-directed needs into educational programs that can answer those needs in a positive way. Underlying any theory of the education of older people is the fact that people change as they become older and their relations with others change. In the important work compiled by Donahue, *Education for Later Maturity,* John E. Anderson (1955) makes the point that an educational program for older people should be broadly conceived, and, as with youth, the very process of development presents unique problems concerning when to present content in relation to the emergence of a need.

The first purpose of education, notes Anderson, is to give older people an understanding of the changes that are taking place and an awareness that they are facing problems in common with other people. The second purpose centers on the imparting of knowledge and skills that will maintain health, retain or increase mental capacity, and enable people to use their own resources more effectively and thus make the most of the facilities available in the environment. The third purpose recognizes the fact that learning, of itself, can be interesting and stimulating. The fourth purpose concerns the richer social experience and better understanding of the world that a longer life gives. Education and guidance provide a real opportunity to build constructively upon the interests that older people show in daydreaming or thinking about the meaning and purpose of life.

Approaches to Preretirement Education

Since the first education course was offered to older people by Tibbitts 25 years ago, there has been a proliferation of such programs, taking place not only in university and college settings, but also in industry, labor unions, public schools, libraries, YW-YMCAs, churches, religious communities, university centers, senior housing projects, multipurpose senior centers, government agencies, and the armed forces. The key to carrying on this unprecedented growth of programs is the preparation of leaders to offer quality programs. Basic aspects of leadership training for preretirement education include objectives, content, and method of training; resources for training; and program evaluation. In training preretirement educators, it is important first to help students develop a frame of reference focused on aging and the *retirement process.* This difficult objective may be met by exposing students to the psychology and sociology of aging; the economic status of older people including social security, Medicare and Medicaid, and other health insurance programs; the health status of older people; housing; income planning; leisure; and community planning and organization for aging. This aspect of the training course should not only provide students with knowledge about the process of aging, but also encourage them to develop a positive philosophy of aging.

A second need is to give students experience in planning, conducting, and evaluating educational programs designed to facilitate the transition of older people from a work to a retirement way of life. Here the emphases are on helping students plan and develop program sessions as well as on providing opportunities to practice what they have learned. Students also acquire skill in identifying and assessing community resources to which older people can turn in an attempt to manage problems of everyday living.

Potential leaders in preretirement education ought to know not only the specific content areas for program development, but also something about effective promotion, community involvement including the use of resources, and evaluation. Sponsorship is directly related to effective promotion of a preretirement education program. Groups of hourly-rated workers sometimes are more likely to participate if their labor unions are involved in conducting the program. Other employees show a preference for programs that are sponsored by management; still others show more inclination to participate when sponsorship includes both union and management support. Delegates to the 1971 White House Conference on Aging endorsed the idea that public education should encourage the support and cooperation of as many interested groups in the community as possible. Preretirement education councils have been highly successful in Great Britain. Membership includes public education, industries and labor organizations, and groups providing services and programs to the elderly, such as committees on the aging, libraries, social agency councils, YM-YWCAs, public housing departments, churches, legal aid, recreation, and so forth. Leaders from such groups may be asked to serve as resource persons in preretirement education programs; others may offer organizational facilities for programs. Leadership qualities should include the abilities to: establish a positive philosophy of aging as a basis for promoting the program, create a congenial atmosphere to help older people overcome their fears and concerns about facing retirement issues and to encourage them to ask questions and to participate in discussion, and make clear that the program is intended to reflect the concerns and interests of participants rather than sponsors.

The training of program leaders includes the skills to conduct group discussion sessions; the breadth of information to assure they can lead and encourage discussion of a variety of solutions to retirement programs; and the need to be informed about community resources available to retired people. Discussion leaders are encouraged to take an inventory of community resources and to interview a sample of people who represent the same occupational, economic, and social characteristics as those with whom they will be working.

The shortage of professionally trained personnel has prompted educators at the University of Michigan and other institutions to train discussion leaders from among personnel directors, union leaders, recreation workers, librarians, and others. Older people themselves may be encouraged to serve as resource persons familiar with their communities. In such roles they can be valuable aides in helping other retirees obtain information about local resources and policies, changing tax benefits; and legislation in such areas as drug prescriptions, legal rights, and consumer information.

Credit courses for graduate students in preretirement education principles and practices are offered at some university centers with gerontology programs. A major training center directing programs to personnel staffs from industry is the University of Chicago Industrial Relations Center. Roosevelt University in Chicago has emphasized training programs for labor leaders. One of the most active centers is the Drake University Pre-Retirement Planning Center, which offers five-day workshops. An AOA model project grant has been awarded to the University of Michigan Institute of Gerontology to train preretirement educators in six midwestern states comprising region V, U.S. Department of Health, Education, and Welfare.

Approaches to Postretirement Education

Another need in the training of leaders is to help them understand that learning should not terminate upon retirement, but should continue throughout life. Problems of living and adjustment do not stop with the cessation of employment. Indeed, if anything, the mature years are a critical time for adjusting to changes in individual and social status, relationships to others, health and well-being, as well as often adverse economic circumstances. In addition, mental health and mental activity are seen to be correlated with successful adjustment to the aging process. To this end, adult educators must themselves assume responsibility for responding to the changing educational needs of retired individuals and their spouses by offering a variety of education programs. Educators may exercise their greatest creativity in program planning in this challenging endeavor, realizing that variety in course format, design, and content, may be as varied as the institutions involved in this growing activity.

National surveys[3] of education for aging indicate an increased awareness among educators of the need to program for, and the potential to serve, older adults. In a survey conducted for the National Council on the Aging, Harris (Harris & Associates, 1975) found that educated older people appeared to have more positive self-images in both mental and physical activities than the less educated. Although this is impressive, the data reveal that research is needed to substantiate findings, to investigate problems, and to study implications for all systems of public education.

Needs assessment is a critical area in programming for older adults, and the literature suggests several strategies, from community surveys to the nominal group process (McElreath, 1976). Hunter (1975) found, in a community survey done in collaboration with Schoolcraft Community College, that older people expressed interest in obtaining information about social security, Medicare, aspects of the law, retirement housing, social services, selecting a place to live, making good use of leisure time, volunteer activity, making the most of retirement income, and ways to maintain health during retirement. Respondents in sizable numbers also expressed interest in participating in cultural events and in being of service to the community. Schools for retirement set up at the college were basically organized to supply information about aspects of aging and to teach retirees skills in solving problems of everyday living.

Programs developed in Detroit-area colleges supported the need for many elderly, particularly urban residents with low educational attainment, to acquire information to help them survive in a hostile, changing environment (Brahce, 1976). A preretirement education program organized in the city of Ann Arbor by the Institute of Gerontology in cooperation with the Kiwanis Club and the Ann Arbor Public Schools Continuing Education Department also supported the continuing need of retired people for basic information that is traditionally regarded as preretirement content. Retired participants indicated a strong desire for information to help them in their struggles with diminishing income, health, and other problems such as how to spend their time. These programs suggest

[3]*National Inventory of Learning Opportunities for Older Adults* by Roger DeCrow for the Adult Education Association of the U.S.A.; *National Survey of Education and Training for Older Persons* by Norman Auburn for the Academy for Educational Development, Inc.; *Older Americans and Community Colleges* by Andrew Korim for the American Association of Community and Junior Colleges.

that older adults require specific information at different stages in post-retirement living, in addition to their need to explore new cultural outlets and leisure pursuits. Useful information for retirees may touch on volunteer roles as well as job opportunities. A program that has proved beneficial to retirees, including nursing-home residents, in all socioeconomic and age categories is an intergenerational project to utilize older people as teacher support staff in the Ann Arbor Public Schools (Brahce, 1975).

Program content is limited only by imagination and creative insight of the planner in meeting the requirements of older adults. It was found that courses, such as legal affairs in later life, home nursing, physical fitness after 50, senior adult forum on social security and income, and medical and health services, that deal with practical informational and functional-support needs are most urgently needed by many older people. At the same time, educators at Schoolcraft Community College and Henry Ford Community College (Dearborn, Michigan) determined that courses could also be designed to solve life-change and adapting problems, like "Living Alone and Liking It" for the widowed or the "Know Thyself" offering in self-awareness.

College programmers have discovered that it is essential to provide short sessions or to have frequent breaks in longer periods. Several colleges have successfully designed the minicourse format, which also is useful in giving prospective older adults some ready insights into new offerings. A project in rural, sparsely populated Upper Michigan supports the idea of short offerings with considerable variety. Traveling short sessions were organized at 15 different sites in a health-and-heritage educational adult delivery system organized by administrators at Suomi College under funding from Title I of the Higher Education Act of 1965. A total of 3,919 senior citizens participated in 143 learning sessions, receiving instruction from a combination of college faculty and community residents, including senior adults. Local people or senior scholars coordinated the sessions in such subjects as: social security measures, understanding grief, weaving skills, first aid techniques, protecting valuables, psychology of aging, physical fitness and exercise, nutrition and diet, Finnish heritage, recollections of a bush pilot in Canada, wild flowers, creative retirement, student folk music, recreational dancing, and the metric system (Puotinen, 1976).

In the Institute of Gerontology Consortium Project, teachers of older adults placed strong emphasis on methodology. They stressed the desirability of group discussion and of maximum involvement of the older adult while relaxing the pace of the delivery of new information and of the time required for completing tasks. More individual attention and personal support was encouraged in classes that were designed specifically for older adults.

Educators, then, are advised to keep up-to-date on research in the field of gerontology. Universities share a responsibility to disseminate findings of research and to interpret significant data for professionals working in the field.

The positive affirmation of the powerful force education can exert on changing the lives of elderly has been demonstrated in the Wayne County Consortium on Aging Project. Through the use of videotape evalution, university researchers learned that college programs designed to help older people improve their self-perceptions and to understand such traumatic changes in their lives as death of the spouse or retirement can be valuable in giving the retirees greater self-confidence, independence, and dignity and a feeling of usefulness in their later years.

As Peterson points out:

The challenge that faces adult educators is to re-orient their thinking in such a way that they acknowledge the educational needs of older people and accept the tenet that individuals of all ages have the potential for development and continued growth. This will place educators in a unique position in relation to other professionals providing services to the older population. Other professionals tend to emphasize the decline that accompanies old age . . . . (Peterson, 1975, p. 50)

The importance of motivation in older adult learning is recognized by gerontologists as being very important for the teacher of older adults and the program planner. As Anderson (1955) noted, older people easily drop into a routine and become complacent about life. Because they have met and solved most of their life problems, there is no great pressure for vocational or personal success. These attitudes are obstacles to learning. The instructor's problem is to change these attitudes by showing older people, through activities that appeal directly to immediate needs, that they can learn.

Studies like the National Center for Education Statistics survey of adult education activities show strong correlation of participation with income, prior education, and age. Those with higher incomes and more years of education take education seriously in adult years. Despite the efforts of educators and gerontologists to stimulate learning activity for those in advanced years, participation remains lowest for these men and women, 6.84% for those 55-64, and 2.43% for those over 65, compared with 11.23% for persons 17-24; 20.06% for the 25-34 group and 13.02 for persons 35-54 (National Center for Education Statistics, 1978).

This study, and that by Florio (Florio, 1978), show that older participants are less motivated to pursue vocational courses, but elect courses giving an enriched intellectual experience, or assistance in managing circumstances of later living; to enhance capacity for performance in contributive, citizenship, and advocacy roles. The studies show that 38% of the older learners choose academic courses in the humanities, 36% elect hobby or recreation type courses; with 22% desiring information and consumer education courses (Florio, 1978).

In a study of attitudes toward pensions and retirement, Harris found generally widespread agreement with the recent change in the mandatory retirement age from 65 to 70 years of age. (Harris, 1979). Many (53%) would have continued working if they would, and 51% indicated they prefer to work at some job or less demanding job as an alternative to retirement.

An issue to be resolved in American society remains to provide those older men and women who realize certain values in work roles with ways to substitute these in leisure activities, such as continuing education (Harris et al., 1979).

A Canadian study that examined perceptions of work and leisure among the elderly found that those who did not hold a emunerated job (e.g., housework), and those who willingly gave up their jobs, defined leisure in terms of enjoyment/fulfillment. Those, however, who were forced to retire tended to define leisure in terms of freedom (Roadburg, 1981). Persons planning leisure programs for the elderly could benefit from further research into the differences for perceptions about leisure, as indicators for motivations to pursue certain educational objectives after retirement (Roadburg, 1981).

LEARNING PROGRESSION
IN LATER YEARS

Evaluation of the Post-retirement Education Model Project courses at Detroit metropolitan-area colleges revealed that senior adults often seek the challenge of more advanced education stimuli, regardless of their levels of educational attainment. Once they have overcome their hesitancy to enter the college classroom (attributed to a fear-of-failure mind-set and often accentuated by being out of school for many years), older people become self-motivated to pursue more difficult, complex courses of study or skill. This is evident for people with only a few years of schooling as well as for those older adults who have done some college work earlier in their careers. After successfully taking classes, some retirees also realize they have sufficient talent to teach classes. This occurrence, in both men and women, is termed the *learning progression phenomenon* (Brahce, 1976, p. 57).

This acceptance of the next challenge apparently follows the educative needs suggested by McClusky (1974). Those adults with limited (elementary level) educational experience who entered the learning setting at the coping scale of course instruction were seen to aspire to enrollment in courses offering them greater intellectual challenges. Many of the retired people who first participated in quiltmaking or leathercraft courses in which they overcame their fears of failure, shyness with the instructor, and general feelings of inadequacy, went on to take a course in art and music appreciation. Others who signed up for a senior adult forum giving basic information about social security were later sufficiently motivated to enroll in a course in Bible literature. Some students who had never touched a musical instrument learned to distinguish artists' works and to play simple tunes on the piano. Retirees who first enrolled in survival courses to help them understand about social and consumer protection services went on to enroll in mini-courses dealing with politics and letter writing at Highland Park Community College and cultural appreciation at Wayne Community College. Retirees who were participating in a senior aid course in conjunction with a part-time work program made definite improvements in cognitive, emotional, and social growth after program evaluation. When a pilot group of senior adults were given a course in drama, however, many dropped out. This was attributed either to being motivated to move too rapidly (in some cases it was believed that they could not feel comfortable enough about their reading skills to read dramatic parts) or to not being given sufficient encouragement by the teacher. Older people who were at the other end of the scale of educational achievement, having completed some high school or college work, displayed a similar desire to pursue more challenging courses after first enrolling in college programs. These men and women decided to try academic (degree) courses after mastering course material designed for people who had been out of school a long time. Here, self-confidence resulted in older people moving without difficulty from age-segregated settings to age-integrated ones.

Max R. Raines (1974), one of the early teachers of community-college community-leadership functions, has developed a theory of *life-centered education*. Its central thesis is that the equitable and humane society has a moral obligation to provide its members with developmental assistance in acquiring those transactional competencies necessary for (1) reconciling personal needs with societal expectations, and (2) discovering meaning in their lives through their essential life roles. Senior citizens head the list of potential target groups for Raine's life-centered education.

PROGRAMMING

Retirement educators face a three-fold task: (1) they must understand the potentiality of education as a life-centered enterprise of profound consequences for older people; (2) they must determine the resources of their colleges or institutions to answer the continuing needs of their older constituents; and (3) they have to rally those resources effectively within their communities to effect a significant educational response.

University courses directed at community service deans and directors of adult education programs have been constructed with this multiple purpose. An effective instructional methodology, as colleges develop interest, financial support, and commitment, has been to invite educators with experience in program design and implementation to share their knowledge and firsthand information with seminar or workshop participants. The university acts as a catalyst for resource and information dissemination, at the same time providing theoretical knowledge about the developing field of gerontology. Gerontology centers also are able to demonstrate training methodologies, such as milieu therapy, that have proved beneficial to people employed in various institutional settings.

Consortia in Programming

Although community college consortia have not been conducive to progressive developments in some academic areas, examples may be cited of innovative programming and the creation of beneficial educational opportunities for older adults through consortia in aging. A series of bibliographies of short stories, poems, novels, essays, and other works of literature were produced through the Southeastern Michigan Consortium on Gerontology and the Humanities. A variety of intergenerational programs and creative works by seniors were prepared through the project, involving Eastern Michigan University and five community colleges, and funded by the National Endowment for the Humanities. Six colleges in Michigan were funded for the second year to produce programs for older adults in the Consortium for Aging and Retirement Education, one of 11 special community service and continuing education projects funded by the Department of Health, Education, and Welfare, under Title I of the Higher Education Act. Informative newsletters, workshops, and conferences have helped disseminate information to participating and other institutions. As a result of the two-year Post-retirement Education Model Project involving the four colleges in the Detroit area and the Institute of Gerontology, instructional materials have been developed to assist faculty and administrators at two-year institutions in program development and teaching strategies. The Michigan Community College Community Services Association has stimulated both research and program development. A massive program-development project was undertaken by the colleges and universities of the state of Wisconsin, resulting in statewide programs in consort with community agencies. In California, regional educational organizations have given attention to interinstitutional coordination of programs. The Northeastern Council for Higher Education, made up of representatives of six community colleges, California State University at Chico, and the University of California at Davis, has established a task force on older Americans. A planning group, the Regional Association of East Bay Colleges and Universities, has prepared a report on the older citizens of East Bay. The San Francisco Consortium of Institutions of Higher Education is reported to be developing a plan so that people over 65 could take courses at reduced fees on member campuses (California Higher Education Study for the Aging, 1975).

Another approach is a program developed by retirees themselves with the help and encouragement of the New School for Social Research in New York City. It is the Institute for Retired Professionals, and it recognizes that "the vast pool of experience and talents in the retired population must somehow be used constructively in retirement for the benefit of retirees as well as society" (Kauffman & Luby, 1975, p. 143). The institute offers an opportunity for many highly trained, retired professionals to renew their educations at the university level without the usual course procedures. Using their experience and talents in a retiree's self-directed program represents a new approach in adult education.

Directed by Leroy E. Hixson, the Institutes for Lifetime Learning seek to eliminate any discomfort a retiree might feel upon returning to a learning setting. The institutes, an activity of the National Retired Teachers Association and its public unit, the American Association of Retired Persons, offer noncredit courses of shorter duration than the average college semester, usually an eight-week semester with one 90-minute class per week (Kauffman & Luby, 1975).

Media Approaches

The electronic media, powerful forces for public opinion and instant communications, are playing a fast-developing market that reaches to the older adult. Educational awareness through public broadcasting is reaching into production capabilities for educational television, cable television, and the audiovisual outlets as well. Videotape series of programs, *Elderview,* are produced as a joint project of the New England Gerontology Center and the Harbor Institute of the University of Massachusetts, Boston. Funds are provided to the New England Center for Continuing Education by the Administration on Aging. Programs are produced through a grant from AOA. The productions are for groups of individuals, classes, or home viewing via cable television. The Georgia Center for Continuing Education, similarly funded by AOA, has produced a series of films titled *New Wrinkles on Retirement.* They consist of eight half-hour programs dealing with issues confronting the retired person or the person who is planning for retirement. The series has been introduced over originating station WFTV Athens/Atlanta and over the statewide Georgia educational television network. The first national television series ever to deal with the subject of aging premiered January 21, 1976, on the Public Broadcasting Service. Eight one-hour programs, *Images of Aging,* were produced by WITF, Hershey, Pennsylvania, with a grant from the Corporation for Public Broadcasting.

In a new media and aging section of the Gerontological Society, the important role of the mass media was depicted and discussed, including analysis of current programming and research needs, at the national annual meeting in New York, October 14–17, 1976. A commission on media and aging was proposed to develop and promote policy, coordinate research, and study media production and distribution.

Colleges like Jackson Community College in Jackson, Michigan, have extended special offerings to senior adults in cooperation with the local cable television outlet. Videotape is being studied as both a training tool and an evaluation method in training and program design in aging at the Institute of Gerontology.

More ways will be found to effect collaboration between labor unions, industry, and the universities/colleges to better use the experience and knowledge of the older worker. As the younger employee force diminishes, more experimentation will result in new educational strategies to provide workers in the middle years to learn new skills, to change work opportunities and objectives.

As the middle and older adults become better educated, more pressures will be placed on academic institutions to provide learning challenges throughout the extended life cycle. The psycho-social values of work will be transferred to leisure pursuits, including education, as more elderly persons provide meaningful role models to younger persons through involvement in volunteer service, teaching-learning, family-centered and community-centered activities.

TRENDS

Expanding forces now operating in retirement education have predictable consequences for training in the field. Several may be singled out:

- As adults reach retirement age in the next decade or so, many of them will have been among the waves of returning GI's who took advantage of educational opportunities. Future retirees therefore will have a higher educational attainment than those now becoming separated from work. Also, the trend toward earlier retirement may be softened with more phased-out retirement. Both events will increase the likelihood of future retirees responding to lifelong educational opportunities.
- More and more women are now working at full- or part-time jobs. Future retirement education will have to make a considerable shift in understanding of spouse relationships, family relationships, and income planning, as more women will be experiencing retirement from work. The whole dimension of sharing years of leisure roles and pursuits will be much different from now on. New educational materials will need to be produced.
- Both men and women will be more interested in obtaining degrees in different fields, or in career change, as the late middle years approach.
- Responsibility for providing retirees not only with pensions, but with lifelong learning aids, will be shared by both labor and industry.
- As legislation to provide lifelong learning options becomes enacted, state and federal education bodies will finally recognize the magnitude of adult learning as a lifelong continuum for people of all socioeconomic groups. More support for education in the later years will be the result.
- Educational institutions, public as well as private colleges and universities, will give credence to the idea of life-centered education. Multidisciplinary programs will become much more common in the

field of gerontology, and professional schools will recognize the need for gerontological content in their specialized fields, from law and political science, to nursing and medical training and including psychiatry.

• Institutions will be under pressure to regard graduates as entitled to lifelong certificates of eligibility instead of terminal degrees.

• Research in many disciplines will accelerate the need for gerontology-center coordination and distribution of information and training materials, including multimedia programs.

• The field of postretirement education will assume more significance and importance as the older population increases and institutions recognize the potential of service to this target population of expanding resource value.

REFERENCES

Anderson, J. E. (1955). Teaching and learning. In W. T. Donahue (Ed.), *Education for later maturity*. New York: Whiteside.

Atchley, R. C. (1971, Spring). Retirement and leisure participation: Continuity or crisis. *The Gerontologist*, pt. 1, pp. 13–17.

Atchley, R. C. (1976). Selected social and psychological differences between men and women in later life. *Journal of Gerontology, 31*(2), 204–211.

Bauer, B. (1973, July/August). *A "new" clientele for a "new" community college.* Paper presented at the Summer Institute on Social Gerontology, University of Michigan, Ann Arbor.

Bottenfield, J. L. (1974, July). *What a community college with limited resources can do in the field of aging.* Paper presented at the Summer Institute in Gerontology, University of Michigan, Ann Arbor.

Brahce, C. I. (1975). Art bridges the age gap. *Innovator, 7*(2), 1, 3–5.

Brahce, C. I. (1976). *Development of postretirement education models with a community college consortium on aging* (Final report). Ann Arbor: University of Michigan.

Brahce, C. I., & Prokop, R. (1980). Commitment, cutbacks, and continuity—Serving older adults in the 1980s. *Update/interface,* September-October.

Butcher, L. J. (1980, March). *Free and reduced tuition policies for older adult students at community, junior, and technical colleges.* Washington, DC: Older Americans Program, American Association of Community and Junior Colleges.

California Higher Education Study for the Aging. *Summary Report.* (1975). Sacramento: Author.

de Beauvoir, S. (1972). *The coming of age.* New York: Putnam.

Donahue, W. T. (1967). Development and current status of university instruction in social gerontology. In R. E. Kushner & M. E. Bunch (Eds.), *Graduate education in aging within the social sciences.* Ann Arbor: University of Michigan.

Feller, R. A. (1973). *Education for the elderly: Part of a comprehensive service program.* Paper presented at the Summer Institute on Social Gerontology, University of Michigan, Ann Arbor.

Glamser, F. D. (1976). Determinants of a positive attitude toward retirement. *Journal of Gerontology, 31,* 104–107.

Gleazer, E. J., Jr. (1974, December/January). After the boom. . .what NOW for the community colleges. *Community and Junior College Journal,* pp. 6–11.

Florio, C. (1978). *Collegiate programs for older adults: A summary report on a 1976 survey.* New York: Academy for Educational Development.

Harris, L., & Associates. (1975). *The myths and reality of aging in America.* Washington, DC: National Council on the Aging.

Harris, L., et al. (1979). *1979 Study of American attitudes toward pensions and retirement.* New York: Johnson and Higgins.

Hunter, W. W. (1975). Preretirement education and planning. In *Education for the Aging.* S. M. Grabowski & W. D. Mason (Eds.), *Learning for aging.* Washington, DC: Adult Education Association of the U.S.A. Syracuse, NY: ERIC Clearinghouse on Adult Education.

Jonas, D., & Jonas, D. (1973). *Young till we die.* New York: Coward.

Kauffman, E., & Luby, P. (1975). Non-traditional education: Some new approaches to a dynamic culture. In S. M. Grabowski & W. D. Mason (Eds.), *Learning for aging.* Washington, DC: Adult Education Association of the U.S.A. Syracuse, NY: ERIC Clearinghouse on Adult Education.

Korim, A. S. (1974). *Older Americans and community colleges: A guide for program implementation.* Washington, DC: American Association of Community and Junior Colleges.

McClusky, H. Y. (1973). Section on Aging. In *Toward a national policy on aging: Final report of the 1971 White House Conference on Aging.* (Vol. 11, pp. 1–10). Washington, DC: U.S. Government Printing Office.

McClusky, H. Y. (1975). Education for aging: The scope of the field and perspectives for the future. In S. M. Grabowski & W. D. Mason (Eds.), *Learning for aging.* Washington, DC: Adult Education Association of the U.S.A. Syracuse, NY: ERIC Clearinghouse on Adult Education.

McElreath, M. P. (1976, March). How to figure out what adults want to know. *Adult Leadership,* pp. 232–235.

Myran, G. A., Huber, R., & Sweeney, S. M. (1971). *Senior citizens services in community colleges* (Research and Report Series, No. 5). East Lansing: Michigan State University.

National Center for Education Statistics. (1978). *Participation in adult education.* Unpublished data. Washington, DC: Author.

Older Americans: An Untapped Resource. (1979). A report by the National Committee on Careers for Older Americans. Washington, DC: Academy for Educational Development, Inc.

Older Americans are a Resource for Community Colleges, Business, Themselves, and Society. (1980, September). Second National Conference Report, Older Americans Program, AACJC (p. 34). Washington, DC: American Association of Community and Junior Colleges.

Peterson, D. A. (1975). The role of gerontology in adult education. In S. M. Grabowski & W. D. Mason (Eds.), *Learning for aging.* Washington, DC: Adult Education Association of the U.S.A. Syracuse, NY: ERIC Clearinghouse on Adult Education.

Puotinen, A. E. (1976). *Heads up—Health and Heritage Educational Adult Delivery System: Upper Peninsula.* Hancock, MI: Suomi College.

Raines, M. R. (1974). *Life-centered education*. (Research and Report Series, No. 6). East Lansing: Michigan State University.

Roadburg, A. (1981). Perceptions of work and leisure among the elderly. *The Gerontologist, 21*(2), 142–145.

Ross, J. K. (1974). Learning to be retired: Socialization into a French retirement residence. *Journal of Gerontology, 29*(2), 211–223.

Streib, G. F., & Schneider, C. J. (1971). *Retirement in American society: Impact and process*. Ithaca, NY: Cornell University Press.

Sussman, M. B. (1972). An analytic model for the sociological study of retirement. In F. M. Carp (Ed.), *Retirement*. New York: Behavioral Publications.

Tibbits, C. (1948). Aging and living: A report of the first course offered to assist people in making adjustments to old age. *Adult Education Bulletin, 13*, 204–211.

Tibbits, C. (1967). Social gerontology in education for the professions. In R. E. Kushner & M. E. Bunch (Eds.), *Graduate education in aging within the social sciences*. Ann Arbor: University of Michigan.

White House Conference on Aging. (1973). *Toward a national policy on aging: Final report of the 1971 White House Conference on Aging* (Vol. 11). Washington, DC: U.S. Government Printing Office.

United States Senate, Special Committee on Aging. (1973). *Older Americans comprehensive services amendments of 1973*. Washington, DC: U.S. Government Printing Office.

15

A 21st CENTURY CHALLENGE TO HIGHER EDUCATION: INTEGRATING THE OLDER PERSON INTO ACADEMIA

BEN E. DICKERSON
DENNIS R. MYERS
Baylor University

WAYNE C. SEELBACH
Lamar University

SUE JOHNSON-DIETZ
Baylor University

An Aging problem? No problem. Put senior citizens back in college. Under such conditions, accustomed to lifelong learning, why shouldn't they remain creative and innovative to very nearly the end of their lives?

Isaac Asimov
(Asimov, 1988)

INTRODUCTION

The Educational Institution in a Social Context

Advanced societies rely heavily on educational institutions to equip their members to be productive participants in an ever-changing social environment. Education accomplishes this task by introducing the individuals to a relatively large number of social roles and inculcating the requirements, knowledge, and skills needed to perform them. Until recently, the focus of education was on individuals 25 years of age and younger. Societal expectations for this age group indicate when formal education begins in terms of chronological age and what should be included in the curriculum.

Because of the longevity revolution and demographic changes that it produces, society is reexamining the purposes of education. On July 4, 1986, the trend toward an aging society was noted by the announcement that there were more people over age 65 than there were people 18 years of age and younger. Likewise, with rapid technological and informational changes, it is now evident that if people are to remain productive they require both formal and informal educational experiences throughout the life course. Although adult education in the 1980s was successful in encouraging adults to complete their education, it is also apparent that efforts have been restricted in purpose. Because of the demographic shift and the traditional orientation toward adult education, society now is in a position of contemplating how to meet new educational needs of their older members.

The Impact of Demographic Changes on the Student Population

The shifting age structure within society is mirrored in student enrollment on college and university campuses. The numbers and percentages of adults attending colleges have increased significantly over the past 20 years. About 50% of all college students are 25 years or older according to a recent College Board study. Carol Aslanian, Director of the Office of Adult Learning Services of the College Board, observed that adults are increasingly being accommodated into mainstream college programs (Aslanian & Brickell, 1980) rather than being segregated in night school or special programs. College and university enrollments among degree-seeking applicants have been declining in recent years while the last of the baby boom generation has completed full-time study. According to the American Association of Retired Persons (AARP), the 18- to 22-year-old applicant pool continues to decrease in size, whereas the older population steadily increases (AARP, 1986).

This precipitous drop in high school graduates is encouraging colleges to explore the market possibilities of older learners. College registrations may actually decline somewhat less than originally thought; the Carnegie Council on Policy Studies predicts enrollments may fall by only 5–15% between 1979 and 1997. In fact, the period between 1989 and 1991 will show no decline in registrations, and 1997 shows an upswing in projected enrollments in younger students (Carnegie Council on Policy Studies, 1980). During the decline in registrations among younger students, graduate enrollment will probably increase (National Center for Education Statistics [NCES], 1988). In spite of some moderations in the expected drop, higher education will have an interest in courting the older adult market. Whether or not colleges or universities proceed in this direction will depend on their readiness to play a critical role in preparing older people for social change and for productive involvement with society.

Greater involvement by older persons in higher education raises these fundamental questions:

- Has society conveyed to higher education what it deems necessary to fill the knowledge and skill gaps for older adults if they are to continue to have contributory roles?
- How do you overcome the perception that participation in the college or university credit programs is "not the thing to do"?
- Once the older adults are "educated" how does this affect the homeostasis of society?
- How can society and educational institutions overcome the tendency to define roles on the basis of chronological age rather than on the basis of one's ability to perform roles regardless of age?

If education is to be responsive to its social purpose, it must consider expanding its institutional boundaries to encompass the entire life course. Higher education can be the arena in which this expansion takes place. The fundamental assumption is that as participation levels increase, greater benefit will accrue for both the older person and higher education, but more important, older people will be adequately prepared to make the societal contribution the future will demand.

A Decision-Making Model for Participation in Higher Education

The decision of the older person to participate in credit course offerings and the inclination of the higher education organization to invite this level of involvement are determined by complex transactions between the older person, the higher education organization, and societal forces. Several assumptions are made about the nature of these transactions:

- The strength of the willingness of the older person and the level of commitment made by the college or university result from a cognitive appraisal process that balances the positive and negative forces internally and externally present.
- The interaction between the older person and the higher education organization is embedded in a matrix of institutional and cultural currents that stimulate or depress this transaction.
- When the adaptational processes of the older person and the college or university negotiate a productive exchange, there is an increased likelihood of future transactions.
- Careful attention to the process of adoption and diffusion of innovations that promote the relationship between the older person and higher education is necessary.

Figure 1 provides a synopsis of the conceptual framework that guides our consideration of credit-seeking behavior in people 55 and older. The contribution of Lewin's (1947) force field analysis and Germain and Gitterman's (1980) ecological perspective guides this approach to understanding formalized participation in traditional higher education by older adults.

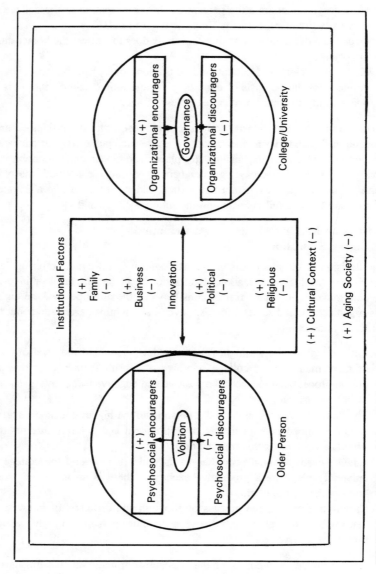

FIGURE 1 A decision-making model for participation in higher education.

Chapter Overview

The focus of this chapter is on the older student, age 55 or older, who is potentially or currently enrolled, either full- or part-time, for the purpose of obtaining an undergraduate, graduate, or professional degree or for reasons other than seeking a degree. First we examine the relationship between the older, credit-seeking student and higher education from the perspective of historical currents and contemporary participation rates. Using the decision-making model as a frame of reference, forces that either discourage or encourage credit-seeking behavior by the older person are identified. Positive and negative patterns of influence on educational participation that emanate from institutional and cultural and societal features are reviewed. Increasing the motivation of the older person to participate and the responsiveness of the college or university raise fundamental questions that require a response by higher education. Thus, we propose guidelines and recommendations for increasing the capacity of societal institutions and higher education to support older, credit-seeking students and thereby facilitate their contribution to American society.

HISTORICAL PERSPECTIVES ON OLDER LEARNERS

Historical trends and adaptational processes within higher education are underway that contribute to the potential for increases in for-credit participation. These trends include the adult education movement, the international impetus to create noncredit, lifelong programs in the United States, and innovations in the types of for-credit courses offered.

The inclination to include the older student in higher education programming is rooted in national and international movements to promote lifelong learning as a rationale for adult education. American higher education has historically, but not exclusively, been directed toward youth and young adults. In tracing the historical record, Harrington (1977) contends that adult education has been a vital part of American higher education. Nonetheless, greater commitment to lifelong learning has been largely a 20th-century phenomenon. In fact, only in the past few decades has a new pattern begun to emerge, a trend referred to by some as the adult education revolution (Harrington, 1977). Long (1986) provided a historic overview of the context within which the idea of formalized, continual education across a life span emerged. Long has observed that during the period of 1880–1919:

> education for adults continued to receive increasing attention as the evening high school, junior college, vocational high school, and university extension developed. It is important to know that the above institutions were unlike the Mechanics Institutes, Lyceum and Chautauqua of early periods. In contrast to the latter, the former were associated with formal educational establishment and reflected increasing recognition of the role of the state in the education of adults. (1986, pp. 10–11)

The 1950s heralded a period of greater visibility for older learners within the adult education enterprise. The American Association of Adult and Continuing Education was established in 1951 and concurrently a section on aging was created. In 1950 Malcolm Knowles, who would become an influential proponent of andragogy, published *Informal Adult Education*. In 1955 a survey of available education programs for older learners was reported by Wilma Donahue (1955). The specialized educational program offerings of the 1960s were oriented toward providing older people with knowledge and skills to cope with the problematic aspects of growing older. Peterson (1985) concluded that in the era of the 1960s "Educational programs emphasized the crisis of adjustment to retirement and the need for outside assistance to overcome the trauma of role change" (p. 84). Programs focused on the needs of older people and the responsibility of social institutions to meet these needs through service programs.

The 1970s were a period of dramatic change and development for the older learner. Research interest and program development oriented toward the older student showed remarkable proliferation. A network of higher education institutions and activities was emerging. McClusky (1971) sounded the theme for a decade of heightened emphasis and responsiveness to the older student by emphasizing the positive outcomes of education and focusing on education as an affirmative enterprise. This orientation pointed program developers to participation in self-actualization themes rather than to the emphasis on social services that characterized the 1960s (Moody, 1976).

Paralleling the changes in the 1970s within adult education for the older student were the international movements to promote lifelong learning. An emphasis on the vitality of the later years marked the education offerings for older people proposed by Pierre Vellas in 1973 at the Université des Sciences Sociales in Toulouse, France. Vellas's proposal for instruction, productive research, and personal development for senior citizens became L'Université du Troisiéne Age (University of the Third Age). By 1983, this educational innovation had been adopted in Belgium, Switzerland, Poland, Italy, Spain, the United States, and Quebec in Canada (Radcliffe, 1985).

The spirit of the University of the Third Age movement struck a responsive note in the United States as is reflected in the establishment of a host of on-campus, noncredit educational programs for the highly educated older person: Elderhostel, Institute for Retired Professionals, New School for Social Research, The Academy of Senior Professionals at Eckert College, and many other programs. These noncredit offerings may serve as a bridge to adult involvement in that they facilitate accommodation by the older person to the demands of traditional higher education. As a result of a project funded by the Older Americans Act, the American Association of Community Junior Colleges encouraged its constituents to integrate the older person into existing programs and also create specialized programs such as Elderhostel. Through this project, an important step in moving beyond noncredit offerings was taken as community and junior colleges assumed a leadership role in making the traditional curriculum available to people over 55.

Educational gerontology developed considerable momentum in the decade of the 1970s. It was the outgrowth of the convergence of adult education and social gerontology (Peterson, 1985). One implication of the emphasis in higher education was the creation of multidisciplinary gerontology centers for research, education, and service. Another development was the initiation of conferences and publications with a specific focus on the older learner (e.g., *Educational Gerontology,* first published in 1976). In a sense, these gerontology centers provided a focal point for integration of the older student on campus. Of particular note is the effort of these gerontology programs to involve the older person in undergraduate and graduate gerontological education.

Innovation in postsecondary education is expected to promote for-credit participation by older learners. Traditional college and university programs require course schedules, classroom modes of delivery, and learning materials and resources that are all highly structured and specified by the institution. These facets of academic life may be impediments for many older learners. Circumvention of some of these barriers may be provided by innovative, nontraditional learning resources such as correspondence study, telecourses, courses by newspaper, credit by examination, and external degree programs. Nontraditional programs include both for-credit and noncredit study.

Correspondence study is probably the original "distance-learning" concept. Because such study is essentially accomplished at home and lacks the support and discipline offered by the traditional classroom, ideal candidates for correspondence study may be the older and self-disciplined learner who is capable of independent motivation and work (Cross, 1982). Many older learners could be expected to perform well in such programs. Quality control has been, and probably will continue to be, a challenge for correspondence programs. Public confidence may require standardization and testing in these programs at the expense of flexibility and imposition of testing generally perceived by the late-life learner as an unfavorable aspect of education. The National University Continuing Education Association publishes a catalog (Ready & Sacchetti, 1986) of independent study programs by correspondence that lists 71 colleges and universities, including many well-known and academically respected schools. These schools offer both for-credit and noncredit studies ranging from high school through master's degree level.

Some distance-learning programs provide independent study, degree-granting plans that require minimum residencies. Syracuse University offers one of the oldest accredited programs of this type. The program consists of intermittent on-campus study periods of short duration and self-paced at-home study. Six degrees are offered, including three at the bachelor's level and three at the master's level. Although the Syracuse program is not directed specifically toward the older learner, older learners may be attracted by the flexibility of this type of program. Like correspondence studies, distance-residency studies may be handicapped by failure to provide for social contact needs and intergenerational relations available in traditional classrooms.

Charner (1984) suggested a distance-learning strategy that he called *meta-*

connection strategy. This strategy refers to the bringing of diverse personnel and facilities, including teachers, peer learners, administrators, and multiple institutions into partnership for the purpose of delivering a comprehensive program of educational services. Two examples can be given of such a strategy. The Union Graduate School of the Union for Experimenting Colleges and Universities in Cincinnati, Ohio, offers a unique design for doctoral-level degrees. As a second example of meta-connected strategy, Empire State College, founded as a part of the State University of New York system, offers an interesting program. Neither program is exclusively oriented toward the older learner, but implications nevertheless exist for the older student.

The Union program is one of the most innovative. One may indeed suspect that such unconventional structures may be controversial within the educational community. Quality control issues again surface, because the Union program is a distance-learning program requiring minimum residency. Innovations include having peer learners as doctoral dissertation committee members, designating the learner (students are referred to as learners, not students) as chair of his or her own dissertation committee, making no core requirements and allowing all work to be planned by the learner in collaboration with advisory people, and using diverse faculty and facilities. This approach is in all respects an "open university." Doctoral-level degrees require an average of 3½ years to complete, and the school's prospectus stresses high academic achievement, including procedures for public inspection of completed dissertations and other work.

Empire State College offers a meta-connected strategy that includes more than 40 campuses within the state of New York. Unlike the Union program, Empire State is not a distance-learning program. Access to programs may be greatly facilitated, however, through operation of many facilities across the state. Implications of this type of program, as with the open university concept, are the flexibility and facilitated access that a meta-system may offer. It is logical that older learners may be especially attracted to more accessible programs.

PARTICIPATION RATES OF OLDER LEARNERS

Estimates of the extent of credit participation in higher education by this "new" older person are constrained by methods that do not permit precise determinations of the extent of for-credit versus noncredit involvement. Survey data from national samples compiled by the National Center for Educational Statistics (NCES, 1969, 1972, 1975, 1978, 1981) or by Harris and Associates (1974, 1981) do not permit measurement of for-credit participation among the population that is 55 or older relative to all other age groups.

Table 1 summarizes the number and percentages of people 55 and older who were involved in the three broad types of post-secondary education. On the basis of this definitional scheme, enrollment in for-credit courses for this age group range from 0.7% (academic degree-seeking) to 15.9% (continuing education, both credit and noncredit) of all post-secondary students. A more specific estimate is precluded

TABLE 1 Participants in Educational Programs Who Are 55 and Older (October, 1982)

Age Group	Type of Post-Secondary Education					
	Academic		Vocational		Continuing	
	Number	Percent	Number	Percent	Number	Percent
Mean total	68	7	114	11	823	82
55–64	56	8	95	14	514	77
65+	12	4	19	6	309	91

Note. Numbers expressed in thousands. Data are from *Participants in Post-secondary Education: October, 1982*, Washington, DC, U.S. Department of Education, National Center for Education Statistics. Copyright 1988.

because for-credit and noncredit participation is aggregated in the continuing education category, and vocational enrollments are assumed to be provided in settings other than higher education institutions. Studies that do examine for-credit participation by the 55 and older age group analyze data drawn from smaller, specialized or geographically restricted samples. These reports of formalized involvement reflect that 1% of all credit-seeking college and university students are 55 years of age or older.

For example, less than 1% of enrollees in higher education in the state of New York were over the age of 60 (New York State Department of Education, 1980), and only 1.1% of older Virginians (McAuley, Arling, Nutty, & Bowling, 1980) were "presently a student." A state-wide study of post-secondary education in California estimated that less than 1% of these participants in continuing education were 60 or older (California Post-Secondary Education Commission, 1981). In one of the earlier estimates of for-credit participation, Weinstock (1978) found that 1.7 million or 3% of the population of America's colleges were age 55 or older. A conservative estimate based on these findings is that this group constitutes 1% of the students enrolled in for-credit college and university settings.

Considering all participants 55 and older who are involved in higher education, what percentage take formal courses? Again, the calculations necessary to address this question are imprecise owing to the for-credit versus noncredit measurement issue previously mentioned. For example, NCES, which provides the most complete data available, defines adult education as education to serve "persons 17 years of age and over on the date of the survey" (NCES, 1988, p. 284). As is reported in Table 2, at least 8% of people 55–64 and 3% of people 65 and older are enrolled in for-credit courses because, by definition, they are degree-seeking.

Further estimation of the percentage of older people within the other two categories cannot be made because of the method of data collection. The most obvious observation is that older people represent a very small portion of credit-seeking students as well as of older adults who participate in all forms of adult education. However, numerous studies point to encouraging shifts in adult education

TABLE 2   Percentage of Participation in Education Programs Among
Adults 55 and Older (October, 1982)

Age Group	Type of Post-secondary Education		
	Academic	Vocational	Continuing
55–64	8%	14%	78%
65 +	3%	6%	91%

Note. Data are from U.S. Department of Education, National Center for
Education Statistics, *Participants in Post-secondary Education: October,
1982.* (This table was prepared May 1986)

participation, which suggest greater for-credit involvement in the future. Across the
NCES surveys from 1969 through 1981, the percentage of participation in educational activities increased from 4.5% to 8.0% for the 55–64 age group and from
1.4% to 3.1% for people 65 and older (Ventura & Worthy, 1982). Greater increases
in proportions of older participants were observed in surveys made between 1974
and 1981 (Harris & Associates, 1974, 1981): 5% in 1974 to 11% in 1981 for the
55–64 age groups, and 2% in 1974 to 5% in 1981 for the 65 and older population.

Based on the NCES data, it can be concluded that from 1969 to 1981 the
number of older learners who were 65 and older tripled with an average growth rate
of 30% every 3 years compared to a growth rate of 12% for other adult students
(NCES, 1981). Projections for educational participation by the 55 and older population group were made by Momeni (1980) based on the trends within the NCES data.
This research concluded that the number of participants in adult education among
those 55 and older could grow at a rate of 4% from 1985 to 1990. Another encouraging indicator is the number of older people who are considered to be potential
credit-seeking students. Based on smaller scale studies such as those completed by
Graney and Hays (1976), approximately 26% of older participants may seek credit.

Although descriptive data such as the type of degree program in which older
people participate are not available, the findings of surveys that reflect course interest and selection among older people involved in adult education (see Table 3) may
suggest participation patterns relevant to the credit-seeking older person.

CHARACTERISTICS OF OLDER LEARNERS

American higher education has never had a substantial number of people aged
55 or older in for-credit courses. Brazziel (1987) observed that in the case of older
people "few individuals at this age participate in higher education and almost none
take degree credit courses" (p. 225). Will this pattern of low involvement in traditional for-credit programs continue? Older people must overcome certain social
forces that discourage their considering higher education, and colleges and universities have organizational features that may discourage the older person. Yet, the
empirical indicators previously mentioned and encouraging shifts in the characteris-

tics of the older person and in the responsiveness of higher education point to a substantial increase in credit-seeking behavior.

Whether or not enrollment activity in this age group will increase significantly will be partially determined by relative strength of factors that affect the relationship between the older person and colleges and universities as that relationship is shaped by institutional, cultural, and societal forces. At the individual level, enrollment activity will vary in relation to the strength or "push" toward participation determined by the older person's appraisal of the competing encouraging and discouraging dynamics interacting with the encouragers and discouragers within the college or university. Conversely, the willingness of the higher education organization to become more responsive to the older person is a function of the governance structure's appraisal of the benefits and costs of classroom participation in the light of the unique characteristics that shape for-credit participation by the older student.

What are the encouragers and discouragers within the older person's life space and the factors within higher education that have the potential for influencing participation? A response to this question begins with a presentation of demographic and psychosocial characteristics of the older person that may affect credit-seeking behavior. This discussion is followed by an examination of the forces that encourage and discourage the responsiveness of colleges and universities. From research on the patterns of the older person's involvement in adult education activities, one can begin to draw a profile of the factors that influence participation in courses for credit. Table 4 lists the factors that encourage and discourage participation.

Encouragers of Participation

The New Elderly   One unique feature of the latter half of this century has been the emergence of a "new" older person with remarkable potential for continued personal growth and productive contributions to society. Neugarten considered the impact of older people on American society in the year 2020 and concluded that

> *as changes in the age distribution become more marked in the decades ahead, there will undoubtedly be general recognition that older persons constitute a*

TABLE 3   Subject Areas in Which Older People Showed Interest in Studying

Subject	% Interested in Subject ($N = 135$)
Liberal arts and sciences	42
Arts and crafts	32
Vocational-technical	13
Business	6
Other	7

Note. Data are from "Senior Students: Higher Education After Age 62" by M. J. Graney and W. C. Hays, 1976, *Educational Gerontology, 1,* 343–359.

TABLE 4 Potential Psychosocial Encouragers and Discouragers of Participation in For-credit Courses

---

Encouragers

Attributes of the "New" Older Person
   Increasing resource potential
   Increasing educational attainment
   Gender
   Life transitions
Educational Predispositions
   Career development
   Intellectual stimulation
   Love of learning
   Learning new social roles
   Self-actualization
   Address developmental needs
Benefits of Education
   Opportunity to express educational predisposition
   Survival skills
   Empowerment
   Status enhancement

Discouragers

Physiological and Psychological Changes
   Decreasing sensory and cognitive ability
   Decreasing energy level
   Performance anxiety
   Lower self-concept
   Decrease of awareness of educational need
   Decreasing interest
Sociological Changes
   Ethnic orientation
   Children do not have college education
   Incongruent demands between student, spouse, employee, and friend roles
   No spouse support
   Feeling out of phase with age group
Resource Deficits
   Income
   Time
   Transportation

---

major resource to the society, a resource that must be utilized for both the good of the older individuals themselves and the good of the country at large. (1981, p. 29)

This untapped cadre of older people is experiencing an unprecedented increase in life expectancy such that people reaching age 65 have a life expectancy of 17 years (18.6 years for women and 14.8 years for men). This increase carries with it "a change in expectations about the quality of life in late adulthood" (Hooyman &

Kiyak, 1988, p. 31). This group of modern pioneers demand a "wide range of options and opportunities with regard to the meaningful use of time" (Neugarten, 1981, p. 30). The options they may select are diverse, reflecting the heterogeneity of interests that characterize the new elderly. The combination of modern health care, economic well-being, and social services produces an older, diverse generation like no other in the history of humankind. This population is characterized by the requisite resources to pursue new interests, including academic ones.

Educational Attainment Perhaps the most significant characteristic of the new older people is their increasing level of educational attainment. This variable is directly and significantly related to subsequent educational participation. Thus, predictions concerning formal involvement in higher education are greatly enhanced by knowing the level of educational attainment of the older person. Table 5 indicates the present level of educational attainment within the 55- to 64-year-old and 65-year-old and older populations. If educational attainment is predictive of future involvement, those with a high school diploma or greater level of educational attainment (63.8% of people 55–64 and 45.9% of people 65 and older) are potential consumers of for-credit courses within higher education.

Data reveal that 16% of students 65 and older who had college degrees and 6% of those who were high school graduates or had some college (1–3 years) reported taking courses at a college or university (Harris & Associates, 1981). Ventura and Worthy (1982) found that having "a higher education level than the median level for the older population, especially having some college experience, predisposes older persons to participate in educational activities" (Ventura & Worthy, 1982, p. 16). Ventura and Worthy predicted that

> *As succeeding age groups with more years of formal schooling reach age 65, the older population will continue its steady rise in level of educational attainment. It is predicted that by the year 2014, approximately three-quarters of the elderly will have at least graduated from high school and less than 10% will have no high school education. (1982, p. 5)*

With these projected increases in educational level, the 55 and older population group should form an even more substantial constituency for enrollment in courses for credit.

Gender The significance of gender as a predictor of credit-seeking behavior in later life is not known. The NCES (1981) survey showed that more women (64%) are older adult education participants. The Harris data did not report this gender difference, and there was some indication of increasing higher education participation among men age 55–64 between 1974 and 1981 (Harris & Associates, 1981). The changing status of women and the rising rates of their participation in the work force will continue to heighten their involvement in higher education.

Educational Predispositions Intrapersonal variables such as educational needs, subject area interests, desires, motivations, and goals also predispose the elder to seek rewards through enrollment in undergraduate or graduate courses.

TABLE 5 Highest Level of Education Achieved or Highest Degree
Earned by Adults 55 and Older (Spring, 1984)

	Age	
Level of Education	55–64	65 +
No high school diploma	36.2	54.0
High school diploma	35.3	25.3
Some college, no degree	12.1	9.2
Vocational diploma	1.7	1.5
Associate's degree	1.9	0.9
Bachelor's degree	7.9	5.9
Master's degree	3.1	2.0
Professional degree	1.2	0.7
Doctoral degree	0.6	0.4

Note. Numbers expressed in thousands. Data are from *Educational
Background and Economic Status* (Current Population Reports, Series
P-70, No. 11), Spring, 1984, Washington, DC: U.S. Department of
Commerce, Bureau of the Census.

Recognition of these predispositions will enable educational planners to more effectively recruit, reward, and retain the older student. In order to ascertain what motivates older learners, most researchers have used surveys to assess needs, interests, desires, reasons, and goals. Because these surveys have been varied, it is difficult to translate their findings into educational planning and practice. As was observed by Merriam and Lumsden (1985), most needs assessments really survey the wants or desires of the older person. What the elderly need in the more psychological and existential sense may not be apparent to those who rely on preference reports from them.

Moody (1987–1988) noted that "Surveys of perceived educational needs are always dependent on a respondent's prior experience with education. But people do not really have a sense of what the need or demand for education might be until actually offered a concrete alternative program" (p. 7). Thus, needs can emerge, not from the present interests of the older person, which are tied to life experience and "what exists," but from new experiences that activate a more fundamental, yet unexpressed, need. A comprehensive understanding of the educational needs of the older population should include qualitative data from older people in the form of their reflections and life review.

Developmental theorists, educational gerontologists, and philosophers are another potent source for identifying needs that can be addressed through the higher education process. Methodologies for determining the predispositions of the older learner should follow Londoner's (1978) three-pronged prescription for needs assessment, which includes gathering information from experts, prospective older learners, and higher education planners. In this way, data will be available to inform those who design educational programs as well as researchers and innovators as they seek to create congruent educational structures for the elderly. There is a substantial body of research on the predispositions of older people who enroll in for-credit and noncredit courses within a college or university setting. In-depth discussion and summaries of research on learning needs (Lowy & O'Connor, 1986), motivations (Londoner, 1985), goals (O'Connor, 1987) and interests (Ventura & Worthy, 1982), are available.

Havighurst (1964) applied the instrumental (learning as a means to a future end) and expressive (learning as an end itself) dichotomy to categorizing learning interests in later life. This typology is helpful to researchers who are interested in predicting the salience of age for learning predispositions. Some researchers (e.g., Londoner, 1971) have argued for the importance of instrumental activities, whereas others (e.g., Bauer, 1975) found that older learners preferred expressive activities. Londoner (1978) pointed out that the assumed dichotomy between instrumental and expressive was not helpful without further understanding of *how* the individual older student perceived the learning activity. What is an instrumental course for one older student may be expressive for another. Lowy and O'Connor (1986) suggested that the dichotomy actually formed one continuum of interest.

O'Connor (1987) concluded that the distinction between instrumental and expressive was heuristic in that respondents did choose between the two categories. O'Connor's sample included older college students (age 60 and older), Elderhostel participants (age 60 and older), and middle-aged college students (age 40–59). More than 85% of the older attendees in regular college programs valued "learning for its own sake," (O'Connor, 1987, p. 515); (i.e., an expressive goal). Only 38% of the middle-aged college students reported an expressive goal. Surprisingly, the middle-aged college students tended to perceive instrumental goals as more important, and, interestingly, there was a much greater tendency among this age group to rate expressive and instrumental as equally important.

Although O'Connor is to be commended for specifically including the older college participant versus the Elderhostel participant in the sample, no information was provided concerning the degree aspirations of the college students. Intuitively, it would seem that the older credit-seeking students would report a more instrumental orientation. However, in his sample of older people in a senior auditors program at the University of Colorado at Boulder, Covey (1980) found that "learning for the sake of learning was the most important reason for enrollment" (Covey, 1980, p. 177). The most frequent response centered around the educational betterment of the individual—enjoyment, bettering oneself, and accomplishment. The least frequent response was "social expectations," such as adaptation to society and occupational training. Some intragroup variance in educational predispositions can be explained by occupational and educational experiences. For example, Hiemstra (1976) observed that the young-old learner may prefer instrumental rather than expressive learning interests.

Whereas some of the typologies have been developed on the basis of predispositions expressed directly by older respondents in empirical studies, other scholars have developed their classification systems more theoretically and have used "ideal type" approaches to classifications. As previously noted, one of the inherent flaws of needs assessment is the dependence on the educational experience of the respondent. The normative approach adopted by authors such as Moody (1976) and McClusky (1971) permits consideration of educational predispositions that may emerge as a function of developmental transition or societal transformation.

McClusky's (1971) functional (or "needs") hierarchical classification system suggests that the most meaningful predisposition is transcendence; in Moody's classification system, it is self-actualization. Moody (1976) proposed four modal patterns for the treatment of the aged and suggested implications for higher education. He envisioned a role for higher education in the self-actualization of the older adult. According to Moody, the fundamental life task is to confront the question of identity. In fact, Moody envisioned an educational purpose integrated with a unique developmental need associated with the later years. Thus the advantage of these typologies and others is to inform higher education as it moves to more accurately and effectively address the predispositions of the older person.

Benefits of Education The opportunity to express these educational predispositions within higher education provides a plentiful assortment of rewarding experiences. Higher education can assist the older person in realizing some of the newly stated goals they desire to achieve. In an article entitled "New Life in a New Job" (Rosenblum, 1989), several older people are named who were able to move beyond retirement because of the apparent help given by colleges or universities. Rosenblum tells a story of one individual whose first career was in dentistry who wanted to "get re-educated in other facets and fields" (pp. 30–31). As a result he enrolled in an anthropology class at Florida Atlantic University and "translated his love in anthropology into a second career" (pp. 30–31). In this same magazine, ten opportunities are identified for older workers who desire to renew themselves. Most of these opportunities suggest a role for higher education if older adults are to be successful. In addition to preparing older people for new career opportunities, higher education can also be helpful in assisting with empowerment skills, status enhancement, new relationships, and new incentives for living productive lives in the later years.

Discouragers of Participation

The small percentage of older adults who are engaged in credit-seeking activity have overcome complex and formidable barriers in their quest for involvement. Accurate recognition of the mosaic that forms these limiting conditions suggests the kinds of educational innovations and compensatory policies and practices that will increase participation. Identification of these barriers to credit-seeking in late adulthood is based primarily on surveys of non–credit-seeking older adults who participate in all forms of adult education. The translation of available survey data is biased by several factors: an absence of national data on nonparticipants; the tendency of respondents to name more socially acceptable barriers, such as "no interest or no time," or institutional facets, rather than an unacceptable factor such as low self-esteem or fear of failure; and a lack of analysis of how the predisposition toward credit-seeking shapes the pattern of barriers to participation. Fortunately, the extensive research that is available on older learners who participate in adult education provides a foundation for future investigations.

The reasons for noncredit enrollment among older adults are complex. Cross (1979) characterized these barriers as situational, structural, and dispositional. Situational barriers exist in the older person's position in interpersonal relations, family, social group, and employment. The referents for the structural barriers are facets within higher education such as scheduling problems, geographic or transportation difficulties, course offerings, or procedural problems (Charner & Fraser, 1986). Dispositional barriers arise from within the individual and include personal characteristics (i.e., gender, educational level, ethnicity, and income), attitudes (i.e., perception of self), and the influence of significant others. Others have adopted the term *attitudinal* or *socio-psychological* (Charner & Fraser, 1986) for this category. The term *discouragers* is used to refer to facets of the person and his or her social environment that limit one's decision to participate in degree-seeking behavior.

Discouragers can arise from physiological, psychological, and sociological changes as well as from resource deficits of the older learner. The discourager category is similar to Cross's (1982) dispositional and Charner and Fraser's (1986) socio-psychological category. In the surveys concerning barriers to higher education among older adults, the dispositional barriers are least frequently mentioned, probably because of the concerns about social acceptability mentioned previously.

Physiological Changes The older person must also overcome the physical changes that occur with chronological age. The most significant of these is hearing loss, which has frequently been mentioned as a barrier to classroom participation (Kingston, 1982a). Also, older persons, especially older *non-students* (Covey, 1980), may perceive themselves as both older and in poorer health than older *students*. Many recent studies emphasize that poor health is not an automatic concomitant of old age but is more related to choosing a detrimental lifestyle (unhealthy diet, smoking, alcohol abuse, etc.) and lack of exercise (MacRae, 1986). Notwithstanding, physiologic changes do occur in aging and these changes, whether objectively or subjectively perceived, may explain some of the inverse correlation between age and interest in further education so frequently reported in the literature.

Psychological Changes Compounding these physical changes are psychological discouragers, such as performance anxiety, which make participation difficult. Underlying the concerns around performance in the academic setting are self-concept issues. For many, the thought of competing with younger cohorts challenges the assumption of competency. Considerable risk-taking is needed to overcome the sense of powerlessness and break the self-fulfilling prophecies that the fear of failure produces. Overall, confidence will rise and fall as a function of the older person's self-concept in the area of educational achievement. One of the most traumatic effects of agism is that older people begin to actually define themselves in terms that are consistent with agist viewpoints.

Sociological Changes As social beings, older people must also deal with the impact of interpersonal issues on their participation. Whether or not their adult children are degree holders may be a factor in participation as well as the extent of their spouses' support for their involvement. Socially, older people may be encouraged to fill the retiree and grandparent role, and they may feel out of phase with their own cohorts if they return to the college campus. Basically, they must overcome the absence of socialization into the student role. As was noted by Darkenwald and Merriam (1982), membership in reference groups exerts powerful pressures on participation as to social roles. The social role of retiree or senior citizen can erode an older person's sense of personal worth.

The effects of ethnicity on education participation are not so evident. The assumption that lower educational attainment levels of blacks and Hispanics contribute to lower participation in higher education has some support. The number of minority students in higher education increased from 15.4% in 1976 to 17.9% in 1986 (NCES, 1988). Asian students accounted for the majority of these increases. However, "the proportion of students who were black fell from 9.4% in 1976 to 8.6% in 1986. The drop in the proportion of black students reflects the declining enrollments of black males" (NCES, 1988, p. 136). As noted by earlier research using NCES data (Heisel, Darkenwald, & Anderson, 1981), the small sample sizes available for adequate analysis of the older ethnic and education participation relationship preclude a clear understanding of this variable. Jackson and Wood (1976) found in their sample of 2,400 persons over the age of 65 that blacks were more likely to participate in educational activities and plan to take courses than was the comparison group of whites.

Resource Deficits   Older people may experience deficits in resources that can significantly deter the decision to enroll. One of the most significant factors involves financial assistance. Less than 15% of federal student aid is used by adult learners. In his excellent analysis of federal financial resources available to the adult learner, Sexton (1980) identified nine barriers to student financial aid that face the adult student. Another resource concern that may face the older person is the availability of time and transportation.

Even in light of the encouraging features of the new older learner, imposing physiologic, psychologic, sociologic, and economic barriers will provide significant reasons for not enrolling.

CHARACTERISTICS OF HIGHER EDUCATION

Encouragers of Higher Education's Acceptance of Older Learners

A list of factors that encourage and discourage college and university inclusion of the older learner is provided in Table 6. The encouragers of involvement include the contribution of older students to the intellectual climate of academia, the creation of a new constituency for the college or university, and the opportunity to offset tuition income losses caused by decreasing enrollments. In addition to these,

TABLE 6   Potential Organizational
Encouragers and Discouragers of
Participation in For-credit Courses
Among People 55 and Older

Encouragers

Enhanced intellectual climate
Creation of new constituency
Offset tuition losses

Discouragers

Accessibility issues
Administrative concerns
Funding constraints
Curriculum design
Faculty detractors

Sprouse (1982) identified several other potential outcomes that may encourage higher education to accept older learners: fulfillment of the university's community-oriented mission; linkage to community agencies; good public relations; leverage for seeking grants; and a new association with a potential source of endowment and funding. As in the case of the psychosocial factors, the organizational attractions to the older person may be offset by the countervailing effects of organizational discouragers.

Enhanced Intellectual Climate   Older students tend to be highly motivated and involved in the educational process (Kasworm, 1980). When this appreciation for the life of the mind is coupled with their experiences, they are uniquely gifted in the ability to provide significant intellectual contributions in the classroom and, ultimately, throughout the intellectual life of the college or university.

Creation of a New Constituency   As was noted by Sprouse (1982), the continual funding of publicly supported higher education organizations is an essentially political process that requires broadly based support. Involving older people creates a new source of political and economic advocacy. If the older students are alumni of the college or university, they can be more effectively engaged in programs that would increase this participation in campus activities and promote their financial support.

Offset Tuition Losses   Older students are a potential source of tuition income that is needed to compensate for declining enrollments (Sprouse, 1982). This encourager is one of the more significant efforts to involve older people in courses for credit, particularly those that are linked to obtaining a degree.

Discouragers of Higher Education's Acceptance of Older Learners

Organizational discouragers reside within the policy and implementing structures that guide and support the higher education institution. These discouragers are related to issues of accessibility, administrative concerns, funding constraints, curriculum design, and faculty support.

Accessibility Concerns   Accessibility barriers can be informational, procedural, and physical. Marketing strategies that have proactively reached out to the older person in an effort to engage them in a degree program have been essentially nonexistent. Information concerning the availability of degree programs and the willingness of institutions to receive the older student are prerequisites in the engagement process. Carp, Peterson, and Roelfs (1974) found that 10% of adult learners reported a lack of information as a barrier to enrollment. When Charner et al. (1978) studied unionized workers, approximately 42% of these subjects reported informational difficulties. In commenting on the information barrier, Charner and Fraser concluded that

> *it may be more critical than reported because many of the other structural problems may ultimately be due to lack of information about the options that do exist. Information does seem to be a bigger problem for adults with lower levels of education and those who are in lower status occupations. (1986, p. 69)*

Pritchard and Tomb (1981) summarized their study concerning the response of retired people to educational programs in universities and colleges. They included all four-year institutions listed in the *National Directory of Educational Programs in Gerontology,* and they listed some major institutions not affiliated with the Association for Gerontology in Higher Education to ensure that at least two institutions in every state were included. Concerning barriers to educational participation, the study reflected the fact that agism, transportation inadequacies, and lack of awareness were the three most frequently cited barriers. Recruitment and other outreach efforts are geared to much younger students, and the strategies reflected this bias.

Bayer (1974) noted that informational brochures and catalogs are "written for the young, suggesting that students come in just four sizes: 18, 19, 20, and 21" (p. 6). Kingston (1982b) concluded that one reason so few older people enroll in degree-granting institutions is the laissez-faire attitude and the apparent unwillingness to recruit the older student or otherwise make the campus attractive to them. Accessibility may also be limited by the complexity of application procedures and admission standards, which cater to the 18-year-old applicant. Sprouse (1982) observed that the older student desires "equal access to educational opportunities by means of simplified registration procedures [and] modified admission requirements" (p. 18).

Physical accessibility is probably the most frequently mentioned discourager. Parking difficulties and movement around campus are very frequently identified by the elderly as presenting a barrier to their full participation. Price and Lyon (1982) noted that the more familiar an older person is with the site, the greater likelihood of attending. Physical accessibility issues such as stairs, inclines, and unavailability of elevators have been mentioned, although many of these are being corrected as accommodations for people who have disabilities are provided. Whereas many studies (e.g., Kingston, 1982a) indicate that a majority of older students are able to deal with the physical accessibility issues without special consideration, older learner involvement could be enriched by attention to concerns around parking and transportation (Covey, 1980).

Administrative Concerns The extent to which a campus is supportive or nonsupportive to the older learner is inextricably tied to the attitudes and actions of the governance or policy-making system. Some key executive administrators may be concerned that involvement of the elder may in some fashion tarnish the reputation of the university or college (Sprouse, 1982). The reasoning is that by involving the older learner, the university is failing to attract the most desirable scholars for its academic program. Older people may be considered inappropriate for the fundamental purpose around which the university is organized. For example, if the institution sees itself as a major research center, key administrators may assume that older students are not very productive as far as knowledge development and are therefore not appropriate for this kind of mission. Sometimes the auspice of the college or university can become a barrier.

Funding Constraints One of the primary concerns of the governance structure is with the cost/benefit ratio of having older people involved in degree programs. Because most administrators must balance scarcity, programs that attempt to meet the specialized needs of elders may be considered an inappropriate use of these limited resources. Older students may even be a financial liability to the institution, as is evidenced by the fallout from tuition waiver programs initiated in most states for older people. After analyzing the impact of these programs, Romaniuk (1984) noted that, although the number of participants under fee waivered programs has remained small, issues of fiscal responsibility of institutions offering these programs must be raised since these programs generate no revenues to cover their costs. In addition to having concerns about reputation, mission, and cost, administrators may feel unprepared to deal with what they perceive to be the specialized needs of this age group. They may be unsure about the liabilities they incur by having large numbers of older learners on their campus. These discouragers and others reflect the overall concern of administrators that they are unprepared for dealing with this age group.

Curriculum Design Older individuals may encounter numerous difficulties as they attempt to involve themselves in the college or university's curriculum. Usually, orientations are geared to a much younger population and do not address the unique challenges faced by the older individual. Smith and Abent (1988) noted that advisement and counseling offerings tended to address traditional issues such as graduation, selection of a major, and career interests rather than helping the older student with reintegration into campus life, helping them identify their expectations and interests, and assisting them in locating those faculty who may be more sensitive to their unique needs. Designing academic programs of work that accommodate for the frequent need to attend part-time requires special attention by academic advisers. Butler and Lewis (1982) noted that older people may become more present-oriented as they grow older. This focus on here and now may make commitments to time-consuming degree programs and lengthy semesters difficult.

There have been some indications that older learners have difficulty adjusting to the demands of the curriculum as a function of these unique learning characteristics. They may require alternatives in the instructional format (e.g., pacing, material organization, multisensory input, and psychological support) in order to function at an optimal level (Arenberg & Robertson-Tchabo, 1977; Peterson, 1986).

Faculty Although the research evidence indicates that faculty essentially have no difficulty with elders in their classrooms (Covey, 1980; Kingston, 1982a), the perception persists that older people may be too demanding or otherwise disruptive in the classroom. Another stereotype concerning the older learner is that they may require specialized testing and other time-consuming practices. Essentially, these concerns reflect a lack of information provided to faculty concerning the characteristics of the older learner. Most faculty development programs do not provide academicians with information concerning the learning characteristics in later life and strategies for creatively using the experiences of older people to enrich rather than detract from the classroom process.

CHARACTERISTICS OF SOCIAL INSTITUTIONS

Hertzler (1929) expressed the importance of institutional analysis with this statement: "For institutions, being both products of and factors in social processes must of necessity be intimately and vitally involved in social organization" (p. 9). Such an approach is appropriate for gaining insight into how discouragers affect educational institutions and how discouraging influences on the older person can be minimized and the encouragers maximized to develop a more flexible structure allowing older learners to be participants. By viewing higher education as a component of the larger society, and by viewing its relationship to other social institutions, the investigator is likely to ask more definitive questions and arrive at more realistic answers in reference to the proper place for the college or university in American society. To demonstrate how this approach works, we look briefly at five institutions and their relations to higher education.

Family

One of the most significant changes in the family structure is that it has become multigenerational. This aspect of family life increases the complexity and longevity of relationships between and among children, parents, and grandparents. For example, it is not uncommon to have a two-decade relationship between grandparent and grandchild and a five-decade relationship between parent and child. These changes will provide higher education with the opportunity to assist in the assimilation of knowledge derived from different historical periods thus improving understanding and acceptance among those of different age cohorts. Another change in the contemporary family is the relatively high rate of divorce and remarriage.

Higher education, with its resources in the humanities and social sciences, can help equip individual family members to understand such destabilizing changes.

Family can also be detrimental to the enrollment of older learners. As the size of the family decreases, the demands for intergenerational caregiving by older people increase, and older cohorts are expected to expend personal and financial resources in a manner that develops and maintains family solidarity. Participation in higher education may be viewed as an inappropriate allocation of these resources and a distraction from familial support. At the federal level, financial incentives for educational participation among the elderly are limited and even discouraged. For example, families who apply for a dependent student loan may be entitled to some exclusion of their resources prior to determining loan eligibility. Older people who apply for the same loan program for themselves do not receive this exclusion. One obvious conclusion of this review of the available financial resources is that support for the older student is not a priority.

Religion

Among religious organizations, there is some indication of a movement toward more productive, contributory roles within churches and synagogues for the older person (Dickerson & Myers, 1988). Because the resources of higher education are needed to enable the older religious member to fulfill these new expectations, there may be greater impetus within the religious institution to promote for-credit involvement. An example of the productive linkage between religion and higher education is the model program for career training of older adults at the University of Massachusetts. In 1983, the archdiocese of Boston requested that the gerontology program at the University provide career preparation of older people affiliated with the archdiocese.

Unfortunately, some religious groups view participation in higher education as a distraction to involvement of older people in the church's mission. Consequently, there is little encouragement to the older person to pursue educational goals. Often the roles that are assigned by the religious organization to older people do not require them to participate in higher education.

Politics

A salient aspect of the political arena is the provision made by both federal and state governments to encourage and support older adults in their learning pursuits. The reader is referred to two resources for in-depth recapitulations of federal and state legislative roles in higher education and the older learner: *The Older Adult and Higher Education: Analysis of State Public Policy* (Romaniuk, 1982) and "Who is Responsible? The Federal Role," in Lowy and O'Connor's *Why Education in the Later Years?* (1986). Notable also were the recent amendments to the Older Americans Act (U.S. Congress, 1987). These amendments required area agencies on aging to (a) develop outreach programs regarding tuition-free postsecondary education, (b) compile information about college and university course offerings, including tuition-waivered and reduced-tuition programs, and (c) disseminate information about educational programs at senior centers, nutrition sites, and other appropriate locations.

Another initiative by state legislators is to make tuition waivers available for older adults desiring to participate in college or university programs. However, tuition waiver policies differ from state to state. Differences are related to the source of the policy (statutory, constitutional, regulatory, or a combination), the minimum age specified by policy, residency requirements, whether the waiver is subject to available classroom space, and whether the waiver is limited with respect to credit (for-credit, noncredit, audit, or a combination). In addition, state policies vary according to income eligibilities and other restrictions or limitations. Table 7 presents data on selected waiver policies to illustrate waiver programs in several states. These states are selected on the basis of their having high proportions of older residents.

This form of educational support appears, to many legislators, to be all that is needed to ensure adequate support for the older adult's participation in higher education. Additionally, state budgets are often reduced by minimizing the amount dedicated to tuition waivers making them no more than a token gesture. Furthermore, such assistance may be counterproductive in that it may influence the motivation of the older adult to pursue academic programs not covered under the tuition waiver plan or may even contribute to a decreased demand for seeking credit (Hays & Hays, 1988).

Business

Business provides an incentive for older adults to continue their education in preparation for second and third career options. For example, business initiatives such as retiree talent banks, job-sharing options, and opportunities to return to work lend themselves to efforts by colleges and universities to equip the older learner to continue in a productive role. Although mandatory retirement is virtually a thing of the past, its influence still discourages older people from contemplating career options after age 60. Likewise, business, in some cases, has made the retirement option so attractive that a significant number of people 60 and older choose premature retirement instead of considering how they might remain in the labor force.

Culture

The posture of cultural institutions in relation to higher education is further complicated by a number of cultural values that permeate society. Harris and Cole (1980) identified five value orientations that affect the elderly: youth orientation, work ethic, independence and self-reliance, education, and progress. These orientations individually and collectively may deter or enhance educational participation. Unfortunately, the emphasis on youth often pushes educational institutions to design programs with primary attention given to the younger generations. Thus, institutions overlook those values that encourage any citizen, regardless of age, to gain as much educational experience as possible.

Internalization of the work ethic among older people is prevalent and may

TABLE 7 State-initiated Tuition-waiver Policies for Older Learners

State	Year Enacted	Source	Minimum Age	Residency Requirements	Subject to Space	Credit Given	Legal Authority
California	1975	Statutory	60	Yes	Yes	For-credit	Educational Code, Article 4, Section 89330-89331
New York	1974	Statutory, regulatory	60	No	Yes	Audit	Ohio Revised Code 3345.27
Ohio	1976	Statutory[1]	60	Yes	Yes	Noncredit	Texas Higher Education Code, Title 3, Sec. 54.210 (See also acts 1975, 64th Leg., p. 265, ch. 111, Sec. 1, eff. Sept. 1, 1975)
Texas	1975	Statutory	60	No	Yes	Audit	

Note. A report on state-initiated tuition-waiver programs is available from The Institute of Gerontological Studies, Baylor University, CSB Box 348, Waco, TX 76798.

[1]Colleges and universities are given broad discretion in issuing rules for implementation of the statute.

either lead the individual into a more active student role or in the direction of a more passive retirement role and limit the risk-taking that credit-seeking requires. Autonomy and self-reliance attitudes may keep older people from assuming a dependent status as a student, especially if losses in other roles make feelings of autonomy precarious. Although education is highly valued by older people, the culture subscribes to the concept of return on "human investment."

> *Instead of viewing the cost of education as a necessary expense like food or clothing, education is now regarded as a capital investment, in much the same way as buildings, machines, or materials are. People invest money to train and educate young persons with a view to a future payoff, but they are not willing to do the same for older people. The obvious reason for this reluctance is that an older person's remaining years are limited, and the return would not be enough to justify such an investment. (Harris & Cole, 1980, p. 76)*

The emphasis on progress that characterizes the current technological age strips older people of status and prestige, which, in earlier times, would have been assigned them as a result of their abilities as historians, storytellers, and purveyors of wisdom (Moody, 1986). The selection of Harris and Cole's value orientations set forth above illustrate the importance of examining cultural influences as encouragers and discouragers of enrollment.

QUESTIONS FACING HIGHER EDUCATION IN AN AGING SOCIETY

Higher education is faced with providing effective leadership in developing new modes of adapting to the shifting demographic trend toward an aging society. Education's effectiveness in this adaptation process depends on its ability to address questions such as those that follow. Responding to these questions will create dilemmas in educational policy, design and resource allocation. Whatever the responses might be, they must be expedient in the light of the rapid growth of highly educated seniors in this post-industrial age.

Why Allocate Educational Resources for Older People?

Those who argue against legislative attention and resource allocation to benefit the older learner present a formidable argument. There is considerable evidence that older people are not interested and do not demand enrollment in for-credit programs. Furthermore, older people who do wish to participate in educational activities prefer that these occur outside the boundaries of the traditional higher education setting. If resources were allocated to the older learner, they would essentially go to an elite "already highly educated" set of older people who could well afford to fund their own self-initiated structures to meet educational needs. Allocation of resources to elders, in the view of some, is a wasteful enterprise at best and may even be detrimental to the future of the nation. The following statement illustrates concern over this resource issue.

What are they going to do—what are they going to do with the education when
they have already retired? I think they're using it as a place to go. We're
trying to educate the ones that can't afford the college system. We're trying to
educate the youth to keep them off of welfare. Those that are already retired,
my God, they're using it as a hobby. (U.S. Congress, 1977, p. 39)

Currently we are experiencing a crisis in our educational system as our youth
consistently perform poorly on achievement tests in comparison with other industrial societies. The available resources should be allocated to correct these educational deficits. One imperative in this regard is that the older student not be required
to take up space that should be saved for younger students. Unfortunately, an important motivation of colleges and universities for including the older student is to
augment waning economic resources—a less than optimal motivation. If colleges
and universities are interested in tapping older students for their endowment possibilities, they should go the route of less costly, noncredit programs rather than
pursuing the for-credit route.

To counter the arguments that older people are a drain on educational resources, one must ascertain that older persons, in fact, must be educationally em-
powered to contribute to this society. The nature of this contribution takes on several
forms. As observed by Naisbitt in *Megatrends* (1982), growth of high technology in
the future will also generate a need for "high-touch" contributions. Because older
people have the benefit of life experience, their tendency to be contemplative can be
harnessed to provide society with high-touch contributions such as reflection on
life's meaning, storytelling, oral history, and so forth (Moody, 1986).

Presently, we are in an age in which self-help will be the lifestyle of the
future. This reality has two implications. First, younger generations will require the
skills possessed by the older generation to assist them in their transition to a self-
help orientation. Second, older people will need to garner new problem-solving
skills in order to avoid excessive dependency on welfare and health resources.
Higher education can promote more effective problem-solving skills such as dealing
with leisure and how to manage on limited resources. Furthermore, higher education will strengthen the democratic participatory skills of older people and make
them more effective citizens of this society. Last, the allocation of educational resources for older people will enable them to be responsive to challenges of the 21st
century.

Should Educational Programming Be Age-Specific
or Age-Irrelevant?

Peterson (1987–1988) observed that "age-segregated instruction, the teaching
of older people in a program designed and offered exclusively for them, has gained
greater popularity than have programs that simply allow older learners to sit in
courses with traditional students" (p. 17). Providing specialized resources for the
older matriculating student is consistent with addressing the discouragers to participation previously discussed. Numerous studies point out the hearing difficulties of

older people. These can be addressed only by age-sensitive interventions. The homogeneity of age-specific and segregated programs makes planning and administration easier.

At this point, integration that results when age is not relevant in educational programming produces a situation of generational mixing. The amount of generational mixing that creates the optimal learning environment is unknown. If age is considered irrelevant, would generational mixing be disruptive and have a negative influence? Consider the impact on younger students of having large numbers of older students in their classes and how this large number of older students would affect campus life.

Proponents of age-irrelevance on the college campus are in concert with the futuristic thinking of Neugarten (1982). Those who argue for this position essentially are indicating that there is no need to design educational programming on the basis of age. This argument is grounded in several recent studies that document that older people prefer age-integrated programming and are capable of adjusting to the same demands that are placed on younger students. Age-irrelevance makes possible a mixing of the generations that is critical for the survival of society.

In fact, higher education may be the one institution that will most promote this linkage between young and old. As older people participate in class, they are able to express the "elder function" (Butler & Lewis, 1982) that is critical for late-life development and promoting positive images of older people with the younger generation. The creation of specialized and segregated programs is essentially stigmatizing and dehumanizing to older people and represents a kind of hand-out approach to education that is quite distasteful to self-reliant, independent cohorts. Sociologists have noted that society is moving away from a strict use of chronological age in terms of relationships, social customs, and careers. If these changes are occurring in other areas, why should they not also occur in higher education?

What Should Be the Relationship Between the Older Learner and Higher Education and Business?

The older student would benefit from close linkage between the business community and higher education in several ways. First, companies might be interested in providing incentives to older workers that would allow them to participate in higher education. For the older worker who is in transition (e.g., because of retirement or the death of a spouse), higher education may provide an opportunity for them to participate in a curriculum that would lead to a new career. In exchange for these fringe benefits, companies could be provided with tax incentives. Furthermore, companies may elect to participate with higher education in providing non-credit and for-credit offerings to their older workers.

Likewise, the disadvantages of the linkage between higher education and business should be considered. Business enterprise is increasingly becoming more involved in adult education and may threaten higher education's predominant role in this area. One of the negative consequences of this shift in the pattern of adult education service delivery is that older people will not have the opportunity to strengthen the citizenship role that has traditionally been a part of liberal arts education (Moody, 1987–1988). Furthermore, adult education provided by an entrepreneurial auspice will tend to not focus on the special needs of ethnic groups or provide older people with the survival skills they may need to deal with scarcity. Advocates of this position would be more in favor of limiting the involvement of business to that of providing incentives and funding for matriculating services provided within the structure of higher education.

GUIDELINES AND RECOMMENDATIONS FOR INTEGRATING THE OLDER PERSON INTO THE COLLEGE OR UNIVERSITY SETTING

Three considerations would be helpful to the educational innovator acting on behalf of students who are 55 or older. It can be expected that new practices or ideas will not be adopted without resistance. Pioneers in innovation and adoption research (e.g., Lionberger, 1960; Rogers & Shoemaker, 1971) suggest that innovations progress through a series of stages before adoption occurs. These stages include awareness, interest, evaluation, trial, and adoption. Advocates for greater responsiveness by higher education would benefit from the guidance that the literature on innovation adoption can provide. Second, a review of the literature reveals that older people involved with higher education prefer to be treated by the college or university in the same way as more traditional students. There should be an effort to normalize the participation pattern of the older person in existing academic programs. Third, the academic mission should be correlated with the type of older adult enrolled for academic study. For example, a senior university dedicated primarily to research will seek out older students prepared to handle graduate-level assignments in their chosen field.

Figure 1 is a paradigm depicting an organized view of the variables affecting the decision made by older adults and higher education at the point of for-credit course involvement. The figure provides intervention points for the educational planner who is developing a strategy to increase involvement of this target population. Among the numerous sources of innovations for integrating older people, two stand out as major references for anyone anticipating assignments in this area: *The Older Adult on Campus: A Policy Manual for College Administrators* (Sprouse, 1982) and "Avoid Detroit's Mistakes: Reposition Your Institution to Respond to Adults" (Smith & Abent, 1988).

Ideas for change at the government level include: tax incentives for businesses that invest in educational support of older, economically disadvantaged people, a GI bill for elderly veterans, and expansion of social security into funding of educational benefits. ACTION, an independent federal agency, can also be used to further educational aims of older people through their Retired Senior Volunteer Program and the Peace Corps. Each of these programs have unique purposes that find older people who are appropriately educated to be extremely useful in accomplishing the agency's mission. In the economic arena, business can be encouraged to provide higher education as an incentive for older people to reenter the work force.

Numerous suggestions can be made for dealing with discouragers within higher education. In the area of accessibility, the following are possibilities: initiate recruitment programs that target industry, that is, go where the college-educated older adults are (e.g., AARP, military installations, and industries that show an interest in the elderly); use the state cooperative extension services to do recruitment and educational counseling; and consider admission based on an individualized assessment process rather than on standardized testing. In the area of funding, apply the concept of barter for assisting older people in paying tuition. Apply the concept of brokering in assisting older people as they access the higher education programs of their choice. With the emergence of a variety of funding sources, particularly for older women, and the availability of credit for life experience opportunities, this type of service would be of particular value to the older person who is unfamiliar with educational resources. Application of the self-help concept to the promotion of higher education for the elderly seems particularly appropriate in dealing with the low self-esteem and performance anxiety discouragers mentioned previously. This innovation would allow the use of peers as providers of supportive structures within the intergenerational campus.

CONCLUSION

In this chapter we have presented the challenge that the longevity revolution has brought to higher education. We reviewed, assessed, and synthesized research through the use of a paradigm depicting the social processes involved in integrating the older adult into credit-producing academic coursework. This compilation of findings represents a usable resource for those desiring to initiate research or implement plans for establishing programs designed to normalize the involvement of older students with the traditional student. We named and discussed variables affecting plans for integrating the older person into higher education and offered guidelines on and examples of new approaches.

Table 8 proposes the impact that the involvement of older people in credit-seeking activities may have across four dimensions of societal benefit. If high levels of involvement become prevalent, then the status of the elderly increases as well as the potential for generational transfers in productive involvement both for society and higher education. In the case of moderate involvement, the benefits are less useful and may produce serious consequences for our aging society. If involvement in higher education were to be maintained or decline to a minimal level, then the outcome would be unacceptable. Higher education has before it the opportunity to benefit present-day elderly people, future generations, and society at large in its effort to produce an inventory of people capable of fulfilling contributory roles.

TABLE 8 The Impact of Higher Education Involvement with the Credit-seeking Older Person on Societal and Educational Outcomes

Outcome Measure	Minimal Credit Involvement & Noncredit Programs	Moderate Credit Involvement & Noncredit Programs	Maximum Credit Involvement
Status of the elderly	Declines	Status quo	Increases
Integration of generations	Increased generational conflict	Intergenerational inequity	Generational transfer
Productive & optimal role	Role-taking	Role-taking/self-stimulation	Role-making and intellectual contribution
Benefit to higher education	Minimal	Economic contribution/passive participation	Intellectual & economic contribution & proactive participation

REFERENCES

American Association of Retired Persons. (1986). *College centers for older learners.* Washington, DC: AARP Institute of Life Long Learning.

Arenberg, D., & Robertson-Tchabo, E. A. (1977). Learning and aging. In J. E. Birren & K. W. Schaie (Eds.), *Handbook on the psychology of aging* (p. 31). New York: Van Nostrand Reinhold.

Asimov, I. (1988, December 19). *Time,* p. 82.

Aslanian, C. B., & Brickell, H. M. (1980). *Americans in transition: Life changes as a reason for adult learning.* New York: College Entrance Examination Board.

Bauer, B. M. (1975). *A model of continuing education for older adults.* Unpublished doctoral dissertation, University of Minnesota, Minneapolis.

Bayer, E. L. (1974). Breaking up the youth ghetto. In D. W. Dyckman (Ed.), *Lifelong learners: A new clientele for higher education.* San Francisco, CA: Jossey-Bass.

Brazziel, W. F. (1987, March/April). Forecasting older student enrollment: A cohort and participation rate model. *Journal of Higher Education, 58*(2), 223-231.

Butler, R. N., & Lewis, M. I. (1982). *Aging and mental health: Positive psychosocial and biomedical approaches* (3rd ed.). St. Louis, MO: Mosby.

California Post-Secondary Education Commission. (1981). *1981 information digest.* Sacramento, CA: Author.

Carnegie Council on Policy Studies in Higher Education. (1980). *Three thousand futures: The next twenty years for higher education.* San Francisco, CA: Jossey-Bass.

Carp, A., Peterson, R., & Roelfs, P. (1974). Adult learning interests and experiences. In K. P. Cross & J. R. Valley & Associates (Eds.), *Planning non-traditional programs: An analysis of the issues of post-secondary education.* San Francisco, CA: Jossey-Bass.

Charner, I. (1984). *Exploring new concepts for post-secondary education.* Washington, DC: National Institute for Work and Learning.

Charner, I., & Fraser, B. S. (1986). *Different strokes for different folks: Access and barriers to adult education and training.* Washington, DC: National Institute for Work and Learning.

Charner, I., Knox, K., LeBel, A., Levine, H., Russell, L., & Shore, J. (1978). *An untapped resource: Negotiated tuition-aid in the private sector.* Washington, DC: National Manpower Institute.

Covey, H. C. (1980). An exploratory study of the acquisition of a college student role by older people. *The Gerontologist, 20*(2), 173-181.

Cross, K. P. (1979). Adult learners: Characteristics, needs and interests. In R. E. Peterson & Associates (Ed.), *Lifelong learning in America* (pp. 9, 23-24). San Francisco, CA: Jossey-Bass.

Cross, K. P. (1982). *Older adults and higher education.* Washington, DC: National Council on the Aging.

Darkenwald, G., & Merriam, S. (1982). *Adult education: Foundations of practice.* New York: Harper & Row.

Dickerson, B. E., & Myers, D. R. (1988). The contributory and changing roles of older adults in the church and synagogue. *Educational Gerontology, 14,* 303-314.

Donahue, W. T. (Ed.). (1955). *Education for later maturity.* New York: Whiteside.

Donley, M., & Gallagher, J. (1988, October 24). *Time*, p. 90.

Germain, C. B., & Gitterman, A. (1980). *The life model of social work practice*. New York: Columbia University Press.

Graney, M. J., & Hays, W. C. (1976). Senior students: Higher education after age 62. *Educational Gerontology, 1*, 343–359.

Harrington, F. (1977). *The future of adult education*. San Francisco, CA: Jossey-Bass.

Harris, D. K., & Cole, W. E. (1980). *Sociology of aging*. Boston, MA: Houghton Mifflin.

Harris, L., & Associates. (1974). *Myth and reality of aging in America*. Washington, DC: National Council on the Aging.

Harris, L., & Associates. (1981). *Aging in the eighties: America in transition*. Washington, DC: National Council on the Aging.

Havighurst, R. J. (1964). Changing status and roles during the adult life cycle: Significance for adult education. In H. Burnes (Ed.), *Sociological backgrounds of adult education* (p. 20). Chicago: Center for the Study of Liberal Education for Adults.

Hays, W. C., & Hays, J. A. (1988, November). *Trends in re-enrollment rates and enrollment choices of older students auditing university courses*. Paper presented at the meeting of the Gerontological Society of America, San Francisco, CA.

Heisel, M. A., Darkenwald, G. G., & Anderson, R. A. (1981). Participation in organized educational activities among adults age 60 and over. *Educational Gerontology, 6*, 227–240.

Hertzler, J. O. (1929). *Social institutions*. New York: McGraw-Hill.

Hiemstra, R. (1976). Older adult learning: Instrumental and expressive categories. *Educational Gerontology, 1*, 343–359.

Hooyman, N. R., & Kiyak, H. A. (1988). *Social gerontology: A multidisciplinary perspective*. Needham Heights, MA: Allyn & Bacon.

Jackson, M., & Wood, J. (1976). *Aging in America: Implications for the black aged*. Washington, DC: National Council on the Aging.

Kasworm, C. E. (1980). The older student as an undergraduate. *Adult Education, 31*(1), 30–47.

Kingston, A. J. (1982a). Attitudes and problems of elder students in the university system of Georgia. *Educational Gerontology, 8*, 87–92.

Kingston, A. J. (1982b). The senior citizen as college student. *Educational Gerontology, 8*, 43–52.

Knowles, M. S. (1950). *Informal adult education*. New York: Association Press.

Lewin, K. (1947). Frontiers in group dynamics: Concept, method and reality in social science. *Human Relations, 1*, 5–41.

Lionberger, H. F. (1960). *Adoption of new ideas and practices*. Ames, IA: Iowa State University Press.

Londoner, C. A. (1971). Survival needs of the aged: Implications for program planning. *International Journal of Aging and Human Development, 2*, 113–117.

Londoner, C. A. (1978). Instrumental and expressive education: A basis for needs assessment and planning. In R. H. Sherron & D. B. Lumsden (Eds.), *Introduction to educational gerontology* (pp. 19–20). Washington, DC: Hemisphere.

Londoner, C. A. (1985). Instrumental and expressive education: A basis for needs assessment and planning. In R. H. Sherron & D. B. Lumsden (Eds.), *Introduction to educational gerontology* (2nd ed., pp. 93–110). Washington, DC: Hemisphere.

Long, H. B. (1986). A brief history of education in the United States. In D. A. Peterson, J. E. Thornton, & J. E. Birren (Eds.), *Education and aging* (p. 6). Englewood Cliffs, NJ: Prentice-Hall.

Lowy, L., & O'Connor, D. (1986). *Why education in the later years?* Lexington, MA: D. C. Heath.

MacRae, P. G. (1986). The effects of physical activity on the physiological and psychological health of the older adult: Implications for education. In D. A. Peterson, J. E. Thornton, & J. E. Birren (Eds.), *Education and aging* (pp. 205–230). Englewood Cliffs, NJ: Prentice-Hall.

McAuley, W. J., Arling, G. A., Nutty, C., & Bowling, C. (1980). *Statewide survey of older Virginians*. Final report: Volume II Research Series No. 3. Richmond, VA.

McClusky, H. Y. (1971). In *Education: Background and issues* (Report for the 1971 White House Conference on Aging). Washington, DC: U.S. Government Printing Office.

Merriam, S., & Lumsden, D. B. (1985). Educational needs and interests of older learners. In D. B. Lumsden (Ed.), *The older adult as learner: Aspects of educational gerontology* (pp. 51–71). Washington, DC: Hemisphere.

Momeni, J. (1980). *Adult participation in education: Past trends and some projections for the 1980's*. Washington, DC: National Institute for Work and Learning.

Moody, H. R. (1976). Philosophical presuppositions of education for old age. *Educational Gerontology, 1,* 1–16.

Moody, H. R. (1986). Late life learning in the information society. In D. A. Peterson, J. E. Thornton, & J. E. Birren (Eds.), *Education & aging* (pp. 122–148). Englewood Cliffs, NJ: Prentice-Hall.

Moody, H. R. (1987–1988). Why worry about education for older adults? *Generations, 12*(2), 5–9.

Naisbitt, J. (1982). *Megatrends: Ten new directions transforming our lives*. New York: Warner Books.

National Center for Education Statistics. (1969). *Participation in adult education: Final report*. Washington, DC: U.S. Government Printing Office.

National Center for Education Statistics. (1972). *Participation in adult education: Final report*. Washington, DC: U.S. Government Printing Office.

National Center for Education Statistics. (1975). *Participation in adult education: Final report*. Washington, DC: U.S. Government Printing Office.

National Center for Education Statistics. (1978). *Participation in adult education: Final report*. Washington, DC: U.S. Government Printing Office.

National Center for Education Statistics. (1981). *Participation in adult education*. Washington, DC: U.S. Government Printing Office.

National Center for Education Statistics. (1988). *Digest of education statistics*. Washington, DC: U.S. Government Printing Office.

Neugarten, B. L. (1981). Growing old in 2020. *National Forum, 61*(3), 28–30, 43.

Neugarten, B. L. (1982). *Age or need? Public policies for older people*. Beverly Hills, CA: Sage.

New York State Department of Education. (Nov., 1980). *Adult participation in postsecondary education*. Albany, NY: Author.

O'Connor, D. M. (1987). Elders and higher education: Instrumental or expressive goals? *Educational Gerontology, 13,* 511–519.

Peterson, D. A. (1985). The development of education for older people in the USA. In

Frank Glendenning (Ed.), *Educational gerontology: International perspectives.* (pp. 81–99). New York: St. Martin's Press.

Peterson, D. A. (1986). Aging and higher education: Older students, older faculty, and gerontology instruction. In D. A. Peterson, J. E. Thornton, & J. E. Birren (Eds.), *Education and aging* (pp. 30–61). Englewood Cliffs, NJ: Prentice-Hall.

Peterson, D. A. (1987–1988). The role of higher education in an aging society. *Journal of the American Society on Aging, 7*(2), 16–18.

Price, W. F., & Lyon, L. B. (1982). Educational orientations of the aged: An attitudinal inquiry. *Educational Gerontology, 8,* 473–484.

Pritchard, D. C., & Tomb, K. (1981). Emerging new service roles for older adults on college and university campuses. *Educational Gerontology, 7*(2–3), 167–175.

Radcliffe, D. (1985). Universities of the Third Age: An international perspective. *Convergence, 18*(1–2), 67–74.

Ready, B. C., & Sacchetti, R. D. (1986). *The independent study catalog: NUCEA's guide to independent study through correspondence instruction 1986–1988.* Washington, DC: Peterson's Guides.

Rogers, E. M., & Shoemaker, F. F. (1971). *Communication of innovations: A cross-cultural approach* (2nd ed.). New York: Free Press.

Romaniuk, J. C. (1982). *The older adult in higher education an analysis of state public policy.* Washington, DC: National Council on the Aging.

Romaniuk, J. C. (1984). Tuition-waiver policies for older adults: What are the assumptions? *Educational Gerontology, 10*(2), 119–133.

Rosenblum, G. (1989). New life in a new job. *New Choices, 29*(1), 27–34.

Sexton, R. F. (1980). *Barriers to the older student: The limits of federal financial aid benefits.* Washington, DC: The National Institute of Work and Learning.

Smith, L. N., & Abent, R. (1988). Avoid Detroit's mistakes: Reposition your institution to respond to adults. In *The admissions strategist: Recruiting in the 80's* (pp. 10–15). New York: College Entrance Examination Board.

Sprouse, B. M. (1982). *The older adult on campus: A policy manual for college administrators.* Washington, DC: National Council on the Aging.

U.S. Congress. (1977). House. *Senior citizen higher education opportunity act.* Washington, DC: U.S. Government Printing Office.

U.S. Congress. (1987). Senate. Special Committee on Aging. *Older Americans Act Amendments of 1987.* Senate Report No. 100-68, 100th Cong., 1st Sess. p. 19. Washington, DC: U.S. Government Printing Office.

Ventura, C. A., & Worthy, E. H., Jr. (1982). *Education for older adults: A synthesis of significant data.* Washington, DC: National Council on the Aging.

Weinstock, R. (1978). *The graying of the campus.* New York: Educational Facilities Laboratories.

16

EDUCATIONAL GERONTOLOGY AND THE FUTURE

JAMES A. THORSON
SHIRLEY A. WASKEL
University of Nebraska at Omaha

PREFACE

I recently had an opportunity to, within a week's time, teach both a Mojahedin from Afghanistan and a 77-year-old American woman how to use instant cash cards with a personal banking machine. It is worth saying parenthetically that both the Afghan man and the American woman might have been the teachers in another setting: One could provide instruction in, say, operating a rocket launcher or cutting the throat of a Russian soldier (he has done both); the other could relate lessons that were learned from living through the Depression and the war years. Both of them were in an informal learning setting, eager to acquire a skill that might add to life's convenience. Any apprehension they had over the technology was overcome by their expectation of success. And, indeed, both did succeed in a very few minutes. The process of adult education was identical for both the younger man and the older woman, and it involved principles of mutual respect, patience, and learning by doing. John Dewey would have been proud. Educational gerontology in this instance was no different than adult learning at any age.

In *The Mirror of Time: Images of Aging and Dying* (1987), philosophers Boyle and Morris cite the dialogue between Socrates and the old man Cephalus that can be found in Plato's *Republic* (7.-330D):

> *Cephalus spoke of a review of life that goes on in the last years before death. This was a call to justice and entailed a consideration of one's past deeds and an attempt, through truth telling and paying one's debts, to right the wrongs of the past.* (p. 32)

Although Boyle and Morris did not make a comparison to Butler's seminal work on the life review (1963), it is nevertheless enlightening to recognize the redating of the emergence of this concept from A.D. 1963 to circa 400 B.C. Thus we see once again that the more things change the more they stay the same. Not every new idea is all that new.

I relate these anecdotes for two reasons. One is the quite serious question of whether a separate educational gerontology really exists, or needs to exist. In many if not most cases, what we are talking about is the application of principles of adult education to older groups that are virtually the same as applications to younger adult groups. The other is the observation that the underpinnings of what we say when we speak of the future are not necessarily based on new ideas. The technology may change but the thing itself may be pretty much the same.

Having said all that, let me also observe that the world in 1989 does indeed look a bit different than it did in 1976 when I wrote the first draft of a chapter on this topic for the first edition of this book, which was then published almost two years later (Thorson, 1978). We thought it necessary at that time, for example, to spend much of the reader's time on a demonstration of demographic projections. There would be a lot more older people in the future, but they would be better educated and more prosperous. Now, it seems tiresome to belabor those concepts or to spend much time at all proving them.

The chapter written for the first edition seemed less appropriate by the time we revised it for the 1985 second edition (Thorson & Waskel, 1985); I asked Shirley Waskel to join me at that time as coauthor, and material dealing with her research on problem solving (1981) was added. The chapter we revised for the second edition now seems inappropriate in light of our present thinking. So, the following is not a revision of previous work at all; it is entirely new material.

INTRODUCTION

Some of the major issues in the literature on education for older adults are public policy and its impact on the growth of late-life learning, self-directed learning as a viable alternative to the traditional mode of learning, attitudes toward access being passé (even if access has not yet been achieved); job training as both instrumental and expressive types of learning, and questioning whether those outside the educational arena also have a role to play in continuous late-life learning.

Although the terminology has changed, there seems to be little change in recent years in public policy regarding the concept of late-life learning. According to Dye (1978), public policy is whatever governments choose to do or not do. Easton (1965) defined public policy as the authoritative allocation of values for the whole society. Easton also stated that government inaction can be considered public policy as well as action could; even inaction has impact on society. The substance of public policy ranges from the trivial to the sublime.

Several authors have stated the need for examining public policy in the arena of late-life education. For instance, Moody (1987) identified retraining of older workers whose work skills are obsolete as an appropriate public policy issue. He also proposed that programs be developed that address issues such as literacy, health care, nutrition, and intergenerational exchange. Questions of public policy invariably involve the questions of who pays and cost-effectiveness. Moody maintained that, with education for aging, all benefit. The more self-reliant people become, the less the monetary burden on society that results from a "do for them" mentality.

Bass (1987), addressing income equality among the elderly, cited Reischauer: "It is possible that current policy will create two distinct classes of retired people in the not-too-distant future" (p. 37). One group, the larger by far, would have Social Security as their main source of income, whereas the other group would have Social Security, private pensions, and other assets. Bass stressed the need for public decisions to address economic problems that will befall the majority who have only Social Security. He suggested that only through a variety of economic and educational policies will tomorrow's society be able to be a learning society for all elderly people.

Moody (1987) emphasized the need to create an aging society that gives people the resources necessary to pursue the things that make life worth living. He suggested that late-life learning is a vehicle for meeting multiple needs while continuing to give the hope that there is value in the last stage of life. In order to begin to come close to this goal, however, it may be necessary to alter people's perceptions of self-development to encompass a birth-to-death continuum and assure people that late life can mean a deepening of sense of self. But for these goals to be achieved, measures must be taken to eliminate the sense of helplessness that can rule an older person's life. As Campbell (1988) aptly said, "I am; therefore, I have value" (p. 3). It may be difficult to convince an older person who has operated out of a self-negating mode for a lifetime to suddenly embrace and live in a self-actualizing way.

If older people do continue to learn, we suspect that much of that learning takes place outside of institutions. Therefore, it seems evident that some type of self-directed learning is practiced. Because one of the prerequisites of this type of learning is involvement with others who have the knowledge or skills that the self-directed learner wishes to obtain, access to resources remains an important consideration. Many in the field, however, are indicating that it is time to move beyond issues of access. Often, discussion of access is limited to institutions, thus limiting the true concept of late-life learning. If access is defined more broadly to include allowing older adults to take charge of their own development, then there is greater possibility of growth and change. It is true that in every stage of development and age category, there are people who are left out of the mainstream, unable to access it because of ignorance. They may, as well, have very legitimate concerns with basic survival. It would be unfair, however, to characterize this as a problem peculiar to older persons.

Institutional barriers include lack of money, fear of failure, problems with schedules, lack of awareness of subsidized educational programs, and inadequate skill proficiency levels (Waskel, 1982). Some of the same barriers may exist for late-life learners who are not involved or interested in institutional learning, but often for different reasons. For instance, lack of money may keep people at a subsistence level and trying to survive. If enough energy is expended for the purpose of survival, even cost-free educational opportunities within the community will be ignored. Fear of failure could keep late-life learners from participating in any kind of learning experience in or out of an institutional setting. Inadequate skill proficiency levels can keep people of all ages outside the institutional education arena. The elderly poor are often seen as having the greatest need for education in self-help, job retraining, or political empowerment. They probably are the people who least benefit from programs designed to aid them.

We would also add to these issues identified by a number of authors in the fields of adult education and gerontology several concepts that go beyond questions of access, public policy, values, and institutional barriers. Silverstone (1988) has observed that the fact that the country's largest birth cohort will attain old age in the not-too-distant future will present the nation with a host of changes never before confronted. That is, there will be new problems, not just variations upon continuing themes. Unless there is a massive in-migration of young people to the United States sometime around the year 2020, for example, there simply will not be enough hands to care for all the frail old people who will then be alive. This is predicated on the assumption that the birth rate will not skyrocket during the next two decades; all indications of that happening are to the contrary. There will be a human resource crisis in basic service occupations.

The social problems now confronted by young people may be new ones. We have no way of knowing if this will cause a cohort effect that will have a continuing influence as the present generation ages. A report broadcast on the "Morning Edition" program on National Public Radio on November 1, 1988 cited a survey of some 7,000 school children in the St. Louis area. The primary concern they expressed was, by a wide margin, personal safety. Should this be the case in other communities—and we suspect that it is—and should it be a continuing area of concern, then self-actualizing behaviors among these individuals as they age will be less likely. As older people of the future, they may be less prone to help each other and more inclined to build walls and lock locks.

Other social issues that will influence learning in late life in the future include the following:

- The next generation of elders will be the first to have grown up within a society influenced by a relatively high divorce rate.
- Older people are for the most part no longer poor.
- Education has been seen, to an unprecedented degree, as a universal right and as a panacea for social ills.
- Technical innovations in communication are commonplace, are increasing in number, and are increasingly affordable.
- Dollars that in other circumstances might have gone for educational expenditures are devoted increasingly to either income support or health care.
- The cohorts of the aged now and in the future have very different attitudes about receiving assistance.

RISING EXPECTATIONS OF THE ELDERLY

One does not have to have attained great age to remember at least a few hearty individuals who refused to accept Social Security checks to which they were entitled. It was not unheard of 30 years ago for values of independence and freedom from government support to be stronger than the desire for money, at least among a minority of the aged. The notion of accepting welfare was even worse. Many older people flatly refused to apply for Aid to the Aged, which, along with Aid to the Blind and Aid to the Totally and Permanently Disabled, was one of the adult welfare categories. The concept behind the introduction of Supplemental Security Income (SSI) in 1974 was that older people would be more inclined to accept aid distributed by the Social Security office than by the welfare office. And, indeed, this was the case. SSI Alert was a program run by community action agencies and area agencies on aging to flush out those elderly isolates who might qualify for welfare payments that had been camouflaged as a Social Security pension. Thousands were found and signed up.

In contrast to an older generation that at least had to be urged to accept help—for whom government aid had to be disguised to make it more palatable—the current cohort of the aged often seems to prefer a handout to a hand up. Spencer (1988) described the amusing phenomenon of older people in Cicero, Illinois, packing an auditorium when a program on AIDS was announced. Sponsors of the seminar were bewildered at such interest from those least likely to be afflicted by AIDS until they found out that the older people had misunderstood: They thought the program was to be on various types of *government* aid for which they might qualify. One wonders what the expectations of the next generation of old people will be. In any event, we are now starting to see editorial cartoons of greedy old people snatching up support that might otherwise have gone to poor children. This might be characterized variously as over-reaction or as a harbinger of generational conflict in the future.

One of the ironies of this change in generational attitudes is the switch in the public stance of the largest older person's lobby. The National Retired Teachers' Association–American Association of Retired Persons (NRTA-AARP) has grown to such a degree that in 1988 it claimed to have 29 million members (and has, for the sake of convenience, dropped the "NRTA" from its logo). Back in the early 1960s, when there were half a million NRTA members and a little over two million members of the AARP, the organizations refused to lobby Congress on behalf of the Kennedy administration's proposed plan for Medicare (Binstock, 1972). Chapters of the United Auto Workers' retirees were organized into the National Council of Senior Citizens so that health insurance for the aged might have an institutional voice of support. The NRTA-AARP was of little more use when the time came to lobby for the Older Americans Act of 1965.

In a complete reversal of field, we now see brochures from the AARP entitled *Know Your Rights—A Program on Medicare's Prospective Payment System* and *Claim Your Share from Medicare*. Both brochures are for adult education programs available from what has now become an advocacy organization. The change in attitudes toward government support from one generation of elders to the next is thus demonstrable. Concurrent with this change in the attitudes of a generation has come a host of changes in relative social well-being. One need only refer to another AARP document (AARP, 1987) for a list of some of these changes:

- The poverty rate among the aged is the lowest (12.4%) it has been in the history of the nation.
- The median net worth of older households was $60,300 in 1984.
- Families headed by people 65 and older had a median income in 1986 of $19,932.
- The major source of income for older families in 1985 was Social Security (35%), followed by assets (25%), wages (23%), pensions (14%), and transfer payments such as SSI (2%).
- Seventy-five percent of the elderly are homeowners, and, of those home-owners, 83% own their houses free and clear.
- Among white older people in 1986, the median number of years of education was 12.1.
- About 10% of the aged have completed 4 or more years of college.

We now have the best educated and most prosperous generation of older people in our history. The cohort following them will be even better off. We would be remiss to fail to note, however, that there are serious pockets of poverty within the older population. In 1986, 31% of elderly blacks lived below the poverty line, and 44% of older people living alone (including many of the widowed) had incomes of less than $7,000. Bass (1987) noted that income inequality may grow in the future, which has potential implications for a learning society. However, competition for resources between the generations can be seen as a more serious potential problem. Binstock (1983) has warned that the relative prosperity of the aged will make them scapegoats. We are now seeing editorials (Samuelson, 1988) pointing out that age alone is not a reasonable criterion for receiving assistance. The majority of older people need little help, and help should go only to those who need it (Thorson & Horacek, 1986b).

We have predicted that it will become increasingly clear that most older people are, in fact, not sick, not poor, not educationally deprived, and not in need of government assistance (Thorson & Horacek, 1986a). The increasing competition for health care dollars to provide care for the frail elderly may leave discretionary spending for such things as educational programs for older people behind and funded by public sources only at a rate at or below current levels.

In terms of a rising level of expectations among the elderly, we have a mixed message for the future. Older people are more prosperous and better educated than ever before, and they are likely to become more so. They may see government aid more and more as their natural right. Advocates for other groups, however, may well point to the very prosperity of the aged as an argument for giving them a smaller slice of the public pie. The great numbers of older people in the health care system of the future may exhaust the government's capacity (and the public's willingness) to pay for much beyond survival maintenance for the most needy. The implication is that private efforts in education for older adults have the best prospects for future growth. In fact, advocacy groups such as the AARP are already becoming a major provider of educational programming.

THE SOCIAL PROBLEM OF ISOLATION

Adapting to change and remaining integrated in society have been identified as important learning tasks for older people of the future (Thorson, 1978); coping with stress by maintaining confidant relationships will be especially important. The problem of isolation has educational implications that are yet to be explored, and, we point to it as an exceedingly important and growing social concern for elders of the future.

Lack of capacity to cope with life's changes is exacerbated by isolation; we can see that support networks hold great importance for the well-being of older people of the future. Yet, we may also predict with confidence that social isolation will be on the increase because of the twin demographic forces of declining birth rates and higher divorce rates. Issues related to coping, socialization, education, and survival are of such importance that we believe they should be examined in some detail.

The classic study of isolation as a stress among the elderly was done some years ago by Lowenthal (1964). She compared 534 people aged 60 and older who had been admitted to mental hospitals with 600 people of similar ages who lived in the community and were healthy. The objective was to determine the extent to which isolation contributed to mental illness and lower morale. In addition to completing several behavioral measures, including a morale scale, the first group was asked to list the number of their social contacts two weeks prior to hospitalization; the community group was asked to indicate the number of contacts they had had two weeks prior to the interview.

Respondents were divided into three categories: pure isolates (very few, if any, social contacts—almost urban hermits), semi-isolates (few social contacts, most of which were superficial), and interactors (high numbers of meaningful social contacts). In the hospitalized group, 52 were identified as pure isolates, 50 as semi-isolates, and 30 as interactors. The remaining subjects did not fall clearly into any of these categories. Lowenthal identified 30 pure isolates and 417 interactors in the community group. Three-fourths of the isolates were men, and three-fourths of the interactors were women. The isolates were 4 times more likely to be single than were others in the population, and 79% were in the lowest socioeconomic group.

The first conclusion from the preliminary data is that, although pure and semi-isolates in the hospitalized group outnumbered those in corresponding categories in the community group by a ratio of more than three to one, it cannot be concluded that all isolates are necessarily going to have mental problems, nor are all people with high levels of social interaction going to be mentally healthy. Isolation is a correlate of mental illness, but there is not sufficient evidence with which to claim an absolute relationship. More than 5% of the institutionalized subjects had high levels of interaction with others prior to hospitalization, and 5% of the group remaining in the community consisted of pure isolates. However, it may be concluded that people with low levels of social contact are more vulnerable to mental problems than are those who remain integrated within the social fabric and have frequent social contacts.

In order to get a clearer picture of the apparent relation between isolation and mental illness, Lowenthal and Haven (1968) investigated the quality of the individual's social interactions and the lifelong patterns of isolation or integration in a follow-up study of 280 surviving subjects from the original community sample. Social isolation seemed to increase sharply at about age 75; more of the isolates in this older group were women who had become widowed. The investigators identified four patterns of isolation among those who had thus become pure (lifelong alienated and defeated) or semi-isolates (chronic blamers and late isolates):

1. *The lifelong alienated.* These were mostly single men who had never attempted to become integrated in society. They represented 28% of the sample; many were alcoholics, and the majority were homeless.
2. *The defeated.* These lifelong marginal isolates had tried and failed to make a place for themselves in society. They represented 24% of the sample; two-thirds of them were men.
3. *Chronic blamers.* These isolates made 20% of the group, and almost all of them were single or divorced and had only casual or superficial contacts with others in society.
4. *Late isolates.* Composing 28% of the group, half of these isolates were over age 80 and a majority were women. About two-thirds were widows who had no children.

Out of the total sample group of 280 in the follow-up study, 112 had some form of psychiatric impairment and 60% were depressed. Social losses such as widowhood were clearly related with poor morale. It appears then that people who have been alone all of their lives have adapted to a solitary existence and have no particular adaptation to make in late life. Those who are used to the presence of others and have interacted with them, however, have a particularly hard time accepting the loss of those contacts in old age.

Lowenthal and Haven (1968), writing about the quality of interaction, introduced another important factor: the confidant. A confidant is a person in whom one may confide, who will listen to your troubles, a close friend or relative who is trusted, a person who is near at hand and willing to listen. A man's confidant is most often his wife, if he has one; a woman's could be her husband, but it is as likely to be an older daughter, sister, or a close friend. The majority (69%) of the 168 psychiatrically unimpaired persons in the follow-up sample had a confidant, compared to only 31% of the impaired group. Again, as with interaction with others, the concept of loss is vital. "The great majority of those who lost a confidant are depressed, and the great majority of those who maintained one are satisfied." The implication is that the presence of an intimate relationship serves as a buffer against the problems caused by losses associated with old age. Much of Lowenthal and Haven's early findings have since been confirmed by more recent research (Kendig, Coles, Pittlekow, & Wilson, 1988).

Other studies demonstrate that isolation is related to physical illness. Berkman and Syme (1979) conducted a study of a random sample of 6,928 adults in Alameda County, California. They were interested in investigating relations between mortality and social and community ties. After nine years of following the group, it was clear that people who lacked social ties were more likely to die than were those who had many connections in the community. A more recent follow-up (Seeman, Kaplan, Knudsen, Cohen, & Guralnik, 1987) has confirmed the earlier Alameda County figures with 17-year longitudinal data among those 70 and older: Social ties and mortality are significantly related.

Four sources of social relationships in the Alameda County studies were identified: marriage, contacts with close friends and relatives, church membership, and group associations. in each case, people with social relationships had lower rates of death than did people without such ties. The more intimate ties of marriage and friendship were found to be more important than church and group membership. The most isolated group of men was found to have an age-adjusted mortality rate 2.3 times higher than that of men with the most social relationships. For women, the most isolated group had a death rate 2.8 times higher than that of the women with the most connections. The association between isolation and mortality was found to be independent of factors such as self-reported health, economic status, smoking, alcohol consumption, physical activity, obesity, and utilization of health services. The implication is clear: Those who maintain friendships and companionship find greater support in the process of adaptation. An implication for gerontology is that older people who lose their social supports will have more difficulty coping with the stresses of late life.

Another indication of the stress associated with isolation and loneliness is found in a comparison of the mortality data between married, single, widowed, and divorced people. Lynch presented this information in his book *The Broken Heart: The Medical Consequences of Loneliness* (1979). Lynch demonstrated that the death rates for almost every cause are lower for married men and women than for those in the single, widowed, or divorced categories. For example, the death rate from coronary disease for married white men is 176; the rate for single men is 237, which is 35% higher. The death rate for widowed white men is 275, which is 56% higher than the rate for married men. The rate for divorced men is 362, or 106% higher than for married men.

There are only a few conditions in which the death rates for those who are alone are lower than for married people. The overall impact of these comparisons is striking. Although widowed people are probably on the average older than the others, and thus should have higher rates of mortality for some of the causes, the age factor does not explain the higher rates for the single and divorced people or the non-disease causes among the widowed. Deaths from homicide generally go down significantly with advancing years. Yet, widowed men have a mortality rate from murder that is 300% higher than that of married men, and the rate for divorced men is fully 650% higher than the rate for married men. Rates for women are smaller, but are proportionately similar. An inescapable conclusion from these data is that lonely people just do not try as hard to stay alive.

Although we hasten to add that we believe that the current generation of elders has adapted well to change (Thorson & Thorson, 1981), and that they perceive a number of stresses differently because of their social situations (Thorson & Thorson, 1986), we see the problem of isolation-induced stress as increasingly problematic in the future. Coping with the stresses of the future will be done well by most older people, but it will be done best by those who remain integrated within a rich social network. Isolates may drop by the wayside, and all the demographic trends point toward older people who are more isolated in the future. High rates of divorce and an increasing proportion of childless people make this issue doubly serious. Thus the socialization motive for educational participation will become even more important. Coping with changing social relationships will also be important because of the inevitability of having to cope with changes in technology.

TECHNOLOGY AND THE FUTURE
OF EDUCATION FOR THE AGED

Much of what is written about the future focuses on a love of machines. A whole branch of our literature—science fiction—has developed such themes. Some of these works tend to be misguided, not so much in their predictions of technological change as in the assumptions that human relationships and desires will somehow also change. One need only thumb through back issues of popular magazines to see articles on what life was predicted to be like in 1970 or 1980: cities on the ocean floor, people being shot back and forth via pneumatic tubes, and travel to other planets for the masses. Authors of such articles seemed to ignore two things: that innovation costs money, and that the best predictor of that which is yet to come is that which has gone on before. The main business of the majority of the world's population for many years to come will be what it has been for thousands of years: to grub a living out of the earth. Not only will few want to live in a space station; no one will be able to afford it.

Just because a technology is possible is no reason to think it will be used. The practical failure of the Concorde airplane is a case in point. It has been possible since the early 1970s to take a flight on either Air France or British Airways that will get one from New York to London or Paris at twice the speed of sound (and at about four times the usual cost). Only a tiny percentage of trans-Atlantic passengers opt for this; most are content to pay much less and fly at a little less than the speed of sound. The technology is there to go fast, and it is useless as a practical matter. In point of fact, the oceanliner—a very old technology—has made a dramatic comeback in the last decade. Perhaps comfort is worth more than speed. The anecdote comes to mind of the speed-reader tearing through *War and Peace* in record time. Asked what the book was about, he replied, "I think it may have been about Russia."

Similarly, much of what one might read about education in the future looks for the machine to provide the quick fix, the flashy technique or the catch phrase to provide something resembling substance. It is all well and good to say that we are in a post-industrial age and entering an era of networking, but one wonders where the true meaning is in these clichés. Visions come to mind of the learner of the future all plugged in to the latest electronic bulletin board searching with futility for something there that is worth knowing. Perhaps we are easily fooled into believing that the medium *is* the message, that the computer can actually have a thought. Although our typewriters and adding machines have been getting quicker for some time now, few would argue that our children can read or do sums better than their counterparts of 30 or 50 years ago. Nor are their thoughts any more profound. Perhaps this is inconsistent with prevailing views, but let us look at the future of adult learning in particular.

Futurists have generally and inexplicably been willing to overlook the obvious when it comes to human behavior. It has always been possible to isolate oneself in a monk's cell and study. Yet, we actually have only a few examples over our history of hermits hidden away among their books. On the contrary, most people consider solitary confinement to be a torture. Why then should adult learning in the future be characterized inevitably as a solitary activity? Yes, we can fill a living room wall with a television screen, and, yes, we can design a computer network that can dial up much of what a person might want to know. However, we have no evidence with which to predict that people of the future will be so misanthropic as to isolate themselves in learning caves. Doubtless those who participate in adult learning activities in the future will have, at least as a part of their motivation, the desire to meet interesting people and go out to dinner after class. The dual goals of love of learning and socialization identified by Houle in 1963 are still operative in 1989 and will continue to have validity in 2009 and 2029. In an extensive study of 560 Elderhostel participants, Brady and Fowler (1988) found intellectual challenge and meaningful social relationships to be the twin motivations identified by most respondents. We see no reason to think that this will change.

Anxiety over learning the latest technology has seemingly been more easily overcome than might have been anticipated (Fuchs, 1987). Being afraid of computers has probably been less of a deterrent to their use than the fact that many adults—older as well as younger—can see no particular purpose or convenience to them. It may be that the concept of accessing information by electronic means has been oversold by educators enamored with technology and the notion of mechanization or the quick fix. The fact is that our technology has in many areas been developed far in advance of any particular use for it. The smashing failure of "teaching machines" is an example. Purchased with Elementary and Secondary Education Act funds during the decades of the 1960s and 1970s, these devices continue to gather dust in school closets throughout the country. Similarly, home computer networks and bulletin boards may provide entertainment for many, but few would argue their value for substantive educational purposes. They may in the future advance to the level of dullness currently achieved by educational television. The serious learner no doubt will continue to rely on books and discussion for many years to come.

Resistance to the use of technology when it is seen to have little purpose has been demonstrated by the market research of commercial organizations. As reported in the *Wall Street Journal* (Guenther, 1988), Citicorp executives have been pleasantly surprised at the almost universal acceptance over the past few years of the instant cash machine. Introduced by the development division of this large banking corporation, it was originally anticipated that this computerized after-hours banking window would catch on very slowly and not be used by many—especially the elderly, who were turned off by technology or apprehensive over the use of an unfamiliar gadget. Guenther reported that its quick acceptance nationwide has justified what was thought of in the banking community as a bold and risky venture by Citicorp. On one hand, the machines have had great success, are seen as a major convenience, and have been marketed to other networks of banks throughout the country. On the other hand, using a personal computer and telephone connection for home banking has not caught on at all. Citibank and Chemical Bank have both, after several years' effort, dropped their Direct Access and Pronto systems, respectively. Again, the technology is there, but the desire is not.

Evidently, few can see any particular use or convenience for home banking. The technology is there, but the need is not. Similarly, home shopping has been pretty much a failure. People want to get out and squeeze the melons; the act of shopping has intrinsic benefits that go beyond the acquisition of goods. We suspect that the same is true of education: High tech learning destroys the satisfaction of socialization.

Merely because even an old technology is present and available is no reason to think that it will be used. As Fisher (1987, 1988) pointed out, much of the nonreading by older adults can be explained by the lack of a perceived need to read. Those who have no use for books will have even less use for computers. Technical innovations that are seen as useful will be embraced and quickly adopted. Like the older American woman and the younger Afghan man learning to use the instant cash machine, people from diverse cultural and educational backgrounds will find new ways of doing old things. Those innovations that lack real utility will fall by the wayside. We should be cautious in our predictions; not every new gadget will sell.

It is important to emphasize that the technologies, not the people, that will fall by the wayside. A journalist named Toffler wrote a book in 1970 in which he predicted that changes in society were coming at an increasingly accelerated pace: The fast pace of new things would eventually come in such a blur that most older people would pretty much have to drop out. Like so many flies stuck in amber, these psychological dropouts could be seen left out of the mainstream, victims of future shock. The experiences of the succeeding years have demonstrated that Toffler was wrong. Older people are keeping up pretty well (Fuchs, 1987).

The real role for innovative technologies in the future will be to provide the means to sustain life, promote independence, and to improve rehabilitation possibilities (Frydenberg, 1988; Haddad, 1987; Levy & Phillips, 1988). Much work has now been done with people with disabilities that has application to assisting the frail elderly. A computerized voice synthesizer, for example, enables a blind journalist to hear back what she has just written (Campbell, 1988). A device called an Optacon lets blind people "feel" normal print. A host of such innovations enable people with disabilities to lead more independent, satisfying lives (Timmerman, 1987). It should be noted that the machines are not providing education, but will increasingly facilitate adult learning by helping people to communicate or get about. The real learning that goes on—now and in the future—involves human interaction. The important educational gerontology takes place one-on-one—in the doctor's office, at the Social Security desk, prior to entering the voting booth. Frydenberg emphasized, "We view the computer as a significant enhancement to rehabilitation programs for the elderly; however we caution against its use as a replacement for the 'high touch' aspect of human care" (1988, p. 600).

It has been demonstrated that educational rehabilitation, based on interaction within a rich environment with other humans, can make the cognitively deprived older person literally bounce back with significantly improved performance (Labouvie-Vief, 1976; Labouvie-Vief & Gonda, 1976). Providing an emphasis on cognitive rehabilitation and the teaching of survival skills may be the real contribution of the educational gerontologist of the future. A host of articles has recently appeared in the gerontological literature dealing with educational strategies for issues such as monitoring cancer risk, coping with disability and blindness, self-management of heart disease and diabetes, ensuring patient rights, and decision making in long-term care settings (Ansello, 1988; Clark et al., 1988; Crews, 1988; Howe, 1988; Keintz, Riner, Fleisher, & Engstrom, 1988; Scharlach, 1988; Tymchuck, Ouslander, Rahbar, & Fitten, 1988). In fact, an increasingly important role for educational gerontology is merely to devise means for the only partially lucid to take their medications in the proper sequence and at the right time (Haddad, 1987; Thorson & Thorson, 1979a, 1979b).

An interesting variation on these health education themes has been taken by Wacks (1988): death education for the aged. Maintaining that eschatological concerns are uppermost in the minds of those nearest to death, Wacks has taught a course, "Life after Death," in senior centers and Elderhostel settings. Our own research (Thorson & Powell, 1988) indicates not only that older people have the least death anxiety, but that their primary concern with the end of life has to do with questions about an afterlife. Perhaps Wacks has identified an educational need that has not heretofore been perceived.

THE ROLE OF EDUCATIONAL INSTITUTIONS

Our social institutions have a tradition of serving those who are easiest to serve, and this will no doubt continue to be the pattern of the future. We have little trouble teaching the young person who is bound for college; it is the nonreader and the dropout that are difficult to teach. Likewise, the 2% to 4% of the elderly who make it onto our college campuses are embraced, but our institutions of higher learning are ill prepared to reach out to the others. The fact that mature adults are returning to campus in unprecedented numbers is reported regularly in the popular press (Crothers, 1988; Tifft, 1988). However, as Peterson (1987) pointed out, age-segregated instruction has gained greater popularity in recent years than has the integration of older people into the regular educational program of the institution. Indeed, the big news in educational gerontology during the past decade has been Elderhostel. Largely self-financing and in many cases almost entirely separate from its institutional sponsorship (one might in fact identify the university's emerging role in this regard as that of a motel), Elderhostel has grown to involve thousands of bright and vigorous older adults in hundreds of creative, innovative learning programs.

A conference was held in 1976 at the New England Center for Continuing Education, sponsored by the University of New Hampshire and the then newly formed Elderhostel organization. Fewer than 100 institutions, mainly small colleges in the Northeastern states, had held programs for older learners for a few weeks the previous summer. The Elderhostel formula was promoted to conferees as a way for institutions to rent their dorm space during the slack summer months—similar to a cheerleading camp. It might also be a way for some professors to earn extra money. Elderhostel has taken off like wildfire since then.

The organization's catalog *Supplement* in April of 1988 ran to 72 pages of course listings in the United States and in 23 foreign countries. It reports that Elderhostel at, for example, the University of Arizona runs 52 weeks per year and, at the University's Nogales campus, the space shortage is such that Elderhostel has had to move over into an off-campus hotel. One wonders how phenomenal this growth might have been had college administrators been told in 1976 that Elderhostel could cost their institutions money, but it would be nice if they could do something for older people anyway. Obviously, the situation has been to the contrary: The institutions are finding Elderhostel to be profitable. One of the fortunate functions of the national organization has been to hold costs down and prevent the universities from unreasonable price gouging.

Older students in the regular institutional program have been welcome as well, but adult students in their 30s and 40s far outnumber older people on campus. Institutions may not be in such desperate straits in terms of enrollment as was once thought. The influx of what were once called nontraditional students has all but made up for the decline of potential students in the 18- to 22-year age cohort. University administrators who had predicted doom only a few years ago are now looking to the decade of the 1990s with some optimism (Harrington & Sum, 1988). However, there is something else going on in addition to the graying of the campus: A higher proportion of younger people—at least among whites—is coming to college. Recently released census data reported in the *Chronicle of Higher Education* (1988) indicates that 19.9% of American adults now hold a college degree, an all-time high. At an earlier time in our history, when only a few upper-class people had been to college, a young person might have to fight to get the chance for higher education. Now, the one thing we know about college-educated adults is that they most always will find a way to send their own children on for further study. A better-educated populace overall not only means more people in general on campus, but also more older people in the classroom eventually.

Thus, we can see both people in midlife and a higher proportion of the available young people starting college, taking the enrollment pressure off of the institutions to a certain degree. Filling half-empty classrooms with older people attending on a tuition-free basis has not been a necessity—not that such programs have ever been very successful. The kind of individual who would attend a university in late life seemingly does not perceive the cost of tuition as much of a barrier.

Tuition-free or full-pay, our campuses in actuality have not attracted a large number of older people into their regular academic programs (Peterson, 1987). Our own institution is a case in point and may be representative of many universities. An urban university that tailors its program to the adult student, the University of Nebraska at Omaha has a more mature student clientele than do many residential campuses (the mean age is 27.1 years). Although the welcome mat is out for older students, out of 15,932 registrants in the most recent semester, only 39 were age 60 or above, and only 14 were 65 and older (Office of Institutional Research, 1988). The campus is geographically central, in a low-crime neighborhood, and is barrier-free architecturally. Professors are accustomed to adult students, and many go out of their way to make them feel welcome. The few who do attend are enthusiastic in their praise of the institution.

A glib explanation for this poor showing might be that the barriers are in the minds of the potential older students—lack of self-confidence in one's abilities, low level of motivation, and so on. Perhaps a more likely rationale is that the product is not needed. As Hiemstra (1976) pointed out, most learning takes place somewhere other than school, and this is especially true for older people. Lumsden (1987) interpreted Hiemstra's work to suggest that "at some point during the adult years, there occurs a shift from a preference for institutionally sponsored educational activities to a preference for self-planned, self-directed learning" (p. 11). All of the evidence on this is not yet in, but Lumsden's contention should stimulate further research in the field. Suffice it to say that many universities' regular academic programs have not attracted too many older people, even in an era when administrators court the adult student.

College centers for older learners—as distinct from Elderhostel programs, which they may sponsor—have enjoyed some limited success (Institute for Lifetime Learning, 1986). Most of them provide specialized counseling and program activities, sometimes seeking to help integrate older students into the regular academic program of the campus, but they are often geared to special programming for seniors. Classes taught by retired faculty especially for other retirees, such as the prototype of these programs at the New School for Social Research, is a frequent pattern. Institutions having such centers are demonstrating a commitment to education for the older adult that goes beyond filling the dorms during slack times.

Surveying these sometimes conflicting trends may make the future role of institutions of higher learning seem to be somewhat ambiguous. No doubt a small but increasing percentage of the aged will in the future find the regular and customary academic program of our colleges and universities attractive. More will be able to afford it, and an increasingly better-educated older population will seek access. Attitudes will cease to be barriers (Waskel & Powell, 1988). Increasingly open to concepts of lifelong learning, and needy for the dollars in tuition and the goodwill of potential donors, the institutions will for the most part welcome older students. Special centers of elderly students and Elderhostel programs will also continue to grow.

Such efforts will continue to be financially self-sufficient. Increases in government funding for the education of the aged will be no more than a pleasant fantasy: Every cent earmarked for the aged will be going into income maintenance or long-term care. In this regard, at least, we see no real change. Federal and state funding for education of older people has always been scarce. School districts may make more than token efforts, but most will be financially preoccupied with repair and replacement of an aging infrastructure.

EDUCATIONAL GERONTOLOGY
AS INTERVENTION

As long ago as 1971, Londoner called for programs of instrumental adult education to provide survival skill training for the elderly. Interpreted in the light of Hiemstra's (1976) research, we might conclude that the truly needed survival skills are learned by the elderly independently, over a lifetime of coping with life's problems and opportunities. The fact that older people are getting along pretty well without much help consistently escapes us.

It is possible that most people we often think of as elderly are not, in fact, old. It has become increasingly clear that 65 is an inappropriate point for defining the onset of old age (Thorson & Horacek, 1986b). The cohort in the 65–74 year age group is about twice as large in absolute numbers as the remaining older population aged 75 and older, and including the young-old in our social statistics that describe the elderly thus skews the data. The young-old have few problems in comparison to the old-old.

The ever-popular 4% fallacy is an example of how inappropriate statistics shape our thinking. For years, gerontologists have cited the fact that only a little more than 4% of the elderly are in nursing homes. The elaboration, however, is hardly ever given: The average nursing home patient is about 82 years old. In other words, the rate for those 65 and older is low because hardly any 65-year-olds are in nursing homes. The institutionalization rate is more like 10% by age 75, and it approaches 30% by age 85 (Palmore, 1977; Wershow, 1976). It should be noted that these are rates for utilization at any one point in time. The *lifetime* probability of entering a nursing home is 48.2%, and it is 63% for those aged 65 and above (Liu & Manton, 1984; McConnel, 1984; Thorson, 1988). The point is a simple one: Aging problems are serious, and they are truly serious for the truly aged. Sixty-five-year-olds really are not elderly; they do about as well as others in late middle age.

Our conclusion is that those precious efforts that can be made in terms of educational interventions on behalf of the elderly ought not be wasted on the young. Waskel (1982) has pointed out that senior centers, churches, Elderhostels, community schools, YMCAs and YWCAs, libraries, museums, labor unions, colleges, private clubs, and the AARP are all providing education for an aging clientele. No doubt they will continue to flourish in the years to come. As Hiemstra (1976) pointed out, these identifiable efforts are the mere tip of the iceberg. A vigorous, prosperous, and well-educated cohort of the young-old will continue to grow and develop with their own independent learning projects. It is the frail older person without resources who will need educational gerontology as an intervention in the future. Within the context of those 85 and older being the fastest-growing age cohort in our population, educational efforts for the frail elderly will need to be doubled and redoubled.

We see a need for the emergence of a new professional: the clinical educational gerontologist. As much a clinician as the physical therapist and the social worker, the clinical educational gerontologist will be able to assess needs and provide educational therapies and interventions in consultation with multidisciplinary teams of service providers. Helping the individual buffeted by the forces of isolation and sensory deprivation, teaching health maintenance regimens to promote independent living, providing educational interventions through a host of means to stimulate vulnerable intellects—these are the real needs in educational gerontology. We are beginning to see growth in the employment categories of specialists in educational therapy (usually in mental hospital settings) and specialists in therapeutic recreation in hospital and nursing home settings. A variation on these themes may emerge in the not-too-distant future: The adult educator who specializes in clinical interventions within a geriatric care setting.

Apart from this growing need for the professional educator skilled in providing interventions and therapies, there may be no particular reason to define a separate educational gerontology. We cannot argue that adult education for most older people is different from any education for other adult groups. Vocational needs might be supplanted somewhat by desires for socialization, but there really is hardly any difference. And, everybody is doing it: stockbrokers, lawyers, politicians, health care practitioners, ministers, morticians, and Tupperware salespeople all provide education of one sort or another to older people, not to mention the information that older people exchange among themselves. It would be hard to argue that the educational approaches appropriate for a 70-year-old are much different from those useful with someone who is 50.

However, teaching self-maintenance and safety skills to an Alzheimer's patient, helping a dying older woman review her life and come to some kind of peaceful resolution of her own personal existential problem, keeping the suddenly widowed 82-year-old man integrated meaningfully in society involve skills that truly go beyond general adult education. Older people of the future will need such assistance. There will be more of us, and we will be more alone.

Education for the young-old has been happening, and it will continue in a thousand different ways without any particular concerted effort on the part of the field. Nurses and counselors will increasingly be called upon to provide therapeutic interventions of an educational nature with the frail elderly. Perhaps this spells the need for the emergence of a new area of specialization: The clinical educational gerontologist. Futurists generally have a fairly dismal record; we have a hard enough time figuring out where we are and where we have been. Where we are going is always uncertain. James Birren, Dean Emeritus of the Andrus Gerontology Center should appropriately have the last word on this topic:

> *Older people will be freely mixing work, leisure, education, and personal growth, without regard for age, in new ways we can scarcely imagine today. (Today, we are seeing babyboomer women have a first child at 40 after many years of work, a development unthinkable just a few years ago; tomorrow's developments will be equally surprising.) (1987, p. 26)*

REFERENCES

American Association of Retired Persons. (1987). *A profile of older Americans.* Washington, DC: Author.

Ansello, E. F. (1988). The intersecting of aging and disabilities. *Educational Gerontology, 14,* 351–363.

Bass, S. A. (1987). Income inequality among the elderly. *Generations, 12*(2), 37–41.

Berkman, L., & Syme, S. L. (1979). Social networks, host resistance, and mortality: A nine-year follow-up of Alameda County residents. *American Journal of Epidemiology, 109,* 186–204.

Binstock, R. H. (1972). Interest-group liberalism and the politics of aging. *The Gerontologist, 12,* 265–280.

Binstock, R. H. (1983). The aged as scapegoat. *The Gerontologist, 23,* 136–143.

Birren, J. E. (1987). Cited in *Aging research on the threshold of discovery* (p. 26). Washington, DC: The Alliance for Aging Research.

Boyle, J. M., & Morris, J. E. (1987). *The mirror of time: Images of aging and dying.* Westport, CT: Greenwood.

Brady, E. M., & Fowler, M. L. (1988). Participation motives and learning outcomes among older learners. *Educational Gerontology, 14,* 45–56.

Butler, R. N. (1963). The life review: An interpretation of reminiscence in the aged. *Psychiatry, 26,* 65–76.

Campbell, E. (1988, December). Perspective on being a blind journalist. *Kids, Kids, Kidz, 1*(1), p. 24.

Campbell, J. (1988). *The power of myth.* New York: Doubleday.

Chronicle of Higher Education. (1988, September 28). Percentage of college grads at all-time high. p. 28.

Clark, N. M., Rakowski, W., Wheeler, J., Ostrander, L., Oden, S., & Keteyian, S. (1988). Development of self-management education for elderly heart patients. *The Gerontologist, 28,* 491–494.

Crews, J. E. (1988). No one left to push: The public policy of aging and blindness. *Educational Gerontology, 14,* 399–409.

Crothers, D. W. (1988, November 3). The mature years: Adult education. *Christian Science Monitor,* pp. 21–22.

Dye, T. R. (1978). *Understanding public policy.* Englewood Cliffs, NJ: Prentice-Hall.

Easton, D. (1965). *A framework for political analysis.* Englewood Cliffs, NJ: Prentice-Hall.

Fisher, J. C. (1987). The literacy level among older adults: Is it a problem? *Adult Literacy & Basic Education, 11,* 41–50.

Fisher, J. C. (1988). Older adult readers and nonreaders. *Educational Gerontology, 14,* 57–67.

Frydenberg, H. (1988). Computers: Specialized applications for the older person. *American Behavioral Scientist, 31,* 595–600.

Fuchs, B. (1987). Teaching elders to be computer friendly. *Generations, 12*(2), 57–59.

Guenther, R. (1988, March 11). At Citicorp's "secret lab," technology is put through the human wringer. *The Wall Street Journal,* p. 29.

Haddad, A. M. (1987). *High tech home care.* Rockville, MD: Aspen.

Harrington, P. E., & Sum, A. M. (1988). Whatever happened to the college enrollment crisis? *Academe, 74*(5), 17–22.

Hiemstra, R. (1976). The older adult's learning projects. *Educational Gerontology, 1* 331–341.

Houle, C. O. (1963). *The inquiring mind.* Madison: University of Wisconsin Press.

Howe, E. G. (1988). Ethical aspects of geriatric patients' rights to refuse treatment and to receive limited medical resources. *Educational Gerontology, 14,* 451–463.

Institute for Lifetime Learning. (1986). *College centers for older learners.* Washington, DC: AARP, Program Department.

Keintz, M. K., Riner, B., Fleisher, L., & Engstrom, P. (1988). Educating older persons about their increased cancer risk. *The Gerontologist, 28,* 487–490.

Kendig, H. L., Coles, R., Pittlekow, Y., & Wilson, S. (1988). Confidants and family structure in old age. *Journal of Gerontology, 43*(2), S31–40.

Labouvie-Vief, G. (1976). Toward optimizing cognitive competence in later life. *Educational Gerontology, 1,* 75–92.

Labouvie-Vief, G., & Gonda, J. (1976). Cognitive strategy training and intellectual performance in the elderly. *Journal of Gerontology, 31,* 327–332.

Levy, S. B., & Phillips, K. (1988). Developments in technology for visually impaired older people. *American Behavioral Scientist, 31,* 601–606.

Liu, K., & Manton, K. G. (1984). The characteristics and utilization pattern of an admission cohort of nursing home patients. *The Gerontologist, 24,* 70–76.

Londoner, C. A. (1971). Survival needs of the aged: Implications for program planning. *International Journal of Aging and Human Development, 2,* 113–117.

Lowenthal, M. F. (1964). Social isolation and mental illness in old age. *American Sociological Review, 29,* 54–70.

Lowenthal, M. F., & Haven, C. (1968). Interaction and adaptation: Intimacy as a critical variable. *American Sociological Review, 33,* 93–110.

Lumsden, D. B. (1987). How adults learn. *Generations, 12*(2), 10–15.

Lynch, J. J. (1979). *The broken heart: The medical consequences of loneliness.* New York: Basic Books.

McConnel, C. E. (1984). A note on the lifetime risk of nursing home residency. *The Gerontologist, 24,* 193–198.

Moody, H. R. (1987). Introduction. *Generations, 12*(2), 5–10.

Office of Institutional Research. (1988, October 28). *Age distribution of fall 1988 on-campus students.* Omaha: University of Nebraska Press.

Palmore, E. (1977). Facts on aging. *The Gerontologist, 17,* 315–320.

Peterson, D. A. (1987). The role of higher education in an aging society. *Generations, 12*(2), 16–18.

Samuelson, R. J. (1988, March 21). The elderly aren't needy. *Newsweek,* p. 68.

Scharlach, A. E. (1988). Peer counselor training for nursing home residents. *The Gerontologist, 28,* 499–502.

Seeman, T. E., Kaplan, G. A., Knudsen, L., Cohen, R., & Guralnik, J. (1987). Social network ties and mortality among the elderly in the Alameda County study. *American Journal of Epidemiology, 126,* 714–723.

Silverstone, B. (1988). Aging in tomorrow's world. *The Gerontologist, 28,* 577–578.

Spencer, T. M. (1988). Escape from Cicero. *Chicago, 37*(10), 118–121, 190.

Thorson, J. A. (1978). Future trends in education for older adults. In R. H. Sherron & D. B. Lumsden (Eds.), *Introduction to educational gerontology* (2nd ed., pp. 203–227). Washington, DC: Hemisphere.

Thorson, J. A. (1988). Relocation of the elderly: Some implications from the research. *Gerontology Review, 1*(1), 28–36.

Thorson, J. A., & Horacek, B. J. (1986a). Aging and long-term care in Nebraska. In J. S. Luke & V. Webb (Eds.), *Nebraska policy choices* (Vol. 1, pp. 106–136). Omaha: University of Nebraska at Omaha, Center for Applied Urban Research.

Thorson, J. A., & Horacek, B. J. (1986b). Self-esteem, value, and identity: Who are the elderly, really? *Journal of Religion and Aging, 3*(1/2), 5–15.

Thorson, J. A., & Powell, F. C. (1988). Elements of death anxiety and meanings of death. *Journal of Clinical Psychology, 44,* 691–701.

Thorson, J. A., & Thorson, J. R. (1979a). Nursing responsibilities in drug administration. In D. Petersen, F. Whittington, & B. Payne (Eds.), *Drugs and the elderly* (pp. 151–162). Springfield, IL: Charles C Thomas.

Thorson, J. A., & Thorson, J. R. (1979b). Patient education and the older drug taker. *Journal of Drug Issues, 9,* 85–89.

Thorson, J. A., & Thorson, J. R. (1981). How to keep elders alive. In M. O'Hara-Devereaux, L. H. Andrus, & C. Scott (Eds.), *Eldercare: A guide to clinical geriatrics* (pp. 331–335). New York: Grune & Stratton.

Thorson, J. A., & Thorson, J. R. (1986). How accurate are stress scales? *Journal of Gerontological Nursing, 12*(1), 21–24.

Thorson, J. A., & Waskel, S. (1985). Future trends in education for older adults. In R. H. Sherron & D. B. Lumsden (Eds.), *Introduction to educational gerontology* (2nd ed., pp. 223–247). Washington, DC: Hemisphere.

Tifft, S. (1988, October 24). The over-25 set moves in: Adults are fast becoming the majority on college campuses. *Time,* p. 90.

Timmerman, S. (1987). Learning to overcome disability. *Generations, 12*(2), 46–48.

Toffler, A. (1970). *Future shock.* New York: Random House.

Tymchuk, A. J., Ouslander, J. G., Rahbar, B., & Fitten, J. (1988). Medical decision-making among elderly people in long-term care. *The Gerontologist, 28,* 59–63.
Wacks, V. Q. (1988). Educating for eschatological concerns of the older adult: A brief report. *Death Studies, 12,* 329–335.
Waskel, S. (1981). The elderly, change, and problem solving. *Journal of Gerontological Social Work, 3*(4), 77–81.
Waskel, S. (1982). Scope of educational programs for older adults. In M. Okun (Ed.), *New directions for continuing education programs for older adults* (pp. 25–34). San Francisco: Jossey-Bass.
Waskel, S., & Powell, F. C. (1988). Use of words to describe aged or elderly: A factor analysis. *Gerontology and Geriatrics Education, 8,* 123–131.
Wershow, H. J. (1976). The four-percent fallacy: Some further evidence and policy implications. *The Gerontologist, 16,* 52–55.

INDEX

Academic institutions:
  college-university links, 279–281
  community college programs, 15, 187,
      198, 273–275, 277–281
  degree levels, 198–199, 228–229
  gerontology programs, 178–180
  integration guidelines, 325–326
  older students in, 314–318
  role of, 277–281, 346–348
  tuition policies, 228, 280, 315, 320, 347
  university programs, 277–281
  (*See also* Educational programs; Training,
      of gerontological practitioners)
Academy of Educational Development, 19,
  136
Accessibility, 233–234, 276, 316–317, 326,
  335
Adams, Ansel, 201, 214
Administration on Aging, 13, 73, 177, 272–
  273, 277, 278
Adult Education Association, 11, 12
Adult education movement, 6–7, 272–275,
  301–304
  (*See also* Educational gerontology)
Advocacy, church and, 121
Aesthetic theory, 203–204, 221
Age and aging:
  behavioral expectations and, 146
  cohort effects, 138–139
  creative decline and, 209–211
  criteria for, 207, 209–211, 248
  definitions of, 124–126, 348
  demographic changes, 188, 298–299
  denial of, 25
  religious activity and, 111
  segregation by, 61, 71, 151–152, 190,
      323, 346
  stereotypes of, 208, 257
  (*See also* Intergenerational interaction; Life

span development; Older adults;
    specific activities, problems, pro-
    grams)
American Association of Retired Persons
  (AARP), 127, 157, 193, 298, 337
American Society on Aging, 11
Andragogical theory, 136, 141
Anthropological models, 259–260
Arts and crafts, 73–75, 78–80, 165
Authority-focused teaching, 139–141
Autistic anxiety, 81

Bass, Scott A., 227–242
de Beauvoir, Simone, 25, 28, 34, 36, 270
Beckett, S., 27–28
Biofeedback, 253
Birren, J. E., 5, 19
Black Elk Speaks (Neihardt), 27, 38
Bolton, Christopher, 135–149
Brahce, Carl I., 10, 164, 269–295
Bridge Project, 75–77
Burkey, F. T., 98–99
Business, 320, 324
Butler, R. N., 26, 43–46, 49, 51

Career training (*see* Training, of gerontology
    practitioners)
Case history methods, 182
Center for Intergenerational Learning, 159–
  160
Charles Stewart Mott Foundation, 14
Charner, I., 303–304
Chautauqua movement, 7, 13
Childhood, 42, 44–45, 247, 260
Church (*see* Religious institutions)
Cognitive dissonance, 50, 63
Cognitive processes:
  anthropological models of, 259–260
  assessment criteria, 258–263

Cognitive processes (*Cont.*):
  behavioral plasticity and, 252–254
  creative behavior and, 210–211
  discontinuity hypothesis, 251
  habitual information processing, 143–144
  idealistic models of, 244–249
  intelligence concepts, 246–249
  learning process and, 135–149
  psychobiological maturation and, 249–254
  reminiscence and, 48–49
  research needs, 243
  social context of, 254–258, 261–262
  (*See also* Learning)
Cohort effects, 138–139, 203
Communication:
  community of generations concept, 61
  creative action and, 203
  historical perspective and, 69
  interinstitutional, 281
  motivations and, 215
Community college programs, 15, 187, 198,
    273–275, 277–281
Community of generations:
  concept of, 59–62
  examples of, 73–82
  learning process and, 62–72
Competence, cognitive, 248, 258
Competition, 156, 232–233, 235
Computers, 343–344
Conflict theory, 229–233
Consortia projects, 286, 290
Contact (*see* Intergenerational interaction)
Coping, 281
  life review and, 46
  religion and, 125–126
  reminiscence and, 48–50
Corbin, D. E., 151–169
Correspondence schools, 303
Crafts, 73–75, 78–80
Creative behavior, 165, 201–223
  arts and crafts programs, 73–75, 78–80
  definitions for, 206–207
  educational intervention and, 54
  intergenerational programs, 73–75, 78–80
  reminiscence and, 52
Crisis, development and, 256–258
Cross, L., 44–45, 47

Death and dying, 198, 228, 251, 345
Decision-making model, 299–301
Defense mechanisms, 25
Denial, of aging, 25

Dependency (*see* Independence)
Depression, 49
Deschooling, 146
Development (*see* Life span development)
Dewey, John, 41
Dialogue educational method, 29–34
Dickerson, Ben E., 297–331
Disabilities, 114–115, 313, 345
Discrimination, 237
Dissonance theory, 50, 63
Dohr, Joy H., 201–226
Driver education, 279

Ebersole, P., 51, 55
Ecological validity, 261–262
Economic factors:
  church attendance and, 115
  conflict theory and, 229–230
  educational goals and, 96
  historical perspective and, 69
  income levels, 99–100, 237–238, 335
  intergenerational interactions and, 151–152
  program growth and, 172
  program participation and, 314
  public policy and, 335
  resource allocation, 227, 232–233, 322–
    323
  role of education, 237–238
  work force participation, 234–236
  (*See also* Funding)
Edna McConnell Clark Foundation, 14
Educational gerontology:
  adaptations of, 191
  age demographics and, 298–299
  background issues of, 174–181
  definitions for, 1–3
  dialogue method, 29–34
  efficacy of, 145
  functionalist theory and, 229–232
  future of, 16–19, 333–350
  geragogy and, 194
  historic developments of, 272–276, 301–
    304
  integration guidelines, 325–326
  intervention and, 53–55, 348–350
  journals of, 12
  personnel requirements, 279
  public policy and, 334–335
  purposes of, 4–6
  redesigning of, 143–147
  responsibility for, 33
  state of knowledge about, 136–137

Educational gerontology (*Cont.*):
   student body compositions, 192–194
   technology and, 342–345
   (*See also* Academic institutions; Educa-
      tional programs; Learning; *specific
      activities, problems, programs*)
Educational programs, 8–14
   academic structures and, 178–180
   acceptance of older learners, 314–318
   accessibility to, 276, 316–317
   adaptations of, 238–239
   age relevance, 323–324
   barriers to, 312–313, 316–318
   categories of, 15, 228
   components of, 1
   conferences and, 10–11
   curriculum design, 195–199
   degree programs, 198–199, 228–229
   early programs, 9–10
   evaluation of, 171–185
   growth problems, 172–174
   implications of, 14–16
   intergenerational programs, 73–82, 154–
      166
   national consultative body for, 181–182
   needs-goals assessment for, 85–107
   planning responsibility, 177
   priorities for, 19
   residential programs, 13
   senior privileges for, 3
   structure of, 286
   (*See also* Educational gerontology; Train-
      ing, of gerontological practitioners;
      specific problems, programs)
Ego integrity, 36, 44, 49, 55, 72, 126
Elderhostel, 13, 17, 302, 343
Elderly (*see* Older adults)
Eliot, T. S., 23–26
Elites, 230
Employment (*see* Work)
Equal opportunity, 233–234
Erikson, Erik, 35–36, 38
Evaluation, of educational programs, 171–185
Exercise, 252, 253, 313
Existential philosophy, 28, 34
Experience:
   child vs. adult, 42
   devaluation of, 30
   development and, 247
   diversity of, 237
   education and, 23–29
   learning and, 67–73, 136

   reminiscence and, 41–56
   self-identity and, 42
   of time, 36–37, 139
Expressive education, 66–101, 311

Family relationships:
   education and, 60, 318–319
   intergenerational tensions, 152–153
   institutionalized elderly and, 118
   mortality rates and, 341
   Federal government, 13, 18–19, 172, 319–
      320
   (*See also specific agencies, programs*)
Finances (*see* Economic factors; Funding)
Frail elderly, 117–118
Freire, Paulo, 33–34
Functionalist theory, 229–232
Funding, 17, 175, 272–274
   advocacy for, 315
   family resources, 319
   government and, 280, 319–320
   priorities for, 173
   retirement training and, 278
   (*See also* Economic factors)

Generations Together, 160–161
Geragogy, 194
Gerontological Society, 291
Gerontology (*see* Educational gerontology;
      related problems, programs, topics)
Girl Scouts, 73–74
Glass, J. Conrad, Jr., 109–134
Goals:
   alternative actions and, 89
   assessment of, 101–104
   education and, 1–21
   functional approach to, 95
   inferred gratification, 93
   instrumental-expressive orientations and,
      87–101
   literature review for, 97–101
   participation assessment and, 95
   proaction and, 145
   purposeful product, 214–217
   survival goals, 96–97
Gray Panthers, 36, 158
Group therapy, 51, 55

Handicaps, 114–115, 313, 345
Hartford, Margaret E., 187–200
Health:
   categories of elderly and, 116–118

Health (*Cont.*):
    cognitive decrement and, 250–252
    educational participation and, 313
    religious activity and, 114–115
    social isolation and, 341
    technology and, 345
    training and, 196
Hearing loss, 313
Homebound elderly, 116–117, 197
Hunter, Woodrow W., 269–295
Hurst, B. M., 141–142

Income, 99–100, 237–238, 335
Independence:
    authority and, 139–140
    creative activity and, 205
    educational intervention and, 144–145
    intellectual competence and, 258
    retirement policy and, 271
    socioeconomic status and, 237
Individuation, 35
Industry, training programs and, 18
Information dissemination, 121–122, 316
Institute of Gerontology, 285, 296
Institutionalized elderly, 117–118
Instrumental education, 86–101, 311
Integration (*see* Participation)
Intelligence:
    assessment criteria, 258–263
    concepts of, 246–249
    creative processes and, 210–211
    reminiscence and, 48–49
Interest, recovery of, 66
Interest groups, 36–37
Intergenerational interaction:
    age segregation, 151–152
    autistic anxiety and, 81
    benefits of, 154–157
    cognitive dissonance and, 63
    common needs and, 154–155
    community of generations concept, 59–83
    economic changes and, 151–152
    educational programming and, 323–324
    learning from young people, 65–67
    learning process and, 62–72
    programs for, 73–82, 154–166
    reminiscence and, 51
Isolation, social problem of, 339–342

Johnson-Dietz, Sue, 297–331
Journals, 12, 55

Jung, Carl, 35, 38
Junto society, 7

Karuza, J., 144–145
Kerr, D., 203–204
Knowledge, theory of, 245
Knowles, M. S., 42, 102, 136, 140–142
Koch, Kenneth, 52
Kuhn, Maggie, 36, 111, 158

Labor force roles, 234–236
Labouvie-Vief, Gisela, 243–268
Leadership, 193, 269–295
Learning:
    andragogy and, 141
    authority-focused methods, 139–141
    barriers to, 312–313, 316–318
    cognitive decline and, 252
    community of generations, 62–72
    deschooling, 146
    experience and, 136
    factors affecting, 137–139
    habitual processing and, 143–144
    homeostasis and, 63
    intergenerational interaction and, 62–64
    learner-focused methods, 141–143
    learning from older adults, 67–73
    learing from young people, 65–67
    learning progression phenomenon, 288–289
    perceptual contrasts and, 63
    proaction and, 142–146
    psychophysiological change and, 313–314
    resource access and, 335
    responsibility for, 33
    self-initiative and, 145
    technology anxiety and, 343
    (*See also* Academic institutions; Educational gerontology; *specific programs*)
Learning society, 2, 15
Libraries, 7, 273
Life review, 26–29, 42–46, 49, 52, 333
Life span development:
    cognitive processes and, 243–268
    community of generations, 59–83
    creative behavior and, 201–223
    criteria for, 258–263
    educational philosophies of, 23–34
    experience and, 247
    idealistic models of, 244–249
    intergenerational understanding of, 71–73

Life span development (*Cont.*):
  learning and, 138
  life crises and, 256–258
  life review and, 45–46
  psychobiological maturation and, 249–255
  religious activity and, 121
  reminiscence and, 41–56
  retirement and, 270–272
  self-actualization and, 72
  self-identity and, 42
  temporal line of, 90–93
  transcendence of past and, 34–39
  time frames of, 207–208
  (*See also* Age and aging)
Londoner, C. A., 85–107
Loss concepts, 125–126, 340–341
Lumsden, D. B., 11–12
Lyceum program, 7

McClusky, H. Y., 5, 10, 14, 59–83
Market forces, 231
Marriage ties, 341
Maturity:
  criteria of, 258–263
  evolutionary view of, 245
  intellectual change and, 247
  (*See also* Life span development)
Mead, Margaret, 190
Media, and education, 18, 275, 291–292
Memory, 43, 137, 247
  (*See also* Cognitive processes; Reminiscence)
Mental health, 250, 339–340
  (*See also* Cognitive processes)
Merriam, S., 41–58
Meta-connection strategy, 303–304
Metal-Corbin, Josie, 151–169
Middle-aged adults, 211
Moody, Harry R., 4–6, 15, 19, 23–39, 50
Morale, 47, 52, 87, 93, 100
Mortality, sociality and, 341
Motivation:
  creative behavior and, 214–217
  instrumental-expressive education, 86–97
  needs-goals assessment and, 86–97
  participation and, 90–96
  retirement training and, 287
  for volunteers, 80–81
Mott Foundation, 14
Music therapy, 54
Myers, Dennis R., 297–331

National Council on the Aging, 158
National Institute of Aging, 173
National Retired Teachers Association (NRTA), 193, 337
Needs:
  assessment of, 101–104
  categories of, 281–282, 312
  definition of, 100
  developmental, 35
  expectations and, 337–339
  functional approach to, 95
  instrumental-expressive motivation, 86–101
  intergenerational kinship of, 154–155
  literature review for, 97–101
  participation and, 347
  planning and, 96
  psychosocial motivation and, 91–96
  for retirement training, 281–282, 285
  statements of, 95
  surveys of, 310
  wants and, 87, 100
Neihardt, J. G., 27
Neugarten, B. L., 116
Newman, S., 154–155
Nursing homes, 74–75, 117–118, 348–349
Nutrition, 196

Obsolescence, 25
Older adults:
  college centers for, 347–348
  economic role of, 234–236
  educational acceptance of, 314–318
  educational characteristics of, 306–314
  expectations of, 337–339
  historical perspectives of, 68–70
  as interest group, 36–37
  leadership positions of, 193, 271
  learning from, 67–73
  privileges of, 3
  as role models, 152, 166
  segregation of, 61, 151–152, 190, 208, 257, 318, 323–324, 246
  stereotypes of, 155, 208
  subgroups of, 116–118
  (*See also* Age and aging; Intergenerational interaction; *specific organizations, problems, topics*)
Older Americans Act, 272–274, 319, 337
Opinionation, 30–31
Oral history projects, 54, 73

Participation:
  accessibility and, 233–234, 276, 316–317, 326, 335
  barriers to, 110–116, 312–313, 316–318
  curriculum design and, 317–318
  decision-making model, 299–301
  discouragers of, 312–313, 316–318
  educational level and, 309
  encouragers of, 307–315
  goals analysis and, 95
  income and, 99–100
  instrumental-expressive motivations, 87–96
  market forces and, 231
  needs and, 347
  psychophysiological change and, 313–314
  psychosocial motivation, 90–96
  rates of, 304–306
  religious activity and, 109–134
  resource access and, 335
  in retirement programs, 287
  social institutions and, 318–322
  social isolation and, 339–342
  social needs and, 86–87
  time perception and, 36
  well-being and, 34
  work force and, 234–236
Perlmutter, M., 138–139
Personality theory, 208–209
Peterson, D. A., 1–21, 100–101, 136
Physiological changes, 249–255
Placement, 193
Planning:
  for creative activities, 220–222
  curriculum design, 195–199
  for intergenerational programs, 162–164
  national consultative body for, 181–182
  needs-goals assessment, 85–107
  responsibility for, 104–106, 177
Platonic theories, 29–32, 249, 333
Poetry, 52, 54
Population studies, 188, 192–194, 298–299
Portillo, Margaret, 201–226
Poverty, 238
Privacy, 154
Proactive learning, 142–146
Productivity, 214–217
  (See also Creative behavior; Work)
Programming, for training, 289–292, 323–324
Public sphere activity, 208–210

Rabinowitz, V. C., 144–145
Race, 112

Recruitment programs, 326
Religious institutions, 109–111
  adult education and, 6, 123–130, 319
  church advocacy role, 121
  model ministry for, 119–123
  objectives of, 118–119
  psychosocial influence of, 113–114
  services and, 120–123
  training for ministry, 126–128
Reminiscence, 26, 43–55
Residential programs, 13
Resource allocation, 227, 232–233, 322–323
Retirement:
  academic institutions and, 277–281
  attitudes toward, 287–288
  as crisis, 36, 257
  educational programs and, 10
  employment training and, 18
  leadership training for, 269–295
  mandatory, 103, 235, 287
  needs-goals assessment and, 103–106
  postretirement education, 284–288
  preretirement training, 283–284
  as process, 269, 283
  social mainstream and, 66
  transition programs, 228
  work force and, 234–235
Retirement homes, 74–75, 117–118, 348–349
Rich, Thomas A., 171–185
Rilke, R. M., 39
Robertson, E. A., 136–137
Romaniuk, J. G., 209–213

Satisfaction, 47, 52, 87, 93, 100
Second-career students, 192–193
Seelbach, Wayne C., 297–331
Segregation, by age, 61, 151–152, 190, 323, 346
Self-actualization, 5, 50, 72, 209
Self-direction, 145
Self-esteem, 55, 211–212
Self-image, 33
Self-realization, 35
Self-reliance (see Independence)
Senior citizens (see Older adults)
Services (see Social services)
Social action theory, 88
Social gerontology (see Socialization; specific problems, topics)
Social integration (see Participation)
Socialization:
  aging population trends, 188–191

Socialization (*Cont.*):
anticipatory socialization, 125
behavioral expectations and, 146
collective social categorizing, 218
creative behavior and, 209, 217–220
educational institutions and, 297–298
educational level and, 237
future of gerontology and, 336
hypothetical constructs, 91
intellectual context and, 254–258, 261–262
isolation and, 339–342
motivations and, 88–96
needs assessment and, 86–96
religious activity and, 109–134
reminiscence and, 55
retirement and, 66, 270, 272
social institutions, 318–322
student body composition and, 192–194
support groups and, 219
theories of schooling, 229–233
(*See also* Intergenerational interaction;
Participation)
Social Security Act, 235
Social services:
attitudes toward older adults and, 4–5
educational programs and, 9–10, 180–181
employment trends, 190
homebound elderly and, 116–117
religious institutions and, 120–123
training and, 195
Socratic method, 29–32
State governments, 275, 280, 319–320
Stein, Edith, 77–78
Stereotypes, 155, 208, 257, 318
Stress, 48–49, 256–258, 339
Support systems, 122–123, 209, 219
Survival goals, 96
Survivor bias, 41

Teaching-Learning Community, 78–80
Technology:
anxiety of, 343
educational gerontology and, 342–345
functionalist view of, 229
media and, 18, 275, 291–292
social obsolescence and, 25
Television, 18, 275, 291
Therapy, 51–55, 253
Thorson, James A., 333–353
Tice, Carol, 79
Time:
cognitive processes and, 254–258

creative association and, 204–205
developmental perceptions, 207–208
educational experience and, 139
experience of, 36–37
perceptions of, 221–222
reminiscence and, 43, 48, 50
temporal lifeline, 90–93
use of, 34
Toffler, Alvin, 188, 190, 244, 344–345
Training, of gerontology practitioners, 187–
200, 269–275
administrative skills, 189
cognitive improvement and, 253
consortia and, 290
evaluation of, 171
graduate follow-up, 183
institutional role, 277–281
media and, 291–292
needs assessment and, 103, 281–282, 285
objectives of, 194–195
practice skills, 196–197
programming for, 289–292
for religious ministry, 126–128
reminiscence and, 51–53
responsibility for, 175
retirement education, 269–275, 283–288
short vs. long-term, 180
task assessment, 282
work force needs and, 178
(*See also* Educational gerontology; Educational programs)
Transcendence concepts, 34–39, 282
Tuition policies, 228, 280, 315, 320, 347

Understanding Aging, Inc., 161–162
Universities, 277–281

Volunteer programs, 5, 78–81, 157, 275
(*See also specific programs*)
Volunteers in Service to America (VISTA),
153

Wants, 87, 100
(*See also* Needs)
Waskel, Shirley, A., 333–353
White House Conference on Aging (1971),
10, 14, 174, 273–274, 283
Withdrawal, 52, 81
Work:
aging trends and, 190
creative satisfaction of, 215–216
educational incentives of, 320, 322
employment training, 18

Work (*Cont.*):
  job placement, 193
  labor force roles, 234–236
  life span development and, 202
  (*See also* Retirement; *specific careers,
    programs*)

Worship, 120
  (*See also* Religious institutions)

Young people:
  learning from, 65–67
  self-actualization and, 72